THE HEBREW BIBLE AND ITS VERSIONS

7

General Editor
Robert P. Gordon, University of Cambridge

LEXICAL DEPENDENCE AND INTERTEXTUAL ALLUSION IN THE SEPTUAGINT OF THE TWELVE PROPHETS STUDIES IN HOSEA, AMOS AND MICAH

Myrto Theocharous

t&t clark

Published by T & T Clark International
A Continuum imprint
80 Maiden Lane, New York, NY 10038
The Tower Building, 11 York Road, London SE1 7NX

www.continuumbooks.com

Visit the T & T Clark blog at www.tandtclarkblog.com

Library of Congress Cataloging-in-Publication Data
A catalog record for this book is available from the Library of Congress.

ISBN: HB: 978-0-567-10564-6

Typeset by Forthcoming Publications Ltd (www.forthpub.com)
Printed and bound in the United States of America

CONTENTS

ABBREVIATIONS

AB	Anchor Bible
ABD	*Anchor Bible Dictionary.* Edited by D. N. Freedman. 6 vols. New York, 1992
AJBI	*Annual of the Japanese Biblical Institute*
AJSL	*American Journal of Semitic Languages and Literature*
ArBib	The Aramaic Bible
ASOR	American Schools of Oriental Research
ASTI	*Annual of the Swedish Theological Institute*
BA	*La Bible d'Alexandrie*
BASOR	*Bulletin of the American Schools of Oriental Research*
BCTP	*Bilingual Concordance to the Targum of the Prophets.* Edited by Johannes C de Moor et al. 21 vols. Leiden, 1995–2005
BDB	Brown, F., S. R. Driver, and C. A. Briggs. *A Hebrew and English Lexicon of the Old Testament.* Oxford, 1907
BETL	Bibliotheca ephemeridum theologicarum lovaniensium
BGU	*Aegyptische Urkunden aus den Königlichen Staatlichen Museen zu Berlin, Griechische Urkunden.* 15 vols. Berlin, 1895–1983
BHS	*Biblia Hebraica Stuttgartensia.* Edited by K. Elliger and W. Rudolph. Stuttgart, 1983
BIOSCS	*Bulletin of the International Organization for Septuagint and Cognate Studies*
BIS	Biblical Interpretation Series
BN	*Biblische Notizen*
BT	*The Bible Translator*
BWAT	Beiträge zur Wissenschaft vom Alten Testament
BZAW	Beihefte zur Zeitschrift für die alttestamentliche Wissenschaft
CBET	Contributions to Biblical Exegesis and Theology
CBQMS	Catholic Biblical Quarterly Monograph Series
ConBOT	Coniectanea biblica: Old Testament Series
Conybeare	Conybeare, F. C., and Stock, St. George. *Grammar of Septuagint Greek.* 1905. Boston, 2004
CP	Classical Philology
CP Herm.	*Corpus Papyrorum Hermopolitanorum* I. Edited C. Wessely. Leipzig, 1905
DBSup	*Dictionnaire de la Bible: Supplément.* Edited by L. Pirot and A. Robert. Paris, 1928–

DCH	*Dictionary of Classical Hebrew*. Edited by D. J. A. Clines. Sheffield, 1993–
DJD	Discoveries in the Judaean Desert
EOM	*Encyclopedia of Midrash: Biblical Interpretation in Formative Judaism*. Edited by Jacob Neusner and Alan J. Avery Peck. 2 vols. Leiden: Brill, 2005
ESAJS	European Seminar on Advanced Jewish Studies
ETL	*Ephemerides theologicae lovanienses*
EvQ	*Evangelical Quarterly*
FAT	Forschungen zum Alten Testament
GKC	*Gesenius' Hebrew Grammar*. Edited by E. Kautzsch. Translated by A. E. Cowley. 2d ed. Oxford, 1910
HALAT	*Hebräisches und aramäisches Lexicon zum Alten Testament*. Edited by Ludwig Koehler and Walter Baumgartner. 3d ed. 6 vols. Leiden, 1967–96
HAR	*Hebrew Annual Review*
HBS	Herders Biblische Studien
HBV	Hebrew Bible and Its Versions
HKAT	Handkommentar zum Alten Testament
Holladay	Holladay, William L., ed. *A Concise Hebrew and Aramaic Lexicon of the Old Testament*. Leiden, 1988
HR	Hatch, Edwin, and Henry A., Redpath, eds. *A Concordance to the Septuagint: and the Other Greek Versions of the Old Testament* (including the Apocryphal Books). 2d ed. Grand Rapids, 1998
HSM	Harvard Semitic Monographs
ICC	International Critical Commentary
IEJ	*Israel Exploration Journal*
JANES	*Journal of the Ancient Near Eastern Society, Columbia University*
Jastrow	Jastrow, Marcus, ed. *A Dictionary of the Targumim, the Talmud Babli and Yerushalmi, and the Midrashic Literature*. New York, 1903. Repr., Peabody, 2005
JATS	*Journal of the Adventist Theological Society*
JBL	*Journal of Biblical Literature*
JBS	Jerusalem Biblical Studies
JETS	*Journal of the Evangelical Theological Society*
JNSL	*Journal of Northwest Semitic Languages*
Joüon	Joüon, P. *A Grammar of Biblical Hebrew*. Translated and revised by T. Muraoka. 2 vols. Subsidia Biblica 14/1–2. Rome, 1991
JPS	Jewish Publication Society
JQR	*Jewish Quarterly Review*
JSJSup	Journal for the Study of Judaism in the Persian, Hellenistic, and Roman Periods: Supplement Series
JSNTSup	Journal for the Study of the New Testament: Supplement Series
JSOTSup	Journal for the Study of the Old Testament: Supplement Series

JSS	*Journal of Semitic Studies*
JTS	*Journal of Theological Studies*
KAT	Kommentar zum Alten Testament
KHC	Kurzer Hand-Commentar zum Alten Testament
LCL	Loeb Classical Library
LEH	Lust, Johan et al., eds. *A Greek–English Lexicon of the Septuagint.* Stuttgart, 1992, 1996
LSJ	Liddell, H. G., R. Scott, and H. S. Jones. *A Greek–English Lexicon.* 9th ed. with revised supplement. Oxford, 1996
LUÅ	Lunds universitets årsskrift
LXX	Septuagint
MBE	Monumenta Biblica et Ecclesiastica
MSU	Mitteilungen des Septuaginta-Unternehmens
MT	Masoretic Text
Muraoka 2002	Muraoka, T. *A Greek–English Lexicon of the Septuagint: Chiefly of the Pentateuch and Twelve Prophets.* 2d ed. Louvain, 2002
Muraoka 2009	Muraoka, T. *A Greek–English Lexicon of the Septuagint.* Louvain, 2009
NAC	New American Commentary
NET	New English Translation
NETS	*A New English Translation of the Septuagint.* Edited by Albert Pietersma and Benjamin G. Wright. Oxford, 2007
NICOT	New International Commentary on the Old Testament
NIDOTTE	*New International Dictionary of Old Testament Theology and Exegesis.* Edited by W. A. VanGemeren. 5 vols. Grand Rapids, 1997
NovTSup	Novum Testamentum Supplements
NRSV	New Revised Standard Version. (1989)
NS	New Series
NT	New Testament
OBO	Orbis biblicus et orientalis
OCHJS	The Oxford Centre for Hebrew and Jewish Studies
OG	Old Greek
OL	Old Latin
OLA	Orientalia lovaniensia Analecta
OT	Old Testament
OTL	Old Testament Library
OTP	*Old Testament Pseudepigrapha.* Edited by J. H. Charlesworth. 2 vols. New York, 1983
OtSt	*Oudtestamentische Studiën*
PAAJR	*Proceedings of the American Academy for Jewish Research*
PFES	Publications of the Finnish Exegetical Society
PSI	*Sylloge inscriptionum graecarum.* Edited by W. Dittenberger. 4 vols. 3d ed. Leipzig, 1915–24
RB	*Revue biblique*
REJ	*Revue des études juives*
ResQ	*Restoration Quarterly*

RevQ	*Revue de Qumran*
SAIS	Studies in Aramaic Interpretation of Scripture
SBL	Society of Biblical Literature
SBLDS	Society of Biblical Literature Dissertation Series
SBLSCS	Society of Biblical Literature Septuagint and Cognate Studies
Schleusner	Schleusner, Johann F., ed. *Novus Thesaurus Philologico-criticus: Sive, Lexicon in LXX et Reliquos Interpretes Graecos, ac Scriptores Apocryphos Veteris Testamenti.* 2d ed. 3 vols. London, 1829
SGFWJ	Schriften der Gesellschaft zur Förderung der Wissenschaft des Judentums
Sokoloff	Sokoloff, Michael. *A Dictionary of Jewish Palestinian Aramaic of the Byzantine Period.* Dictionaries of Talmud, Midrash, and Targum II. Ramat-Gan, 1990
SOTS	Society for Old Testament Studies
SSEJC	Studies in Scripture in Early Judaism and Christianity
SSS	Semitic Study Series
StBL	Studies in Biblical Literature
STDJ	*Studies on the Texts of the Desert of Judah*
TDNT	*Theological Dictionary of the New Testament.* Edited by G. Kittel and G. Friedrich. Translated by G. W. Bromiley. 10 vols. Grand Rapids, 1964–76
TDOT	*Theological Dictionary of the Old Testament.* Edited by G. J. Botterweck and H. Ringgren. Translated by J. T. Willis, G. W. Bromiley, and D. E. Green. 8 vols. Grand Rapids, 1974–
TLOT	*Theological Lexicon of the Old Testament.* Edited by E. Jenni, with assistance from C. Westermann. Translated by M. E. Biddle. 3 vols. Peabody, 1997
TP	Twelve Prophets
TWOT	*Theological Wordbook of the Old Testament.* Edited by R. L. Harris and G. L. Archer Jr. 2 vols. Chicago, 1980
VT	*Vetus Testamentum*
VTSup	Vetus Testamentum Supplements
WO	*Die Welt des Orients*
ZNW	*Zeitschrift für die neutestamentliche Wissenschaft und die Kunde der älteren Kirche*

ACKNOWLEDGMENTS

The Septuagint has always been the "ecclesiastical text" of the Greek Orthodox Church, to be read in the liturgy "untranslated," but certainly not to be studied in an academic setting. That was more or less how I perceived this word "Septuagint," so, when a course was offered at Wheaton College by Dr. Karen Jobes on this ancient version, I was fascinated by the possibility of actually examining this text more deeply. Karen's class marked the beginning of my journey in Septuagint studies and led me to Cambridge, where my interest was matched and "fanned" by Professor Robert Gordon, a wonderful mentor and friend whose insights and comments educated and guided me through the three years of my research.

The present work is my doctoral dissertation, which was submitted to the University of Cambridge and examined by two scholars I greatly admire: Dr. Jennifer M. Dines and Dr. Sebastian P. Brock. Their helpful remarks and insightful ideas were taken into consideration for the purposes of this publication.

I am thankful to the Langham Foundation for providing the bulk of my financial and personal support in Cambridge and for adding me to their global family of biblical scholars. I am also grateful to the Greek Bible College and to many faithful friends for their generous gifts.

Most of my research was carried out at Tyndale House in Cambridge, where my colleagues were an indispensable part of my academic progress and spiritual formation. I would like to thank especially the warden, Dr. Peter J. Williams, for readily offering his feedback when I needed to test new ideas and for his ongoing mentorship; our librarian, Dr. Elizabeth Magba, for her gentle assistance and for never refusing my requests for new book orders; Joshua Harper, for his willingness to proofread the entire work; Robert Crellin, for offering his language expertise; Dr. Mary Hom, for great conversations and advice of every kind; and, last but not least, my carrel mate, Seulgi Byun, for battling side by side on Septuagint issues and many more.

I owe my initiation into British rituals, especially that of high tea, to Professor John Emerton. His friendship, regular warm hospitality at St. John's College, and his valuable insights on my work have been a landmark of this journey.

I would like to express my gratitude to the faculty of the Greek Bible College in Athens for laying my academic foundations, especially Professor Jeffrey W. Baldwin for his ceaseless encouragement as I have continued my studies. I can think of many professors from Wheaton College from whom I inherited my love for the Scriptures, especially Dr. Gregory K. Beale and Dr. Daniel I. Block.

Apart from the numerous friends I have left unmentioned, to whom I owe a great deal, I thank my mother, Xenia Theocharous, a woman of great faith who passed her love for God and the Scriptures on to me. Her presence was the "invisible hand" in my path.

Finally, I dedicate this work to the memory of my father, Antonis Theocharous, who found life before his death in the comforting pages of the Greek Bible.

Soli Deo Gloria

Chapter 1

INTRODUCTION

Intertextuality

The literary study of "intertextuality" was first developed by Julia Kristeva in the 1960s.[1] Kristeva investigated how meaning, rather than being directly transferred from writer to reader, is communicated by certain "codes" imparted to both the writer and the reader by other texts. Thus, in the field of literary criticism, "intertextuality" has mainly referred to philosophical theories of language relations.[2]

Intertextuality in Biblical Studies
In Biblical Studies, however, "intertextuality" is rarely used with such philosophical connotations.[3] Instead, scholars have adopted the term for their examination of how one biblical text depends on another, and intertextuality has come to be used as a synonym for "echo" or "allusion." Miscall says that "'Intertextuality' is a covering term for all possible

1. Julia Kristeva, *Desire in Language: A Semiotic Approach to Literature and Art* (trans. Thomas Gora, Alice Jardine, Leon Roudiez; New York: Columbia University, 1980).
2. For a brief history of how the term arose in literary criticism, see George Aichele and Gary A. Phillips, "Introduction: Exegesis, Eisegesis, Intergesis," *Semeia* 69 (1995): 7–18; Donald C. Polaski, *Authorizing an End: The Isaiah Apocalypse and Intertextuality* (BIS 50; Leiden: Brill, 2001), 32–35; John Strazicich, *Joel's Use of Scripture and Scripture's Use of Joel: Appropriation and Resignification in Second Temple Judaism and Early Christianity* (Leiden: Brill, 2007), 3–14; Leroy A. Huizenga, *The New Isaac: Tradition and Intertextuality in the Gospel of Matthew* (NTSup 131; Leiden: Brill, 2009), 45–58; Abi T. Ngunga, "Messianism in the Old Greek of Isaiah: An Intertextual Analysis" (Ph.D. diss., University of Aberdeen, 2010), 16–23.
3. Timothy K. Beal, "Ideology and Intertextuality: Surplus of Meaning and Controlling the Means of Productions," in *Reading Between Texts: Intertextuality and the Hebrew Bible* (ed. Danna Nolan Fewell; Louisville: John Knox, 1992), 27.

relations that can be established between texts. The relations can be based on anything from quotes and direct references to indirect allusions to common words and even letters to dependence on language itself."[4]

In the last decades there has been a growing interest among biblical scholars in identifying these relations between texts and authors. Studies in intertextuality have involved examining the connections between one OT book and another,[5] the use of OT texts in the NT[6] and in Midrash,[7] and so on.

Huizenga has noted that, in previous intertextual studies, not enough attention has been given to extra-biblical interpretations associated with the texts to which allusion is made. Huizenga's criticism of Hays, a major representative of NT intertextual studies, is that he

> downplays the fields of tradition and interpretation that lie between Israel's Scripture and Paul's use of that Scripture... In effect, Hays's approach does not thus fully consider the possibility that an allusion to an Old Testament text could be an allusion to a radical interpretation thereof. This is problematic, for the semiotic matrix within which the New Testament writers lived and moved and had their being was not merely Scripture *qua* Scripture, but rather the entire cultural encyclopedia of early Judaism in all its diversity, within which Old Testament Scripture was interpreted.[8]

---

4. Peter D. Miscall, "Isaiah: New Heavens, New Earth, New Book," in Fewell, ed., *Reading Between Texts*, 44.

5. E.g. Robert Alter, *The Art of Biblical Narrative* (London: George Allen & Unwin, 1981); Michael Fishbane, *Biblical Interpretation in Ancient Israel* (Oxford: Clarendon, 1985); Robert Alter, *The World of Biblical Literature* (London: SPCK, 1992); James D. Nogalski, "Intertextuality and the Twelve," in *Forming Prophetic Literature: Essays on Isaiah and the Twelve in Honor of John D. W. Watts* (ed. James W. Watts and Paul R. House; JSOTSup 235; Sheffield: Sheffield Academic, 1996), 102–24; Johannes C. de Moor, ed., *Intertextuality in Ugarit and Israel: Papers Read at the Tenth Joint Meeting of The Society for Old Testament Study and Het Oudtestamentisch Werkgezelschap in Nederland en België; Held at Oxford, 1997* (Leiden: Brill, 1998); Richard L. Schultz, *The Search for Quotation: Verbal Parallels in the Prophets* (JSOTSup 180; Sheffield: Sheffield Academic, 1999); Polaski, *Authorizing an End*; Strazicich, *Joel's Use of Scripture*.

6. E.g. Richard B. Hays, *Echoes of Scripture in the Letters of Paul* (New Haven: Yale University Press, 1989), and "Who Has Believed Our Message?," in *The Conversion of the Imagination: Paul as Interpreter of Israel's Scripture* (Grand Rapids: Eerdmans, 2005), 34–45.

7. E.g. Daniel Boyarin, *Intertextuality and the Reading of Midrash* (Indiana Studies in Biblical Literature; Bloomington: Indiana University Press, 1990).

8. Huizenga, *The New Isaac*, 61.

Huizenga is looking not just for echoes of scripture, but, as Craig Evans says, for echoes of *interpreted* scripture.[9] A crucial element that Huizenga adds to his study is that of post-biblical tradition. He quotes James A. Sanders:

> One must often rummage around in the Targums, midrashim, and Jewish commentaries to learn how a passage of Scripture functioned for Matthew. He was sometimes dependent on a particular interpretation or understanding of a passage of Scripture: indeed, he would have had that interpretation in mind even as he read or cited a text.[10]

For the present study, the translator of the LXX TP should be considered from a similar perspective: the same considerations must be taken into account when identifying sources of influence. The LXX translator probably lived in the second century B.C.E.,[11] at a time when the bulk of what we know as the Hebrew Scriptures will have been known and studied. Moreover, it is reasonable to assume that he was exposed not only to Jewish writings and ideas, but also to the Greek literature available in his time, which formed part of his intertextual matrix.[12]

Intertextuality and Translation

Interest in intertextuality has mainly focused on original compositions rather than translations, since a translation, by definition, is expected to reproduce the original text without introducing additional material to it. However, scholars have noted that even the most "literal" of translations involve some degree of interpretation, thus providing information on how the translator went about interpreting his source text.[13] Even though

---

9. Craig A. Evans, "Listening for Echoes of Interpreted Scripture," in *Paul and the Scriptures of Israel* (ed. Craig A. Evans and James A. Sanders; JSNTSup 83; SSEJC 1; Sheffield: JSOT, 1993), 51.

10. Huizenga, *The New Isaac*, 62, quoting James A. Sanders, "Isaiah in Luke," in *Luke and Scripture: The Function of Sacred Tradition in Luke–Acts* (ed. Craig A. Evans and James A. Sanders; Minneapolis: Fortress, 1993), 16.

11. See the discussion below on Judeo-Hellenistic milieu.

12. There are inescapable difficulties in our investigation. As Polaski notes, "the state of our historical knowledge makes it impossible to be clear which texts the reader might be expected to know; it is virtually certain the reader would have known texts to which we have no access. Thus this reader's 'solutions' to problems in the text or even to certain figures in the text must rely on *our* knowledge of texts and traditions of that time" (Polaski, *Authorizing an End*, 44–45).

13. E.g. James Barr, *The Typology of Literalism in Ancient Biblical Translations* (MSU 15; Göttingen: Vandenhoeck & Ruprecht, 1979).

the translator of LXX TP is not the author of an entirely new composition, he is a reader of the Hebrew Scriptures and we are the witnesses of his translation-cum-interpretation; in fact, we are the witnesses of the earliest extant reading of the Hebrew text. Our task is much harder than witnessing an author composing an original work. Our translator is heavily constrained by his source text and by his task of translating from Hebrew to Greek. Nevertheless, his "reading" is betrayed in the way he resignifies[14] the text, and especially in places where his *Vorlage* is obscure.[15]

Most of the time, the Hebrew sign finds its Greek counterpart relatively easily: אִישׁ is ἀνήρ, for example. However, at times, the translator stumbles upon difficult signs or syntactical relationships which he has to decipher. The semiotician Michael Riffaterre notes the inadequacy of linguistic competence in any reader of the poetic genre and emphasizes the role of literary competence:

> [H]is linguistic competence enables him to perceive ungrammaticalities;[16] but he is not free to bypass them... Literary competence is also involved: this is the reader's familiarity with the descriptive systems, with themes, with his society's mythologies, and above all with other texts... [I]t is this literary competence alone that will enable the reader to respond properly and to complete or fill in...[17]

According to Riffaterre, the "intertextual" reading proceeds as follows: "It [i.e. the sign] is first apprehended as a mere ungrammaticality, until the discovery is made that there is another text in which the word is grammatical; the moment the other text is identified, the dual sign becomes significant purely because of its shape, which alone alludes to that other code."[18]

He further adds that

---

14.   Resignification is the transformation of an antecedent text or tradition.

15.   When the Greek text does not strictly represent the Hebrew, Barr considers the deviation as "composition": "in that case it may be an original Greek composition of the translator, a reminiscence of some other scriptural passage, a quotation of a non-biblical Greek proverb, or something of the kind" (*The Typology of Literalism*, 287).

16.   An "ungrammaticality" is anything in the text which visibly distorts the representation which the context leads the reader to expect. It can be a deviant grammar or lexeme. See Michael Riffaterre, *Semiotics of Poetry* (London: Methuen, 1980 [1978]), 2.

17.   Ibid., 5.

18.   Ibid., 82.

any ungrammaticality within the poem is a sign of grammaticality else-where, that is, of belonging in another system. The systemic relationship confers significance. The poetic sign has two faces: textually ungram-matical, intertextually grammatical; displaced and distorted in the mimesis system, but in the semiotics grid appropriate and rightly placed.[19]

John Strazicich says that the job of the reader, and in our case the trans-lator, is to perceive these clues or "ungrammaticalities" in the text and to make the proper connection to the presumed intertext, in order to under-stand the author's intent, through the use of the allusion.[20] What we are after, however, is not the author's clues and his intent but the translator's *idea* of the author's intent. Various places in the text provide the oppor-tunity for the translator to express his idea of what the author intended by drawing on other texts. Marguerite Harl notes that at times the translator does resort to "analogical ('intertextual') interpretations, due to the links with parallel passages elsewhere in the LXX. This method of interpreting a passage by reference to another one within the same work has been practiced in Antiquity for all great writings."[21]

Similarly, Robert Hanhart observes that sometimes

> the translators explained the Hebrew original from analogous formulations in the OT witnesses themselves; it is thus a question concerning the possibility of illuminating such analogous statements by translating in a way that was not explicitly represented in the statement of the original… The act of translation leads necessarily to the question about analogous formulations in the context of the original as a whole as received by the translator.[22]

Intertextuality in the LXX

The Aims. The study of intertextuality has been applied to the Septua-gint version for various reasons. There was a need to understand the hermeneutical method of the Greek translators by observing how they interpreted one text in the light of another, and to establish whether there

---

19. Ibid., 164–65.
20. Strazicich, *Joel's Use of Scripture*, 12–13.
21. Marguerite Harl, "La Bible d'Alexandrie," in *X Congress of the IOSCS, Oslo 1998* (ed. Bernard A. Taylor; SBLSCS 51; Atlanta: SBL, 2001), 192.
22. Robert Hanhart, "The Translation of the Septuagint in Light of Earlier Tradition and Subsequent Influences," in *Septuagint, Scrolls and Cognate Writ-ings: Papers Presented to the International Symposium on the Septuagint and Its Relations to the Dead Sea Scrolls and Other Writings (Manchester, 1990)* (ed. George J. Brooke and Barnabas Lindars; SBLSCS 33; Atlanta: Scholars Press, 1992), 358–59.

is a discernible theology behind the translation.[23] Another question was whether similarity of vocabulary and expression could reveal something about the identity of the translator of a specific book, and even help decide whether two or more books shared the same translator.[24] Some studies aimed at determining whether the Greek translator of a LXX book was aware of other LXX books and used them in the process of translation.[25] This could also answer the question of the chronological order in which the various LXX books were translated.[26] Another approach is

23. E.g. Jean Koenig, *L'Herméneutique Analogique du Judaïsme Antique* (VTSup 33; Leiden: Brill, 1982); Gilles Dorival, "Les phénomènes d'intertextualité dans le livre grec des Nombres," in Κατὰ τοὺς ο´ *"selon les Septante": Trente études sur la Bible grecque des Septante. En hommage à Marguerite Harl* (ed. Gilles Dorival and Olivier Munnich; Paris: Cerf, 1995), 253–85; Joachim Schaper, "Messianism in the Septuagint of Isaiah and Messianic Intertextuality in the Greek Bible," in *The Septuagint and Messianism* (ed. M. A. Knibb; BETL 195; Leuven: Peeters, 2006), 371–80; Ngunga, *Messianism in the Old Greek of Isaiah*.

24. E.g. H. St J. Thackeray, "The Greek Translators of Ezekiel," *JTS* 4 (1903): 398–411, "The Greek Translators of Jeremiah," *JTS* 4 (1903): 245–66, and "The Greek Translators of the Prophetical Books," *JTS* 4 (1903): 578–85; Arie van der Kooij, "The Septuagint of Psalms and the First Book of Maccabees," in *The Old Greek Psalter: Studies in Honour of Albert Pietersma* (ed. Robert J. V. Hiebert, Claude E. Cox, and Peter J. Gentry; JSOTSup 332; Sheffield: Sheffield Academic, 2001), 229–47.

25. E.g. Joseph Ziegler, *Untersuchungen zur Septuaginta des Buches Isaias* (Alttestamentliche Abhandlungen 12/3; Münster i. W.: Aschendorffschen, 1934), 103–34; Johann Cook, "Intertextual Relationships Between the Septuagint of Psalms and Proverbs," in Hiebert, Cox, and Gentry, eds., *The Old Greek Psalter*, 218–28; Mirjam Croughs, "Intertextuality in the Septuagint: The Case of Isaiah 19," *BIOSCS* 34 (2001): 81–94, and "Intertextual Readings in the Septuagint," in *The New Testament Interpreted: Essays in Honour of Bernard C. Lategan* (ed. Cilliers Breytenbach, Johan C. Thom, and Jeremy Punt; NovTSup 124; Leiden: Brill, 2006), 119–34; Arie van der Kooij, "Isaiah and Daniel in the Septuagint: How Are These Two Books Related?," in *Florilegium Lovaniense: Studies in Septuagint and Textual Criticism in Honour of Florentino García Martínez* (ed. H. Ausloos, B. Lemmelijn, and M. Vervenne; BETL 224; Leuven: Peeters, 2008), 465–73; Larry Perkins, "Greek Exodus and Greek Isaiah: Detection and Implications of Interdependence in Translation," *BIOSCS* 42 (2009): 18–33; Cécile Dogniez, "L'indépendance du traducteur grec d'Isaïe par rapport au Dodekapropheton," in *Isaiah in Context: Studies in Honour of Arie van der Kooij on the Occasion of His Sixty-Fifth Birthday* (ed. Michaël N. van der Meer et al.; VTSup 138; Leiden: Brill, 2010), 229–46, and, in the same volume, Johann Cook, "The Relationship Between the Septuagint Versions of Isaiah and Proverbs," 199–214.

26. E.g. I. L. Seeligmann, *The Septuagint Version of Isaiah: A Discussion of Its Problems* (Ex oriente lux 9; Leiden: Brill, 1948; repr., ed. R. Hanhart and H. Spieckermann; FAT 40; Tübingen: Mohr Siebeck, 2004), 222–30; Tyler F.

represented by Cécile Dogniez, who examined the links between the LXX translation of Deutero-Zechariah and other parts of Scripture in order to see whether intertextual echoes in the MT itself have had any effect on the translation of the LXX. The purpose was to discover whether the Greek translator had recognized the same links which modern scholars have identified in the Hebrew text.

Dogniez's particular interest, however, concerned cases where the Greek version creates new forms of intertextuality, either absent from the MT or present in the MT but made more explicit in the Greek. The examination of such cases is also a major concern of the present study. These intertextual resonances are evaluated in order to determine whether they are the consequence of thematic or lexical coincidences, incomprehension, vague reminiscence, or the result of the translator's hermeneutical engagement with the biblical text.[27]

Influence from Greek or Hebrew? One difficulty faced by many LXX scholars in their quest for evidence of intertextuality is that of determining with certainty whether the influence on a Greek translator was coming from the Hebrew or the Greek version of a specific LXX book. In the present study, the cases examined offer no indisputable evidence that the Greek translator of the TP was influenced by the LXX version of any book. The influences demonstrated in the translation can be explained solely on the basis of reminiscence of biblical texts in their Hebrew form. In this connection, Dogniez alerts us to the fact that, even when Greek lexical links are present, this could be coincidental if these were words in common use.[28] This, however, does not prove that the translator was unaware of existing Greek versions of other books, but only that such influence is rarely provable. In fact, Robert Hanhart has examined a few cases where the wording of certain passages in the LXX could not exist without the knowledge of the Greek version of the passages from which the influence was derived.[29] One of his examples is the allusion to Lev 26:5 in Amos 9:13:

Williams, "Towards a Date for the Old Greek Psalter," in Hiebert, Cox, and Gentry, eds., *The Old Greek Psalter*, 248–76; J. M. Dines, "The Twelve Among the Prophets" (paper presented as a Grinfield Lecture on the Septuagint, Oxford, March 1, 2007).

27. Cécile Dogniez, "L'intertextualité dans la LXX de Zacharie 9–14," in *Interpreting Translation: Studies on the LXX and Ezekiel in Honour of Johan Lust* (ed. F. García Martínez and M. Vervenne; BETL 192; Leuven: Peeters, 2005), 82–83.

28. Ibid., 89.

29. Hanhart, "The Translation of the Septuagint," 339–79.

Lev 26:5	Amos 9:13
LXX: καὶ καταλήμψεται ὑμῖν ὁ ἀλοητὸς τὸν τρύγητον And for you the threshing shall overtake the vintage	LXX: καὶ καταλήμψεται ὁ ἀλοητὸς τὸν τρύγητον And the threshing shall overtake the vintage
MT: וְהִשִּׂיג לָכֶם דַּיִשׁ אֶת־בָּצִיר Your threshing shall overtake the vintage [NRSV]	MT: וְנִגַּשׁ חוֹרֵשׁ בַּקֹּצֵר the one who plows shall overtake the one who reaps [NRSV]

While the Hebrew formulation is different in these two texts, the Greek translator of Amos recognizes the allusion and renders the verse virtually as it has been rendered in LXX Leviticus.[30] The Greek translator of the TP never uses καταλαμβάνω for נגשׁ. Examples like this, where the LXX expression cannot be accounted for by common translation practice, are, according to Barr, the most convincing type.[31] Of course, agreements such as these are more likely to have come from memory of oral Greek recitations, and not from a copy of the Greek Torah functioning as a reference source consulted by the translator of the TP (see Chapter 2). Dogniez likewise notes that intertextuality may be on the level of reminiscence rather than through direct dependence of one text on another.[32]

LXX TP

LXX Translator
This study is conducted with the assumption that a single translator was responsible for LXX TP. This was suggested by Thackeray[33] and Ziegler[34]

30. Ibid., 360–61. His example of Daniel's use of LXX Num 24:24 is also convincing.
31. James Barr, "Did the Greek Pentateuch Really Serve as a Dictionary for the Translation of the Later Books?," in *Hamlet on A Hill: Semitic and Greek Studies Presented to Professor T. Muraoka on the Occasion of His Sixty-Fifth Birthday* (ed. M. F. J. Baasten and W. Th. van Peursen; OLA 118; Leuven: Peeters, 2003), 541. Less convincing is Muraoka's example of the verb πτερνίζω in LXX Hos 12:4 for עקב as having been borrowed from LXX Gen 27:36. However, the rendering could be explained as etymologically derived (cf. metathesis in LXX Mal 3:8, 9 and LXX Jer 9:3); see Muraoka's "Towards a Septuagint Lexicon," in *VI Congress of the IOSCS: Jerusalem 1986* (ed. Claude E. Cox; SBLSCS 23; Atlanta: Scholars, 1986), 265–68. For some more examples, see *BA* 23, no. 1:11–16.
32. Dogniez, "L'intertextualité dans la LXX de Zacharie 9–14," 96.
33. Thackeray, "The Greek Translators of the Prophetical Books," 579.
34. Joseph Ziegler, "Die Einheit der Septuaginta zum Zwölfprophetenbuch," in *Sylloge: Gesammelte Aufsätze zur Septuaginta* (MSU 10; Göttingen: Vandenhoeck & Ruprecht, 1971), 29–42; originally published as *Die Einheit der LXX zum*

but questioned by Howard[35] and Harrison.[36] However, Muraoka's latest defence of the unitary hypothesis has been sufficiently convincing to provide the basis for an approach to LXX TP by various Septuagint scholars.[37]

Moreover, in this study we shall not be questioning Tov's theory of a common translator for the TP, Jeremiah, and Ezekiel,[38] which represents a modified version of Thackeray's theory. However, no conclusions have been based on this assumption in so far as it reaches beyond the TP (see the cases of Hos 9:14 and Amos 4:13).

LXX Vorlage

On the basis of frequent interchanges between ד and ר, as well as י and ו, the Hebrew *Vorlage* of the Septuagint as a whole is believed to have been written in the Aramaic square script, probably very similar to that of many of the Qumran scrolls.[39] At the same time, Gelston proposes that the Hebrew *Vorlage* used by the translator of Amos displayed an unclear handwriting or was damaged, resulting in frequent minor misreadings.[40]

We have reason to assume that the Hebrew *Vorlage* of the LXX TP was very similar to the consonantal text of the MT, this mainly because of the lack of extensive minuses or pluses, as well as being based on

---

Zwölfprophetenbuch (Beilage zum Vorlesungsverzeichnis der Staatlichen Akademie zu Braunsberg im WS 1934/35; Braunsberg, 1934).

35. George Howard, "Some Notes on the Septuagint of Amos," *VT* 20 (1970): 108–12.

36. C. Robert Harrison, "The Unity of the Minor Prophets in the LXX: A Reexamination of the Question," *BIOSCS* 21 (1988): 55–72.

37. T. Muraoka, "In Defence of the Unity of the Septuagint Minor Prophets," *AJBI* 15 (1989): 25–36, and "Is the Septuagint Amos viii 12 – ix 10 a Separate Unit?," *VT* 20 (1970): 496–500. Some works assuming the unity of the LXX TP are: J. M. Dines, "The Septuagint of Amos: A Study in Interpretation" (Ph.D. diss., Heythrop College, University of London, 1992), 14; *BA* 23, no. 1:9–10; James K. Palmer, "'Not Made with Tracing Paper': Studies in the Septuagint of Zechariah" (Ph.D. diss., University of Cambridge, 2004), 17; W. E. Glenny, *Finding Meaning in the Text: Translation Technique and Theology in the Septuagint of Amos* (VTSup 126; Leiden: Brill, 2009), 261–62.

38. Emanuel Tov, *The Septuagint Translation of Jeremiah and Baruch: A Discussion of an Early Revision of the LXX of Jeremiah 29–52 and Baruch 1:1–3:8* (HSM 8; Missoula: Scholars Press, 1976), 1–14. Also James A. Arieti, "The Vocabulary of Septuagint Amos," *JBL* 93 (1974): 342.

39. Emanuel Tov, "Some Reflections on the Hebrew Texts from which the Septuagint was Translated," *JNSL* 19 (1993): 117.

40. A. Gelston, "Some Hebrew Misreadings in the Septuagint of Amos," *VT* 52 (2002): 499–500.

observations on translation technique.[41] While this may not be an appropriate presupposition for other books, such as LXX Ezekiel or LXX Jeremiah,[42] for the LXX TP the assumption that the Greek translator was working from an MT-family text is justified. In his NETS introduction to the LXX TP, Howard notes that "one should probably not look to a different parent text as the cause for most differences."[43] He also quotes Tov's remarks: "Although there are thousands of differences between 𝔐 and the translations, only a fraction of them was created by a divergence between 𝔐 and the *Vorlage* of the translation. Most of the differences are created by other factors that are not related to the Hebrew *Vorlage*."[44]

Similarly, Dines notes that "[i]n the case of Amos, it is unlikely that the Hebrew text being rendered into Greek was radically different from MT (by comparison with, say, Jeremiah or Job), although it is by no means identical."[45]

While Glenny agrees for LXX Amos,[46] Palmer found that LXX Zechariah was normally consonantally identical with the MT.[47]

However, assuming an MT-type base for LXX TP is only a presupposition, not an attested fact, one should proceed with caution. Jan Joosten states that

> [w]here the LXX diverges from the MT we must always reckon with the possibility that the Greek simply reflects a different Hebrew text. For Hosea, as for the Hebrew Bible in general, the scrolls from Qumran have been an eye-opener in this regard: several variants of the Greek version which had been claimed to be due to the translator can now be shown to have existed in Hebrew manuscripts. For the evaluation of the translator's exegesis such cases make a real difference. Furthermore, we do not possess the original Greek translation as it left the hands of the translator.

41. For LXX Amos and consequently for the rest of the TP, see James A. Arieti, "A Study in the Septuagint of Amos" (Ph.D. diss., Stanford University, 1972). His conclusions agree with G. E. Howard's for the whole of the TP, "To the Reader of the Twelve Prophets," in NETS, 777–81. J. Joosten calls the translation technique of the Greek TP "creatively faithful"; see Joosten's "A Septuagintal Translation Technique in the Minor Prophets: The Elimination of Verbal Repetitions," in García Martínez and Vervenne, eds., *Interpreting Translation*, 217.

42. Tov, "Some Reflections on the Hebrew Texts," 116–17.

43. Howard, "To the Reader of the Twelve Prophets," 777.

44. E. Tov, *Textual Criticism of the Hebrew Bible* (Minneapolis: Fortress, 1992), 123.

45. Dines, "The Septuagint of Amos," 17.

46. Glenny, *Finding Meaning in the Text*, 14.

47. Palmer, "'Not Made with Tracing Paper,'" 18, 176.

Divergences between the Greek and the Hebrew may be due to scribal errors in the transmission of the Greek, or to conscious alterations of the Septuagint text.[48]

At the same time, Joosten admits that "the extent of our ignorance should not be exaggerated. Each of the 'unknown' domains has in fact been much researched, and usable results have been obtained."[49] While not overlooking the element of uncertainty in all this, the present study uses the MT as its point of departure unless internal or external factors point to a Hebrew *Vorlage* different from the MT (for example, see the cases of Amos 1:3 and 1:15).[50] As regards the textual history of the TP in its Hebrew and Greek witnesses,[51] the scope of the present study permits discussion of texts and issues only as they become relevant in relation to specific texts.

Translation Technique
Any conclusions on the Hebrew *Vorlage* of the LXX are subject to conclusions relating to translation technique. The importance of the analysis of translation technique cannot be overemphasized, and Tov rightly warns against rash retroversions of presumed variants: "one should first attempt to view deviations as the result of the inter-translational factors described here. Only after all possible translational explanations have

48. Jan Joosten, "Exegesis in the Septuagint Version of Hosea," in de Moor, ed., *Intertextuality in Ugarit*, 63–64. The problems arising in the transmission of the Greek are also highlighted by Peter J. Gentry, "Old Greek and Later Revisors: Can We Always Distinguish Them?," in *Scripture in Transition: Essays on Septuagint, Hebrew Bible, and Dead Sea Scrolls in Honour of Raija Sollamo* (ed. Anssi Voitila and Jutta Jokiranta; JSJSup 126; Leiden: Brill, 2008), 301–27.

49. Joosten, "Exegesis in the Septuagint Version of Hosea," 64.

50. For the LXX addition in Hos 13:4, see Barry A. Jones, *The Formation of the Book of the Twelve: A Study in Text and Canon* (SBLDS 149; Atlanta: Scholars Press, 1995), 93–95.

51. See the following studies: J. Ziegler, "Einleitung," in *Duodecim prophetae,* vol. XIII (Septuaginta Vetus Testamentum Graecum; Göttingen: Vandenhoeck & Ruprecht, 1943), 1–145; Arieti, *A Study in the Septuagint of Amos*, 1–21; L. A. Sinclair, "Hebrew Text of the Qumran Micah Pesher and Textual Tradition of the Minor Prophets," *RevQ* 11 (1983): 253–63; R. E. Fuller, "The Minor Prophets Manuscripts from Qumran, Cave IV" (Ph.D. diss., Harvard University, 1988), and "Textual Traditions in the Book of Hosea and the Minor Prophets," in *The Madrid Qumran Congress*, vol. 1 (ed. J. Trebolle Barrera and L. V. Montaner; Leiden: Brill, 1992), 247–56; Palmer, "'Not Made with Tracing Paper,'" 15–17; Glenny, *Finding Meaning in the Text*, 10–14.

been dismissed should one turn to the assumption that the translation represents a Hebrew reading different from MT."[52]

Even the "Helsinki school,"[53] whose name has come to be synonymous with the study of "translation technique," acknowledge that "'[t]rans-lation technique' is not a very appropriate term to describe the whole procedure or process of translation, which is the focus of translation-technical studies, but a more suitable term has not yet been found."[54] It is not until Aquila that one may talk about a preconceived technique.[55]

In the absence of a communicative term, the need to clarify what is meant by "translation technique" was felt by Aejmelaeus in 1998, when she suggested that "'translation technique' be understood as simply designating the relationship between the text of the translation and its *Vorlage*."[56] Despite her focus on syntactical relationships and while criticizing reliance on a statistical approach, she recognizes the value of a multi-angled approach for understanding the technique of each translator: "In this endeavour there is room for all kinds of approaches—for the linguistic and the more theological approach, for statistical representa-tion of data as well as sampling of unique cases. Every possible kind of observation is valuable and complements in its way the portrait of the individual behind the text."[57]

Before describing "translation technique" in the LXX, one should remember that the LXX is not a single translation but a collection of translations with different types of translation technique in evidence. Thus it is imperative to acquire a sense of how each translator approached his text before considering other explanations for peculiarities in his renderings. Like Tov, Theo A. W. van der Louw stresses the importance of approaching the LXX in this way:

---

52. E. Tov, *The Text-critical Use of the Septuagint in Biblical Research* (2d ed.; JBS 8; Jerusalem: Simor, 1997), 40.

53. For a survey of the various schools of thought on "translation technique," see Glenny, *Finding Meaning in the Text*, 31–44. For his observations on the translation technique of LXX Amos, see pp. 44–69.

54. Raija Sollamo, "Introduction," in *Helsinki Perspectives on the Translation Technique of the Septuagint* (ed. Raija Sollamo and Seppo Sipilä; PFES 82; Göttingen: Vandenhoeck & Ruprecht, 2001), 7; also Anneli Aejmelaeus, "What We Talk About When We Talk About Translation Technique," in Taylor, ed., *X Congress of the IOSCS*, 531–32.

55. However, studies in Aquila show that he also made use of various approaches in interpreting his text. See Tim Edwards, "Aquila and the Rabbis on Hapax Legomena in the Psalms" (paper presented at ESAJS "Greek Scripture and the Rabbis" Conference, OCHJS, Yarnton Manor, Oxford, June 21, 2010).

56. Aejmelaeus, "What We Talk About," 532.

57. Ibid., 552.

If one wants to determine whether a 'deviation' stems from a different *Vorlage*, it should first be excluded that the 'deviation' has its roots in translational factors. In order to do so we must know which techniques were used, how and why.[58]

The linguistic orientation of this method stipulates that linguistic explanations of certain renderings are sought before either text-critical or cultural and theological factors are called in. This procedure can offer a helpful correction to the methods used in Septuagint research, since they force the researcher to explain more precisely which 'free renderings' result from linguistic demands and which are the result of the translator's exegesis or a different parent text.[59]

With reference to the Greek translator of the TP, it is apparent from the outset that he follows the word order of the Hebrew *Vorlage*, giving the impression of a very "literal" translation.[60] This, however, renders it by no means slavish.[61] In fact, the Greek translator was able to exercise freedom within the boundaries of an often faithful word order.[62] Arieti's study on Amos has shown this "freedom" at work in many of the tendencies of the Greek translator. He finds that additions result from paraphrasing, whether supplying the subject or object where it is unclear in the Hebrew, or inserting words or phrases in order to clarify the sense, and suchlike.[63] At times there are double translations of a single Hebrew word, and at other times the translator abbreviates.[64] Similarly, de Waard gives examples of how the Greek translator of Amos explicates the Hebrew text. He brings agents (e.g. ἀνήρ in Amos 7:7),[65] implicit

58. Theo A. W. van der Louw, *Transformations in the Septuagint: Towards an Interaction of Septuagint Studies and Translation Studies* (CBET 47; Leuven: Peeters, 2007), 8.

59. Ibid., 17.

60. In LXX Zechariah Palmer generally sees a faithful word order, but also observes divergences in several places; "'Not Made with Tracing Paper,'" 36–37. In LXX Amos the translator displays a conscious effort to follow the word order of his Hebrew *Vorlage*; see Glenny, *Finding Meaning in the Text*, 44–46.

61. See Jones, *The Formation of the Book of the Twelve*, 83–91; also Arie van der Kooij, "The Septuagint of Zechariah as Witness to an Early Interpretation of the Book," in *The Book of Zechariah and Its Influence* (ed. Christopher Tuckett; Aldershot: Ashgate, 2003), 53.

62. James Barr describes the translation technique of various LXX books as "variations within a basically literal approach"; see his *The Typology of Literalism*, 281.

63. Arieti, *A Study in the Septuagint of Amos*, 30.

64. Ibid., 44–45.

65. Jan De Waard, "Translation Techniques Used by the Greek Translators of the Book of Amos," *Bib* 59 (1978): 340.

referents (e.g. λόγον κυρίου in Amos 5:1)[66] and general information that is inferred (e.g. καὶ ὑπολειφθήσονται οἱ κατάλοιποι in Amos 6:9)[67] out into the open.[68] Additionally, vocabulary choices, as Muraoka emphasizes, reveal much about the translator's skill, competence and subtle sense of aesthetics.[69] At times, as many scholars observe, the translator's agenda of providing an intelligible text for his readers led him to "manipulate" his Hebrew text,[70] or to interpret it in the light of the TP as a whole.[71]

However, any study on translation technique should presuppose some degree of faith in the translator and his task. Although we do not have access to the translator's mental processes, we can begin with the assumption, as Dines suggests, that the text made some sense, even if obscure or mysterious to the translator:

> [I]t just does not seem credible to imagine him like a schoolchild faced with a Greek or Latin unseen, writing nonsense out of sheer desperation. Of course, we do not have access to what the translator thought or intended. But he should be allowed a presumption of seriousness (the Prologue to Ben Sira reveals one ancient translator's seriousness of purpose and awareness of the problems); the text he has produced should be first examined as making sense rather than nonsense.[72]

This, however, should not be taken to the extreme position that every divergence is the result of conscious exegetical processes or pre-existing traditions. As Palmer concludes, "[t]here seems to be an element of ignorance in the translation too, and we must not let an analytical

---

66. Ibid., 342.

67. Ibid., 343–44.

68. Joosten notes the translator's use of clarifying additions in LXX Hosea; see his "Exegesis in the Septuagint Version of Hosea," 77. See also Aaron W. Park's analysis of LXX Amos: *The Book of Amos as Composed and Read in Antiquity* (StBL 37; New York: Lang, 2001), 138–77.

69. Takamitsu Muraoka, "Translation Techniques and Beyond," in Sollamo and Sipilä, eds., *Helsinki Perspectives*, 22. Also evident in Arieti's article, "The Vocabulary of Septuagint Amos."

70. Tov, *The Text-critical Use of the Septuagint*, 162–71; Dines, "The Septuagint of Amos," 308–9; David A. Baer, *When We All Go Home: Translation and Theology in LXX Isaiah 56–66* (JSOTSup 318; HBV 1; Sheffield: Sheffield Academic, 2001), 29; Palmer, "'Not Made with Tracing Paper,'" 55; Glenny, *Finding Meaning in the Text*, 85–86. The phenomenon is also traced in Qumran writings; see Shemaryahu Talmon, "Aspects of the Textual Transmission of the Bible in the Light of Qumran Manuscripts," *Textus* 4 (1964): 128.

71. Van der Kooij, "The Septuagint of Zechariah," 60.

72. Dines, "The Septuagint of Amos," 37.

schematisation dictate that the translator is either scholar or slave."[73] Indeed, the translator's mind is only partly open to us. All we have available to examine is his documented reading of the consonantal Hebrew text.

Reading Tradition or Not?
When we are faced with disagreements between the MT and the LXX, the inevitable question arises: What do these divergences mean? Assuming the Hebrew *Vorlage* of the LXX is similar to an MT-type text, as is the case for the TP, the divergences are the result of a different *reading* of the unpointed text. Apart from the casual use of *scriptio plena*, vowels were not marked. Occasionally, the consonantal text may have been divided in different places,[74] and vowels different from those in the MT may have been assumed by the LXX translator. Earlier in the twentieth century, Wutz proposed a theory already suggested by Tychsen in the eighteenth century,[75] namely that the Septuagint was translated from a *Vorlage* that consisted of a Hebrew text transcribed in Greek letters, including the Hebrew vowels normally read.[76] However, no transcriptions of this kind, apart from Origen's in the third century C.E., are known to have existed.[77] Other approaches seek to take account of translator competence extending even to the tradition of vocalization. Tov holds that the Septuagint presupposes the knowledge of a reading tradition from public readings of the Torah,[78] and van der Kooij assumes that the translators were scribes who were trained in the reading of the Hebrew text.[79]

---

73. Palmer, "'Not Made with Tracing Paper,'" 176.
74. E.g. LXX Hos 6:5 (καὶ τὸ κρίμα μου ὡς φῶς) read ומשפטי כאור instead of MT ומשפטיך אור. However, there is not much evidence of scriptio continua for Hebrew texts, as Alan Millard has noted: "'Scriptio Continua' in Early Hebrew: Ancient Practice or Modern Surmise?," *JSS* 15 (1970): 2–15.
75. O. G. Tychsen, *Testamen de Variis Codicum Hebraicorum Vet. Test. MSS* (Rostock, 1772).
76. F. X. Wutz, *Die Transkriptionen von der LXX bis zu Hieronymus* (BWAT 2,9; Stuttgart: Kohlhammer, 1933).
77. See the evaluation of the theory by Natalio Fernández Marcos, *The Septuagint in Context: Introduction to the Greek Versions of the Bible* (trans. Wilfred G. E. Watson; Leiden: Brill, 2000), 61–62.
78. Tov, *The Text-critical Use of the Septuagint*, 107–10.
79. Arie van der Kooij, *The Oracle of Tyre: The Septuagint of Isaiah XXIII as Version and Vision* (VTSup 71; Leiden: Brill, 1998), 121–22; criticized by Stefan Schorch, "The Septuagint and the Vocalization of the Hebrew Text of the Torah," in *XII Congress of the IOSCS: Leiden, 2004* (ed. Melvin K. H. Peeters; SBLSCS 54; Leiden: Brill, 2006), 44–45.

According to James Barr, one could postulate two methods by which the translator went about producing his version. Under Method A,

> [k]nowing the variety of possibilities, the reader worked by a process of semantic/syntactic scanning, looking at each word within a series and considering what meanings and functions they, as spelt, might have within that context. When he decided on a meaning through this process, he was also able to provide the full phonic realization of the words… The essential point is that the semantic/syntactic scanning preceded the full pronunciation of the words and *provides* the basis for it.[80]

On the other hand,

> [i]n Method B the reader, having before him the then written or "consonantal" text, asked for, or had available, the full pronounced form for each word (in traditional terms, the "vocalization"; or, in more modern terms, the reading tradition)… Under Method B the translator knew, or obtained from someone else who knew, the "correct" vocalization (more exactly, the pronunciation of the entire word), and used this, along with the written text, as combined datum for the rendering of the text into Greek.[81]

While Method A leaves evidence of its existence when things go very wrong, it is not the same with Method B. When things go badly (i.e. large semantic/syntactic divergence between MT and LXX), Method B commonly implies the recognition of more variants.[82] Barr, by using various examples and especially the ד/ר variations, shows that these differences between the Hebrew and the Greek "could have taken place *only where the text is visually read but without an oral tradition of its pronunciation*."[83] Although Barr does not argue that Method A was the one solely or exclusively used by all or some of the translators of the LXX, he does observe that it explains a considerable number of cases. Moreover, Method A has a lot to commend it, especially since this would

---

80. James Barr, "'Guessing' in the Septuagint," in *Studien zur Septuaginta - Robert Hanhart zu Ehren* (ed. D. Fraenkel et al.; MSU 20; Göttingen: Vandenhoeck & Ruprecht, 1990), 21.

81. Ibid.

82. L. H. Schiffman notes that "[o]ften exegesis has been introduced into LXX readings such that they do not constitute real variants with MT": "The Septuagint and the Temple Scroll: Shared 'Halakhic' Variants," in Brooke and Lindars, eds., *Septuagint, Scrolls and Cognate Writings*, 292.

83. Barr, "'Guessing' in the Septuagint," 29 (emphasis original). For possible confusion of consonants, see Armand Kaminka, *Studien zur Septuaginta an der Hand der Zwölf Kleinen Prophetenbücher* (SGFWJ 33; Frankfurt: Kauffman, 1928), 24–30. For Septuagint Amos, see Gelston, "Some Hebrew Misreadings," 493–500.

have been the normal way of reading and translating any Hebrew text other than Scripture. This is the way in which an ancient dragoman might have approached business or government documents.[84] I would agree with Barr, without necessarily saying that there are no discernible "traditions" in the LXX translation. From a similar standpoint to that of van der Kooij,[85] I would argue that Jewish tradition *did* affect the LXX vocalization of the Hebrew text, for this was probably not a disinterested translator but one who moved in Jewish circles, and the Scriptures were not commercial documents but sacred texts to which he would have had prior exposure. Most probably, Method A was often guided by the translator's *presuppositions* of what the text was saying (see on Amos 7:1 in Chapter 5) and not from possession of a *complete* phonic tradition in his memory.[86] Moreover, we should allow that traditions have a starting point, and they may just as well have begun in the process of translation.[87]

Rabin argues that the Greek Pentateuch displays features of the dragoman practice of ancient Egypt more than it displays features of the targumic model, and this renders the LXX important for the reconstruction of the Hebrew *Vorlage*.[88] Others have argued for a closer

84. Barr, "'Guessing' in the Septuagint," 25, 28.

85. Van der Kooij, *The Oracle of Tyre*, 112.

86. A similar view to mine is proposed by Stefan Schorch, who argues that the pointing depends to a large extent on parabiblical traditions current in Second Temple Judaism. However, these traditions are eclectic and cover only parts of the biblical text. "This feature explains why the translators of the Torah produced a translation that is very faithful in some parts, while it failed in others." Schorch's study was limited to Genesis, but some of his conclusions can be applicable to the TP; see Schorch, "The Septuagint and the Vocalization of the Hebrew Text of the Torah," 54. Anneli Aejmelaeus also notes that familiarity with popular Pentateuchal stories triggered more freedom in the Greek translation of those passages: *Parataxis in the Septuagint: A Study of the Renderings of the Hebrew Coordinate Clauses in the Greek Pentateuch* (Annales Academiae Scientiarum Fennicae Dissertationes Humanarum Litterarum 31; Helsinki: Suomalainen Tiedeakatemia, 1982), 172–73.

87. Aaron Schart thinks that "[a]s long as there are no clear indicators that suggest otherwise one must presume that a different vocalization occurred unintentionally" ("The Jewish and the Christian Greek Versions of Amos," in *Septuagint Research: Issues and Challenges in the Study of the Greek Jewish Scriptures* [ed. Wolfgang Kraus and Glenn Wooden; SBLSCS 53; Atlanta: SBL, 2006], 164).

88. Chaim Rabin, "The Translation Process and the Character of the Septuagint," *Textus* 6 (1968): 21–26. This is the view of Elias J. Bickerman ("The Septuagint as a Translation," *PAAJR* 28 [1959]: 8) and Sebastian Brock ("The Phenomenon of the Septuagint," *OtSt* 17 [1972]: 11–36). For an evaluation of their theories, see Benjamin J. Wright, "The Jewish Scriptures in Greek: The Septuagint in the Context

relationship between the targums and the LXX and have claimed similarities in the exegetical methods employed in these versions.[89] For the
LXX TP, one can see a combination of devices employed in the production of the translation: ad hoc renderings, stylistic ploys, and interpretive/
midrashic manipulations of the text.

Judeo-Hellenistic Milieu
Scholars have tentatively placed the translation of LXX TP around the
middle of the second century B.C.E. in Egypt.[90] Although Dines recognizes the possibility of a Palestinian provenance, she rejects it.[91] Some of
the translator's methods are attested in Egypt as well as Palestine, which
makes the question of provenance more difficult. His translation displays
techniques attested in Alexandrian word-analysis (see "Etymologizing"
in Chapter 2),[92] and his vocabulary, as Egyptian papyri have shown, is at
home within the contemporary Greek linguistic context (see Chapter 2).[93]

of Ancient Translation Activity," in *Praise Israel for Wisdom and Instruction:
Essays on Ben Sira and Wisdom, the Letter of Aristeas and the Septuagint* (JSJSup
131; Leiden: Brill, 2008), 197–212.
  89. E.g. Z. Frankel, *Über den Einfluss der Palästinischen Exegese auf die
Alexandrinische Hermeneutik* (Leipzig: Barth, 1831; repr., Farnborough: Gregg
International, 1972); Pinkhos Churgin, "The Targum and the Septuagint," *AJSL* 50
(1933): 41–65; Geza Vermes, "Bible and Midrash: Early Old Testament Exegesis,"
in *Cambridge History of the Bible*, vol. 1 (ed. P. R. Ackroyd and C. F. Evans;
Cambridge: Cambridge University Press, 1970), 203; D. W. Gooding, "Two Possible Examples of Midrashic Interpretation in the Septuagint Exodus," in *Wort, Lied
und Gottesspruch: Beiträge zur Septuaginta. Festschrift für Joseph Ziegler herausgegeben von Josef Schreiner* (ed. Josef Schreiner; Forschung zur Bibel 1; Würzburg:
Echter Verlag Katholisches Bibelwerk, 1972), 39–48, and "On the Use of the LXX
for Dating Midrashic Elements in the Targum," *JTS* 25 (1974): 1–11; Koenig,
L'Herméneutique Analogique; Leo Prijs, *Jüdische Tradition in der Septuaginta: Die
grammatikalische Terminologie des Abraham ibn Esra* (Leiden: Brill, 1948; repr.,
Hildesheim: Georg Olms, 1987); E. Tov, "Midrash-Type Exegesis in the Septuagint
of Joshua," in *The Greek and Hebrew Bible: Collected Essays on the Septuagint*
(VTSup 72; Leiden: Brill, 1999), 153–64.
  90. Dines, "The Septuagint of Amos," 311–13; Glenny, *Finding Meaning in the
Text*, 262–264.
  91. Dines, "The Septuagint of Amos," 313.
  92. David Weissert, "Alexandrinian Analogical Word-Analysis and Septuagint
Translation Techniques," *Textus* 8 (1973): 31–44.
  93. For LXX Pentateuch, see John A. L. Lee, *A Lexical Study of the Septuagint
Version of the Pentateuch* (SBLSCS 14; Chico: Scholars Press, 1983). For LXX
Isaiah, see Michaël N. van der Meer, "Papyrological Perspectives on the Septuagint
of Isaiah" (paper presented at Colloquium on "The Old Greek of Isaiah: Issues and

However, with eight Septuagint or Septuagint-related mss found at Qumran and a ninth at *Naḥal Ḥever* (Greek TP scroll), we can no longer treat the LXX as solely an Alexandrian phenomenon.[94] Lindars notes that

> [t]he Minor Prophets scroll from Naḥal Ḥever gives further evidence that the Greek scriptures were used in Palestine… All this supports the growing consensus that the Jews in Palestine belonged to the larger culture region in which Greek style and language predominated, at least in the educated classes. It can be assumed that the Septuagint was used in the synagogues of the Hellenists in Jerusalem (Acts 6:9).[95]

Various affinities with Qumran writings, such as hermeneutical approaches to the biblical text, have been noted by various scholars.[96] For example, the LXX translator's attitude to prophecy appears to have been close to that observed in Jewish writings, especially Qumran writings, in that he understood the text to be speaking primarily about the times of the LXX translator; moreover, many of the prophecies were yet to be fulfilled (see the sections on Amos 5:24 and 7:1).[97]

As far as intertextuality is concerned, it has been observed that sometimes a single lexematic association would place two texts in a parallel relationship, in the eyes of the ancient reader, as Friedrich Avemarie has shown for the Qumran writings and the NT.[98] George Brooke has also discussed intertextuality in the Qumran documents and in the NT and notes that

Perspectives," Colloquium, University of Leiden, Leiden, April 10–11, 2008). However, their discoveries are applicable to the LXX TP when the vocabulary is shared. Of course, we assume that the language of the Egyptian documents probably resembled other Levantine Greek that did not survive from antiquity.

94.   Eugene Ulrich, "The Septuagint Manuscripts from Qumran: A Reappraisal of their Value," in Brooke and Lindars, eds., *Septuagint, Scrolls and Cognate Writings*, 49.

95.   Barnabas Lindars, "Introduction," in Brooke and Lindars, eds., *Septuagint, Scrolls and Cognate Writings*, 4.

96.   See the volume dedicated to this topic: Brooke and Lindars, eds., *Septuagint, Scrolls and Cognate Writings*.

97.   See Dines, "The Septuagint of Amos," 38–39; van der Kooij, "The Septuagint of Zechariah," 55–57; Schart, "The Jewish and the Christian Greek Versions of Amos," 166–67.

98.   Friedrich Avemarie, "Interpreting Scripture Through Scripture: Exegesis Based on Lexematic Association in the Dead Sea Scrolls and the Pauline Epistles," in *Echoes from the Caves: Qumran and the New Testament* (ed. Florentino García Martínez; Studies on the Texts of the Desert of Judah 85; Leiden: Brill, 2009), 83–102.

the scrolls found at Qumran attest how scribes in copying its books often behaved intertextually themselves, introducing phraseology that was reminiscent of other passages of scripture. This may happen both deliberately as two scriptural texts with related subject matter are associated with one another; or it may happen unconsciously as the idiomatic phraseology of one passage comes to influence the scribe as he works on another.[99]

Moreover, Brooke has shown that exegetical techniques later accepted by the rabbis (e.g. *gezerah shavah*) are already observed in Qumran documents regardless of genre.[100] It would not, therefore, be unreasonable to expect similar approaches to the biblical text on the part of the LXX translators.

As Brooke reports for Philo, Qumran and the targums, the scope of the ancient interpreter is very broad, and he treats the Bible as a whole.[101] A broad context vision is also a characteristic of the LXX translators, as Tov confirms: "it should be stressed that the translators' concept of context was more comprehensive than ours. They referred not only to the relationship between the words in their immediate context but also to remote contexts. Furthermore, the translator might introduce any idea that the source text called to mind."[102]

Such an approach creates a larger context for the interpretation of biblical passages, or even individual words.

Concluding Methodological Observations and Summary

In the light of the above, we are justified in looking for "intertexts" outside the TP. Indeed, intertextuality operating solely within the LXX TP has not been included in the present study, nor have instances where the LXX TP may have exercised influence on other biblical books. Nevertheless, the aim of this study is to cover the broad intertextual spectrum, examining all manifestations of influence on the Septuagint of the TP, ranging from lexical sourcing to intertextual allusions.

---

99. George J. Brooke, "Shared Intertextual Interpretations in the Dead Sea Scrolls and the New Testament," n.p. Online: http://orion.huji.ac.il/symposiums/ 1st/papers/Brooke96.html. Cited January 16, 2011.

100.   George J. Brooke, *Exegesis at Qumran: 4QFlorilegium in Its Jewish Context* (JSOTSup 29; Sheffield: JSOT, 1985), 8–79.

101.   Ibid., 8–79, esp. 28 and 36. Also Jones, *The Formation of the Book of the Twelve*, 9.

102.   Tov, *The Text-critical Use of the Septuagint*, 26.

For my evaluation of intertextual links I have taken into account criteria such as are highlighted by Dines:[103]

1. A resemblance between two texts must not be explicable as independent renderings of similar *Vorlagen*.[104]
2. It must not be traceable to a passage in the Pentateuch used independently by each translator.
3. It must not be the outcome of each translator's normal translational practice.
4. One rendering must fit its presumed Hebrew, and thus its context, more appropriately than the other, so that dependence is plausible only in one direction.[105]

I use the eclectic Old Greek[106] text of the TP edited by J. Ziegler,[107] which I compare with the MT[108] (for Chapters 3, 4 and 5), identifying differences between the two which appear to be intertextually significant, or which have been considered as such by other scholars. It was not possible to include all the material generated in this research. The chapters are laid out as follows:

In Chapter 2, "Lexical Sourcing," I begin by looking at vocabulary agreements with the LXX Pentateuch, using Tov's thesis as a starting point and attempting to recover any discernible dependence on the LXX Pentateuch for the lexical sourcing of the *entire* LXX TP.

For Chapter 3 and following, the scope had to be narrowed to a selection of cases from Hosea, Amos and Micah because of space limitations. However, my findings may have implications for the longer Greek collection of the TP (see the section "LXX Translator"). Chapter 3 focuses on the use of standard translations or expressions also found in other LXX books.

Chapter 4 deals with connections between specific passages triggered by the presence of "catchwords," and Chapter 5 examines allusions[109] to

---

103. Dines was influenced by Seeligmann's work in developing her criteria.

104. This point seems to suggest that the necessary work of textual criticism must be done first in order to ensure that intertextuality is the product of the LXX translation and was not already found in the Hebrew *Vorlage* used by the translator.

105. Dines, "The Twelve Among the Prophets," 5.

106. Old Greek, Greek, LXX and Septuagint are used interchangeably, and the LXX order of books is followed as well as the LXX names of books unless only the MT text is intended.

107. *Duodecim Prophetae.*

108. For the MT, the *Codex Leningradensis* in the standard edition of *BHS* was used.

109. Beal offers a variety of suggestions from different scholars on how "allusion" is defined. The ones I find most helpful and sufficiently flexible are: an

specific biblical stories, events or characters. These are broad categories, and the lines of demarcation are not absolute. Various cases display elements which belong in more than one category, but for the purposes of the present study a working division had to be made.

This study highlights the need for more exhaustive research on the entire corpus of the LXX TP in order to acquire a more thorough understanding of the translator's linguistic and literary competence, as well as his working methods.

"allusion" can be "a 'text-linking device' which transgresses the boundaries of the text in which it is found," or "a 'device for the simultaneous activation of two texts'." Beal notes that "the question of whether or not the author *intended* to allude need not be raised in determining what is an allusion and what is not." Timothy K. Beal, "Glossary," in Fewell, ed., *Reading Between Texts*, 21.

Chapter 2

LEXICAL SOURCING:
WAS THE GREEK PENTATEUCH
USED AS A LEXICON BY THE GREEK TRANSLATOR
OF THE TWELVE PROPHETS?

Introduction: The Problem and Its History

Many scholars have noticed that the vocabulary of the LXX Pentateuch
is also reflected in other LXX books. At the beginning of the twentieth
century, Thackeray observed that translation equivalents in various
books agreed with the LXX Pentateuch. LXX Isaiah, for example, displays
some affinity with LXX Exodus, and this served as one of his arguments
for an early date for the translation of Isaiah.[1] Around the same time,
F. W. Mozley noted similar affinities between LXX Pentateuch and the
Greek Psalter and made the following bold statement: "This only seems
certain about the date and relative order of the books of the LXX, that the
Pentateuch came first, about 250 B.C.E. It was probably, Hebrew and
Greek, our translator's text-book in learning Hebrew, and serves him to a
great extent in place of [*sic*] dictionary."[2]

Thackeray, however, proposed his theory that the LXX translation
developed within the Jewish synagogue in Alexandria,[3] a theory picked
up by Gerleman who says that similarities in LXX vocabulary may be
partly attributable to liturgical practice in the Jewish synagogue.[4] Seeligmann describes this theory of a Targum-like liturgical provenance for the
LXX, developed mainly by Kahle, as arising from the custom of giving a
Greek paraphrase after every Hebrew sentence or two. He says:

1. Thackeray, "The Greek Translators of the Prophetical Books," 583.
2. F. W. Mozley, *The Psalter of the Church: The Septuagint Psalms Compared
with the Hebrew, with Various Notes* (Cambridge: Cambridge University Press,
1905), xii–xiii.
3. H. St. J. Thackeray, *The Septuagint and Jewish Worship: A Study in Origins*
(The Schweich Lectures 1920; London: Oxford University Press, 1921).
4. G. Gerleman, *Studies in the Septuagint*. Vol. 2, *Chronicles* (LUÅ I/43 3;
Lund: Gleerup, 1946), 22.

Such a paraphrase, more or less improvised during the service, could never display the strict uniformity of a written text; however, with time, a tradition consolidates for the rendering of certain expressions. When the need was gradually felt to replace these improvised oral recitations by a written translation, various written residues came into being, which at first circulated side by side.[5]

Seeligmann, in agreement with Mozley's theory, concludes for LXX Isaiah that "the Pentateuch—or, more precisely, the traditional explanation of it—exercised a profound influence on the translator's way of thinking and his working method."[6] However, Seeligmann still raises some unanswered questions:

> [D]id the translator—or translators—derive such renderings as those discussed above, from already existing, written translations, or from his— or their—memory of unconsolidated oral tradition? To what extent did he improvise on the basis of direct reminiscences of the Hebrew text of the Pentateuch; [*sic*] that is, what evidence is there of the extent to which this text was still a vital possession of the Alexandrian circle to which our translator belonged?[7]

Flashar,[8] Kaminka,[9] Ziegler,[10] Walters,[11] and Allen[12] also note affinities between the Greek Pentateuch and other LXX books, but in 1981 Emanuel Tov expanded this thesis that the Greek Pentateuch influenced the rest of the LXX books. He lists several Greek renderings adopted by later translators, which allegedly originated in the LXX Pentateuch, the first part to be translated as a single entity.[13] While past observations were restricted to individual books, Tov now incorporates the entire LXX in a systematic way.

---

5. Seeligmann, *The Septuagint Version of Isaiah*, 47.

6. Ibid., 188.

7. Ibid., 191–92.

8. M. Flashar, "Exegetische Studien zum Septuaginta Psalter (IV)," *ZAW* 32 (1912): 161–89.

9. Kaminka, *Studien*, 17–20.

10. Ziegler, *Untersuchungen*, 134–75.

11. P. Walters, *The Text of the Septuagint: Its Corruptions and Their Emendation* (ed. D. W. Gooding; Cambridge: Cambridge University Press, 1973), 150–53.

12. L. C. Allen, *The Greek Chronicles: The Relation of the Septuagint of I and II Chronicles to the Masoretic Text*. Part 1, *The Translator's Craft* (VTSup 25; Leiden: Brill, 1974), 23–26.

13. Emanuel Tov, "The Impact of the LXX Translation of the Pentateuch on the Translation of the Other Books," in *Mélanges Dominique Barthélemy: Études Bibliques Offertes à l'Occasion de son 60e Anniversaire* (ed. Pierre Casetti, Othmar Keel, and Adrian Schenker; OBO 38; Göttingen: Vandenhoeck & Ruprecht, 1981), 577–93.

Tov's Thesis

Since Tov's proposal is our point of departure, it is worth outlining briefly his position. Tov begins with the following assumptions: (a) the Torah was translated first, and (b) it would have been familiar to the translators of the rest of the LXX books in Greek, owing to its liturgical use in the synagogue.[14] As a result, he holds that it is only natural that the vocabulary of the Greek Pentateuch would have influenced subsequent translations of biblical books. This influence, according to Tov, is detected at four different levels:

1. The *vocabulary* of the Greek Pentateuch was perpetuated in the translation of the later books.
2. The Greek Pentateuch served as a *lexicon* for later translators who often turned to it when they encountered "difficult" Hebrew words which occurred also in the Pentateuch.
3. *Quotations* from, and *allusions* to, passages in the Hebrew Pentateuch occurring in the later books of the Bible were often phrased in the Greek in a manner identical to the translation of Pentateuchal passages in the LXX.
4. The *contents* of the Greek Pentateuch often influenced the wording of later translations on an exegetical level.[15]

It is in the Pentateuch, according to Tov, that formal equivalences between Greek and Hebrew words are first established. Yet, he also allows for the possibility that the foundations of this "matching" were already laid in the generations which preceded formal translation.[16] The lack of variation in these equivalences persuades Tov that post-Pentateuchal books are dependent on the vocabulary of the Pentateuch. To support this, he compiles a list of "influential" Hebrew–Greek identifications, with a special emphasis on neologisms. Tov defines "neologisms" as words which were coined by the translators (or by a preceding generation) in order to represent objects or ideas which could not be adequately expressed by the existing vocabulary.[17] Ten of these "neologisms" are used in the Greek TP.

---

14. Ibid., 578. However, Tov admits that there is no sound evidence for the liturgical use of the Greek Pentateuch, or of the other Greek books.
15. Ibid.
16. Ibid., 579.
17. Ibid., 592 n. 9.

With a view to testing Tov's thesis, Johan Lust examines the LXX translation of Ezekiel and modifies the theory.[18] In studying Papyrus 967, Lust suspects that a reviser, and not the translator, may have used the Pentateuch as a dictionary. The Three may have been more influenced by the vocabulary of the Pentateuch, and LXX Ezekiel shows more affinities with them than with the LXX Pentateuch.[19] Nevertheless, he concedes that certain elements of vocabulary must have arisen in the liturgy of the Jewish community and that, in the case of cultic vocabulary, it is quite possible that no synonyms were allowed.[20] However, he questions the criteria by which Tov's word selection was made and argues that a similar list of words *not* rendered in the same way outside the LXX Pentateuch could be compiled.[21] He further suggests that:

> a good domain in which the dependency of a translation of a particular book, such as Ezekiel, upon the Pentateuch can be checked is undoubtedly to be found in the passages in which the Hebrew text of that particular book displays affinities with passages in the Pentateuch, especially when this Hebrew text uses rare expressions that are hardly or not found elsewhere. In these circumstances one may expect a translator to search for lexicographical guidance in the works of his predecessors.[22]

However, Lust is still operating under the assumption of the primacy of the Greek translation of the Pentateuch over the rest of the books, as do the rest of the participants in the debate. This point, among others, was about to be challenged by James Barr.[23] Barr begins with an attempt to envisage a situation where the LXX Pentateuch was functioning as a "lexicon":

> While it is possible that people knew the entire Hebrew text by heart, and possible also that some knew the entire Greek Pentateuch by heart, to know them *both* by heart, in such a way as to say, when faced with an unusual word in Hosea or Proverbs, 'Oh, yes, that occurs near the end of Numbers and is there rendered with the Greek word x' is, in the absence of written concordances, no easy task, and one that does not necessarily fit very easily with one's picture of the way in which the translators worked.[24]

---

18.   Johan Lust, "The Vocabulary of the LXX Ezekiel and Its Dependence Upon the Pentateuch," in *Deuteronomy and the Deuteronomic Literature* (ed. Marc Vervenne and Johan Lust; BETL 133; Leuven: Peeters, 1997), 529–46.

19.   Ibid., 534, 545.

20.   Ibid., 532, 536, 542.

21.   Ibid., 532.

22.   Ibid., 544–45.

23.   Barr, "Did the Greek Pentateuch Really Serve as a Dictionary?," 523–43.

24.   Ibid., 526.

This matching may not be as difficult as Barr envisages. Nowadays, people may still be found who can recite passages from the ancient biblical text, while at the same time knowing how they have been translated into their own language. Nevertheless, Barr goes on to challenge Tov's thesis on similar grounds to those of Lust, adding a helpful note on the topic of "neologisms." According to Tov, neologisms strengthen his thesis: "it is noteworthy that several of the neologisms of the Greek Pent. were perpetuated in the later books of the LXX, a situation which underlines the dependence of the latter on the former."[25]

Barr, however, argues that, apart from words which have a particularly Jewish motivation behind their coinage, others may simply be *Koine* words which happen not to be recorded before the third century. This does not necessarily mean that they were coined by the LXX translators of the Pentateuch,[26] since genuinely new *Koine* words may not have been documented before the LXX translation.

In order to substantiate his challenge to the primacy of the LXX Pentateuch over other LXX books, Barr uses the example of the Targum of Job discovered alongside fragments of the Targum of Leviticus at Qumran. Barr suggests that more marginal books may have been translated first if their language was harder than that of the Pentateuch and if, unlike the Pentateuch, they were not continually read. To exemplify this, Barr uses Isaiah's "unsystematic" translation style to suggest that Isaiah could have been the first to be translated. In this way, borrowing could have worked in the opposite direction.[27]

No research in this area can disregard the points made by Lust and Barr. In this study I will attempt to evaluate the vocabulary of the Greek TP from within Tov's assumption of the primacy of the Greek Pentateuch in order to see whether there is indeed a demonstrable influence from the LXX Pentateuch on the LXX TP. For the purpose of this study I have divided the words I will be examining into four categories: (a) neologisms, (b) Greek words with a "forced meaning," (c) etymologizing, and (d) suitable Greek equivalents available in a Hellenistic context.

25. Tov, "The Impact of the LXX," 580.
26. Barr, "Did the Greek Pentateuch Really Serve as a Dictionary?," 538.
27. Ibid., 539–40.

Neologisms

ἀνεμοφθορία–שדפון

ἀνεμοφθορία occurs three times in the LXX (Deut 28:22; 2 Chr 6:28; Hag 2:17).[28] The word means "damaging by wind"[29] and appears in parallel to ὤχρα ("mildew")[30] in Deut 28:22 and ἀφορία ("failure of agricultural crops")[31] in Hag 2:17.

The adjective ἀνεμόφθοροι (שדופת) is used five times in Pharaoh's dream (LXX Gen 41:6, 7, 23, 24, 27) about the seven thin and scorched ears of grain (στάχυες οἱ λεπτοὶ καὶ ἀνεμόφθοροι) swallowing up the plump and full ears (cf. LXX Isa 19:7; LXX Hos 8:7). Harl says that ἀνεμόφθορος ("spoiled by the wind") is a compound adjective which does not occur prior to the LXX and may be regarded as a *hapax* modelled on the Hebrew שדופת קדים ("blasted by the east wind"). Aquila's preference is to keep the two words separated: ἐφθαρμένοι καύσωνι ("destroyed by a hot wind").[32] Philo uses the adjective for "damaged crops": ἐπάρατοι πάντες οἱ καρποί, τῷ γὰρ καιριωτάτῳ τῆς ἀκμῆς ἀνεμόφθοροι γενήσονται (*Praem.* 1.141). Although not attested prior to the LXX, ἀνεμόφθορος appears in a papyrus from 100 B.C.E., probably referring to damaged crops: ἢ ἀνεμόφθορος ἢ ἄλλη τις ποτ.υ.πα.ος φθορ[ὰ (*P.Köln.* VI. 275, 14).[33]

In order to determine whether the Greek translator of Hag 2:17 was influenced by LXX Deut 28:22, we must examine the translation of these two verses. If we observe the word order of the MT and the LXX in Hag 2:17, we find that בשדפון comes first and corresponds to ἐν ἀφορίᾳ, while ובירקון comes second and corresponds to καὶ ἐν ἀνεμοφθορίᾳ. Last in the list is ובברד corresponding to καὶ ἐν χαλάζῃ.[34] The first two identifications do not occur in the LXX Pentateuch. When שדפון occurs

28. Though Tov mentions only the first two occurrences; see his "The Impact of the LXX," 585.

29. *Muraoka 2009*, 49. "Blasting, blight," *LEH* 47.

30. *Muraoka 2009*, 751.

31. *Muraoka 2009*, 109.

32. *BA* 1:273. Symmachus has πεφρυγμένοι ἀνέμῳ.

33. ἀνεμόφθορα, referring to damaged crops, occurs in a papyrus from the Byzantine era (*P.Cair.Masp.* I. 67002, 2, 26).

34. Tov and Polak suggest that ובירקון corresponds to ἐν ἀφορίᾳ and בשדפון to καὶ ἐν ἀνεμοφθορίᾳ (Emanuel Tov and Frank Polak, eds., *The Revised CATSS Hebrew/Greek Parallel Text* [Jerusalem, 2005]; accessed via *Bible Works 8*, 2009–2010). However, the translator's lack of consistency in rendering these words is obvious and it is thus unnecessary to assume a different word order.

again in Amos 4:9, it is rendered as πύρωσις, which suggests that the translator did not have a fixed Greek equivalent for שדפון in mind. The same can be said for ירקון, which is rendered once as ἀνεμοφθορία (Hag 2:17) and once as ἴκτερος (Amos 4:9), while in the LXX Pentateuch ירקון is represented by ὤχρα (Deut 28:22) and ἴκτερος stands for קדחת (Lev 26:16). What seems to be the case in the Greek translation of the TP is that the translator was aware of the Pentateuchal curses in Greek and applied the terminology variably when he needed to translate Hebrew words relating to curses. He does not observe the exact Greek equivalents these Hebrew words have been assigned in the LXX Pentateuch.[35] If there has been influence from the Greek Pentateuchal curse list in this case, then it falls short of consistent, direct equivalence in strict lexical fashion.

δεκτός–לרצון

In Mal 2:13, δεκτόν translates רצון. Apart from רצון, δεκτόν translates the *Qal* passive participle of רצה in LXX Deut 33:24 and the *Qal* infinitive construct of רצה in Prov 15:28[MT16:7]. δεκτόν is also used for the *Niphal* of רצה in Lev 1:4. In the TP, the Greek translator uses forms of προσδέχομαι to render רצה forms in Hos 8:13; Amos 5:22; Mic 6:7; Mal 1:8, 10 and 13. On one occasion in Hag 1:8 the translator uses εὐδοκήσω for ארצה. The treatment of רצה by the Greek translator of the TP shows that he understood the root's basic meaning as "be pleased with, accept favourably,"[36] and does not seem to be dependent on any particular rendering of the LXX Pentateuch. In cultic contexts the translator understands the word as referring to God's favourable acceptance of offerings, while elsewhere he relates the word to pleasure or satisfaction.

The variety of Greek terms used for רצון in other LXX books, such as ἐπιθυμία (Gen 49:6), θέλησῃ (2 Chr 15:15; Prov 8:35), θέλημα (Esth 1:8; Ps 29[MT30]:6; Dan [Th] 8:4), ἀρεστόν (Ezra 10:11; Neh 9:24, 37),

---

35. The lack of strict observance in the order of the Deuteronomic curses is also evident in later Christian times in two inscriptions found in Euboia:
τοῦτον τε θεὸς [πατάξαι]
[ἀπ]ορίᾳ καὶ πυρετῷ καὶ ῥείγει καὶ [ἐρ]εθ[ι]σμ[ῷ] καὶ ἀνεμοφθ[ορίᾳ]
[καὶ παραπληξίᾳ] καὶ ἀορασίᾳ καὶ ἐκστάσει διανοίας· [καὶ εἴη ἀφανῆ]
[τὰ κτ]ήματα αὐτοῦ, μὴ γῆ βατή, μ[ὴ θάλα]ττα πλ[ωτ]ή, μ[ὴ παίδων]
[γονή]· μηδὲ οἶκος αὔξοιτο [μη]δὲ καρπῶν ἀπολαύ[οι μηδὲ οἴκου],
[μὴ φ]ωτός, μὴ χρήσεως μηδὲ κτήσεως, ἐπισκό[πους δὲ ἔχοι]
['Ερε]ινύας. (Aegean Islands [general], IG XII,9 [Euboia] document 955, 6–12; see also 1179, 25).
36. BDB 953.

εὐδοκία (Pss 5:13; 18[MT19]:15), προσδεκτόν (Prov 11:20; 16:15) and others, as well as the interchange of equivalents within single books, indicates a basic knowledge of רצון.

At the same time, Tov is right in isolating δεκτόν as a neologism used only in the Septuagint and NT. Extra-biblical descriptions of "acceptable offerings" use only the verbal form (e.g. δέκτο [third singular aorist indicative middle] in Homer, *Iliad* 2.420; 15.88; δέξεσθαι [infinitive future middle] in Sophocles, *Electra* 443; δέξαι [second singular aorist imperative middle] in Aristophanes, *Lysistrata* 204; δέχονται [third plural present indicative middle passive] in Pindar, *Pythia* 5.86), but the verbal adjective δεκτός is absent. This may suggest that such a cultic term was used exclusively by the Jewish community, though it is difficult to prove that it was the creation of the Greek translators of the Pentateuch.

θυσιαστήριον–מזבח

Here we are dealing with a stereotype. Out of 437 occurrences of θυσιαστήριον, only four times does it stand for a Hebrew word other than מזבח (2 Chr 14:4 [במה]; Ezra 7:17 [Aram. מדבח]; Ps 82[MT83]:13 [ms. B—נאה]; Hos 3:4 [מצבה]). The most common word for "altar" since Homer was βωμός. Yet in the LXX we witness the peculiar phenomenon of the dominance of θυσιαστήριον, a term which is still unattested in extra-biblical sources.[37] Inscriptions with θυσιαστήριον come from Christian times when the term was probably adopted for the Christian altar or table of offerings.[38]

Suzanne Daniel brings Philo's comments on the word θυσιαστήριον to our attention.[39] Philo's etymological *midrash* shows that he believed the word to have originated in the Scriptures and to carry a special significance:

37. The only possibility of an extra-biblical occurrence, as mentioned by Suzanne Daniel, is the adjective θυσιαστήριος which occurs in Fragment of Timaeus (fourth- to third-century B.C.E. historian) and is established on the basis of Pindar's scholia. However, θυσιαστήριον is the reading offered by Boeckh and is not at all certain. See Suzanne Daniel, *Recherches sur le Vocabulaire du Culte dans la Septante* (Études et Commentaires 61; Paris: C. Klincksieck, 1966), 26. See also Hans-Josef Klauck, "θυσιαστηριον. Eine Berichtigung," *ZNW* 71 (1980): 274–77, who concludes that θυσιαστήριον is part of a special Judeo-Christian vocabulary.

38. I.Eph. 4130 (Keil) [this inscription has the symbol of the *menorah* next to the word]; I. Hadrianoi 121 (E. Schwertheim, ed., *Die Inschriften von Hadrianoi und Hadrianeia* [Bonn: Habelt, 1987], 80).

39. Daniel, *Recherches sur le Vocabulaire du Culte*, 27.

διὸ καὶ κέκληκε θυσιαστήριον, ἴδιον καὶ ἐξαίρετον ὄνομα θέμενος αὐτῷ παρὰ τὸ διατηρεῖν, ὡς ἔοικε, τὰς θυσίας, καίτοι τῶν κρεῶν ἀναλισκομένων ὑπὸ πυρός· ὡς εἶναι σαφεστάτην πίστιν, ὅτι οὐ τὰ ἱερεῖα θυσίαν ἀλλὰ τὴν διάνοιαν καὶ προθυμίαν ὑπολαμβάνει τοῦ καταθύοντος εἶναι, ἐν ᾗ τὸ μόνιμον καὶ βέβαιον ἐξ ἀρετῆς.[40]

Colson notes that Philo must have broken the word into two parts: τηρεῖν = "keep" and θυσίας = "sacrifices."[41] The emphasis of –τήριον (τηρεῖν), for Philo, is not on the sacrifice which gets consumed but on the motives of the one who offers the sacrifice. It is not the flesh that is preserved, but the person. Similarly, in *De vita Mosis* 2.106, Philo says that

τὸν δ' ἐν ὑπαίθρῳ βωμὸν εἴωθε καλεῖν θυσιαστήριον, ὡσανεὶ τηρητικὸν καὶ φυλακτικὸν ὄντα θυσιῶν τὸν ἀναλωτικὸν τούτων, αἰνιττόμενος οὐ τὰ μέλη καὶ τὰ μέρη τῶν ἱερουργουμένων, ἅπερ δαπανᾶσθαι πυρὶ πέφυκεν, ἀλλὰ τὴν προαίρεσιν τοῦ προσφέροντος.[42]

It appears that, for Philo, θυσιαστήριον is a special term originating in the Jewish Scriptures to designate their βωμός. Of course, Philo is often concerned about the deeper meaning of words, and his comments should not be taken at face value. However, the fact that he gives so much attention to the word could be an indication that it was uncommon outside Jewish circles and demanded an explanation. At the same time, he does not seem to give similar attention to θυμιατήριον ("censer") in 2.105, which is a common term also found outside the biblical literature.

According to Suzanne Daniel, θυσιαστήριον is derived from the verb θυσιάζειν or θύειν rather than the noun θῦμα, "victim," or θύτηρ, "priest," with which θυτήριον, a common Greek term, is connected. For Daniel, the availability of θυτήριον makes the formation of θυσιαστήριον all the more surprising.[43]

As Tov points out, it might be possible to distinguish in this case between the two stages in the formation of a stereotype.[44] We do not know the exact point in the Pentateuch where מזבח was first identified as θυσιαστήριον, or whether the translator(s) created the word.[45] The phenomenon unique to the LXX Pentateuch which we do see is some intentionality in the distinction between θυσιαστήριον and βωμός. βωμός

40. Philo, *Spec.* 1.290.
41. Philo, *Spec.* 1.290 (Colson, LCL, 267 n. c).
42 Philo, *Mos.* 2.106.
43. Daniel, *Recherches sur le Vocabulaire du Culte*, 28.
44. Emanuel Tov, "Three Dimensions of LXX Words," *RB* 83 (1976): 541.
45. Lee mentions θυσιαστήριον as an example when he observes that "[t]here are however some clear cases of formations that are likely to have been confined to the Biblical vocabulary" (*A Lexical Study*, 52).

is always used for pagan altars (with the exception of Num 3:10).[46] θυσιαστήριον seems to be reserved for Yahweh's altar. This could mean that: (a) the translator(s) of the Pentateuch used the term θυσιαστήριον for Yahweh's altar in order to differentiate between the holy and the profane or simply so that they could specify which βωμός they were referring to; or, (b) a corrector of LXX Pentateuch changed the terminology for holy altars from βωμός to θυσιαστήριον in order to differentiate between holy and profane. While the distinction could have been introduced by a corrector, there is no reason to assume this.[47] In scenario (a) θυσιαστήριον is a uniquely Jewish term and the selective use of the word for Yahweh's altar would have successfully communicated the distinction between Jewish and pagan. If θυσιαστήριον were also used in pagan vocabulary, it would have functioned synonymously to βωμός and the distinction introduced in LXX Pentateuch would not have been readily understandable. In scenario (b) a corrector inherits a text which has βωμός alone or a text which has both terms used interchangeably regardless of context. He would then have to restrict θυσιαστήριον to Yahweh's altar and βωμός to pagan altars.

However, it is not clear why he would do this unless θυσιαστήριον *already* carried a special significance against βωμός for the corrector and his audience. Would this corrector be operating at a time when θυσιαστήριον had acquired a higher register or holier significance? This is doubtful, since the trend we observe outside the LXX Pentateuch is that this distinction was becoming blurred and θυσιαστήριον seems to be used indiscriminately whenever מזבח occurs, for both Israelite and pagan altars. It is likely, then, that the distinction between θυσιαστήριον and βωμός originated with the Greek translation of the Pentateuch, which probably preceded the translation of the rest of the biblical books. By the time of the translation of several of the other LXX books, the "exclusive" sense of θυσιαστήριον was lost and it simply became the Greek symbol for מזבח.[48]

---

46. Wevers notes: "Unique, however, is the rendering here of τὸν βωμόν for המזבה, since this is otherwise used only for non-Israelite altars; in fact, at 18:7 it is translated by τοῦ θυσιαστηρίου. That the tradition was troubled by the use of τὸν βωμόν for the altars in the tabernacle is clear from various attempts to substitute or add a reference to του θυσιαστηριου (possibly direct influence of 18:7?) in F V Byz *b z* +"; see John William Wevers, *Notes on the Greek Text of Numbers* (SBLSCS 46; Atlanta: Scholars Press, 1998), 37.

47. Daniel thinks that both terms, θυσιαστήριον and βωμός, originated in the LXX translation (*Recherches sur le Vocabulaire du Culte*, 30).

48. So Lust, "The Vocabulary of the LXX Ezekiel," 535; Daniel, *Recherches sur le Vocabulaire du Culte*, 22–23. Hanhart holds that the distinction remained strong

At the same time, the above findings do not necessitate that the Greek translator of the TP consulted the LXX Pentateuch for the purpose of rendering מזבח: θυσιαστήριον may simply have become the most familiar Greek word for "altar" in Jewish circles. If, on the other hand, θυσιαστή-ριον originated with the Greek translators of the Pentateuch, not with generations preceding the translation, their "neologism" is more likely to have exercised its influence indirectly on the translator of the TP.

μακρόθυμος–ארך אפים

μακρόθυμος means "able to bear up under provocation,"[49] and it occurs twice in the LXX Pentateuch, translating ארך אפים (Exod 34:6; Num 14:18). The same identification is true in other LXX books (e.g. Neh 9:17; Ps 7:11; Prov 14:29; 15:18), including the TP (Joel 2:13; Jon 4:2; Nah 1:3). Once it translates קר רוח, "cool in spirit" (Prov 17:27) and once it translates ארך רוח (Eccl 7:8). In Dan [Th] 4:27[MT24] it translates the Aramaic ארכה.

The adjective μακρόθυμος is absent from Greek sources prior to the LXX. However, the verb μακροθυμέω is used by Astrampsychus (*Astrampsychi oraculorum decades* 38.10; 42.8; 81.5; 90.7; *Sortes* 78.2) around the fourth century B.C.E., and later by Plutarch (*De genio Socrates* 593F8), with the meaning "persevere." μακροθυμία ("long-suffering, patience") is found in Menander (*Fragmenta* 549.2), Strabo (*Geographica* 5.4.10.15) and Plutarch (*Lucullus* 32.4.2; 33.1.4).[50] A parallel formation of μακρόθυμος, ὀξύθυμος ("quick to anger"),[51] is found in many writers prior to the LXX (e.g. Euripides, *Medea* 319, Aristophanes, *Equites* 706; Hippocrates, *De morbis popularibus* 2.5.16.2; Aristotle, *Ethica Eudemia* 1221b.12; *Rhetorica* 1368b.20), which suggests that it would not be unlikely for μακρόθυμος to have existed alongside it.

Although μακρόθυμος looks to be a calque of ארך אפים,[52] it need not necessarily have been created by the translators. Since, as has been

through to the latest translations, and that inconsistencies in this observance cannot be used as evidence against this assertion. Hanhart, "The Translation of the Septuagint," 346–47. Van der Kooij's analytical study of βωμός in the LXX shows that only 1 Maccabees seems to follow the LXX Pentateuch's strict distinction between βωμός and θυσιαστήριον. Arie van der Kooij, "On the Use of βωμός in the Septuagint," in Baasten and van Peursen, eds., *Hamlet on a Hill*, 601–7.

49. *Muraoka 2009*, 439.

50. LSJ 1074.

51. LSJ 1235.

52. θυμός, as אפים, can be used in various ways with the sense of breath, life, spirit, strength, soul, anger, wrath, and so on (LSJ 810).

shown, the word is likely to have existed in the translators' Greek environment, it could simply have been chosen to represent ארך אפים owing to its remarkable affinity with the Hebrew.

ὀρθρίζω–השכים

ὀρθρίζω ("to rise from bed in the morning")[53] is another neologism, according to Tov.[54] In the Pentateuch, the identification with השכים is very common (e.g. Gen 19:2, 27; 20:8; Exod 8:16; 9:13; Num 14:40), and in the TP it is only found in Zeph 3:7. However, that the translator here was probably familiar with the root meaning of the Hebrew word, and was not dependent on the Pentateuch for his rendering, is indicated by the fact that the Greek translator renders the participial משכים as ὀρθρινή in Hos 6:4 and 13:3.

ὀρθρίζω is also found in LXX Hos 5:15, representing the *Piel* of שחר ("look early, diligently for"),[55] but this does not mean that ὀρθρίζω was understood to have the precise meaning of שחר. Instead, the translator "etymologized" the *Piel* שָׁחֵר from the noun שַׁחַר which he always translates by ὄρθρος (Hos 6:3; 10:15; Joel 2:2; Amos 4:13; ἐπαύριον in Jon 4:7).[56]

It might be supposed that שכם is represented by other Greek words as well: ἀνίστημι (Gen 21:14; 22:3; 26:31; 28:18; 32:1; Josh 6:12, 15; Job 1:5; Isa 37:36[B]), ἐγείρω [middle] (Isa 5:11), ἐξανίστημι (Isa 37:36 [mss. A S]) and ὄρθρος (Jer 7:25; 25:4; 33[MT26]:5; 39[MT32]:33; 42[MT35]:14; 51[MT44]:4). However, as Gehman argues, ὀρθρίζω is almost always identified with שכם, so we should understand that the two were regarded as having the same signification (*Hiphil*, rise early, make an early start).[57]

The adjective ὀρθρινός (LXX Hos 6:4; 13:3) is found in various extra-biblical texts (e.g. Hippocrates, *Prorrheticon* 2.4.11; Aratus, *Phenomena* 1.948; Phaedimus, *Epigrammata* 7.739.5), but ὀρθρίζω is absent from Greek literature prior to the LXX. Lee, in the light of Moeris' discussion of the two forms ὀρθρίζω and ὀρθρεύω, thinks that the word must have been used outside the LXX, and that it must be entirely due to chance that

---

53. *Muraoka 2009*, 504–5. Additional meanings offered are, "to seek and turn in eager anticipation" and "to act eagerly"; "to rise up early," LEH 445.

54. Tov, "The Impact of the LXX," 586.

55. BDB 1007.

56. So E. Tov, "Greek Words and Hebrew Meanings," in *Melbourne Symposium on Septuagint Lexicography* (ed. Takamitsu Muraoka; SBLSCS 28; Atlanta: Scholars Press, 1990), 121.

57. H. S. Gehman, "Hebraisms of the Old Greek Version of Genesis," *VT* 3 (1953): 147; Tov, "Greek Words and Hebrew Meanings," 120.

we have no non-biblical examples of it.[58] It is therefore quite reasonable to suppose that later translators had access to this word, and were not dependent on the Pentateuch for the rendering.

LSJ mentions ὀρθρεύω with the meaning "lie awake before dawn."[59] To this definition, the LSJ Supplements add "rise early, make an early start" on the basis of Tob 9:6.[60] According to Horsley, ὀρθρίζω has gradually taken the place of ὀρθρεύω.[61] If Lee and Horsley are right, then ὀρθρίζω may have been a variant of ὀρθρεύω since, as Tob 9:6 shows, the two could have very similar meanings. If the Greek translator of the TP knew the meaning of שכם, then the equivalent ὀρθρίζω would have been the most appropriate choice.

παραπικραίνω–המרה

The only instance of παραπικραίνω ("to embitter, to provoke")[62] in LXX Pentateuch is in Deut 31:27, where the plural *Hiphil* masculine participle of מרה, מַמְרִים ("rebellious"), is rendered as παραπικραίνοντες, as if from מרר ("be bitter") or מר ("bitter, bitterness").[63] The preferred reading in Deut 32:16 is ἐξεπίκραναν for יכעיסהו, supported by Alexandrinus, but Vaticanus has παρεπίκραναν. παραπικραίνω is another neologism, according to Tov.[64] In the Greek TP, it is only found in Hos 10:5 as a result of a misreading:

MT	LXX
לְעֶגְלוֹת בֵּית אָוֶן יָגוּרוּ	τῷ μόσχῳ τοῦ οἴκου Ων παροικήσουσιν
שְׁכַן שֹׁמְרוֹן כִּי־אָבַל	οἱ κατοικοῦντες Σαμάρειαν ὅτι ἐπένθησε
עָלָיו עַמּוֹ וּכְמָרָיו עָלָיו	ὁ λαὸς αὐτοῦ ἐπ᾽ αὐτόν καὶ καθὼς παρεπίκραναν
יָגִילוּ עַל־כְּבוֹדוֹ	αὐτόν ἐπιχαροῦνται ἐπὶ τὴν δόξαν αὐτοῦ
כִּי־גָלָה מִמֶּנּוּ׃	ὅτι μετῳκίσθη ἀπ᾽ αὐτοῦ

It is obvious that וכמריו was broken down into three parts: the ו conjunction rendered as καί, the כ preposition rendered as καθώς, and

---

58. Lee, *A Lexical Study*, 46.
59. LSJ 1250.
60. LSJ, Supplement, 231.
61. G. H. R. Horsley, *New Documents Illustrating Early Christianity: A Review of the Greek Inscriptions and Papyri Published in 1976*, vol. 1 (Sydney: Macquarie University Press, 1981), 86.
62. LEH 466. Muraoka gives three definitions: "to invite harsh reaction of, infuriate," "to add to the harshness and bitterness of" and "to feel bitter about sth"; *Muraoka 2009*, 530.
63. BDB 600.
64. Tov, "The Impact of the LXX," 586. Also Cécile Dogniez and Marguerite Harl (*BA* 5:319).

a third plural perfect form related to מר was read.[65] In the majority of cases in the LXX where παραπικραίνειν occurs, it translates some form based on the two consonants מר: מָרַד (Ezek 2:3), מָרָה *Qal* (3 Kgdms 13:21, 26; Pss 5:11; 77[MT78]:8; 104[MT105]:28; Lam 1:18, 20), מָרָה *Hiphil* (Deut 31:27; Pss 77[MT78]:17, 40, 56; 105[MT106]:7, 33, 43; 106[MT107]:11; Ezek 20:13 [ms. A], 21) and מְרִי (Ezek 2:5, 6, 7, 8; 3:9, 26, 27; 12:2, 3, 9, 25; 17:12; 24:3; 44:6). Tov, in his examination of biliteral exegesis of Hebrew roots in the LXX, treats מר as an example of this phenomenon. He notes that "words of the מר"ה group have *often* been rendered as παραπικραίνω ('to embitter'), a verb that is related to the adjective πικρός, 'bitter' (usually reflecting מר). This frequent LXX equivalence was apparently influenced by its first occurrence in the Greek Pentateuch, in the present verse (i.e. Deut 31:27)."[66]

Tov shows how this Septuagintal exegesis was done in Ezek 2:3 and Ps 9:28[MT10:7]. It appears that the Greek translator of the TP does something similar in Hos 10:5. He knows מר as πικρός (LXX Zeph 1:14; ὀδύνη in Amos 8:10 and Zech 12:10) and connects it with παραπικραίνειν.[67] Nevertheless, Tov insists that the identification of מרה with παραπικραίνειν was fixed in LXX Deut 31:27 and then influenced subsequent translations. However, it is not necessary to hold that all the LXX translators knew this identification. Rather, they may have been familiar with the neologism παραπικραίνειν, which could have been invented in LXX Deuteronomy, and they may have used it as the closest equivalent to a מר root verb but without explicit identification with the usage in Deuteronomy.[68]

πολυέλεος–רב חסד

πολυέλεος, another neologism according to Tov, renders רב־חסד in Exod 34:6 and Num 14:18. Outside the Pentateuch, the above equivalence is found in Neh 9:17, Pss 85[MT86]:5, 15 and 102[MT103]:8. In Ps 144[MT145]:8 πολυέλεος translates גדל־חסד[ו]. In the Greek TP it occurs only twice for רב־חסד, as part of the wordpair μακρόθυμος καὶ πολυέλεος (Joel 2:13; Jon 4:2).

---

65. It is just possible that כמריו was thought to contain an infinitive construct with suffix. LEH suggests that מרה was read (466).

66. Emanuel Tov, "Biliteral Exegesis of Hebrew Roots in the Septuagint?," in *Reflection and Refraction: Studies in Biblical Historiography in Honour of A. Graeme Auld* (ed. R. Rezetko et al.; Leiden: Brill, 2007), 471.

67. So Walters, *The Text of the Septuagint*, 150–53.

68. Dogniez and Harl point out that the prefix παρα- in front of verbs like παραπικραίνω, παροργίζω and παροξύνω indicates "transgression" or "excess"; *BA* 5:330.

It is possible that πολυέλεος was originally coined in order to corre-spond to the wordpair רב־חסד. However, both Hebrew words in the wordpair would have been familiar to the Greek translator of the TP, which makes it unlikely that the LXX Pentateuch was consulted directly. Rather, it seems more reasonable to suppose that πολυέλεος (like μακρό-θυμος) was a divine epithet circulating in the Jewish community, perhaps originally introduced by a translator, and that it so readily lent itself to the translation of רב חסד that no further consultation of the Pentateuch was necessary.

πρωτότοκος–בכור

In the TP בכורי is rendered by πρωτότοκά μου in Mic 6:7 and על־הבכור is rendered by ἐπὶ πρωτοτόκῳ in Zech 12:10. These are the only two places where this Hebrew word occurs in the Twelve. Moreover, only five times out of 141 does the word πρωτότοκος (used both adjectivally and substantivally) represent something other than בכרה, בכר, בכור, ראשון (Gen 25:25); בכורים: or בכירה (Exod 34:19, 20); פטר (1 Chr ראש 5:12; 11:11 [ms. A]). However, πρωτότοκος is not the only word used for בכר-root words. Equivalents are παιδίον (Deut 25:6), πρεσβύτερος (Job1:13, 18), πρεσβυτέρα (Gen 19:31, 33, 34, 37; 29:26), πρωτογενής (Exod 13:2), πρωτόγονος (Mic 7:1), and others.

No dependence on the LXX Pentateuch (e.g. Gen 4:4; Exod 4:22; Lev 27:26; Num 1:20) is apparent, since the Greek translator felt free to use πρωτόγονος for בכורה (cf. Sir 36:11), instead of πρωτότοκος, in LXX Mic 7:1, and he was also flexible in contextualizing the meaning of בכורה in Hos 9:10, rendering כבכורה בתאנה בראשיתה as ὡς σκοπὸν ἐν συκῇ πρόιμον.

Tov places πρωτότοκος (proparoxytone)[69] in his list of neologisms,[70] and, indeed, a survey of extra-biblical Greek literature (e.g. Homer, *Il.* 17.5; Pythagoras, *Fragmenta astrologica* 11.2, 143.18–20; Plato, *Theaet.* 151.c.5) shows that, with only one exception, the active form πρωτοτόκος (paroxytone) is attested prior to the LXX, referring to a female "bearing or having borne her first-born."[71] The exception is a Jewish burial inscription (fifth century B.C.E.) from Tell el Jehudieh (Leontopolis), which reads: ὠδεῖνι δὲ Μοῖρα πρωτοτόκου με τέκνου πρὸς τέλος ἦγε βίου

69. For the mechanisms of determining Greek accents, see Philomen Probert, *Ancient Greek Accentuation: Synchronic Patterns, Frequency Effects, and Prehistory* (Oxford: Oxford University Press, 2006).
70. "The Impact of the LXX," 582.
71. LSJ 1545.

(lines 5f.).[72] This inscription opens up the possibility of the use of πρωτότοκος prior to the LXX.

Michaelis notes that the usual word for "first-born" in extra-biblical sources is πρωτόγονος, which can also mean "first in rank."[73] There was no need, therefore, to promote πρωτότοκος, since πρωτόγονος was available with a passive sense.[74] As already noted, the Greek translator of the TP uses both πρωτότοκος (Mic 6:7 and Zech 12:10) and πρωτόγονος (Mic 7:1). Although πρωτότοκος may have existed prior to the LXX, Michaelis holds that it was the LXX which was responsible for the promotion of the term, but he does not suggest that it was the LXX translators who created it.[75] There seems to be no clear motivation for the LXX translators to coin this word, given that πρωτόγονος was already being used. Nevertheless, it so happens that πρωτότοκος is primarily a Septuagintal term in advance of any Christian writing.[76]

φάρμακος–(מ)כשף

כשף is a verb for "practising sorcery,"[77] and its *Piel* participle is translated by τὰς φαρμακοὺς ("the women practising sorcery") in Mal 3:5 (מכשפים). It is peculiar how the masculine participle is rendered as feminine in the Greek. One could argue that the Greek translator of Malachi was influenced by the feminine form in the Hebrew of Exod 22:17, מכשפה לא תחיה, and not Deut 18:10, which has the masculine version, מכשף.[78] However, in Mal 3:5, מנאפים is also turned into the feminine participle τὰς μοιχαλίδας. Perhaps the context of Nah 3:4 involving a feminine figure practising sorcery and fornication had some influence over the "feminizing" of the participles in Mal 3:5: ἀπὸ πλήθους πορνείας πόρνη καλὴ καὶ ἐπιχαρὴς ἡγουμένη φαρμάκων ἡ πωλοῦσα ἔθνη ἐν τῇ πορνείᾳ αὐτῆς καὶ φυλὰς ἐν τοῖς φαρμάκοις αὐτῆς.

Walters argues that the correct accentuation should be restored in the LXX to distinguish between φάρμακος ("poisoner, sorcerer, magician"

---

72. Wilhelm Michaelis, "πρωτότοκος, πρωτοτοκεῖα," *TDNT* 6:872.

73. Ibid., 6:871. See also his treatment of πρωτότοκος as it relates to the NT descriptions of Christ: Wilhelm Michaelis, "Der Beitrag der Septuaginta zur Bedeutungsgeschichte von πρωτότοκος," in *Sprachgeschichte und Wortbedeutung: Festschrift Albert Debrunner* (ed. G. Redard; Berne: Francke, 1954), 313–20.

74. Michaelis, *TDNT* 6:871 n. 1.

75. Ibid., 6:872.

76. Philo and Josephus use the word with reference to the Old Testament.

77. BDB 506.

78. The association of women with sorcery is also found in *1 En.* 7:10 (from second century B.C.E.). The legend recorded there has it that sorcery was something that the 200 angels taught the women with whom they had sexual relations.

[common gender]), used in the LXX (twelve times), Revelation and Hermas, and φαρμακός ("scapegoat") used by Hipponax (*Fragmenta* 8.2; 104.49) and Aristophanes.[79] φάρμακος and related terms represent other Hebrew words as well: להטים, לט ("secrecy, mystery") in Exod 7:11, 22; 8:3, 14; חובר ("the one who binds") in Ps 57[MT58]:6; חרטמים, חרטם in Exod 9:11 and Dan 2:27. However, כשף (thirteen times) is always represented by φάρμακος or related words.

Tov has φάρμακος in his list of neologisms, and so does Walters.[80] Apart from drug or medicine, φάρμακον refers to an enchanted potion, philtre, charm or spell,[81] and φάρμακος is the "mixer(s) of magical potions."[82] Le Boulluec and Sandevoir discuss the three terms for "sorcerers" in LXX Exod 7:11 (ἐπαοιδός, φάρμακος, σοφιστής) and note that ἐπαοιδός ("enchanter") is one figure under the more general heading of φάρμακος ("magician, sorcerer").[83] The practices of all three groups are called φαρμακεῖαι, thus φάρμακος could be used as the hypernym under which the other terms fall. φάρμακος is thus a less restrictive equivalent for the root כשף. Again, the question which arises is whether this word was used in the Jewish community before the LXX translation was produced or whether it was the product of LXX Pentateuch, indirectly or directly influencing other translators.

χωνευτός–מסכה

The above identification is found only once in the TP, in Nah 1:14. A variation is χώνευμα in Hos 13:2 and Hab 2:18. In the LXX, both χωνευτός and χώνευμα translate מסכה, but χωνευτός also represents מצק (3 Kgdms 7:4[MT16], 19[MT33]) as well as נסך in Dan 11:8. Tov categorizes χωνευτός as a neologism, and the same seems to be true for χώνευμα.[84] The participle κεχωνυμένα/κεχωνευμένα is normally used extra-biblically for "molten" things, although it does not occur often (Diodorus Siculus, *Bibliotheca historica [lib. 1–20]* 16.45.6; Josephus, *Ant.* 3.144; 8.79; *P.Cair.Zen.* 742.4). Notwithstanding our limited evidence for extra-biblical usage of χωνευτός and χώνευμα, it appears that these were particularly Jewish terms. However, it is difficult to say whether the term was coined by the Greek translators of the Pentateuch

79. Walters, *The Text of the Septuagint*, 95.
80. Tov, "The Impact of the LXX," 583; Walters, *The Text of the Septuagint*, 95.
81. LSJ 1917.
82. John William Wevers, *Notes on the Greek Text of Exodus* (SBLSCS 30; Atlanta: Scholars Press, 1990), 98.
83. *BA* 2:36.
84. Except for *P.Leid.X.* 21B; see LSJ 2014.

or a preceding generation, or whether LXX Pentateuch influenced other LXX books in this word choice.

The Birth of Neologisms

As we have seen, Tov admits that a generation preceding the Greek translation of the Pentateuch may have been responsible for the coinage of these words, but it is difficult to establish at what point they originated or whether any of these words are contained in "an as yet unpublished papyrus fragment" and thus do not belong in the LXX Pentateuch "neologism" category. It is also possible that such words may have been in oral use but never written down.[85] Therefore, one should be cautious with this designation. Bickerman says that the deliberate coinage of new words began later:

> Later, when the art of artistic rendering of Greek literary masterpieces was created in Rome, Latin translators often coined new words for the adequate rendering of Greek terms. *Nova novis rebus verba*. Following the illustrious example of Cicero, even the modest authors of the Old Latin versions of Scripture dared to fabricate new words.[86]

Bickerman notes how Origen and Jerome sometimes assumed that certain words were created by the Seventy, but that was, according to Bickerman, an anachronistic assumption: "The dragoman rarely coins new words. In distinction from Latin, it would be difficult in Greek with its long literary tradition going back to Homer, and the "Seventy" were not sure of their Greek. Following the pattern set by professional interpreters, the "Seventy" rather forced the meaning of common Greek vocables."[87]

While the LXX translator may have shared some characteristics of the ancient dragoman, the two were by no means identical. The LXX translator may have reflected more on how to render his community's religious concepts than he would have reflected on common commercial terminology. Thus, we cannot share Bickerman's bold assertion. The creation of neologisms is actually approved by Demetrius (probably the student of Aristotle) who says: "the creation of a new word is thought clever, as though it were the creation of a new usage. So the creator of new words is like those who originally created language."[88]

---

85. Also in E. Tov, "Compound Words in the LXX Representing Two or More Hebrew Words," *Biblica* 58 (1977): 199–201.
86. Bickerman, "The Septuagint as a Translation," 19–20.
87. Ibid., 20–21.
88. *Style*, 95 (Innes, LCL).

Greek Words with a "Forced Meaning"

A few words in Tov's list seem to be used with a different meaning in the LXX from that which they normally have in extra-biblical sources. Bickerman suggests that, rather than word-creation, the translators "forced" the meaning of existing Greek words to fit their Hebrew counterparts, thus ending up with "Jewish Greek." The following words may come into this category.

ἀνάθημα (-εμα)–חרם

In Mic 4:13 the *Hiphil* form וְהַחֲרַמְתִּי is rendered as καὶ ἀναθήσεις and in Zech 14:11 חרם is rendered as ἀνάθεμα. Moreover, the translator uses ἄρδην for חרם in Mal 3:23[MT24]:

וְהִכֵּיתִי אֶת־הָאָרֶץ חֵרֶם   καὶ πατάξω τὴν γῆν ἄρδην

ἄρδην means "utterly, wholly"[89] and is used to describe the destruction of cities in Greek literature (e.g. Plato, *Respublica* 421a; *Leges* 677c). The use of ἄρδην suggests that the translator understood חרם to mean "*total* [destruction]."

However, ἀνάθεμα, as Harl points out, is found in the poetry of Theocritus for something "dedicated to a purpose," but the understanding that ἀνάθεμα meant "doomed to destruction" may be the innovation of the LXX.[90] The identification of חרם with ἀνάθεμα appears for the first time in Lev 27:28 and is defined in v. 29 as something appointed for death, a text which could have been definitive for its understanding, that is, its pejorization:[91] καὶ πᾶν ὃ ἐὰν ἀνατεθῇ ἀπὸ τῶν ἀνθρώπων οὐ λυτρωθήσεται ἀλλὰ θανάτῳ θανατωθήσεται. More translations of חרם forms in LXX Pentateuch are ὀλεθρευθήσεται (Exod 22:19), ἀφωρισμένη (Lev 27:21), ἐξωλεθρεύσαμεν (Deut 2:34; 3:6) and ἀφανισμῷ ἀφανιεῖς (Deut 7:2). Interestingly, apart from חרם forms, no other Hebrew words stand behind ἀνάθεμα in the LXX. The fact that ἀνάθεμα had acquired the sense of "doomed to destruction," making it an appropriate equivalent for חרם, does not prove a *direct* dependence of the Greek translator of the TP on LXX Pentateuch.[92]

---

89. *Muraoka 2009*, 90.

90. *BA* 3:214.

91. For the pejorization of terms and semantic change in general, see Hans Henrich Hock, *Principles of Historical Linguistics* (Trends in Linguistics: Studies and Monographs 34; Berlin: de Gruyter, 1986), esp. 301–3.

92. Palmer distinguishes between "direct" influence of LXX Pentateuch on LXX Zechariah on the one hand and "indirect" cultural influence of LXX Pentateuch

It is quite possible that ἀνάθεμα was used orally in this "levitical" sense in Greek-speaking Jewish circles, before being put down in writing.[93] Therefore, the Greek translator of the TP may well not have had specific Greek Pentateuchal texts in mind when rendering חרם.[94]

γλυπτόν–פסל

Forms of γλυπτόν occur five times in the TP to render either פסיל or פסל (Hos 11:2; Mic 1:7; 5:12; Nah 1:14; Hab 2:18). Other Hebrew words translated by γλυπτόν in the LXX are מסכה ("molten metal, image") and עצב ("idol"). γλυπτός is a verbal adjective meaning "carved" and it is used attributively, qualifying ὁμοίωμα, in LXX Deuteronomy (4:16, 23, 25). However, for the most part it is used as a neuter singular substantive both in the LXX Pentateuch (Exod 34:13; Lev 26:1; Deut 7:5, 25; 12:3; 27:15) and throughout the LXX corpus. The issues are whether this usage as a substantive is purely a Septuagintal phenomenon, and, if so, whether it arose first in the LXX Pentateuch and was then adopted by other books.[95]

In extra-biblical usage, γλυπτός is mainly used as an adjective (Theophrastus, *De lapidibus* 5.3; 8.4; 41.4; Asclepiades, *Epigrammata* 5.194.4), with γλύμμα ("engraved figure") performing the substantival function (Posidippus, *Epigrammata* 11.6; 12.6; cf. Exod 28:11; Sir 38:27; 45:11; Isa 45:20; 60:18). However, it is possible that some Peloponnesian inscriptions (although very fragmentary) testify to the substantive use of γλυπτόν (Peloponnesos, IG V,1 [Lakonia and Messenia] document 315, 5; Peloponnesos, SEG 1–41 [excl. Olympia] document 11:344, 3; 11:385a, Add; 17:167; 36:367, 4). Hayward notes that "[t]he Greek word usually reserved for statues in honour of deities is ἄγαλμα, a word which the translators of LXX Pentateuch never used (although their successors,

---

on LXX Zechariah on the other. He states that "words or ideas are used widely without the users having read the texts in which they originally occurred." Palmer, "'Not Made with Tracing Paper,'" 78.

93. Also ibid.

94. Lust draws attention to the possibility that a reviser, and not the translator, used the Pentateuch as a dictionary. He mentions Jerome's comment on Ezek 44:29 that Aquila, Symmachus and Theodotion replaced ἀφόρισμα by ἀνάθεμα, for חרם. However, the limited scope of this study does not permit a full investigation of this proposal; Lust, "The Vocabulary of the LXX Ezekiel," 534.

95. Wevers prefers γλυπτόν (papyrus 963 [second century C.E.]) in Deut 5:8. He regards the B text as secondary, influenced by the familiar parallel forms of the Decalogue in Exod 20. Moreover, εἴδωλον never renders פסל in Deuteronomy, whereas γλυπτόν is its regular equivalent; John William Wevers, *Text History of the Greek Deuteronomy* (Abhandlungen der Akademie der Wissenschaften in Göttingen; MSU 13; Göttingen: Vandenhoeck & Ruprecht, 1978), 133.

the translators of Isaiah, did once use the word to represent פסילים at Isa. 30.22)."[96]

Therefore, it is rather peculiar that the dominant rendering of פסל forms throughout the LXX is the not-so-common γλυπτόν. We should note that, while γλυπτόν is used both as an adjective and a substantive in LXX Deuteronomy, there is no adjectival use in the rest of the LXX. This situation may point to the possibility that γλυπτόν was not yet standardized as a substantive at the time of the Greek translation of Deuteronomy, since both uses are attested in this book. By the time of the translation of the rest of the non-Pentateuchal books, γλυπτός had come predominantly to be used as a substantive.[97] However, in the places where it is used as a substantive, it would be difficult to demonstrate a conscious, direct borrowing from the LXX Pentateuch by the Greek translator of the TP.

διαθήκη–ברית

The matching of these two words in the TP occurs in the following verses: Hos 2:20; 6:7; 8:1; 10:4; 12:2; Amos 1:9; Obad 7; Zech 9:11; 11:10; Mal 2:4, 5, 8, 10, 14; 3:1. These represent all the occurrences of ברית in the TP. Moreover, there are no other Hebrew words represented by διαθήκη in these books. Tov discusses this stereotype at some length for the entire LXX corpus, concluding that 99% of the occurrences of ברית are rendered by διαθήκη. He assumes that "at a certain stage in the translating process, διαθήκη was used automatically as an equivalent of ברית whenever that occurred in the translator's *Vorlage*."[98]

This phenomenon, also observed in other stereotypes such as νόμος[99]– תורה, and προσήλυτος–גר, leads to Tov's distinguishing of two stages in the adoption of Greek words to render Hebrew in the LXX. In this case, the first stage is the occasion of the first mapping of διαθήκη–ברית. Here, one's principal concerns in analysis are the etymological background of the Greek word, its use outside the LXX and the "exegetical motivations" of the Greek translator in using this Greek word as an equivalent for ברי.

---

96. Robert Hayward, "Observations on Idols in Septuagint Pentateuch," in *Idolatry: False Worship in the Bible, Early Judaism and Christianity* (ed. Stephen C. Barton; London: T&T Clark International, 2007), 41–42.

97. Paul Harlé argues that the word-pair γλυπτὸν καὶ χωνευτόν may have originated in LXX Deut 27:15 and functioned thereafter as a single object of abomination, rather than as two distinct terms (e.g. LXX Judg 17:3), *BA* 7:227.

98. Tov, "Three Dimensions," 534.

99. A similar approach to that of διαθήκη–ברית applies in this case also. Due to space limitations, νόμος will not receive a separate treatment.

The second stage begins when the word came to be used as a stereo-typical rendering for ברית in the TP and other books. At this stage, according to Tov, the meaning of the Greek has to be expressed as ברית, since it represented that word in all its usages.[100] Tov states: "we believe that if a certain Greek word represents a given Hebrew word in most of its occurrences, almost by implication it has become a mere symbol for that Hebrew word in the translation."[101]

What is difficult to determine with stereotypes, is the point at which the first stage began. Who was the first to identify the Greek διαθήκη ("testament") with the Hebrew ברית ("covenant") and what were the reasons? Of particular relevance to our concerns here is the fact that διαθήκη may already have been a term used in the Greek-speaking Jewish community to denote ברית, from which the Greek translators were reluctant to deviate.

κατάσχεσις–אחזה

The word אחזה ("possession, inheritance, property")[102] does not occur in the TP, but LXX Zech 11:14 seems to have misread אחוה for אחזה and rendered κατάσχεσις.[103] Muraoka defines κατάσχεσις as the "act of hold-ing in possession" (e.g. Num 32:5; Deut 32:49) or as "that which one possesses" (e.g. Gen 17:8; 48:4; Lev 25:24), and he marks this second meaning as unattested prior to the LXX. He also notes κληρονομία as a possible synonym (Ps 2:8).[104] Harl states that the occurrence of κατάσχε-σις in LXX Gen 17:8 marks the first occurrence of the word,[105] and similarly Harlé, commenting on LXX Lev 25:24, notes that the word does not occur outside the LXX.[106] Wevers observes that "[t]he noun originally means 'a holding back, a retention,' comp κατέχω, but in the LXX it means 'possession, inheritance.' It is ideally suited to render אחזה which has a similar lexical history with a root meaning of 'grasping, holding on to,' hence a possession, a property."[107]

אחזה is the principal Hebrew word behind κατάσχεσις, but not the only one. In LXX Ezekiel κατάσχεσις translates מורשה ("possession"—33:24;

100. Ibid., 541.
101. Ibid., 538.
102. BDB 28; *DCH* 1:187–88.
103. So LEH 328.
104. *Muraoka 2009*, 385.
105. *BA* 1:169–70.
106. *BA* 3:200.
107. John William Wevers, *Notes on the Greek Text of Genesis* (SBLSCS 35; Atlanta: Scholars Press, 1993), 232.

36:2, 3, 5), and in other places נחלה ("possession"—LXX Num 32:32; 33:54; 36:3; LXX Ezek 36:12).[108]

Apart from κατάσχεσις, κτῆσις (Gen 23:4, 9, 20; 36:43; 49:30; 50:13; Lev 14:34; 25:10, 13) and κληρονομία (2 Chr 31:1; Ezek 46:18) also serve as Greek equivalents for אחזה.

In the Greek TP, κληρονομία is more common than κατάσχεσις. It usually translates נחלה but many times it depends on "etymological exegesis" from the root ירש ("take possession of, inherit").[109] This is obvious with מורשת in Mic 1:14, מרשה in Mic 1:15 and ראשה in Zech 4:7. Could a similar "etymologizing" have taken place with אחז? It is difficult to know since this root does not occur in the TP. However, it is a plausible explanation since common Greek equivalents for אחז in the LXX include ἀντέχειν, ἐπιλαμβάνειν, καταλαμβάνειν, κατέχειν, κρατεῖν, λαμβάνειν, συνέχειν, etc.

On the evidence of the existing sources, the only meaning of κατάσχεσις in extra-biblical literature is "holding back, restraining, retention,"[110] sometimes used of "breath" (Hippocrates, *De diaeta i-iv* 64.15; Aristotle, *Problemata* 961b.23). This suggests that the meaning "possession" was available to the Greek translator of the TP within a community where it was used in this manner. This usage could have been introduced by the translators of the LXX Pentateuch or by a previous generation.

Etymologizing

As we have already seen in the treatment of παραπικραίνω, the biliteral exegesis of Hebrew roots in the LXX was sometimes favoured by the Greek translators. One example of this phenomenon is ἐκλεκτός:

ἐκλεκτός—בריא

בריא, an adjective meaning "fat, fleshy,"[111] occurs twice in the TP (Hab 1:16; Zech 11:16), both times translated by ἐκλεκτός ("chosen, selected for a task or a destiny").[112] However, this is not the only Hebrew word translated by ἐκλεκτός in the TP. Other words are בר ("grain, corn"—Amos 5:11)[113] and חמדה ("desire"—Hag 2:7; Zech 7:14).[114]

---

108. מושב in Num 15:2 (ms. A), 1 Chr 4:33 and מגרש in 1 Chr 13:2.
109. BDB 439.
110. LSJ 915.
111. *DCH* 2:263.
112. *Muraoka 2009*, 212.
113. BDB 141.
114. BDB 326.

HR gives up to twenty Hebrew words being translated by ἐκλεκτός,[115] with the root בחר standing behind most of the occurrences. One should keep in mind that some of the words listed may have been misread by the Greek translator (e.g. בד read as בר/ברר in LXX Ezek 19:14). What becomes evident from HR's list is that many of these words have it in common that they begin with ברה : בר (Song 6:9, 10; Amos 5:11), ברר (*Qal*—1 Chr 7:40; 9:22; Neh 5:18; Isa 49:2; *Niphal*—2 Kgdms 22:27; Ps 17[MT18]:27; *Hithpael*—2 Kgdms 22:27; Ps 17[MT18]:27), ברברים (3 Kgdms 5:3), ברומים (Ezek 27:24), ברי (Job 37:11) and בריא (Gen 41:2, 4, 5, 7, 18, 20; 3 Kgdms 5:3; Hab 1:16; Zech 11:16).

The most plausible scenario is that the above words have been connected to ברר (verb = "separate" [1 Kgdms 17:8],[116] noun = "chosen one" [Neh 5:18; 1 Chr 7:40; 9:22; 16:41]), a meaning widely attested in Qumran as well.[117] בר would have been enough for the translators to "etymologize," connecting the word to ברר. Tov says that "in the weak verbs…, often only two radicals were needed for semantic identification."[118] Therefore, in the TP, the Greek translator connected both בר in Amos 5:11 and בריא in Hab 1:16 and Zech 11:16 with ברר ("choose, select")[119] and thus rendered ἐκλεκτός. This "etymologizing" practice seems to be in agreement with what other Greek translators of LXX books have also done independently.

*Greek Equivalents Readily Available from
the Hellenistic Context*

In this category, I list alphabetically the remainder of the Greek–Hebrew equivalents proposed by Tov which are found in the TP. The treatment of these words shows that they could have been selected independently of any knowledge of the LXX Pentateuch:

ᾅδης–שאול
ᾅδης is almost a stereotype for the Hebrew שאול throughout the Septuagint, with the exception of θάνατος (2 Kgdms 22:6; cf. Pss 17[MT18]:5; 114[MT116]:3) and ἐν βάθει βόθρου (Ezek 32:21 [שאול מתוך]). While Tov decides to disregard obvious agreements, such as אשה–γυνή and

---

115. HR 437.
116. Perhaps ברה ("choose") is the root here. See *DCH* 2:260.
117. *DCH* 2:276.
118. Tov, "Biliteral Exegesis," 463. He also mentions בר as an example of biliteral exegesis on p. 467.
119. BDB 140.

צפרדע–βάτραχος, in his study of the influence of LXX Pentateuch on other LXX books, Lust asks: "[H]ow are we to know, e.g., that ᾅδης, listed in Tov's first series of examples, was not felt to be an obvious equivalent of שאול?"[120] In the TP, שאול is always rendered as ᾅδης (Hos 13:14[×2]; Amos 9:2; Jon 2:3; Hab 2:5). ᾅδης is also the Greek rendition for words or expressions such as אבני־בור (Isa 14:19); יורד־בור (Isa 38:18); דומה (Pss 93[MT94]:17; 113:25[MT115:17]); מָוֶת (Prov 14:12; 16:25; Isa 28:15); מות (Job 33:22); צלמות (Job 38:17). As Lust also notes, probably "the Greek language did not offer a better equivalent,"[121] which makes it difficult to argue for the dependence of the Greek translator of the TP on LXX Pentateuch for the rendering of this word.

ἀκαθαρσία–טמאה, ἀκάθαρτος–טמא
Lust views this example in the same category as αδης–שאול and applies the same conclusions.[122] For the TP also, the above correspondence is true (Hos 9:3; Amos 7:17; Mic 2:10; Zech 13:2), but ακαθαρ- words were not the translator's only choice. Various forms of μιαίνομαι are also employed for טמא (Hos 5:3; 6:10; 9:4; Hag 2:13, 14) and μιαίνομαι forms for the טמא root are just as popular in LXX Pentateuch (e.g. Gen 34:5; Lev 5:3; 11:43; 13:8; Num 5:19). Moreover, ἀκαθαρσία is used to render נבלת as well (Hos 2:12; Nah 3:6 [ונבלתיך read as a noun]). The fact that μίανσις, the closest synonym to ἀκαθαρσία, is extremely rare in extra-biblical Greek literature might suggest why for the Greek translator of the TP ἀκαθαρσία was the choice closest at hand. It is, therefore, unnecessary to ponder a dependence on LXX Pentateuch for rendering טמא.

ἀπαρχή–תרומה, ראשית
The plural ἀπαρχαί is found in Mal 3:8, translating תרומה. By contrast, ראשית is rendered in many different ways (πρόιμον [Hos 9:10]; ἀρχὰς [Amos 6:1]; πρῶτα [Amos 6:6]; ἀρχηγὸς [Mic 1:13]). It is clear that for ראשית no attempt was made to consult the LXX Pentateuch, so we shall only concern ourselves here with תרומה.
    Compared to the synonyms ἀφαίρεμα (Exod 29:27; 35:21; Lev 7:14)—which is absent in extra-biblical literature and categorized as a neologism by both Tov and Lust[123]—and εἰσφορά (Exod 30:13, 14, 15,

120. Lust, "The Vocabulary of the LXX Ezekiel," 532.
121. Ibid., 533.
122. Ibid., 534 n. 14.
123. Tov, "The Impact of the LXX," 580–81; Lust, "The Vocabulary of the LXX Ezekiel," 534.

16), which has no cultic connotations outside the LXX, ἀπαρχή is the most common Greek word used for primal or first-fruit offerings in extra-biblical sources (e.g. Thucydides, *Historiae* 3.58.4; Euripides, *Fragmenta* 516; Euripides, *Phoenissae* 857 [primal offering of the war's spoils]; Sophocles, *Trachiniae* 183). ἀπαρχή would thus be the word most readily available to the Greek translator of the TP who knew the meaning of תרומה ("contribution, offering [for sacred uses]").[124]

ἀπαρχή is also used to translate תנופה (Exod 39:1[MT38:24]) and חלב (Num 18:12, 29, 30, 32), but תנופה never occurs outside the Pentateuch except in Isa 19:16 and 30:32 where it has nothing to do with offerings. Perhaps if תנופה occurred outside the Pentateuch in contexts of cultic offerings, we would find that it was also translated by ἀπαρχή. חלב with the sense of "offering," but not rendered as ἀπαρχή, occurs only in Ezek 44:7 and 15, with the literal translation στέαρ.[125] However, from the available data there is no indication that the Greek translator of Mal 3:8 sought help from LXX Pentateuch in rendering תרומה.

βιβλίον–ספר

The identification of βιβλίον and ספר is found twice in the TP (Nah 1:1; Mal 3:16). Although this identification is the most popular in the LXX, one can find βιβλίον translating דבר (Dan [Th] 12:4 [ms. A]), מגלה (Jer 43[MT36]:14, 20, 25, 29 [ms. A]), מדרש (2 Chr 13:22) and תורה (Neh 10:35 [ms. B]). Other Greek nouns used for ספר are βίβλος/βύβλος (e.g. Gen 5:1; Exod 32:32; Josh 1:8; Ps 68[MT69]:29),[126] γράμμα (e.g. Josh 15:15, 16; Isa 29:11), ἐπιστολή (Isa 39:1) and συγγραφή (Job 31:35). ספר can be used to refer to a letter of instruction (2 Kgdms 11:14; 3 Kgdms 20[MT21]:8), a legal document (Deut 24:1; Jer 39[MT32]:11) or a book or scroll (Josh 18:9; Isa 30:8).[127]

Is βιβλίον broad enough to denote all the above categories covered by ספר? Schrenk says that both βίβλος and βιβλίον can also denote an epistle or document.[128] Specifically, a βίβλος or βιβλίον is made out of βίβλος (see Josephus, *Ant.* 2.246), which is material from the papyrus plant. Papyrus material replaced the wooden tablet in Greece from the

---

124. BDB 929.

125. Lust asks why only ראשית and תרומה were chosen by Tov as the Hebrew equivalents of ἀπαρχή; "The Vocabulary of the LXX Ezekiel," 535.

126. For βίβλος/βύβλος and βιβλίον in the LXX and other works, Schrenk notes that "it is impossible to establish any material distinction between the two terms"; Gottlob Schrenk, "βίβλος, βιβλίον," *TDNT* 1:615.

127. BDB 706.

128. Schrenk, *TDNT* 1:617.

sixth century B.C.E.[129] Therefore, in Hellenistic times, the papyrus scroll must have been the most popular writing material, especially in Egypt, and βιβλίον was the most common word for the "roll of a book," a "book," or a "writing" in the *koine*.[130] In the LXX, πυξίον is reserved for the tablet (לוּחַ—Exod 24:12; Hab 2:2; Isa 30:8). βιβλίον would therefore be the most natural word for the Greek translator to adopt for סֵפֶר, and its use does not provide proof of dependence by the translator on the LXX Pentateuch.

δῶρον–שֹׁחַד

In the TP, δῶρον translates שֹׁחַד in Mic 3:11, but it also translates התנוּ in Hos 8:9 (perhaps etymologizing from נתן–δίδωμι; cf. παραδοθήσονται in Hos 8:10 for יתנוּ) and מַשְׂאֵת ("gift, offering")[131] in Amos 5:11. The noun שֹׁחַד is always rendered as δῶρον in the LXX.

The question that arises is: How many options for Greek equivalents of שֹׁחַד did the Greek translator of the TP have to choose from? He uses δόματα ("gifts") in Hos 9:1 for the Hebrew אֶתְנָן ("hire of harlot"), which suggests another possibility: the translator may have connected התנוּ with אֶתְנָן in Hos 8:9 (ἠγάπησας δόματα [Hos 9:1]—δῶρα ἠγάπησαν [Hos 8:9]). In Hos 10:6, the translator uses ἐν δόματι for בְּשָׁנָה, which suggests that he read the preposition בְּ with שָׁנָה, perhaps confusing ת for שׁ, thus getting תְנָה.[132] Malachi 1:3 strengthens this possibility since לִתְנוֹת there is rendered εἰς δόματα (לְ preposition with etymologizing of תְנוֹת from נתן). δώρημα is very rare in the LXX and found only in Sir 34:18. δωρεά, absent in the Greek TP, would have been another choice for the Greek translator (e.g. 1 Esd 3:5; 2 Macc 4:30; *3 Macc.* 1:7; Wis 7:14; Dan 2:48; 11:39), but not as common as δῶρον. δόσις is also rare (e.g. Gen 47:22—"allotment"; 1 Esd 2:4; Prov 21:14). Büchsel notes that "Philo distinguishes between δόμα, δόσις on the one side as less valuable and δῶρον,

129. Ibid., 615.
130. Ibid., 617.
131. *DCH* 5:499.
132. Muraoka states that בְּאֶתְנָה was read on the basis of a confusion arising in the Palaeo-Hebrew script in which "the sequence את could be mistaken for שׁ"; "…if the LXX Vorlage had read as the MT, it is difficult to see how our translator failed to connect the word with the familiar root בוש"; T. Muraoka, "Hebrew Hapax Legomena and Septuagint Lexicography," in *VII Congress of the IOSCS* (ed. C. Cox; SBLSCS 31; Atlanta: Scholars Press, 1989), 211. *BA* recognize the division into the preposition בְּ and another word which is rendered on the basis of the context (ξένια in the same verse). *BA* 23.1:136.

δωρεά on the other as more valuable" (*Cher.* 84; *Leg. All.* 3.196; so, too, δίδωμι and δωρέομαι, *Decal.* 17).[133]

However, Philo's distinctions do not necessarily mean that for the Greek translator of the TP, or of any other LXX book, these words were not synonymous. They could have been parallels or they might have had a slightly different nuance (cf. James 1:17).

To summarize: of all the words for gift, δῶρον seems to be the one used most frequently. Moreover, there is no indication that שחד was difficult for the translator, necessitating his consulting of the LXX Pentateuch. Even if the word had been unknown, the translator could have understood from the parallels in Mic 3:11 that a "bribe" is meant, and δῶρον would have been the word most readily available to represent it.

ἐγκρυφίας–עוגה

ἐγκρυφίας is a "cake baked in ashes of coal fire"[134] and occurs eight times in the LXX (Gen 18:6; Exod 12:39; Num 11:8; 3 Kgdms 17:12, 13; 19:6; Hos 7:8; Ezek 4:12), representing עגה ("cake of bread")[135] and, once, מעוג ("cake"[136]—3 Kgdms 17:12). עגה has no other Greek equivalents in the LXX.[137]

ἐγκρυφίας is common in *Hippocrates et Corpus Hippocraticum* (*De diaeta acutorum* 21.5; *De morbis popularibus* 7.1.3.38; *De diaeta i-iv* 42.15; 79.9; *De mulierum affectibus i-iii* 34.23; 121.29). In the *Fragments* of Diocles (191.8) we are told that it was baked on coals. The word is also found in Archestratus (fourth century B.C.E.) in *Fragmenta* 4.15 and *Fragmenta et tituli* 135.15. Erotianos, explaining Hippocratean terms in the first century C.E., says that ἐγκρυφίας is made of fat, flour and water, and that it is cooked in hot ashes (*Vocum Hippocraticarum collectio* 56.2).[138] It would not be unreasonable to expect a translator familiar with the term עגה to use ἐγκρυφίας to represent it. This does not exclude the possibility that he had heard the biblical stories featuring עגה being told in Greek and using the word ἐγκρυφίας for the bread in question.

133.   Friedrich Büchsel, "δῶρον, δωρέομαι, δώρημα, δωρεά," *TDOT* 2:166–67.
134.   *Muraoka 2009*, 188.
135.   BDB 728.
136.   BDB 728.
137.   A Greek word parallel to ἐγκρυφίας is ἐγκρίς ("kind of cake"), used in the description of the manna (Exod 16:31 [צפיחת]; Num 11:8 [לשד]).
138.   For more sources, see LSJ 474.

ἐνώτιον–נזם

In the Pentateuch, the above equivalence is found in Genesis (24:22, 30, 47; 35:4) and Exodus (32:2, 3; 35:22), and in the Greek TP the word ἐνώτιον ("earring")[139] occurs once in Hos 2:15, translating נזמה ("[her] ring, nose-ring, earring").[140] נזם and ἐνώτιον are always equivalents in the rest of the LXX (e.g. Judg 8:24; Prov 11:22; Ezek 16:12).

ἐνώτιον is also used outside the LXX by authors such as Aeschylus (*Fragmenta* 102.1), Aristophanes of Byzantium (*Fragmenta* 91.1), Diodorus Siculus (*Bibliotheca historica [lib. 21–40]* 25.15.1.7) and Dorotheus (*Fragmenta Greca* 410.28),[141] so it was an option available to the Greek translator of the TP for representing "earring."

Although נזם is broader than "earring," it is the context which decides whether "ring for the finger," "nose-ring," or "earring" is intended. Nose-ring and earring can be denoted by the same Greek word (ὥσπερ ἐνώτιον ἐν ῥινὶ ὑός [LXX Prov 11:22] or καὶ ἔδωκα ἐνώτιον περὶ τὸν μυκτῆρά σου... [LXX Ezek 16:12]), while a ring for the finger is translated by δακτύλιος (e.g. Gen 38:18; Esth 8:8; Jdt 10:4; Isa 3:20). δακτύλιος was also used for the larger rings on the ark of the covenant (Exod 25:12, 14, 15) and the altar (Exod 27:4, 7). τροχίσκος is used once for a "hoop" earring (עגיל) in Ezek 16:12. In the majority of cases where ἐνώτιον occurs, it is contextually clear that an earring or a nose-ring is intended. The Greek translator of Hos 2:15 may have chosen ἐνώτιον for נזם simply on the basis of its common Hebrew usage.

ἐπιδέκατον–מעשר

The identification of מעשר with ἐπιδέκατον is found twice in the TP, in Amos 4:4 and Mal 3:8. מעשר occurs once more in the TP, where it is rendered as ἐκφόρια (Mal 3:10). ἐκφόρια seems to be a broader term used for everything the land yields (Hag 1:10—יבול; paraphrased in LXX Hag 1:11), and it is used as such by Herodotus (*Hist.* 4.198.8). However, it is not clear why the Greek translator of Mal 3:10 chose it for מעשר instead of ἐπιδέκατον. Perhaps it arises from his understanding of the whole verse, which is different from that indicated in the MT. While the MT appears to be an exhortation to the people to bring their tithes into the temple and experience God's blessing, in the LXX the people seem to be informed that they have brought all the produce of the land, not just the tithes, into the treasuries, but this will be plundered from the temple: καὶ

---

139. *Muraoka 2009*, 243; LSJ 579.
140. BDB 633.
141. For more sources, see LSJ 579.

εἰσηνέγκατε πάντα τὰ ἐκφόρια εἰς τοὺς θησαυρούς καὶ ἔσται ἡ διαρπαγὴ ἐν τῷ οἴκῳ μου.

The Greek translator's choice of ἐκφόρια for מעשר in Mal 3:10 appears to be interpretive and should not be taken as an indicator that he is ignorant of the meaning of the Hebrew word.

ἐπιδέκατον is very common in extra-biblical literature. It is found in financial payments in the Documentary papyri with the general sense of "a tenth" as interest or instalment (e.g. *P.Amh.* II,33,20, 32; *P.Eleph.* 14 rp, 26; *P.Hal.* 1, r, 3, 63), but in some writers it is used for the tithe given to the gods (Andocides, *De mysteriis* 96.11; Xenophon, *Hellenica* 1.7.10.3; 1.7.21.1; Demosthenes, *Contra Macartatum* 71.10). Naturally, this term was available to the Greek translator to denote the concept of "tithe." Any translator with the knowledge of the number ten (עשר = δέκα) would not have had trouble identifying the word מעשר with the common Greek word used for "tenth/tithe" (ἐπιδέκατον), especially when מעשר occurs in cultic contexts.[142] Moreover, the translator's use of ἐκφόρια for מעשר in Mal 3:10 betrays some degree of freedom on his part rather than narrow dependence on LXX Pentateuch.

ἑρπετά–רמש

The collective רמש means "creeping things,"[143] and it is always translated by ἑρπετά. Sometimes it is used for sea animals (Ps 103[MT104]:25), but generally it is distinguished from בהמה, חיה, עוף, צפור and דג. In the TP, the identification of ἑρπετά and רמש occurs twice, in Hos 2:20 and Hab 1:14, but it is also found in Hos 2:14 and 4:3 as a plus. Twelve times in the LXX ἑρπετόν translates שרץ ("swarming things").[144] ἑρπετόν is a common word in the Greek world for "creeping things, reptiles"[145] (e.g. Herodotus, *Hist.* 1.140.12; 4.183.18), and there are no synonyms more adequate for רמש that the Greek translators of the LXX could have used for this class within the animal kingdom.

θυμίαμα–קטרת

In Mal 1:11, θυμίαμα translates מקטר ("incense"),[146] the only place in the TP where θυμίαμα occurs. קטרת is not found in the TP. However, it seems that the translator understands the קטר root as relating to sacrifices

---

142. The Greek translator of Isaiah used ἐπιδέκατον for עשיריה in 6:13.
143. BDB 943.
144. HR 548.
145. LSJ 691.
146. BDB 883.

(Hos 2:15; 4:13) or the burning of incense (Hos 11:2; Hab 1:16). θυμιάζω and nouns related to it are common in extra-biblical sources. As a result, θυμίαμα would have been an obvious choice for the Greek translator in the rendering of מקטר.

κίδαρις–מצנפת

κίδαρις occurs twice in Zech 3:5 for צניף. In the *Letter of Aristeas* (98.1) κίδαρις is part of the description of the High priest: Ἐπὶ δὲ τῆς κεφαλῆς ἔχει τὴν λεγομένην κίδαριν. In Paeon (*Fragmenta* 1.4) κίδαρις is identified as the typical Persian term for the head dress: Κρέων δὲ ἐν τῷ πρώτῳ τῶν Κυπριακῶν κορδύλην φησὶ καλεῖσθαι τὸ πρὸς κεφαλῇ προσείλημα, ὃ δὴ παρὰ Ἀθηναίοις καλεῖται κρώβυλον, παρὰ δὲ Πέρσαις κιδάριον.

Palmer, following Cimosa, says that "[w]hen the Torah was translated it was, whatever the exact reasons for its translation, done in a context where Jews already spoke about their religion in Greek and would inevitably come to use regular terms to refer to particular Hebrew concepts or well-known passages."[147]

Especially for vocabulary relating to the temple, Palmer sees no direct influence from the LXX Pentateuch,[148] but concludes that "[i]n a cultural context which produced the temple at Leontopolis, there was a strong interest in matters relating to the priesthood and tabernacle (ποδήρη and κίδαρις in 3:4–5)."[149]

λέβης–סיר

λέβης ("cauldron")[150] translates סיר four times in the TP (Amos 4:2; Mic 3:3; Zech 14:20, 21). Other Hebrew words behind λέβης in the LXX are כיר and דוד (1 Kgdms 2:14; 2 Chr 35:13). The Greek translator of the TP is aware of the double meaning of סיר, that of "thorn, hook"[151] (Hos 2:8; possibly Hos 4:17, 18) and that of "pot"[152] (Amos 4:2; Mic 3:3; Zech 14:20, 21). Thus in Hos 2:8, where Yahweh threatens to block Israel's way with סירים, the translator adjusts contextually, without any demonstrable dependence on the LXX Pentateuch, by rendering ἐν σκόλοψιν. Moreover, λέβης is very common in Greek extra-biblical sources.

---

147. Palmer, "'Not Made with Tracing Paper,'" 78.
148. Similar conclusions are reached by Cécile Dogniez who notes that the Greek translator of Deutero-Zechariah has not gone to the Pentateuch to get his vocabulary; Dogniez, "L'intertextualité dans la LXX de Zacharie 9–14," 88–89.
149. Palmer, "'Not Made with Tracing Paper,'" 78.
150. *Muraoka 2009*, 427.
151. BDB 696.
152. BDB 696.

λειτουργέω–שרת

λειτουργέω in the LXX is mainly a cultic term used for temple service.[153] In the TP, the *Piel* participle of שרת, found in contexts of cultic service, is always translated by λειτουργοῦντες (Joel 1:9, 13 [×2]; 2:17). λειτουργέω was commonly used in Greek literature for various types of service: public service or public duties, religious service or ritual, serving a master, and so on.[154] Although λειτουργέω is the most popular rendering for שרת-root words, other equivalents used are: διακονία (A—Esth 6:3), διάκονος (Esth 1:10), δουλεύω (Isa 56:6), θεράπων (Exod 33:11), and others. Strathmann notes that in the LXX there is no trace of the "technical political" use of λειτουργέω, and only a few exceptions to the general or popular use of the word are found. Usually the object of the ministry in the LXX is the tent, the house, the altar, God's name or God himself, not the city, the state, the people, the citizens or specific individuals.[155] Strathmann concludes that "[t]he LXX translators obviously felt a need to try to fix a regular and exclusive term for priestly ministry, and thereby to show that the cultic relation to God is something special as compared with all the other relations of service in which men might stand."[156]

However, the concentration of this Greek rendering in cultic contexts in the LXX does not necessarily suggest an intentional effort on the part of the translators to restrict its usage. Philo uses the word for both the cult and official public functions (καὶ ἀγορανομίας καὶ γυμνασιαρχίας καὶ τὰς ἄλλας λειτουργίας ὑπομένοντας [*Prob.* 6]).[157] Moreover, although a specialized cultic use of λειτουργέω existed in extra-biblical sources, Strathmann insists that the LXX translators would not have adopted the term from there:

> If the words were known to the translators as technical terms in the pagan cultus, and if they had this fact in view, they would surely have avoided them. It is more likely that they were thinking of the older official or technical political use in which the words denoted a ministry on behalf of the whole which was legally ordered and which was invested with great solemnity in its chief forms. For them, of course, the recipient of the service is God, not the people, though the service promotes the national welfare, which depends on the gracious disposition of God.[158]

153. See H. Strathmann, "λειτουργέω," *TDNT* 4:215–31.
154. LSJ 1036–38.
155. Strathmann, *TDNT* 4:221.
156. Ibid., 221–22.
157. For the New Testament, see Karen H. Jobes, "Distinguishing the Meaning of Greek Verbs in the Semantic Domain of Worship," *Filología Neotestamentaria* 4 (1991): 186.
158. Strathmann, *TDNT* 4:222.

The certainty by which Strathmann expresses what the LXX translators would have adopted and what they would have avoided is surprising. Since the cultic usage of λειτουργέω is attested in extra-biblical sources, there is no reason to assume that it had received any special treatment or acquired any special significance in the LXX. Moreover, there is no compelling reason to assume that this equivalent for the שרת root came from the LXX Pentateuch, and not from the vocabulary of the translator's environment.

λυχνία–מנורה

In Zech 4:2 and 11, λυχνία translates מנורה, and this is a stereotypical identification throughout the LXX.[159] *A priori*, at least, λύχνος might have been another option. However, it is unlikely that the translator of Zechariah has chosen λυχνία over λύχνος on the basis of the LXX Pentateuch. Muraoka defines λυχνία as "lampstand" and λύχνος as "lamp."[160] Liddell and Scott identify λύχνος as a "portable light, lamp."[161] For an item from the temple furniture, on the basis of extra-biblical usage, it is to be expected that λυχνία would have been preferred over λύχνος. Moreover, λυχνία is commonly attested in the Duke Documentary papyri from Egypt (e.g. BGU VIII, 1854, 11; *P.Bacch.* 1 rp, 2, 46; 2 rp, 10; 4 rp, 9; 5 rp, 8), and in inscriptions from the third century B.C.E. (e.g. *SIG* 1106.118).[162]

μαντεία–קסם

The קסם root occurs four times in the TP. Once the *Qal* infinitive construct in מקסם is represented by (ἐκ) μαντείας (Mic 3:6), twice the *Qal* masculine participle plural הקסמים is represented by οἱ μάντεις (Mic 3:7; Zech 10:2), and once the imperfect third masculine plural verb יקסמו is rendered by ἐμαντεύοντο (Mic 3:11). קסם means "divination" or "practising divination,"[163] and in the LXX the identification of קסם with μαντ- root words holds, with the exception of Ezek 13:8 where καὶ αἱ μαντεῖαι ὑμῶν translates וחזיתם. Other Greek words which have been used to translate the קסם root in the LXX are ἀποφθεγγόμενοι (הקסמים) in Ezek 13:9, στοχαστής (קסם) in Isa 3:2 and οἰώνισμα (קסם) in 1 Kgdms 15:23.

159. HR 891.
160. *Muraoka 2009*, 437.
161. LSJ 1068.
162. LSJ 1068.
163. BDB 890.

The word μάντις ("seer, prophet") goes back to Homer (e.g. *Il.* 13.69; 16.859; 19.420), and the noun μαντεία, which means "prophetic power, power of divination,"[164] is attested in the Homeric Hymns (Hymni Homerici, *In Mercurium* 472). They are common words throughout Greek literature.

It is interesting, however, that while προφητεία and μαντεία could function as synonyms, μαντεία seems to have negative connotations and is mainly used for pagan diviners. It is only used for Israelite prophets when condemning them (e.g. Jer 34[MT27]:9; 36[MT29]:8). προφητεία is used for pagan diviners only when it is explicitly qualified as false, whereas μαντεία would not need such qualification. The negative connotations of μαντεία are carried over into the NT where μαντεύομαι is only used of the girl possessed by the "spirit of divination" in Acts 16:16. Trench argues that the "inspired writers abstain from words, whose employment would tend to break down the distinction between heathenism and revealed religion."[165] He also notes that even pagans recognized the superior nature of προφήτης over μάντης, and refers to *Timaeus* of Plato where μάντης is connected to ecstatic irrationality:[166]

ἱκανὸν δὲ σημεῖον ὡς μαντικὴν ἀφροσύνη θεὸς ἀνθρωπίνη δέδωκεν· οὐδεὶς γὰρ ἔννους ἐφάπτεται μαντικῆς ἐνθέου καὶ ἀληθοῦς, ἀλλ' ἢ καθ' ὕπνον τὴν τῆς φρονήσεως πεδηθεὶς δύναμιν ἢ διὰ νόσον, ἢ διά τινα ἐνθουσιασμὸν παραλλάξας. (71e)

προφήτης, however, should not, according to this dialogue, be put in the same category on the grounds that the person possessing the ability to discern through a sound mind is the *interpreter* of the divinations:

ὅθεν δὴ καὶ τὸ τῶν προφητῶν γένος ἐπὶ ταῖς ἐνθέοις μαντείαις κριτὰς ἐπικαθιστάναι νόμος· οὓς μάντεις αὐτοὺς ὀνομάζουσίν τινες, τὸ πᾶν ἠγνοηκότες ὅτι τῆς δι' αἰνιγμῶν οὗτοι φήμης καὶ φαντάσεως ὑποκριταί, καὶ οὔτι μάντεις, προφῆται δὲ μαντευομένων δικαιότατα ὀνομάζοιντ' ἄν. (72a-b)

To summarize: there is no indication that קסם was a problem to the Greek translator of the TP. Furthermore, it seems possible that μαντεία was preferred for pagan prophecy or false prophecy as a fitting equivalent for קסם owing to the existing negative connotations that the word may have had in the Greek world, and not necessarily because this distinction was established by the LXX Pentateuch.

---

164.   LSJ 1079.
165.   R. C. Trench, *Synonyms of the New Testament* (new ed.; London: Kegan Paul, Trench, Trübner, 1915), 18.
166.   Ibid., 22.

μέτρον–איפה

In the TP, μέτρον translates איפה in Amos 8:5; Mic 6:10; Zech 5:6, 7, 8, 9 and 10. μέτρον is also used to translate קו or קוה in Zech 1:16. In the LXX as a whole, it translates nine different Hebrew roots.[167]

There do not seem to be many Greek options for איפה from which the Greek translator could choose. In Sir 42:4, איפה is translated by ζυγός,[168] perhaps to match the common doublet ζυγοῦ καὶ σταθμίων (cf. LXX Lev 19:35; Prov 11:1; 16:11; 20:23; Sir 28:25; Amos 8:5; Mic 6:11; Isa 40:12; 46:6; Ezek 5:1). μέτρον is a common word which would have been a readily available rendering in contexts relating to "measures." If the Greek translator of the TP was ignorant of the meaning of איפה, he could have guessed it from a verse like Amos 8:5, where it occurs among synonyms. It is possible that, after this choice was made in Amos 8:5, it was faithfully maintained in the translation of Micah and Zechariah, even at the expense of the context (μία γυνὴ ἐκάθητο ἐν μέσῳ τοῦ μέτρου [5:7]). However, it is possible that μέτρον in Zech 5 was understood to be the instrument with which one measures.

μόλιβ(δ)ος–עפרת

μόλιβος ("lead")[169] occurs twice in the Greek TP (Zech 5:7, 8) translating עפרת ("lead").[170] μόλιβος always translates עפרת, except in two passages (Num 31:22; Ezek 22:20) where it translates בדיל ("alloy, tin, dross").[171] עפרת, on the other hand, is not translated by any other Greek word except μόλιβος.

בדיל is understood by the Greek translator in Zech 4:10, as shown by the fact that he correctly translates it with the adjective κασσιτέρινον. However, he could not have borrowed this Greek equivalent from the LXX Pentateuch, since בדיל occurs only once, in Num 31:22, where it is translated by μόλιβος. This suggests a weakness in Tov's selection of words, since he needs to account also for word identifications which are not valid in the LXX Pentateuch. A better explanation in this case is that the Greek translator of the TP had independent knowledge of the meaning of this Hebrew word.

167. HR 918.
168. HR Appendix 2, 178.
169. LEH 407; LSJ 1142.
170. BDB 780.
171. BDB 95.

ὄψιμος–מלקוש

The Hebrew word מלקוש ("latter rain, spring rain")[172] occurs eight times in the Hebrew Bible, three of them in the TP (Hos 6:3; Joel 2:23; Zech 10:1). The word is always translated by ὄψιμος ("far on in time, late").[173] ὄψιμος also renders אפיל at Exod 9:32.

ὄψιμος is attested in Homer (*Il.* 2.325) as well as in Xenophon, where one finds it together with its antonym πρόιμος/πρώιμος, referring to the times of sowing crops (*Oeconomicus* 17.4.3, 5; 17.5.4).[174] The word-pair πρώιμος/ὄψιμος is also present in Eudoxus (*Selenodromium secundum cyclum duodecim annorum* 7.186.19), as also where ὄψιμος occurs in the TP. In Zech 10:1, there is no Hebrew word matching πρόιμος, which suggests that the translator adopted the entire wordpair when rendering מלקוש. Palmer suggests that the other occurrences of the word-pair in the TP might have influenced LXX Zechariah or its Hebrew *Vorlage*. He also notes that the end of the verse עשב בשדה is translated by βοτάνην ἐν ἀγρῷ, while the same phrase in Deuteronomy (11:15) is rendered χορτάσματα ἐν τοῖς ἀγροῖς. Palmer concludes that "[a]t the very least this would weigh against a fully conscious use of LXX-Deut by the LXX-Zech."[175]

As Dogniez says, the two terms are common in agricultural Greek vocabulary, and are also used in a similar manner in the NT:[176] ἰδοὺ ὁ γεωργὸς ἐκδέχεται τὸν τίμιον καρπὸν τῆς γῆς μακροθυμῶν ἐπ᾽ αὐτῷ ἕως λάβῃ πρόϊμον καὶ ὄψιμον (Jas 5:7). The above data suggest that the Greek translator of the TP could have just as easily adopted these terms from his Greek environment.

παράδεισος–עדן גן

The word παράδεισος ("enclosed park, pleasure ground") is an oriental word first used by Xenophon with reference to the parks of the Persian kings and nobles. By the third century B.C.E., the word had become as ordinary as κῆπος ("garden") or ἀμπελών ("orchard"), and the frequent presence of παράδεισοι in the papyri shows that they were a common feature of agriculture in Ptolemaic Egypt.[177] An area planted principally

172.   BDB 545.
173.   *Muraoka 2009*, 517.
174.   See LSJ 1282 for more sources and Shipp's discussion of both ὄψιμος and πρώιμος; G. P. Shipp, *Modern Greek Evidence for the Ancient Greek Vocabulary* (Sydney: Sydney University Press, 1979), 427–28.
175.   Palmer, "'Not Made with Tracing Paper,'" 75–76.
176.   BA 5:189.
177.   E.g. *P.Rev.Laws* 33.11; *P.Cair.Zen.* 33.3; *OGI* 90.15 (LSJ 1308); Lee, *A Lexical Study*, 53–54. G. B. Caird, "Homeophony in the Septuagint," in *Jews,*

or solely with vegetables or flowers would have been identified as a κῆπος. However, a παράδεισος was "an area of cultivated ground containing chiefly fruit-trees, at times also other types of tree, vines, and possibly other plants, and perhaps protected by a wall," meaning that "orchard" would therefore be a better translation and would also explain why this word was chosen over κῆπος for the Garden of Eden in Gen 2 and 3.[178]

In the LXX, עדן is sometimes rendered as Εδεμ (Gen 2:8, 10) and sometimes as τρυφή (Gen 3:23, 24). The fact that Εδεμ is not an accurate transliteration of עדן may suggest that Εδεμ was already a circulating name for the place mentioned in Gen 2 and 3 before the LXX translation was made. In the TP, παράδεισος, with τρυφή instead of Εδεμ, occurs once in Joel 2:3 for the phrase כגן־עדן. Elsewhere in the TP where גנה occurs, the Greek translator renders it as κῆπος (Amos 4:9; 9:14). Is it the presence of עדן in Joel 2:3 which directed the translator's choice towards παράδεισος in this instance? Does the combination of the words imply a larger orchard which would be better reflected by παράδεισος instead of κῆπος? It does not appear so in Ezek 36:35, where כגן־עדן is rendered as ὡς κῆπος τρυφῆς.[179] Moreover, in LXX Jeremiah, both παράδεισος and κῆπος translate גנה in almost identical verses, showing that the two words were interchangeable:

Jer 36[MT29]:5   καὶ φυτεύσατε παραδείσους καὶ φάγετε τοὺς καρποὺς αὐτῶν

Jer 36[MT29]:28   καὶ φυτεύσατε κήπους καὶ φάγεσθε τὸν καρπὸν αὐτῶν

They could even have been considered synonymous in Sir 24:30–31:

κἀγὼ ὡς διῶρυξ ἀπὸ ποταμοῦ καὶ ὡς ὑδραγωγὸς ἐξῆλθον εἰς παράδεισον εἶπα ποτιῶ μου τὸν κῆπον καὶ μεθύσω μου τὴν πρασιάν καὶ ἰδοὺ ἐγένετό μοι ἡ διῶρυξ εἰς ποταμόν καὶ ὁ ποταμός μου ἐγένετο εἰς θάλασσαν

While LXX Genesis never refers to the Garden of Eden as κῆπος, in Josephus the word κῆπος is used (*Ant.* 1.38, 45, 51), as well as παράδεισος (*Ant.* 1.37), when the Garden of Eden is described, thus showing the interchangeability of the two terms. Philo, however, prefers παράδεισος throughout.

Greeks and Christians: Religious Cultures in Late Antiquity: Essays in Honor of William David Davies (ed. Robert Hamerton-Kelly and Robin Scroggs; Leiden: Brill, 1976), 79.

178.   Lee, *A Lexical Study*, 55–56.

179.   Some Lucianic witnesses have εγενετο ως παραδεισος.

Perhaps the reason why the Greek translator of the TP chose παράδεισος when עדן was present and κῆπος when גנה stood alone, was that παράδεισος and τρυφή were more commonly found occurring together in Greek literature (Ctesias, *Fragmenta* 3c,688,F fragment 1b line 348; Clearchus, *Fragmenta* 43a.2; Diodorus Siculus, *Bibliotheca historica* 14.80.2.4), than are κῆπος and τρυφή (Plutarch, *Lucullus* 39.2.8; cf. LXX Ezek 36:35).

It is possible that παράδεισος was preferred when the Garden of God was in mind, but there is no indication of this in the LXX TP.[180]

ποταμός–יאר

In the Greek TP, ποταμός ("river")[181] translates יאר six times (Amos 8:8 [×2]; 9:5 [×2]; Nah 3:8; Zech 10:11) and נהר nine times (Mic 7:12; Jon 2:4; Nah 1:4; 2:7; Hab 3:8 [×2], 9; Zeph 3:10; Zech 9:10), while for נחל the translator consistently uses χείμαρρος (Amos 5:24; 6:14; Mic 6:7; Joel 4:18). In the LXX ποταμός is also used for נחל (3 Kgdms 8:65; 2 Chr 20:16; 32:4; Prov 18:4; Ezek 47:6, 7, 9, 12), and once for פלג (Ps 64[MT65]:10). Sometimes יאר is rendered as διῶρυξ, διώρυγος, διώρυχος (Exod 7:19; 8:1; Isa 19:6; 33:21). As Schmidt points out, ποταμός would have been the generic term used for river:

> Ποταμός ist die allgemeine Benennung der natürlichen fliessenden Gewässer, die wir namentlich der Grösse nach durch die Wörter Strom, Fluss und Bach zu unterscheiden pflegen. Auch Nebenflüsse heissen in Beziehung auf den Hauptfluss wiederum ποταμός; dagegen wird das Wort in der klassischen Sprache nicht von einem künstlich gegrabenen Kanale, διῶρυξ, angewandt.[182]

Although יאר denotes the Nile (Gen 41:1; Exod 1:22; 2:3, 5; 4:9; 7:15; 8:5, 7; 17:5; Sir 39:22; 47:14; Amos 8:8; 9:5; Zech 10:11; Isa 19:7, 8; 23:3, 10; Jer 26[MT46]:7, 8; Ezek 29:3, 9; 4QParGenEx 3:3) and its streams (Exod 7:19; 8:1; 4 Kgdms 19:24; Isa 7:18; 19:6; 37:25; Ezek 29:3, 4, 5, 9, 10; 30:12; Nah 3:8; Ps 77[MT78]:44; 4QpNah 3:9), it is used more generally of other rivers or streams (Isa 33:21; perh. 4QapPs^b 1:4; 4QBer^a 5:10; Dan 12:5, 6, 7).[183]

---

180. See Marguerite Harl, *La Langue de Japhet: Quinze Études sur la Septante et le Grec des Chrétiens* (Paris: Cerf, 1994), 148–49.

181. *Muraoka 2009*, 579.

182. Heinrich J. Schmidt, *Synonymik der Griechischen Sprache* (4 vols.; Leipzig: Teubner, 1876–86), 1:633.

183. *DCH* 4:71–72.

In the TP, the translator does not appear to have understood יאר as having a specific referent (see the anarthrous rendering in LXX Amos 8:8; 9:5, and the pluralized rendering in LXX Zech 10:11) and, therefore, ποταμός seems to have been the commonest equivalent the translator could deploy for "river," without any obvious dependence on LXX Pentateuch.

προσκυνέω–השתחוה

Every time השתחוה (akin to שוח, שחח [cf. שחי in Isa 51:23])[184] occurs in the TP it is rendered with forms of προσκυνέω. This can be regarded as a stereotype, since the identification προσκυνέω–השתחוה is true for the majority of the 288 cases of προσκυνέω.[185] Other words which are used for השתחוה are κύπτειν (Ps 9:31[MT10:10]; Isa 2:9), κατακάμπτειν (Ps 37[MT38]:7) and ταπεινοῦν (Ps 9:31; Isa 2:11, 17; 5:15; 25:12; 26:5). Although, in respect of meaning, these words partly overlap with προσκυνέω, they are not proper synonyms. Jobes sees προσκυνέω as carrying three senses: worship, paying political homage, and entreaty.[186] These senses allow for a certain flexibility in the use of προσκυνέω in different contexts, similar to that of השתחוה in Hebrew, making the two words very appropriate equivalents, and even stereotypes. For example, in LXX Zeph 2:11, the sense of both προσκυνέω and השתחוה may not have been that of "worship" but of "political homage." Since both words can carry the latter meaning, the stereotyping can function successfully:

ἐπιφανήσεται κύριος ἐπ' αὐτοὺς καὶ ἐξολεθρεύσει πάντας τοὺς θεοὺς τῶν ἐθνῶν τῆς γῆς καὶ προσκυνήσουσιν αὐτῷ (וישתחוו־לו) ἕκαστος ἐκ τοῦ τόπου αὐτοῦ πᾶσαι αἱ νῆσοι τῶν ἐθνῶν

προσκυνέω is a common word in extra-biblical sources, with meanings such as "make obeisance," "fall down and worship" and "prostrate oneself before superiors."[187] It is found in Aesop (*Fab.* 193.1.2, 3, 7), Aeschylus (*Prom.* 936; *Pers.* 499), Pythagoras (*Fragmenta* 162.22), Euripides (*Tro.* 1021; *Orest.* 1507), Sophocles (*Oed. tyr.* 327), Herodotus (*Hist.* 1.134.5; 7.136.3) and many others. There is no indication that the Greek translator of the TP depended on the LXX Pentateuch, rather than his linguistic environment, in choosing προσκυνέω as the equivalent for השתחוה.

---

184. BDB 1005.
185. In Daniel LXX and Theodotion, προσκυνέω represents the Aramaic סגד.
186. Jobes, "Distinguishing the Meaning," 186.
187. LSJ 1518.

מצבה–στήλη

The identification of στήλη with מצבה is found in various Pentateuchal texts (e.g. Gen 28:18, 22; Exod 23:24; Lev 26:1; Deut 7:5). The Greek translator of the TP uses στήλη for מצבה three times (Hos 10:1, 2; Mic 5:12). מצבה ("pillar, as monument, personal memorial")[188] is accurately represented by στήλη in the LXX, but sometimes it is rendered as θυσιαστήριον (Hos 3:4), λίθος (Exod 24:4) or στῦλος (Jer 50[MT43]:13). στήλη usually renders מצבה, but sometimes it translates מצבת (Gen 35:14, 20; 2 Kgdms 18:18), נציב (Gen 19:26) and במה (Lev 26:30; Num 21:28; 22:41; 33:52).

στήλη served various functions: from memorial gravestones (Homer, *Il.* 16.457) to cultic monuments (Herodotus, *Hist.* 3.24). Sometimes στήλη is found in parallel to βωμός (Thucydides, *Hist.* 6.55.1.4; Polybius, *Hist.* 10.40.7.7), which could explain why LXX Hos 3:4 interpreted מצבה as θυσιαστήριον. It seems to function as an altar in Gen 28:18 and 35:14 as well as in Herodotus' descriptions (*Hist.* 3.24). Cultic observances were inscribed on a στήλη (Lysias, *In Nicomachum* 17.7) and were set up in sanctuaries (Demosthenes, *In Neaeram* 76.2–3) or sacred enclosures (Polybius, *Hist.* 4.33.2.3). The above references show that there must have been a significant semantic overlap between στήλη and מצבה in its various uses, thus rendering the two as appropriate equivalents for the LXX translators.[189] There is no indication of influence from the LXX Pentateuch on LXX TP for the rendering of מצבה.

שלם–σωτήριον

σωτήριον can have two main meanings: "deliverance, security" or a "thank-offering for deliverance."[190] The most common Hebrew word behind σωτήριον is שלם ("peace offering")[191] and the majority of occurrences are found in the Pentateuch with reference to the "peace offering," זבח השלמים or simply השלמים (e.g. Exod 20:24; 24:5; Lev 3:1; 4:10; Num 6:14; 7:17; Deut 27:7). Outside the Pentateuch, σωτήριον mainly renders the root ישע.

One of the meanings of שלום is "deliverance, salvation,"[192] therefore the identification of שלם with σωτήριον in the LXX would be an acceptable one. Among various nouns or adjectives rendering שלם throughout

188.   BDB 663.
189.   For a discussion of στήλη, see also Daniel, *Recherches sur le Vocabulaire du Culte*, 39–40.
190.   *Muraoka 2009*, 668.
191.   BDB 1023.
192.   *HALAT* 4:1419.

the LXX (e.g. ἀνταπόδοσις, εἰρηνικός, ὁλόκληρος, πλήρης, τέλειος), σωτήριον is the one mainly reserved for the cultic term "peace offering." There are, however, some exceptions where σωτήριον or σῴζω renders שׁלם outside cultic contexts: (a) in Gen 41:16 Joseph assures Pharaoh that God will give him a favourable answer (LXX σωτήριον / MT אֶת־שְׁלוֹם) to his dream, and (b) in LXX Prov 11:31 the verb ישׁלם is translated as σῴζεται.

The equivalence σωτήριον–שָׁלֵם in the Prophets is rare, being found three times in Ezekiel (45:15; 46:2, 12) and once in the TP (Amos 5:22). The שׁלם root is given various equivalents in the TP (ἀνταποδώσομεν [Hos 14:3]; Σαλωμων [Amos 1:6, 9]; ἀνταποδώσω [Joel 2:25]; ἀνταπο-δίδωτε [Joel 4:4]; κατάρχων ὑδάτων [read as מים שׁלם—Nah 1:12]); εἰρήνην [Nah 2:1]), which shows that the translator is aware of the range of meanings this root could have, and is not dependent on a particular Pentateuchal rendering.

The rendering σωτήριον seems to appear in the context of "sacrifice" in Amos and Ezekiel. This suggests that σωτήριον was an established cultic term for the שׁלם offering, and not εἰρηνικός, which is found only in Kingdoms. Fohrer points out that εἰρηνικός is used for the "peace-offering" throughout Kingdoms, never σωτήριον, and he attributes this difference to the fact that Kingdoms comes from different hands.[193] It is obvious that σωτήριον as a technical term had no influence over these books; or, perhaps in an attempt to follow the Hebrew שׁלם more closely, εἰρηνική θυσία was preferred (cf. 1 Kgdms 10:8; 11:15; 13:9; 2 Kgdms 6:17, 18; 3 Kgdms 3:15; 8:63; 4 Kgdms 16:13). Outside Kingdoms, εἰρηνική θυσία is only found in LXX Prov 7:14, but not in extra-biblical texts.

Why was σωτήριον a more popular term for the "peace offering" than εἰρηνική θυσία in the LXX as a whole? It is possible that σωτήριον became part of Jewish cultic terminology because it was already used in this way in the surrounding Greek world. The plural σωτήρια was used to designate "salvation-offerings":

Δοκεῖ μοι, ὦ ἄνδρες, ἐπεὶ περὶ σωτηρίας ἡμῶν λεγόντων οἰωνὸς τοῦ Διὸς τοῦ σωτῆρος ἐφάνη, εὔξασθαι τῷ θεῷ τούτῳ θύσειν σωτήρια ὅπου ἂν πρῶτον εἰς φιλίαν χώραν ἀφικώμεθα. (Xenophon, *Anab.* 3.2.9; cf. 5.1.1; Attica, *IG* II/III² 1 [1–1369] doc. 661,18, 23; 807,7; 930,13, 14; 950,9)

Perhaps σωτήριον was adopted for שׁלם offerings because it was part of an existing cultic terminology in the Greek language. In his study of σωτήριον in LXX Leviticus, Büchner concludes that the translator

---

193. Georg Fohrer, "σωτήριος," *TDNT* 7:1022.

points the reader via familiar contemporary Greek ritual ultimately to the Hebrew ritual. Because of his community's unfamiliarity with the latter, the translator gives it a Greek face... The translator's didactic purpose went beyond language to culture so that he could bring his readership to the שלמים via an Alexandrian version of the meat sacrifice.[194]

However, it is difficult to say that the choice of σωτήριον for שלם in Amos 5:22 came via LXX Pentateuch and not directly from knowledge of the Hebrew word and the Jewish cult.

χύτρα–פ(א)רור

The word χύτρα ("earthen pot")[195] is most common in the TP (Mic 3:3; Joel 2:6; Nah 2:11) where it translates קלחת in Mic 3:3 and פארור in the others. Apart from Joel 2:6 and Nah 2:11, פארור (with an א) occurs nowhere else in the Hebrew Bible. Its meaning is uncertain and seven suggestions are noted in *DCH*, all on the basis of context in Joel 2:6 and Nah 2:11: "paleness," "darkness," "redness," "glow," "pot" (as an alternative form of פרור), "furrow (of face)" and "brightness."[196]

It is possible that the translator read פרור ("cooking-pot"),[197] the word for χύτρα in Num 11:8 and Judg 6:19, because he was more familiar with this word, or because it was in his *Vorlage*. He tends to prefer λέβης for סיר (Amos 4:2; Mic 3:3; Zech 14:20, 21) and he uses χύτρα for קלחת (Mic 3:3). The difference between the two types of pots may be ascertained from Sir 13:2, where it appears that χύτρα was made out of clay and λέβης from metal: βάρος ὑπὲρ σὲ μὴ ἄρῃς καὶ ἰσχυροτέρῳ σου καὶ πλουσιωτέρῳ μὴ κοινώνει τί κοινωνήσει χύτρα (פרור)[198] πρὸς λέβητα αὕτη προσκρούσει καὶ αὕτη συντριβήσεται.

The translator of the TP read פארור as פרור, and, since פרור is rare, we cannot discount the possibility that other passages where the word occurs may have informed his rendering (see Num 11:8; Judg 6:19; [χύθρα] 1 Kgdms 2:14). However, if he was ignorant of the meaning of פרור and needed to consult other texts, he could have derived the meaning of פרור from the *Hebrew* context in the above references, without requiring the knowledge of how earlier translators had rendered it.

---

194.   Dirk Büchner, "The Thysia Soteriou of the Septuagint and the Greek Cult: Representation and Accommodation," in Ausloos, Lemmelijn, and Vervenne, eds., *Florilegium Lovaniense*, 99.

195.   LEH 670; *Muraoka 2009*, 738.

196.   *DCH* 6:647.

197.   *DCH* 6:759.

198.   HR Appendix 2, 196.

Quotations and Allusions

In Tov's section entitled "Quotations and Allusions" only one example is cited for the TP.[199] This involves Hos 12:4–5 and requires a much broader analysis than the words treated above, so it will be dealt with separately in another chapter (see Chapter 4).

Conclusion

The aim of this portion of our study was to examine the set of Greek–Hebrew identifications proposed by Tov as evidence for the lexical influence of LXX Pentateuch on other LXX books and to test whether this is the only way to explain the presence of these identifications in the TP. The words fall into four categories: neologisms, Greek words with a "forced meaning," renderings resulting from etymologizing, and Greek equivalents readily available in the Hellenistic context. This last category is by far the largest. The present analysis shows that the vast majority of the words proposed by Tov are likely to have been known and accessible to the Greek translator of the TP, who would then naturally use them in translating specific Hebrew words independently of the LXX Pentateuch. This comes very close to the conclusions of Lee in his study on the Greek of the LXX Pentateuch, who found that the bulk of the vocabulary chosen by the translators of the Pentateuch reflected the Greek of the period.[200]

In the case of neologisms one could argue that, while Tov's thesis is not disproved, no indisputable proof could be found that the words were coined by the LXX translators of the Pentateuch. For the Greek words adopted but used with a "forced" meaning it was concluded that they were quite conceivably peculiar to the Jewish community prior to the writing down of the LXX Pentateuch. Finally, in the case of words which arose through "etymologizing," the translator seems to have worked independently of any obvious influence from LXX Pentateuch.

Tov's argument may be seen to hold, however, for a few words such as θυσιαστήριον and γλυπτόν. Here the treatment of the Greek words is different in the LXX Pentateuch from that in most of the other books. This difference may be an indicator of the existence of the LXX Pentateuch in written form before the use of particular words was standardized. Moreover, *indirect* influence (i.e. knowledge of oral Greek tradition of the Pentateuch) may be argued for words such as ἀνεμοφθορία

199. Tov, "The Impact of the LXX," 589.
200. Lee, *A Lexical Study*, 145.

(Deut 28:22), μακρόθυμος and πολυέλεος (Exod 34:6; Num 14:18), and ἀνάθεμα (Lev 27:28–29), owing to their associations with well-known texts. However, these identifications were probably not adopted from written translations but from oral tradition.

This study does not claim to have exhausted the investigation on this issue. Further work needs to take other considerations into account, such as possible affinities between the Three and the vocabulary of the LXX Pentateuch, arising from the incorporation of later readings via Origen into our LXX text. It would also be important to examine whether revision in the *Naḥal Ḥever* scroll of the TP displays a preference for Greek Pentateuchal terms. Finally, the same question could be investigated for pre-hexaplaric manuscripts such as the Washington Codex.

Chapter 3

STANDARD TRANSLATIONS

One type of intertextuality observed in the LXX TP is that of "standard translations." By "standard translations" I mean pre-existing, familiar, formulaic expressions which have become part of the religious jargon of the Greek translator and have their origin in a text other than the one being translated.

In each case presented in this section, the Greek translator of the TP deviates from his Hebrew *Vorlage* and translates by using a Greek expression known from other biblical passages. This expression is usually found in three or more places, all of them possible candidates for the source text from which the Greek translator of the TP may have borrowed the expression. At the same time, when more than two passages share the same expression it is very difficult to determine the direction of borrowing. Since "quotation" implies that the original source is well known and/or explicitly attributed, "standard translation," and not "quotation," is a more appropriate label for these expressions. In a "standard translation," even if one is able to identify the original source of the expression, there is no certainty that our Greek translator had "quoted" this expression directly from its original location; he may have quoted instead from a secondary source or from common oral usage. Use of a common expression does not presuppose knowledge of the source from which it originated, as is often the case with English clichés.

Translators may also use Greek variations of a given expression. The reason for this may be that they work from their memory and therefore do not reproduce an expression in an identical manner, or it may be that an expression exists in various Greek forms. A particular variation may be more aesthetically fitting for a specific context. For example, in the case of LXX Hos 4:13, ὑποκάτω δένδρου συσκιάζοντος, ὑποκάτω δένδρου συσκίου and ὑποκάτω δένδρου δασέος are used as three versions of the same Hebrew expression: תחת אלון ואלה כי טוב רענן (note that כל is ignored in all variations). The familiarity of the Greek translator with this Deuter-onomistic phrase used for idolatrous worship under shady trees (e.g. Deut 12:2), a recurring theme in biblical literature, is behind the creative rendering δένδρου συσκιάζοντος for אלה in LXX Hos 4:13.

Knowledge of Deuteronomistic expressions is also obvious in the case of LXX Hos 5:11. Here the Greek translator understood the pejorative sense of צו to be a reference to idols, and instead of rendering the word "literally" he preferred to use μάταια, a standard term used to describe idols. The expression ὀπίσω τῶν ματαίων ("after the vain things") appears in various places in the LXX, among which are 4 Kgdms 17:15 and Jer 2:5, where the fuller expression "they walked after the vain things," in both the Hebrew and Greek, is found. The stock phrase introduced by the LXX translator in Hos 5:11 elucidates what is implicit in the Hebrew: what Hos 5:11 refers to is idolatry, in line with the familiar Deuteronomistic motif known to the translator from various biblical texts.

The intentionality behind the introduction of such standard translations into the text varies from case to case. For example, there is a conscious effort to adopt a standard translation in LXX Mic 1:6 and 3:12. The term introduced in these texts is ὀπωροφυλάκιον, for עי and עיין respectively. The term ὀπωροφυλάκιον had probably originated in the Greek translation of Isaiah where its proper Hebrew counterpart מלונה is found. LXX Isaiah's expression, ὀπωροφυλάκιον, has become standard since various LXX texts show familiarity with it. ὀπωροφυλάκιον seems to have functioned as a euphemistic standard translation rendering the more negative עי wherever it occurred in the biblical texts.

This type of intertextuality adds significantly to our understanding of the translator's reading process. The use of standard translations shows that the translator presupposes similar themes behind corresponding texts. For the translator, Deuteronomistic themes are present in Hosea, and Isaiah's message concerning the fate of Zion is also found on the lips of Micah in relation to Samaria (1:6) as well as Zion (3:12).

The freedom displayed by the translator in incorporating stock expressions into the text, instead of giving a literal rendering of the Hebrew, suggests that he does not regard these expressions as "foreign" elements which could interfere with the message of the text. Rather, his freedom reveals his understanding of a thematic unity between different texts, which permits the use of parallel language.

Hosea 4:13

Hosea 4:13

MT	LXX
עַל־רָאשֵׁי הֶהָרִים יְזַבֵּחוּ	ἐπὶ τὰς κορυφὰς τῶν ὀρέων ἐθυσίαζον
וְעַל־הַגְּבָעוֹת יְקַטֵּרוּ תַּחַת אַלּוֹן	καὶ ἐπὶ τοὺς βουνοὺς ἔθυον ὑποκάτω δρυὸς
וְלִבְנֶה וְאֵלָה	καὶ λεύκης καὶ δένδρου συσκιάζοντος
כִּי טוֹב צִלָּהּ עַל־כֵּן עַל־כֵּן תִּזְנֶינָה	ὅτι καλὸν σκέπη διὰ τοῦτο ἐκπορνεύσουσιν

בְּנוֹתֵיכֶם וְכַלּוֹתֵיכֶם
תְּנָאַפְנָה
They sacrifice on the tops of the mountains, and make offerings upon the hills, under oak, poplar, and terebinth, because their shade is good. Therefore your daughters play the whore, and your daughters-in-law commit adultery. [NRSV]

αἱ θυγατέρες ὑμῶν καὶ αἱ νύμφαι ὑμῶν μοιχεύσουσι
They were offering sacrifice on the tops of the mountains and were sacrificing upon the hills, under an oak and a white poplar and a thickly shading tree, because shelter is a good thing. Therefore your daughters will play the whore, and your daughters-in-law will commit adultery. [NETS]

Ezekiel 6:13

MT

וִידַעְתֶּם כִּי־אֲנִי יְהוָה
בִּהְיוֹת חַלְלֵיהֶם בְּתוֹךְ
גִּלּוּלֵיהֶם סְבִיבוֹת מִזְבְּחוֹתֵיהֶם
אֶל כָּל־גִּבְעָה רָמָה
בְּכֹל רָאשֵׁי הֶהָרִים
וְתַחַת כָּל־עֵץ רַעֲנָן
וְתַחַת כָּל־אֵלָה עֲבֻתָּה מְקוֹם
אֲשֶׁר נָתְנוּ־שָׁם רֵיחַ נִיחֹחַ
לְכֹל גִּלּוּלֵיהֶם

And you shall know that I am the LORD, when their slain lie among their idols around their altars, on every high hill, on all the mountain tops, under every green tree, and under every leafy oak, wherever they offered pleasing odor to all their idols. [NRSV]

LXX

καὶ γνώσεσθε διότι ἐγὼ κύριος ἐν τῷ εἶναι τοὺς τραυματίας ὑμῶν ἐν μέσῳ τῶν εἰδώλων ὑμῶν κύκλῳ τῶν θυσιαστηρίων ὑμῶν ἐπὶ πάντα βουνὸν ὑψηλὸν καὶ ὑποκάτω δένδρου συσκίου (καὶ ὑποκάτω δένδρου συσκίου) οὗ ἔδωκαν ἐκεῖ ὀσμὴν εὐωδίας πᾶσι τοῖς εἰδώλοις αὐτῶν

And you shall know that I am the Lord, when your wounded are in the midst of your idols around your altars, on every lofty hill and under a shady tree, where they gave an odour of fragrance to all their idols. [NETS]

Deuteronomy 12:2

MT

אַבֵּד תְּאַבְּדוּן אֶת־כָּל־הַמְּקֹמוֹת
אֲשֶׁר עָבְדוּ־שָׁם הַגּוֹיִם אֲשֶׁר
אַתֶּם יֹרְשִׁים אֹתָם אֶת־אֱלֹהֵיהֶם
עַל־הֶהָרִים הָרָמִים
וְעַל־הַגְּבָעוֹת
וְתַחַת כָּל־עֵץ רַעֲנָן

You must demolish completely all the places where the nations whom you are about to dispossess served their gods, on the mountain heights, on the hills, and under every leafy tree. [NRSV]

LXX

ἀπωλείᾳ ἀπολεῖτε πάντας τοὺς τόπους ἐν οἷς ἐλάτρευσαν ἐκεῖ τὰ ἔθνη τοῖς θεοῖς αὐτῶν οὓς ὑμεῖς κληρονομεῖτε αὐτούς ἐπὶ τῶν ὀρέων τῶν ὑψηλῶν καὶ ἐπὶ τῶν θινῶν καὶ ὑποκάτω δένδρου δασέος

You shall with destruction destroy all the places, there where the nations whom you are about to dispossess serve their gods on the high mountains and on the dunes and beneath every leafy tree. [NETS]

The first striking thing in the Greek translation of Hos 4:13 is the rendering of אלה by δένδρου συσκιάζοντος. The editors of La Bible d'Alexandrie argue that the only way to explain this rendering is in connection with LXX Ezek 6:13.[1] This view has been suggested by Muraoka and is predominantly based on the ground that a single translator was involved in the translation of both the TP and Ezekiel α (chs. 1–27): "...parallel or related passages may affect the rendering of a particular passage. The probability of such influence must be fairly high when the passages concerned are believed, on other grounds, to be ascribable to a single translator."[2]

The Relationship of the Greek TP, Jeremiah and Ezekiel
Thackeray was the first to argue for an affinity between the Greek translation of the TP, Jeremiah α (1–28) and Ezekiel α (chs. 1–27).[3] Thackeray's position of different translators for Jeremiah was questioned in 1976 by Emanuel Tov, who holds that the differences between Jeremiah α and β (chs. 29–51) arise because Jeremiah β is a revised text. According to Tov, one translator was responsible for the entire book of Jeremiah, and this Old Greek version is now only obvious in Jeremiah α. He disapproves of assumptions of multiple authorship of LXX books, and instead moves towards "translator-reviser" theories.[4] He acknowledges how influential Thackeray, "the 'father' of theories of multiple authorship for the individual books of the LXX," has been on the work of other scholars.[5] However, he agrees with Ziegler that similarities between two parts of a book considerably weaken Thackeray's thesis. For Tov, it is "very questionable methodology to assign important agreements between two sections of one and the same book to a secondary factor."[6] Instead, Tov sees the similarities as pointing to an underlying unity, and explains the differences as coming from a redactor's hand. Despite the disagreements between Thackeray's approach and Tov's, they both agree on the relatedness of the Greek translations of Jeremiah α, Ezekiel α and the TP:

> Important similarities between Jer a', Ez and the MP regarding renditions and rare words suggest that the three are closely related. Jer b' is excluded from this group because it normally presents other translation equivalents... It should be added, however, that if we are correct in assuming that

---

1. *BA* 23.1:91.
2. Takamitsu Muraoka, "Literary Device in the Septuagint," *Textus* 8 (1973): 21.
3. Thackeray, "The Greek Translators of Jeremiah," 245–66, and "The Greek Translators of Ezekiel," 398–411.
4. Tov, *The Septuagint Translation of Jeremiah and Baruch*, 1–14.
5. Ibid., 3.
6. Ibid., 4–5.

Jer a', the MP and Ez a' were produced by one person, it is unlikely that this translator embarked upon the translation of one complete book (the MP), one half book (Jer), and either another half book (Ez a') or another whole book (Ez). Rather, it stands to reason that this translator embarked on the translation of the *whole* of these three books.[7]

Tov is aware of the "tentative character" of his conclusions, and further work is needed to determine the nature of these books and their relationships.[8] At the same time, the question that arises is whether one should favour a reading from an allegedly "related" book (e.g. Ez a'), because it has exercised influence on the Greek TP, over similar readings from other allegedly "unrelated" books. It will become obvious that expressions similar to the one used in LXX Hos 4:13 can be found in various biblical and extra-biblical books. In other words, we are not forced to say that a translator is exclusively influenced by an expression he has already used elsewhere when that expression appears to be already part of his wider literary context. In studying the various possibilities which might have given rise to the reading δένδρου συσκιάζοντος in Hos 4:13 we shall evaluate all factors equally and allow the data to suggest what the reasons behind this rendering might be. No extra weight will be given to books which allegedly come from the same hand.

LXX Hosea 4:13
The verse begins with the standard Greek phrase (ἐπὶ τὰς κορυφὰς τῶν ὀρέων), which follows its Hebrew equivalent perfectly (cf. Mic 4:1; Joel 5). The two verbs are understood as active imperfects and the parallelism is preserved with a faithful representation of the Hebrew.

The first tree in the list is אלון, which the Greek translator renders as δρῦς. δρῦς in the LXX usually represents both אלון (eleven times) and אלה (ten times).[9] Elsewhere in the LXX אלון has been rendered as βάλανος (Gen 35:8; Judg 9:6; Isa 2:13; 6:13) and ἐλάτινος (Ezek 27:5), but the Greek translator of the TP is consistent in identifying אלון with δρῦς (Amos 2:9; Zech 11:2). δρῦς is the reading of the Three as well.

The second tree in the list is לבנה and is rendered by λεύκη. Ziegler thinks that the LXX has derived this rendering through "etymologizing."[10] λεύκη is the white poplar commonly used for chaplets (Eupolis,

---

7. Ibid., 135.
8. Ibid., 150.
9. HR 349–50.
10. J. Ziegler, *Beiträge zum griechischen Dodekapropheton* (Nachrichten von der Akademie der Wissenschaften; Göttingen: Vandenhoeck & Ruprecht, 1943), 354.

Fragmenta 14.4; Aristophanes, *Nubes* 1007; Demosthenes, *De corona* 18.260) and often mentioned in Theophrastus' botanical works: ὥσπερ καὶ νῦν τὰ ἀλσώδη καὶ φίλυδρα, λέγω δ' οἷον πλάτανον ἰτέαν λεύκην αἴγειρον πτελέαν (Theophrastus, *Historia plantarum* 3.1.10–12). Symmachus and Theodotion have πεύκη ("pine") instead of λεύκη, a tree which is just as common throughout ancient Greek literature. Ziegler points us to Isa 41:19 and 60:13, where λεύκη and πεύκη are interchanged in representing תדהר.[11] The formal and phonic similarity of the two Greek tree names may have been a cause of confusion.

The third tree, אלה, is usually rendered by either τερέμινθος (Josh 24:26; Judg 6:11, 19 [ms. B]), τερέβινθος (Isa 1:30; 6:13) or δρῦς (Judg 6:11, 19 [ms. A]; 2 Kgdms 18:9, 10, 14; 3 Kgdms 13:14; 1 Chr 10:12). As already mentioned, δρῦς is used in the LXX for both אלה and אלון, an indication that perhaps these words were treated as by-forms. The Greek translator of the TP consistently identifies אלון with δρῦς (Amos 2:9; Zech 11:2), and it is possible that for him אלון and אלה are related terms. Faced with this "repetition" in Hos 4:13, the translator would not want to repeat δρῦς, so he strives to complete the tree list with something else. Since אלה does not occur anywhere else in the TP, there is no way for us to know whether he had a meaning for this word in mind. However, seeing that אלה is treated somewhat synonymously with אלון elsewhere in the LXX, we may assume that the same could have been true for the Greek translator of the TP.

Instead of repeating δρῦς, the Greek translator generalizes by his free rendering of δένδρου συσκιάζοντος.

δένδρου συσκιάζοντος

Various suggestions as to how this rendering came about have been made by different scholars.

Ziegler's Explanation. Ziegler looks at the Greek versions and attempts to derive an explanation which accounts for the renderings of each of the dendrological terms in the verse. The following are the principal Greek versions on Hos 4:13:

Trees (MT)	LXX	A	Σ	Θ
אלון	δρυὸς	δρυὸς	δρῦν	δρυὸς
לבנה	λεύκης	λεύκης	πεύκην	πεύκης
אלה	δένδρου συσκιάζοντος	τερεβίνθου	πλάτανον ἐπισκιάζουσαν	τερεβίνθου (Syh) δένδρου συσκιάζοντος (86)

11. Ibid.

Ziegler thinks that the original LXX reading was εὐσκιάζοντος rather than
συσκιάζοντος, and was the translation of כי טוב צלה.[12] Ziegler mentions
that Bahrdt (*Schleusner*, I:875) had already suggested this idea; however,
Bahrdt's suggestion was intended to explain the reading ἐπισκιάζουσαν
of Symmachus. He thought that εὐσκιάζουσαν was what Symmachus
had originally written—a conjecture with which Schleusner agrees.[13]
Apparently, Ziegler has adopted this explanation for the LXX as well,
and he has added the suggestion that ὅτι καλὸν σκέπη was a secondary
duplicate translation of the same Hebrew phrase.[14] This would also
explain Symmachus' πλατανον επισκιαζουσαν, translating the entire ואלה
כי טוב צלה. For Ziegler it is hard to explain why Symmachus would
insert επισκιαζουσαν since πλάτανος is already a "shady" tree.

Ziegler also offers the alternative explanation that the LXX adopted
συσκιάζοντος because δένδρον on its own would be too plain. He mentions
Isa 2:13 as a parallel where δένδρον is not let stand on its own: καὶ ἐπὶ
πᾶν δένδρον βαλάνου Βασαν (ועל כל-אלוני הבשן).[15]

Muraoka disagrees with Ziegler's conjecturing of ευσκιαζοντος and
the "double rendering" theory.[16] Moreover, in Isa 2:13, it is obvious that
δένδρον is a plus and adds nothing to the sense of the verse. The reason
for its insertion is probably stylistic, in order to create rhyme with the
parallel κέδρον:

> καὶ ἐπὶ πᾶσαν κέδρον...
> καὶ ἐπὶ πᾶν δένδρον...

It is indeed hard to know whether Theodotion had any influence on the
LXX reading, especially since the sources conflict on what Theodotion
actually read (τερεβίνθου [Syh], δένδρου συσκιάζοντος [86]).[17]

If δένδρου συσκιάζοντος is the Old Greek, Symmachus possibly
replaced δένδρον with πλάτανος because the context consists of a list
of trees, and δένδρον, being a generic term and not a type of tree, was
simply not fitting. In this case, Symmachus was probably "tidying up"
the Greek without slavishly following the Hebrew; otherwise he would

12. Ibid.
13. From Schleusner's reference to Bahrdt's work (C. F. Friederico Bahrdt,
Apparatus Criticus ad Formandum Interpretem Veteris Testamenti, vol. 1 [Leipzig:
Schwickerti, 1775]) in I:875.
14. Ziegler, *Beiträge*, 354.
15. Ibid.
16. Muraoka, "Literary Device," 23–24.
17. Peter Gentry points to various examples where the work of the Three has
influenced the transmission of the OG and alerts us to the fact that it is not always
clear where the dividing line is between OG and the work of the Three; Gentry,
"Old Greek and Later Revisors," 301–27.

not have ἐπισκιαζουσαν and would have chosen a better Greek equivalent for אלה.[18] πλάτανος (564 times)[19] and δρῦς (621 times) are much more common in Greek literature than τερέβινθος (158 times) or τερέμινθος (nine times), and since δρῦς is already included as the first tree in the verse, πλάτανος would be the next likely candidate to have entered Symmachus' mind when completing this tree list.[20]

Muraoka's Explanation. Muraoka does not discuss the other Greek versions, but focuses on the LXX reading and its variants. His goal is to understand how Ezekiel's translator functioned in 6:13, as that would by implication shed light on how this same translator, assuming it is the same one for both the Twelve and Ezekiel α, handled Hos 4:13.

On the basis of the rendering of עבת by κατάσκιον in Ezek 20:28, Muraoka assumes that עבתה lies behind συσκίου in 6:13.[21] However, we do not know how רענן is understood by the translator, since it does not occur elsewhere in Ezekiel. רענן has an equal probability with עבתה of standing behind συσκίου, especially since it is rendered in a similar manner by other LXX books (συσκίου—3 Kgdms 14:23; σύσκιος—Song 1:16; κατασκίου—Jer 2:20; εὔσκιος—Jer 11:16). Moreover, we know that עץ is probably behind δένδρον in Ezek 47:7, so it would make more sense to have the following correspondence in Ezek 6:13:

ותחת כל־עץ רענן   καὶ ὑποκάτω δένδρου συσκίου

Muraoka, however, holds a different view. He sets out the readings of Vaticanus and Alexandrinus in comparison to the Hebrew text of Ezek 6:13 as follows:

1	אל כל־גבעה רמה	B₁ ἐπὶ πάντα βουνὸν ὑψηλὸν
2	בכל ראשי ההרים	A₁ + καὶ ἐν πάσαις κορυφαῖς τῶν ὀρέων
3	ותחת כל־עץ רענן	B₂ καὶ ὑποκάτω δένδρου συσκίου
4	ותחת כל־אלה עבתה	A₂ + καὶ ὑποκάτω πάσης δρυὸς δασείας

After identifying συσκίου with עבתה, Muraoka concludes that both B₂ and A₂ are translations of ותחת כל־אלה עבתה and that ותחת כל־עץ רענן was lacking in the translator's *Vorlage*. The latter Hebrew phrase "may

---

18. Indications of similar readings by Symmachus are found in Exod 39:20[MT34] (συσκιάζον for מסך), Ezek 28:16 (συσκιάζον for סכך) and Ezek 6:13 (σύσκιον for רענן). His usual rendering for אלה is δρῦς (*HR* 349–50), never τερέβινθος/τερέμινθος.

19. Word counts by TLG (*Thesaurus Lingua Graeca*) database.

20. Symmachus is known for his high concern for Greek style, smoothing out lexical inconsistencies and preserving clear diction through sober exegetical expansions. See Karen H. Jobes and Moisés Silva, *Invitation to the Septuagint* (Grand Rapids: Baker, 2000), 40–41.

21. Muraoka, "Literary Device," 23.

easily have been added to the Heb. text by a later hand on the basis of a number of parallel passages such as Dt. 12:2, III Kg. 14:23."[22]

Under a Leafy Tree

Instead of adopting Muraoka's contrived interpretation of the data, it is easier to keep the Hebrew text as it is and attempt to explain the Greek text on other grounds. The phrase תחת כל־עץ רענן is very common in the Hebrew Bible (Deut 12:2; 1 Kgs 14:23; 2 Kgs 16:4; 17:10; 2 Chr 28:4; Isa 57:5; Jer 2:20; 3:6, 13). Except for Isa 57:5 (ὑπὸ δένδρα δασέα), all these LXX books faithfully translate this common phrase by καὶ ὑποκάτω παντὸς ξύλου (renderings for רענן vary). Only Deut 12:2 is translated by ὑποκάτω δένδρου (δασέος), ignoring כל yet still maintaining the generic function of the indefinite δένδρον. LXX Isaiah 57:5 could be aware of LXX Deuteronomy's Greek rendering, and perhaps Ezekiel's Greek translator, knowing the Greek Pentateuch, might have adopted ὑποκάτω δένδρου, by ignoring כל and using the rarer δένδρον instead of the common ξύλον. Moreover, since the Greek translator of Ezekiel seems to have abbreviated lines 1 and 2 of the Hebrew into ἐπὶ πάντα βουνὸν ὑψηλὸν, it is probable that he has done the same with lines 3 and 4 into καὶ ὑποκάτω δένδρου συσκίου.[23]

Hosea's Greek translator seems to display the same affinity with LXX Deut 12:2 by the use of ὑποκάτω and δένδρου, of which the latter is a unique occurrence in the whole of the Greek TP. It is very likely that the Greek translator of Hosea was reminded of Deut 12:2 because of the parallel content:

Deut 12:2	Hos 4:13
אַבֵּד תְּאַבְּדוּן אֶת־כָּל־הַמְּקֹמוֹת אֲשֶׁר	
עָבְדוּ־שָׁם הַגּוֹיִם אֲשֶׁר אַתֶּם יֹרְשִׁים	
אֹתָם אֶת־אֱלֹהֵיהֶם	
[עַל־הֶהָרִים] הָרָמִים [וְעַל־הַגְּבָעוֹת]	[עַל]־[רָאשֵׁי] הֶהָרִים [וְעַל־הַגְּבָעוֹת] יְזַבֵּחוּ
[וְתַחַת] כָּל־(עֵץ רַעֲנָן)	יְקַטֵּרוּ [תַחַת] אַלּוֹן וְלִבְנֶה וְאֵלָה כִּי טוֹב צִלָּהּ
	עַל־כֵּן תִּזְנֶינָה בְּנוֹתֵיכֶם וְכַלּוֹתֵיכֶם תְּנָאַפְנָה

22. Ibid.

23. Lust criticizes a system which has arbitrary rules for *pluses* and *minuses* in ascertaining the correct Hebrew text. "The system is such that the shorter text, most often represented by the Septuagint, is almost automatically accepted as the authentic one. The possibility of parablepsis or intentional shortening is hardly considered"; J. Lust, "The Use of Textual Witnesses for the Establishment of the Text," in *Ezekiel and His Book: Textual and Literary Criticism and Their Interrelation* (BETL 74; Leuven: Leuven University Press, 1986), 9.

The two texts have obvious lexical parallels (indicated above by being enclosed in square brackets). Moreover, there are additional conceptual parallels: the use of עבד in Deut 12:2, which is represented by the sacrifices (זבח) and "smoke/incense" offerings (קטר) in Hos 4:13. The worship of other gods (אלהים) in Deut 12:2 is also present (or implied) in the preceding verse (Hos 4:12) through the use of מתחת אלהיהם. The words within the round brackets in Deut 12:2 would be the phrase "adopted" by the LXX translator of Hos 4:13. It is very likely, as already mentioned, that the combination of ὑποκάτω and δένδρου was known from the Greek version of Deuteronomy, while רענן is rendered by Hosea's Greek translator by συσκιάζοντος instead of δασέος (LXX Deut 12:2). Variations on רענן are observed even with texts containing the entire phrase תחת כל־עץ רענן, therefore some freedom to paraphrase this well known phrase must have been permissible.[24]

On the other hand, δένδρον may have been chosen for another reason. If the Greek translator of Hosea wanted to mention the Deuteronomic "leafy tree" (עץ רענן) in the common Greek style, it would be more natural for him to choose δένδρον instead of ξύλον. A survey of Greek literature shows that ξύλον never occurs with a σκιά-root adjective, but δένδρον does very often (examples are quoted later). ξύλον συσκιάζον may have been an awkward pair but δένδρον συσκιάζον would have been a familiar one.

Wolff highlights the connection between Hos 4:13 and Deut 12:2: "For the first time there is a description of the cultic places, especially the high sanctuaries, which is basically identical with their description in Dtn 12:2… Hosea names the most important kinds of trees, instead of using the general expression 'under every green tree'."[25]

For Wolff, the expected expression "under every green tree," appropriate to the context, does not get mentioned. Instead, certain trees are enumerated. This same expectation of the Deuteronomic expression was probably there in the Greek translator's mind as well. Since אלה was most likely understood as δρῦς by the translator of the Greek TP, a repetition would not be aesthetically agreeable.[26] By moving into the generalization of "a leafy tree," the translator brings out the sense of

---

24. That the Greek translator of Hosea understands רענן as being related to "overshadowing" or "protection" is indicated by his use of πυκάζουσα in Hos 14:9; see LEH 536.

25. Hans Walter Wolff, *Hosea* (Hermeneia; Philadelphia: Fortress, 1974), 85–86.

26. It could be argued that his choice of "tree" for אלה was due to the Aramaic influence of אילן, which means "tree" (*Jastrow*, 49). Even if that had been the case, the translator would naturally have preferred his usual ξύλον to δένδρον.

Hos 4:13 as he understood it in the light of the sanctuary laws of Deuteronomy. Nevertheless, one could argue that his choice of συσκιάζοντος was influenced by συσκίου in LXX Ezek 6:13.

σκιά-root Adjectives

There are many σκιά-root adjectives in the LXX. As a substantive, συσκιάζον is found in LXX Exod 25:20, together with σκιάζον in 38:8 and the verb ἐπισκιάζω in 40:35. συσκιάζον is used as an adjective for the covering of the ark of the covenant in LXX Num 4:5. It is obvious that translators of LXX books are not bound by consistency in their use of σκιά-root words, and one should not expect such mechanical translation practice (e.g. Jer 2:20 [κατασκίου]—Jer 11:16 [εὔσκιον]).

Outside the LXX, σκιά-root adjectives are numerous. The verb form συσκιάζω first shows up in Hesiod (Hesiod, *Opera et dies* 613) followed by Aeschylus' adjective form σύσκιος (τοὺς ἀλσώδεις καὶ συσκίους τόπους τοὺς τοῖς θεοῖς ἀνειμένους [Aeschylus, *Fragmenta Tetralogy* 10C.92.2]), and Euripides' preferred form of συσκιάζον (ἦν δ᾽ ἄγκος ἀμφίκρημνον, ὕδασι διάβροχον, πεύκαισι συσκιάζον [Euripides, *Bacchae* 1052]). σύσκιον in relation to δένδρον is common as well:

> Οὗτός ἐστι σύσκιος δένδρεσιν ἐμπεπλεγμένοις ἐν ἀλλήλοις, ὡς ὅτι μάλιστα πυκνοτάτοις. (Scylax, *Periplus Scylacis* 108.34)

> καὶ περιὼν τὴν χώραν ὅπου κατίδοι τόπους δένδρεσι συσκίους καὶ καταρρύτους ὕδασι τούτους κατεσκεύασεν ἑστιατόρια. (Theopompus, *Fragmenta* 31.9)

> εἶναι δὲ τῆς νήσου τὴν μὲν πρώτην εἰσβολὴν αὐλωνοειδῆ, σύσκιον ὑψηλοῖς καὶ πυκνοῖς δένδρεσιν ὥστε τὸν ἥλιον μὴ παντάπασι διαλάμπειν διὰ τὴν συνάγκειαν. (Dionysius Scytobrachion, *Fragmenta* 8.69)

> ἕτερος ναὸς Ἄμμωνος πολλοῖς καὶ μεγάλοις δένδροις σύσκιος. (Diodorus Siculus, *Bibliotheca historica* 17.50.4.3)

> ἄλσει πυκνῶν καὶ συσκίων δένδρων περιεχόμενον. (Plutarch, *Aristides* 11.8.2)

Philo uses the verb συσκιάζω numerous times,[27] as well as the passive participle συσκιαζόμενος (*Plant.* 1.116; *Decal.* 1.125) and the active participle συσκιάζων (*Abr.* 1.174; *Decal.* 1.44; *Spec.* 4.183).

Conclusion

All the above examples show that variations of the σκιά-root were common, even within the same author, and that δένδρον instead of ξύλον was

---

27. *Leg.* 2.66; 3.27, 158; *Sacr.* 1.30; *Deus* 1.30; *Sobr.* 1.6; *Somn.* 1.83, 87, 104, 109; *Ios.* 1.166; *Mos.* 2.128; *Spec.* 2.75; *Aet.* 1.64; *Legat.* 1.105, 332.

the common "tree" word modified by these adjectives. Descriptions of "shady" or "leafy" trees are found throughout ancient Greek literature, and it would be difficult for one to argue for an exclusive borrowing from LXX Ezek 6:13 by the Greek translator of Hosea.

However, the Greek translator of Hosea introduces the generic "shady tree" in the context where it would be expected to occur. It is obvious that the translator recognizes the pattern of idolatrous worship under shady trees, such as is reflected in Deut 12:2—among other scriptural passages—behind what Hos 4:13 describes. δένδρου συσκιάζοντος and variations of this phrase seem to have been standard expressions familiar to the Greek translator of Hosea, and this is obvious in other LXX texts where כל is ignored in the Hebrew (Deut 12:2; Isa 57:5; Ezek 6:13).

Hosea 5:11

Hosea 5:11

MT	LXX
עָשׁוּק אֶפְרַיִם רְצוּץ מִשְׁפָּט כִּי הוֹאִיל הָלַךְ אַחֲרֵי־צָו	κατεδυνάστευσεν Εφραιμ τὸν ἀντίδικον αὐτοῦ κατεπάτησεν κρίμα ὅτι ἤρξατο πορεύεσθαι ὀπίσω τῶν ματαίων
Ephraim is oppressed, crushed in judgment, because he was determined to go after vanity. [NRSV]	Ephraim has overpowered his opponent; he has trampled judgment, because he began to go after the vain things. [NETS]

4 Kingdoms 17:15

MT	LXX
וַיִּמְאֲסוּ אֶת־חֻקָּיו וְאֶת־בְּרִיתוֹ אֲשֶׁר כָּרַת אֶת־אֲבוֹתָם וְאֵת עֵדְוֹתָיו אֲשֶׁר הֵעִיד בָּם וַיֵּלְכוּ אַחֲרֵי הַהֶבֶל וַיֶּהְבָּלוּ וְאַחֲרֵי הַגּוֹיִם אֲשֶׁר סְבִיבֹתָם אֲשֶׁר צִוָּה יְהוָה אֹתָם לְבִלְתִּי עֲשׂוֹת כָּהֶם	καὶ τὰ μαρτύρια αὐτοῦ ὅσα διεμαρτύρατο αὐτοῖς οὐκ ἐφύλαξαν καὶ ἐπορεύθησαν ὀπίσω τῶν ματαίων καὶ ἐματαιώθησαν καὶ ὀπίσω τῶν ἐθνῶν τῶν περικύκλῳ αὐτῶν ὧν ἐνετείλατο αὐτοῖς τοῦ μὴ ποιῆσαι κατὰ ταῦτα
They despised his statutes, and his covenant that he made with their ancestors, and the warnings that he gave them. They went after false idols and became false; they followed the nations that were around them, concerning whom the LORD had commanded them that they should not do as they did. [NRSV]	And his testimonies that he testified to them they did not keep but went after the worthless things and were rendered worthless and after the nations that were around them of whom he had commanded them not to do in accordance with these. [NETS]

One need only look at modern English translations to see the confusion generated by Hos 5:11:

KJV: Ephraim *is oppressed* and broken in judgment, because he willingly walked after the *commandment*.

RSV: Ephraim *is oppressed*, crushed in judgment, because he was determined to go after *vanity*.

NEB: Ephraim *is an oppressor* trampling on justice, doggedly pursuing what is *worthless*.

NIV: Ephraim *is oppressed*, trampled in judgment, intent on pursuing *idols*.

NAS: Ephraim *is oppressed*, crushed in judgment, because he was determined to follow *man's command*.

NLT: The people of Israel *will be crushed* and broken by my judgment because they are determined to worship *idols*.

עָשׁוּק *and* רְצוּץ

As with the divergences in the English translations, the first disagreement between the LXX and the MT lies in the renderings of עָשׁוּק and רְצוּץ. The MT has vocalized these as passive participles, whereas the LXX has translated these as aorist active verbs.

While the Greek translator of the TP often renders Hebrew passive participles with corresponding Greek ones (e.g. Obad 2; Hag 1:6; Mal 1:14), he does not always follow this practice, but sometimes shows flexibility (e.g. Jon 2:6; Hab 2:19; Mal 1:13). Brockington indicates that the vocalization רָצוֹץ and עָשׁוֹק was preferred by the translators of the NEB,[28] which may well be how the LXX translator also vocalized the text, ending up with active verbs. Muraoka supports the idea that the LXX translator read the words as infinitive absolutes, as in 4:2.[29] Other commentators, however, propose the readings עָשֵׁק and רֹצֵץ behind the LXX renderings.[30]

Additionally, the LXX has the plus, τὸν ἀντίδικον αὐτοῦ ("his adversary"). This may have arisen because the Greek renderings of עָשׁוּק and

28. L. H. Brockington, *The Hebrew Text of the Old Testament* (Cambridge: Cambridge University; Oxford: Oxford University Press, 1973), 246.

29. Takamitsu Muraoka, "Hosea V in the Septuagint Version," *Abr-Nahrain* 24 (1986): 131.

30. See D. Barthélemy, *Critique Textuelle de l'Ancien Testament*. Vol. 3, *Ézéchiel, Daniel et les 12 Prophètes* (OBO 50/3; Göttingen: Vandenhoeck & Ruprecht, 1992), 522. Harper adopts the LXX reading as original and reads the participles as active, "thus furnishing another charge in the indictment against Ephraim, for which punishment is coming"; William Rainey Harper, *A Critical and Exegetical Commentary on Amos and Hosea* (repr., ICC; Edinburgh: T. & T. Clark, 1936 [1905]), 276.

רצוץ lacked an object. Wolff thought that the accusative object τὸν ἀντίδιχον is added to the first verb in order to form a parallel with משפט (χρίμα).[31] ἀντίδιχος is a general term for opponent used in both legal settings (LXX Prov 18:17) and more widely for enemies (e.g. Est 8:11; Isa 41:11; Jer 27[MT50]:34). Muraoka thinks that the word was "added freely," and he translates it by "plaintiff," as in Lysias 7,13.[32] It appears that ἀντίδιχος in the New Testament is always related to a legal setting. It refers to the person who brings accusations against another or who takes one to court (Matt 5:25; Luke 12:58; 18:3; 1 Pet 5:8 [referring to the devil]). The addition of ἀντίδιχος in LXX Hos 5:11 gets rid of any ambiguity as to who the oppressor is, and intensifies the accusation against Ephraim.

In the Hebrew Bible, the word-pair עשוק and רצוץ is found in Deut 28:33 in the curses for disobedience. These passive participles refer to Israel, and the agent of their oppression is "a people they do not know." In 1 Kgdms 12:3–4, the word-pair is used to describe unjust social administration. Upon Israel's request for a king, Samuel asks whether he has "defrauded" or "oppressed" anyone (ואת־מי עשקתי את־מי רצותי) and the people assure him that he had not. In other words, Samuel was a just administrator.

In the TP this word-pair relates to contexts where justice is violated. In Amos 4:1 it refers to unjust social dealings, where the "cows of Bashan" are accused of "oppressing" (העשקות) and "crushing" (הרצצות) the poor. Here, the LXX translator uses Greek equivalents similar to the ones in LXX Hos 5:11: αἱ καταδυναστεύουσαι πτωχοὺς καὶ καταπατοῦσαι πένητας. The active feminine participles are preserved in the Greek and the context makes clear that the oppressors are the elite Israelites. It is possible that the Greek translator related Hos 5:11 to Amos 4:1, which helped steer the reading of the word-pair in Hos 5:11 in the same direction.

עשק on its own occurs in Hos 12:7[MT8] where Ephraim (the subject is unclear) is known for his "love of oppression" with unjust balances (ἐν χειρὶ αὐτοῦ ζυγὸς ἀδικίας καταδυναστεύειν ἠγάπησε). Once more, this verse implies that Ephraim is not the oppressed one. Instead, justice is distorted by Ephraim, an idea parallel to LXX Hos 5:11 where χρίμα (משפט) is the object of "crushed." Moreover, in the prophets in general, עשק is found in the context of oppression of orphans and widows (Mic 2:2; Zech 7:10; Mal 3:5; Jer 7:6; Ezek 22:7, 12, 29). Thus the idea of

---

31. Hans Walter Wolff, *Joel and Amos* (trans. Waldemar Janzen, S. Dean McBride, Jr., and Charles A. Muenchow; Hermeneia; Philadelphia: Fortress, 1977), 104 n. c.

32. Muraoka, "Hosea V," 132.

Ephraim as *oppressor* rather than *oppressed* seems to have been more common, and may have coloured the lens through which Hos 5:11 was read by the Greek translator.[33]

This view of Ephraim may be evident in LXX Hos 8:3 as well. In a similar manner, Ephraim (Israel) is turned into the victimizer rather than the victim in the LXX.

Whereas the MT presents Israel as the one pursued *by* the enemy, in the Greek Israel does the pursuing.

זָנַח יִשְׂרָאֵל טוֹב אוֹיֵב	ὅτι Ισραηλ ἀπεστρέψατο ἀγαθά, ἐχθρὸν
יִרְדְּפוֹ׃	κατεδίωξαν

צו

The second part of Hos 5:11 has been difficult for modern translators due to the presence of צו, a rare word in the Hebrew Bible. The LXX translator renders the phrase הואיל הלך אחרי־צו by ἤρξατο πορεύεσθαι ὀπίσω τῶν ματαίων, which could have been influenced by 4 Kgdms 17:15 or other texts where variations of this expression occur (4 Kgdms 16:2, 26; Jer 2:5; Amos 2:4). Before examining this possibility we should look into the meaning of צו and see what else might have caused this Greek rendering.

The only other place צו occurs is in Isa 28:10 and 13, where its meaning is also unclear:

Isaiah 28:10

כִּי צַו לָצָו צַו לָצָו קַו לָקָו קַו לָקָו	θλῖψιν ἐπὶ θλῖψιν προσδέχου ἐλπίδα ἐπ' ἐλπίδι
זְעֵיר שָׁם זְעֵיר שָׁם׃	ἔτι μικρὸν ἔτι μικρὸν

Isaiah 28:13

וְהָיָה לָהֶם דְּבַר־יְהוָה	καὶ ἔσται αὐτοῖς τὸ λόγιον κυρίου τοῦ θεοῦ
צַו לָצָו צַו לָצָו קַו לָקָו קַו לָקָו	θλῖψις ἐπὶ θλῖψιν ἐλπὶς ἐπ' ἐλπίδι
זְעֵיר שָׁם זְעֵיר שָׁם לְמַעַן יֵלְכוּ	ἔτι μικρὸν ἔτι μικρόν ἵνα πορευθῶσιν
וְכָשְׁלוּ אָחוֹר וְנִשְׁבָּרוּ	καὶ πέσωσιν εἰς τὰ ὀπίσω καὶ κινδυνεύσουσιν
וְנוֹקְשׁוּ וְנִלְכָּדוּ׃	καὶ συντριβήσονται καὶ ἁλώσονται

The modern translations of Isaiah have rendered צו by "precept," "mutter," "meaningless gibberish," "order," etc. The LXX translator of Isaiah, however, has related צו to one of the three words he usually renders by θλῖψις which are of similar appearance or sound (צר [26:16; 30:20; 63:9], צרה [8:22; 30:6; 33:2; 37:3; 65:16], שואה [10:3]).

צו in Hos 5:11 is understood by some commentators to mean "command" or "precept." Sweeney says that "it is intended here to refer to

---

33. רצץ is less common but it can also be used for the oppressed (Judg 10:8; 2 Chr 16:10; Job 20:19; Isa 58:6).

Israel's attempt to abide by its agreements with Judah in that it could refer to the stipulated border between the two countries."³⁴ Mays, following Duhm and Rudolph, agrees with the conjectural emendation of צו into צרו ("his enemy").³⁵ Barthélemy, however, argues that the meaning of the word צו here is "excrement," and that the vocalization is probably concealing a derogatory name for idols. He says that usually גלולים is used foe idols, the term being regarded as a more acceptable designation for "excrement." For a "polished" translation of Hos 5:11b, Barthélemy proposes: "because he liked to walk behind filth."³⁶

With no other occurrence of the word in the Hebrew Bible, outside Isaiah, to inform the Greek translator of the TP, it is possible that he resorted to a word similar in sound or appearance, as Isaiah's translator seems to have done. However, as we have already noted, this is not the only possible explanation for the rendering of צו in LXX Hos 5:11.

μάταια

The Hebrew words which the Greek translator of the TP usually renders by μάταια are: און (Hos 6:8); כזב (Hos 12:2; Amos 2:4; Mic 1:14; Zeph 3:13); הבל (Jon 2:9; Zech 10:2); שוא (Mal 3:14); אליל (Zech 11:17).

Kaminka, following a series of scholars, suggested that שָׁוְא was read by the LXX translator in the place of צו in Hos 5:11,³⁷ and this emendation has been proposed by the editors of *BHS*, citing the LXX, Peshiṭta and Targum:

34. Marvin A. Sweeney, *The Twelve Prophets*, vol. 1 (Berit Olam; Minnesota: Liturgical, 2000), 66. Also Duane A. Garrett, *Hosea, Joel* (NAC 19A; Nashville: Broadman & Holman, 1998), 152.

35. James Luther Mays, *Hosea: A Commentary* (OTL; London: SCM, 1969), 85 n. b.

36. Barthélemy, *Critique Textuelle*, 524. Similarly Andersen and Freedman: "The word *ṣ'h* means 'excrement,' and is derived from the root *ṣw'*, 'to stink.' In Hos 5:11 traditional renderings like 'he walked behind a commandment' are not suitable (contra Good...). The filth of drunkenness is meant. The complete idiom means to join a cult by following a detestable god, called 'Shit'"; *Hosea: A New Translation with Introduction and Commentary* (AB 24; New York: Doubleday, 1980), 410.

37. Examples of צ–שׁ confusion are Amos 8:1 and Mic 7:1; see Kaminka, *Studien*, 30. Initially, J. Wellhausen, *Die Kleinen Propheten: Übersetzt und Erklärt* (Berlin: de Gruyter, 1963), 112; originally published Georg Reimer, 1892; also W. Nowack, *Die kleinen Propheten* (HKAT 3/4; 2d ed.; Göttingen: Vandenhoeck & Ruprecht, 1903), 42; Karl Marti, *Das Dodekapropheton* (KHC; Tübingen: J. C. B. Mohr, 1904), 50; Ernst Sellin, *Das Zwölfprophetenbuch* (KAT 12; Leipzig: Deichert, 1922), 50; Harper, *A Critical and Exegetical Commentary on Amos and Hosea*, 276; Andersen and Freedman, *Hosea*, 410; *BA* 23.1:102.

Targum:
The people of the house of Ephraim are oppressed, crushed by their judgements, because their judges have turned to go astray after the money of falsehood.

Peshiṭta:
Ephraim is oppressed and broken in judgment, because he willingly went after vain things.

As far as the Peshiṭta translators are concerned, Gelston holds that they turned to the Septuagint for help in rendering צו, as they often do when uncertain,[38] and this would be a reasonable conclusion, given the rarity of צו. The Targumic reading, however, appears more complex.

Targum Hosea 5:11

Kaminka thought that the Targum agrees with the LXX.[39] However, the expression "mammon of deceit" (ממון דשקר), which stands in the place of צו in Hos 5:11, is very common in the Targums, usually rendering the Hebrew noun בצע ("gain made by violence, unjust gain, profit"),[40] but also appearing in places where שחד ("bribe") occurs (2 Sam 14:14; Isa 5:23).[41] The Targum of 2 Sam 14:14 reads as follows: "For *the death of one dying, behold it is* like waters that are poured out to the ground *that it is not possible for them that they be gathered up. Thus it is not possible for judges of the truth to receive the mammon of falsehood, and he devises* plans so as not to scatter from him an exile."[42]

This passage shows that ממון דשקר is related to unjust judges; a truthful judge would never receive ממון דשקר.[43] It is unjust judges that *Tg.* Hos 5:11 describes, and their mark is that they pursue the "mammon of falsehood." The sons of Samuel in *Tg.* 1 Sam 8:3 are described in a similar way to *Tg.* Hos 5:11: "And his sons did not walk in his ways, and

---

38. A. Gelston, *The Peshiṭta of the Twelve Prophets* (Oxford: Clarendon, 1987), 167.

39. Kaminka, *Studien*, 37.

40. BDB 130.

41. On Jesus' familiarity with this targumic expression, see Bruce Chilton, *A Galilean Rabbi and His Bible: Jesus' Own Interpretation of Isaiah* (London: SPCK, 1984), 116–23.

42. Daniel J. Harrington, S. J., and Anthony J. Saldarini, *Targum Jonathan of the Former Prophets* (ArBib 10; Edinburgh: T. & T. Clark, 1987).

43. The Targum explains the second utterance of the woman as a "(hidden) reference to the court, i.e. to David himself. Hebrew אלהים is equated with דינא, 'court'. Since David had a reliable court (cf. 2 Sam. 8:15), he was considered incorruptible"; Eveline van Staalduine-Sulman, *The Targum of Samuel* (SAIS 1; Leiden: Brill, 2002), 569.

they turned aside after *the mammon of falsehood* and took the bribe and perverted judgment."

A passage which has even more elements in common with *Tg.* Hos 5:11 is *Tg.* 1 Sam 12:3b: "Whose ox have I taken, and whose ass have I *confiscated*, and whom have I wronged, and whom have I oppressed, and from whose hand have I received *the mammon of falsehood, and from whom have I withheld my eye in judgment?*"

As noted earlier, 1 Sam 12:3 is the verse where the word-pair עשק and רצץ, also found in Hos 5:11, occurs with reference to Samuel's just administration. It is obvious that the Targumist has related Hos 5:11 to unjust judges who pursue ממון דשקר, an act which typically describes the unrighteous judge.[44] The expression ממון דשקר is used twice again in the *Tg.* TP, in Amos 5:12 and Hab 2:9, without the Hebrew שוא in the *Vorlage*. Moreover, the Targumic שקר ("lie, falsehood, vanity")[45] on its own may represent many different Hebrew words.[46] In the light of the above, we shall agree with Barthélemy's conclusions that *Tg.* Hos 5:11 reflects a large paraphrase, including this common stock phrase, and that there is no reason to assume that the Targumist had read anything other than צו.[47] Instructive are the comments of Cathcart and Gordon in their introduction to the Targum of the TP:

> many a non-Masoretic reading has been reconstructed in the modern period by scholars whose skill in retroversion has not been matched by awareness of the characteristics of *Tg.* which render such exercises generally inadvisable. Even where the Targumic reading seems clearly to differ from MT, moreover, there is always the possibility that *Tg.* is making a "silent" emendation which shows what the Targumist thought the reading should be, and not what was actually in his Hebrew text (*Vorlage*).[48]

צוא

The predominant view supported by Kaminka and others requires the alteration of the consonant צ to שׁ (i.e. שׁו/שׁוא was allegedly read by the Greek translator). However, assuming that צו was in the Greek translator's *Vorlage*,[49] we shall consider another explanation for the Greek

---

44. "The Sam and Hos references especially link the expression with bribery of judges"; Kevin J. Cathcart and Robert P. Gordon, *The Targum of the Minor Prophets* (ArBib 14; Edinburgh: T. & T. Clark, 1989), 40 n. 18.

45. *Jastrow*, 1626.

46. *BCTP* 20:251–255.

47. Barthélemy, *Critique Textuelle*, 524.

48. Cathcart and Gordon, *The Targum*, 11.

49. צו is attested in CD IV, 19–20 in what seems to be a quotation from Hos 5:11: ...אשר הלכו אחרי צו...

reading which does not require the emendation of the consonantal text. A similar-looking word which the translator could have considered when encountering צו in Hos 5:11 is the adjective צוֹאִי ("polluted"). This is found in Zech 3:3 and 4 with reference to Joshua's "filthy" garments, which are a symbol of iniquity.

צאה is present in Deut 23:14 with reference to human excrement (אֶת־צֵאָתְךָ) which the Israelites are instructed to cover up so that the Lord will not see anything indecent as he walks through their camp and so be caused to turn away from them. The word is also found in Ezek 4:12, where human excrement is used as fuel (בְּגֶלְלֵי צֵאַת הָאָדָם) for the baking of barley cake. In close proximity to the צו-passages of Isaiah (28:10, 13), צאה occurs (28:8) with reference to the filth on the tables of the drunk priests and prophets who have over-indulged. We shall examine the possibility that the Greek translator of Hosea recognizes צו as a word for "filth" or "dung" and understands it as a reference to idols. Instead of rendering the word literally, he chooses another Greek pejorative word commonly used for idols: μάταια.

Emerton on צו

Emerton has examined the meaning of the word צו in its Isaianic context, and his study will illuminate our investigation.[50] He looks at Isa 28:10 and 13 with the purpose of discussing the different interpretations of these difficult verses and proposing the most plausible one. He begins by examining the ancient versions, as well as some later Jewish interpreters, and then moves on to the evaluation of seven different types of interpretation of the verses, some of which exist in more than one form. Emerton concludes that,

> the fact that *ṣaw* and *qaw* begin with the same letters as *ṣōʾâ* and *qîʾ* only two verses before v. 10 leads us to suspect that there may be a relationship between Isaiah's words in v. 8 and what is probably the mocking imitation of them in v. 10... Isa. 28.10, 13 probably contains a mocking imitation of Isaiah's words condemning the filth or dung and vomit mentioned in v. 8; and v. 13 uses the same words to compare the devastation after the Assyrian invasion.[51]

This interpretation has its earliest support in the Greek versions and the Peshiṭta, a factor which has encouraged Emerton towards his view.

---

50. John A. Emerton, "Some Difficult Words in Isaiah 28.10 and 13," in *Biblical Hebrew, Biblical Texts: Essays in Memory of Michael P. Weitzman* (ed. Ada Rapoport-Albert and Gillian Greenberg; JSOTSup 333; HBV 2; Sheffield: Sheffield Academic, 2001), 39–56.

51. Ibid., 56.

While Symmachus understands צו in Isaiah as ἐντολή ("command") from צוה, Theodotion renders it by δεισαλία ("filth"), which is similar to his translation in v. 8 by ἐμετοῦ δεισαλίας ("of filth of vomit"). Similarly, Aquila's rendering in v. 8 is ἐμετοῦ ῥύπου ("of uncleanness of vomit").[52] 1QIsaᵃ has צי instead of צו in Isa 28:10 and 13,[53] which Kutscher compares to Theodotion's rendering.[54] Emerton also notes that the versions have read צא in Isa 30:22, which refers to idols, as "filth":

MT:

וְטִמֵּאתֶם אֶת־צִפּוּי פְּסִילֵי כַסְפֶּךָ וְאֶת־אֲפֻדַּת מַסֵּכַת זְהָבֶךָ תִּזְרֵם כְּמוֹ דָוָה צֵא תֹּאמַר לוֹ

LXX:

καὶ ἐξαρεῖς τὰ εἴδωλα τὰ περιηργυρωμένα καὶ τὰ περικεχρυσωμένα λεπτὰ ποιήσεις καὶ λικμήσεις ὡς ὕδωρ ἀποκαθημένης καὶ ὡς κόπρον ("as dung") ὥσεις αὐτά.[55]

Theodotion:

(ὡς) ὀδυνηρὰν δεισαλίας, "(as) painful filth."

Aquila:

ταλαιπώρου ῥύπου, "of filth of one in distress."

The Peshiṭta has also identified צו with filth in Isa 28:13: "the word of the Lord was for them dung upon dung...and vomit upon vomit..."[56] The Targum, however, appears to have connected צו with "command" in both vv. 10 and 13.[57]

In the case of לשמצה in Exod 32:25, which is treated in several versions as לשם plus צה or perhaps צו, Emerton demonstrates how "Aquila, Symmachus and the Vulgate, Peshiṭta and Targum in Exod. 32.25 attest knowledge of a noun צא, צה, or צו as a by-form of צאה meaning 'filth' or 'dung'."[58] To this he adds the rendering of the Vulgate in Hos 5:11

---

52. Ibid., 40.

53. Donald W. Parry and Elisha Qimron, *The Great Isaiah Scroll (1QIsaᵃ): A New Edition* (STDJ 32; Leiden: Brill, 1999), 45.

54. E. Y. Kutscher, *The Language and Linguistic Background of the Isaiah Scroll (1QIsaᵃ)* (Leiden: Brill, 1974; Hebrew ed. Jerusalem: Magnes, 1959), 278 (Hebrew 211), cited by Emerton, "Some Difficult Words," 40.

55. For the LXX reading Emerton suggests that "κόπρον 'dung' is either a translator's gloss or an example of a double rendering of ṣ', as a noun meaning 'dung' and as a form of the verb *yāṣāʾ*." Ibid., 41.

56. M. P. Weitzman, *The Syriac Version of the Old Testament: An Introduction* (University of Cambridge Oriental Publications 56; Cambridge: Cambridge University Press, 1999), 228.

57. Emerton, "Some Difficult Words," 42.

58. Ibid., 53–54.

(*sordem*) and arrives at his conclusion that "vv. 10 and 13 use צַו and קָו as synonyms, probably by-forms, of צָאָה and קִיא in v. 8."[59] If Emerton is correct, then it is possible that the Greek translator of Hos 5:11 was familiar with צַו as a by-form of צוֹא as well.

צַו *and the Rabbis*

In the Midrashic literature צַו is mostly read as a form of "command":

AND HE COMMANDED (WAYYEẒAW) alludes to idolatry, as you read: Because he willingly walked after ẓaw—i.e. idols (Hos. V, II). (*Gen. Rab.* XIV.6)

AND WHEN JACOB MADE AN END OF CHARGING HIS SONS; And his sons did unto him according as he commanded them. The first was an exhortation against idolatry, as in the verse, Because he willingly walked after zaw—idolatry (Hosea V, II). (*Gen. Rab.* C.2)

'Commanded' implies [an injunction against] idolatry, as it is written, Because he willingly walked after the commandment (Hos. V, 11). (*Song Rab.* I.2,5)

At the same time, צַו with reference to "filth" is also present: "'And [He] commanded': this indicates idolatry, as it is said, Because he willingly walked after filth (Hos. V, II)" (*Deut. Rab.* II.25). In this last case, Freedman and Simon see a play upon the words וַיְצַו ("commanded") and צַו ("filth"), and note that "filth" functions as a synonym for idolatry.[60] Is it possible that the connection of צַו to idolatry in Hos 5:11 found in the Midrashim goes back to the time of the LXX translator of Hosea?

ὀπίσω τῶν ματαίων

In the OT, one forms the impression that so many Hebrew words

had been waiting to pour their negative content into the Greek μάταιος... The distinctiveness of μάταιος in the LXX is—purely lexically—that it is constantly used for the other world. The gods of the ἔθνη are primarily μάταια, i.e., the very gods who in the Greek world are supposed in some way to be the guarantors of that which escapes the μάταιον.[61]

---

59. Ibid., 54.
60. H. Freedman and Simon Maurice, eds., *Midrash Rabbah* (10 vols.; London: Soncino, 1939), 7:54 n. 2. צַו in Hos 5:11 is connected to idolatry in the Talmud as well (*b. Sanh.* 56b).
61. O. Bauernfeind, "μάταιος," *TDNT* 4:521–22.

However, as Barr reminds us, μάταιος/ον does not carry the meanings of all those Hebrew words in itself, but has distinct meanings according to the context in which it is used.[62] When used in the particular expression πορεύεσθαι ὀπίσω τῶν ματαίων, μάταιος may have a particular reference to "idols."

The expression ὀπίσω τῶν ματαίων ("after the vain things") appears in various places in the LXX. The fuller expression "they walked after the vain things" is found in 4 Kgdms 17:15 and Jer 2:5, where the Hebrew and Greek are identical in both passages:

וַיֵּלְכוּ אַחֲרֵי הַהֶבֶל   καὶ ἐπορεύθησαν ὀπίσω τῶν ματαίων
וַיֶּהְבָּלוּ   καὶ ἐματαιώθησαν

In 4 Kgdms 17:15 μάταια appears to refer to the gods of the nations or their idols. Verses 15 and 16 exhibit parallelism as follows:

A1)   καὶ τὰ μαρτύρια αὐτοῦ ὅσα διεμαρτύρατο αὐτοῖς οὐκ ἐφύλαξαν
B1)   καὶ ἐπορεύθησαν ὀπίσω τῶν ματαίων καὶ ἐματαιώθησαν καὶ ὀπίσω
       τῶν ἐθνῶν τῶν περικύκλῳ αὐτῶν ὧν ἐνετείλατο αὐτοῖς τοῦ μὴ
       ποιῆσαι κατὰ ταῦτα
A2)   ἐγκατέλιπον τὰς ἐντολὰς κυρίου θεοῦ αὐτῶν
B2)   καὶ ἐποίησαν ἑαυτοῖς χώνευμα δύο δαμάλεις καὶ ἐποίησαν ἄλση καὶ
       προσεκύνησαν πάσῃ τῇ δυνάμει τοῦ οὐρανοῦ καὶ ἐλάτρευσαν τῷ Βααλ

A1 and A2 state the disobedience to God's law, while B1 and B2 describe how the disobedience was executed. B2 describes the making of idols and their worship (specifically Jeroboam's calves), which is a detailed description of the parallel B1 (καὶ ἐπορεύθησαν ὀπίσω τῶν ματαίων…).

Jeremiah 2:5 is repeated in a slightly different way in v. 8b, where the worship of Baal is condemned:

וְהַנְּבִיאִים נִבְּאוּ בַבַּעַל   καὶ οἱ προφῆται ἐπροφήτευον τῇ Βααλ
וְאַחֲרֵי לֹא־יוֹעִלוּ הָלָכוּ   καὶ ὀπίσω ἀνωφελοῦς ἐπορεύθησαν

A clear reference in Jeremiah where μάταια (הבלים) functions synonymously with idols is 8:19b:

מַדּוּעַ הִכְעִסוּנִי בִּפְסִלֵיהֶם   διὰ τί παρώργισάν με ἐν τοῖς γλυπτοῖς αὐτῶν
בְּהַבְלֵי נֵכָר   καὶ ἐν ματαίοις ἀλλοτρίοις

In addition, a case where "idols" translates הבלים (Jer 14:22) shows the synonymity of the two terms (cf. Jer 10:3, 8, 14–15; see also Jer 9:15; 16:19):

---

62. See James Barr's criticism in *The Semantics of Biblical Language* (Oxford: Oxford University Press, 1961), 38.

הֲיֵשׁ בְּהַבְלֵי הַגּוֹיִם מַגְשִׁמִים   μὴ ἔστιν ἐν εἰδώλοις τῶν ἐθνῶν ὑετίζων

Elsewhere in the LXX we observe a similar connection of μάταια to idols. In Lev 17:7 where Targum Pseudo-Jonathan has "idols" and Onkelos and Neophiti have "demons," the LXX has μάταια for שׂעירם, a rendering "obviously intended as a judgment, a term of derision; the שׂעירם are worthless non-entities, vain things."[63] This same Hebrew word (שׂעירים[ל]) is rendered by a doublet in 2 Chr 11:15: τοῖς εἰδώλοις καὶ τοῖς ματαίοις ("to idols and to vanities").

μάταια refers to idols in Isa 2:20 and 30:15, and Ezek 8:10 makes the identification as well:

וָאָבוֹא וָאֶרְאֶה וְהִנֵּה כָל־תַּבְנִית	καὶ εἰσῆλθον καὶ εἶδον καὶ ἰδοὺ μάταια
רֶמֶשׂ וּבְהֵמָה שֶׁקֶץ וְכָל־גִּלּוּלֵי בֵּית	βδελύγματα καὶ πάντα τὰ εἴδωλα οἴκου
יִשְׂרָאֵל מְחֻקֶּה עַל־הַקִּיר סָבִיב סָבִיב	Ισραηλ διαγεγραμμένα ἐπ᾽ αὐτοῦ κύκλῳ

μάταια in LXX TP

Idols seem to be in mind in LXX Amos 2:4 where Judah is accused of disobeying God's law and of being deceived by the μάταια which they have made, after which their fathers also walked:

וְחֻקָּיו לֹא שָׁמָרוּ	καὶ τὰ προστάγματα αὐτοῦ οὐκ ἐφυλάξαντο
וַיַּתְעוּם כִּזְבֵיהֶם	καὶ ἐπλάνησεν αὐτοὺς τὰ μάταια αὐτῶν ἃ ἐποίησαν
אֲשֶׁר־הָלְכוּ אֲבוֹתָם אַחֲרֵיהֶם	οἷς ἐξηκολούθησαν οἱ πατέρες αὐτῶν ὀπίσω αὐτῶν

This verse seems to parallel 4 Kgdms 17:15–16, but μάταια could also refer to what people say in different contexts (Zeph 3:13; Zech 10:2). However, ἃ ἐποίησαν is a plus in LXX Amos 2:4 and is reminiscent of 3 Kgdms 15:12: את־כל־הגללים אשר עשו אבתיו. In LXX Hos 5:11, however, the reference is most probably to idols or foreign gods, not words, since the expression is normally used that way (4 Kgdms 17:15; Jer 2:5; cf. Judg 2:12; Jer 8:2; 9:13). After establishing that "vanities" can refer to idols, especially in the context of the phrase "walk after vanities," we must now examine whether it was common to associate idols with "filth."

εἴδωλα, גלולים *and "Filth"*

Robert Hayward examines the sense of εἴδωλον and points out the disparity between the Hebrew פסל and the Greek εἴδωλον in the Ten Commandments of Exod 20:4 and Deut 5:8. While פסל signified something "hewn, sculpted, or cut into shape," εἴδωλον signified the exact

---

63. John William Wevers, *Notes on the Greek Text of Leviticus* (SBLSCS 44; Atlanta: Scholars Press, 1997), 265.

opposite, namely, "a phantom; an unsubstantial form; an image of the sort reflected in water or a looking-glass; a mental image or idea; or a likeness."[64] He thinks that the use of εἴδωλον, instead of the more appropriate ἄγαλμα, originated with the translation of the Song of Moses in Deut 32, and has הבל as its background (Deut 32:21). However, because the LXX translators were aware of the identification of פסל and הבל from Jer 8:19, they adopted εἴδωλον for פסל, as well as for six more Hebrew words.[65]

One of the words translated by εἴδωλα is גלולים: "The Hebrew word גלולים is found only twice in the Pentateuch, at Lev. 26.30 and Deut. 29.16. On both occasions, LXX have rendered it as 'idols'. The Hebrew word is strongly pejorative, carrying with it notions of uncleanness, filth and defilement which are thereby directly related to pagan cult objects."[66] גלולים is Ezekiel's favourite term for idols which he probably picks up from Leviticus. Milgrom holds that Ezekiel, in 6:3–6, was modelling himself on Lev 26:30–31.[67] He further comments that

> the word derives from *gālāl* 'dung, dung balls' (*ʾAbot R. Nat.*[2] [recension b] 38; Ibn Janaḥ; Radak; cf. 1 Kgs 14:10; Ezek 4:12, 15; Zeph 1:17) and the denominative *gālal* 'be dirty' (2 Sam 20:12; Isa 9:4). The vocalization has been assimilated to *šiqqûṣîm* 'detested objects', with which it is occasionally paired (Deut 29:16; 2 Kgs 23:24; Ezek 7:20). It appears thirty-nine times in Ezekiel where it is frequently associated with the word *ṭāmēʾ* 'impure' (20:7, 18, 31; 22:3–4; 23:7, 30; 36:18, 25; 37:23). That it is Ezekiel's favorite term for idols is shown, in contrast, by his use of *ʾĕlîlîm* only once (30:13, for another people) and the other derisive term *šiqqûṣîm*, seven times (5:11; 7:20; 11:18; 20:7, 8, 30; 37:23).[68]

Lust suggests a broader meaning for גלולים on the basis of the variety of Greek equivalents chosen by Ezekiel's Greek translator.[69] The equivalent εἴδωλα usually occurs in contexts where reference is made to material cultic objects.[70] However, the most common equivalent for

64. Hayward, "Observations on Idols," 41–42.
65. Ibid., 40–45. HR, 376, lists fifteen Hebrew words translated by εἴδωλον.
66. Hayward, "Observations on Idols," 50.
67. Jacob Milgrom, *Leviticus 23–27* (AB 3B; New York: Doubleday, 2000), 2319. Johan Lust, however, supports the view that the prophet Ezekiel may have coined the word himself, since it hardly ever occurs in pre-exilic biblical literature; Lust, "Idols? גלולים and εἴδωλα in Ezekiel," in Ausloos, Lemmelijn, and Vervenne, eds., *Florilegium Lovaniense*, 317.
68. Milgrom, *Leviticus 23–27*, 2319.
69. The variety of Greek equivalents and their spread across the book is an argument against any hypothetical multiple translation theory, according to Lust, "Idols?," 319–20.
70. Ibid., 332–33.

גלולים is ἐνθυμήματα ("thoughts, mental images"), similar to διανοήματα or ἐπιτηδεύματα. Lust also notes that Aquila, in several instances, prefers κάθαρμα, "that which is thrown away in cleansing," or "refuse, slag." Elsewhere he has εἴδωλα/-οις/-ων.[71] Aquila appears to have understood some connection between גלולים, idols and filth. This, however, does not indicate that the other versions failed to recognize such a meaning. It may simply mean that, in some cases, Aquila avoided concealing the pejorative meaning of the word.

In analyzing the Hebrew word גלולים, Daniel Bodi prefers to work from a single root גלל. Rather than postulating two different roots גלל/גל, "to be round"/"heap of stones" and "excrement," and to relate the latter to the term גלולים, it seems more appropriate to assume a single root גלל/גל with two possible meanings which belong, however, to the same semantic field. The basic meaning would be "excrement," since excrements of human or animal origin manifest the feature of rotundity.[72]

The association of the root(s) גלל/גל with "excrement" (צאה) is most evident in Ezek 4:12–15, and, according to Bodi, it is crucial for the message of Ezekiel. The prophet is instructed to eat the bread over a fire made of human dung (והיא בגללי צאת האדם). This act would function as a symbol of how the people would soil themselves among the nations. Bodi says: "[c]ette double acception du terme *gll* permet à Ézéchiel d'exploiter surtout sa deuxième signification, celle d''excrément', parce qu'elle permet de parler de 'souillure' (cf. Ez 4,12.15). De même la pratique de l'idolâtrie représente une souillure et impureté que YHWH ne peut tolérer."[73]

Bodi mentions the connecting of גלולים with צאה by Ibn Ezra. Ibn Ezra explains the גלולים in Lev 26:30 with reference to the excrements of Ezek 4:12 and 15, and thinks that, because of this connection of idols with excrement, גלולים is a term of derision.[74] Ibn Ezra says that גלולים is "a derogatory term for idol-worship, from 'as one removes dung' [1 Kgs 14:10]."[75]

All of the above seems to indicate that idols were commonly associated with "filth." It is possible that Ezekiel's wide polemic use of גלולים had promoted a common way of thinking and referring to idols in terms of "filth."

---

71. Ibid., 332.
72. Daniel Bodi, "Les *gillûlîm* chez Ézéchiel et dans l'Ancien Testament, et les différentes pratiques cultuelles associées à ce terme," *RB* 100 (1993): 481.
73. Ibid., 510.
74. Ibid., 489.
75. Abraham ibn Ezra, *The Commentary of Abraham Ibn Ezra on the Pentateuch*. Vol. 3. *Leviticus* (trans. Jay F. Schachter; Hoboken, N.J.: KTAV, 1986), 163.

Euphemistic Rendering?

If צו was indeed understood by the Greek translator of Hosea as a reference to filth (related to צאה), then why was it not translated literally? A possible answer is that in LXX Hos 5:11 we have a case of "euphemistic translation." De Waard presents two definitions for "euphemism": "a euphemism is a figure by which a less distasteful word or expression is substituted for one more exactly descriptive of what is intended. Or, a euphemism is a figure of speech in which an unpleasant or coarse phrase is replaced by a softer or less offensive expression."[76]

In the case of LXX Hos 5:11, the meaning of צו was not communicated by a socially acceptable synonymous term, but instead was replaced with what the translator thought was the referent *intended* by the text, namely, "idols." Euphemism is a virtually universal feature of human language and the subjects which people normally have difficulty talking about are listed by Ellingworth and Mojola as follows: "sexual acts, sexual organs, menstruation, and pregnancy; certain other bodily organs and functions, such as excretion; disease and death; and in some cultures wealth or poverty, and supernatural powers."[77]

Ellingworth and Mojola show how the simple replacement of the offensive expression with an acceptable one would not be able to solve the translational problem, since a variety of expressions may be available. Instead, the problem is deciding which one is the appropriate expression in order to preserve "referential accuracy" as well as "naturalness."[78]

The choice of ματαίων is the most appropriate because:

a. It is referentially accurate. If צו (understood as "filth") refers to idols and μάταια refers to idols, then the substitution of "filth" with "vanities" would be a successful one in that the same referent is preserved.

b. "Naturalness" is achieved with reference to the context. As already observed, "to walk after vanities" is a familiar expression used to show the idolatrous rebellion of Israel and was therefore readily suggested to the Greek translator as he read הלך אחרי־צו. Not only was צו replaced by "vanity," but it was also "pluralized" in order to match the familiar expression of "walking" ὀπίσω τῶν ματαίων.

76. Jan de Waard, "Do You Use 'Clean Language'? Old Testament Euphemisms and Their Translation," *BT* 22 (1971): 107.

77. Paul Ellingworth and Aloo Mojola, "Translating Euphemisms in the Bible," *BT* 37 (1986): 139. Cf. Shalom M. Paul, "Euphemistically 'Speaking' and a Covetous Eye," *HAR* 14 (1994): 193–204.

78. Ellingworth and Mojola, "Translating Euphemisms," 139–43.

Jerome and Jeroboam

For Jerome the meaning of צא is "filth." In his Vulgate he translates Hos 5:11 as: *calumniam patiens Ephraim fractus iudicio quoniam coepit abire post sordem.* His comments on *sordem*, however, show that he does not deviate much from the sense communicated by the LXX. He identifies "filth" with "idols" since these are related to, or acquired from, "filthy" people. Jerome explains that Ephraim is oppressed by the Assyrians because Jeroboam (representing Ephraim) began to walk after idols and to abandon God by making golden calves. In explaining the LXX reading, Jerome says that Jeroboam (i.e. Ephraim) has oppressed his enemy Rehoboam (i.e. Judah) by abandoning the Jerusalem temple and following the images of the "filthy" Egyptians.[79]

Jerome's interpretation of Hos 5:11, for both the Hebrew and the LXX, takes him to Jeroboam's idolatrous rebellion. This is a natural connection for Jerome to make in the light of 4 Kgdms 17, the chapter which explains the reasons behind the Assyrian invasion (see vv. 7–23). The chapter climaxes with vv. 21–23 laying responsibility for the exile of Israel on Jeroboam, who functions as the archetype of royal rebellion:

> When he had torn Israel from the house of David, they made Jeroboam son of Nebat king. Jeroboam drove Israel from following the LORD and made them commit great sin. The people of Israel continued in all the sins that Jeroboam committed; they did not depart from them until the LORD removed Israel out of his sight, as he had foretold through all his servants the prophets. So Israel was exiled from their own land to Assyria until this day. [NRSV]

The expression in LXX Hos 5:11b (πορεύεσθαι ὀπίσω τῶν ματαίων) makes one wonder whether the connection to Jeroboam's rebellion noted by Jerome was already made in the Greek translator's mind, although that is difficult to establish. The expression is common in the LXX and often refers to Jeroboam's rebellion, but it is hard to know whether it had become a stock expression independent of a clear reference to Jeroboam's sin. Forms of πορεύομαι and μάταιον together are found in 3 Kgdms 16:2 with reference to Jeroboam's ways:

> ἀνθ᾽ ὧν ὕψωσά σε ἀπὸ τῆς γῆς καὶ ἔδωκά σε ἡγούμενον ἐπὶ τὸν λαόν μου Ισραηλ καὶ ἐπορεύθης ἐν τῇ ὁδῷ Ιεροβοαμ καὶ ἐξήμαρτες τὸν λαόν μου τὸν Ισραηλ τοῦ παροργίσαι με ἐν τοῖς ματαίοις αὐτῶν

---

79. Jerome, *Comm. Os.* Col. 0863B–0864A (Patrologia Latina Database).

Similarly, in 3 Kgdms 16:26:

καὶ ἐπορεύθη ἐν πάσῃ ὁδῷ Ιεροβοαμ υἱοῦ Ναβατ καὶ ἐν ταῖς ἁμαρτίαις αὐτοῦ αἷς ἐξήμαρτεν τὸν Ισραηλ τοῦ παροργίσαι τὸν κύριον θεὸν Ισραηλ ἐν τοῖς ματαίοις αὐτῶν.

LXX Amos 2:4, as already discussed, seems to echo 4 Kgdms 17:15–16, in the chapter which traces Israel's destruction back to Jeroboam's rebellion.[80] LXX Amos 2:4–5 is the oracle against Judah, and the reason given for the judgment is that they have not kept God's commands but followed after vanities just as their fathers did. This is mentioned in 4 Kgdms 17:19: "Judah also did not keep the commandments of the LORD their God but walked in the customs that Israel had introduced" [NRSV]. Jeremiah 2:5 is also connected to 4 Kgdms 17 through its identical language with 4 Kgdms 17:15, in both the Hebrew and the Greek.

Conclusion

Rather than restricting the allusion of the phrase πορεύεσθαι ὀπίσω τῶν ματαίων to one exclusive individual, incident or text, it is safer to conclude that what is introduced or elucidated by the Greek translator of Hos 5:11 is the attribution of Ephraim's condemnation to the sin of idolatry, in accordance with Deuteronomistic ideology reflected in this stock phrase. The LXX translator understood the pejorative sense of צו to be a reference to idols, as "filth" words often are, and was able to communicate this through the choice of μάταια, a word fitting the common expression "to walk after vanities."

Micah 1:6 and 3:12

Micah 1:6

MT	LXX
וְשַׂמְתִּי שֹׁמְרוֹן לְעִי הַשָּׂדֶה	καὶ θήσομαι Σαμάρειαν εἰς ὀπωροφυλάκιον ἀγροῦ[81]
לְמַטָּעֵי כָרֶם וְהִגַּרְתִּי	καὶ εἰς φυτείαν ἀμπελῶνος καὶ κατασπάσω
לַגַּי אֲבָנֶיהָ	εἰς χάος τοὺς λίθους αὐτῆς
וִיסֹדֶיהָ אֲגַלֶּה	καὶ τὰ θεμέλια αὐτῆς ἀποκαλύψω

---

80. The connection to 4 Kgdms 17:15b is also noted by Wolff, *Joel and Amos*, 164.

81. Sinclair argues that LXX Micah reflects a Hebrew *Vorlage* similar to that of 1QpMic because of the lack of the article before שׂדה. 8ḤevXII gr has added the article to match a proto-MT Hebrew text (οπω]ροφυλακιον του α[γρ]ου); Sinclair, "Hebrew Text of the Qumran Micah Pesher," 260.

Therefore I will make Samaria a
heap in the open country, a place
for planting vineyards. I will pour
down her stones into the valley, and
uncover her foundations. [NRSV]

And I will make Samaria an orchard-
guard's shed in the field and a planting of a
vineyard. And I will pull down her stones
into a chasm, and her foundations I will
uncover. [NETS]

Micah 3:12

MT	LXX
לָכֵן בִּגְלַלְכֶם צִיּוֹן שָׂדֶה	διὰ τοῦτο δι' ὑμᾶς Σιων ὡς ἀγρὸς
תֵחָרֵשׁ וִירוּשָׁלַם	ἀροτριαθήσεται καὶ Ιερουσαλημ
עִיִּין תִּהְיֶה	ὡς ὀπωροφυλάκιον ἔσται
וְהַר הַבַּיִת לְבָמוֹת יָעַר	καὶ τὸ ὄρος τοῦ οἴκου εἰς ἄλσος δρυμοῦ

Therefore because of you Zion
shall be plowed as a field;
Jerusalem shall become a heap of
ruins, and the mountain of the
house a wooded height. [NRSV]

Therefore, on your account Sion shall be
plowed as a field, and Ierusalem shall
become like a garden-watcher's hut, and
the mountain of the house shall become a
grove of a thicket. [NETS]

The choice of εἰς ὀπωροφυλάκιον for לְעִי in Mic 1:6 is "corrected" by the
other Greek versions (α' εις σωρους σ' θ' εις βουνους Syh), a pointer to the
LXX translator's peculiar rendering of this word. The same is true for
Mic 3:12 where ὀπωροφυλάκιον translates עִיִּין (α' [ως] λιθολογια σ' βουνοι
θ' εις ερημωσιν Syh; εβρ' [εις] λιθολογια[ν] Eus.dem. p.393). This peculiar
rendering raises the question whether the Greek translator of Micah was
influenced by LXX Isa 1:8 and 24:20, the only places in the OT where
ὀπωροφυλάκιον corresponds accurately to its Hebrew equivalent מלונה.
The task before us, however, must not be restricted to the examination of
the relationship between LXX Micah and LXX Isaiah. ὀπωροφυλάκιον
occurs in a few more places in the OT and, for any conclusion to be
meaningful, all occurrences must be taken into account. The rest of these
occurrences are as follows, in the LXX canonical order:

Psalm 78[MT79]:1

MT	LXX
אֱלֹהִים בָּאוּ גוֹיִם בְּנַחֲלָתֶךָ	ὁ θεός ἤλθοσαν ἔθνη εἰς τὴν κληρονομίαν σου
טִמְּאוּ אֶת־הֵיכַל קָדְשֶׁךָ	ἐμίαναν τὸν ναὸν τὸν ἅγιόν σου
שָׂמוּ אֶת־יְרוּשָׁלַם לְעִיִּים	ἔθεντο Ιερουσαλημ εἰς ὀπωροφυλάκιον

O God, the nations have come into
your inheritance; they have defiled
your holy temple; they have laid
Jerusalem in ruins. [NRSV]

O God, nations came into your inheritance;
they defiled your holy shrine; they made
Ierusalem into a fruit-watcher's hut.
[NETS]

Isaiah 1:8

MT	LXX
וְנוֹתְרָה בַת־צִיּוֹן	ἐγκαταλειφθήσεται ἡ θυγάτηρ Σιων
כְּסֻכָּה בְכָרֶם	ὡς σκηνὴ ἐν ἀμπελῶνι
כִּמְלוּנָה בְמִקְשָׁה	καὶ ὡς ὀπωροφυλάκιον ἐν σικυηράτῳ
כְּעִיר נְצוּרָה	ὡς πόλις πολιορκουμένη.

And daughter Zion is left like a
booth in a vineyard, like a shelter
in a cucumber field, like a besieged
city. [NRSV]

Daughter Sion will be forsaken like a
booth in a vineyard and like a hut in a
cucumber field, like a besieged city.
[NETS]

Isaiah 24:20

MT

נוֹעַ תָּנוּעַ אֶרֶץ כַּשִּׁכּוֹר וְהִתְנוֹדְדָה
כַּמְּלוּנָה וְכָבַד עָלֶיהָ פִּשְׁעָהּ
וְנָפְלָה
וְלֹא־תֹסִיף קוּם

LXX

ἔκλινεν καὶ σεισθήσεται
ὡς ὀπωροφυλάκιον ἡ γῆ ὡς ὁ μεθύων
καὶ κραιπαλῶν καὶ πεσεῖται
καὶ οὐ μὴ δύνηται ἀναστῆναι
κατίσχυσεν γὰρ ἐπ᾽ αὐτῆς ἡ ἀνομία

The earth staggers like a drunkard,
it sways like a hut; its transgression lies heavy upon it, and it falls,
and will not rise again. [NRSV]

The earth has bent over, and it will be
shaken like a hut, like the one who drinks
too much and is intoxicated, and it will fall
and will not be able to rise, for lawlessness
has prevailed upon it. [NETS]

Jeremiah 33[MT26]:18

MT

מִיכָיָה הַמּוֹרַשְׁתִּי הָיָה נִבָּא בִּימֵי
חִזְקִיָּהוּ מֶלֶךְ־יְהוּדָה
וַיֹּאמֶר אֶל־כָּל־עַם יְהוּדָה לֵאמֹר
כֹּה־אָמַר יְהוָה צְבָאוֹת צִיּוֹן שָׂדֶה
תֵחָרֵשׁ וִירוּשָׁלַיִם
עִיִּים תִּהְיֶה
וְהַר הַבַּיִת לְבָמוֹת יָעַר

Micah of Moresheth, who
prophesied during the days of King
Hezekiah of Judah, said to all the
people of Judah: 'Thus says the
LORD of hosts, Zion shall be
plowed as a field; Jerusalem shall
become a heap of ruins, and the
mountain of the house a wooded
height.' [NRSV]

LXX

Μιχαιας ὁ Μωραθίτης ἦν ἐν ταῖς ἡμέραις
Εζεκιου βασιλέως Ιουδα
καὶ εἶπεν παντὶ τῷ λαῷ Ιουδα
οὕτως εἶπεν κύριος Σιων ὡς ἀγρὸς
ἀροτριαθήσεται καὶ Ιερουσαλημ
εἰς ἄβατον [var. ὀπωροφυλάκιον] ἔσται
καὶ τὸ ὄρος τοῦ οἴκου εἰς ἄλσος δρυμοῦ

There was Michaias the Morasthite in
the days of King Hezekias of Iouda, and he
said to all the people of Iouda: 'Thus did
the Lord say, Sion shall be plowed like a
field; and Ierousalem shall become
untrodden, and the mountain of the house a
forest grove'. [NETS]

Extra-Biblical Attestation

Before analyzing the biblical occurrences we should note that ὀπωροφυλάκιον is not found outside the LXX,[82] though other forms of this word
are attested elsewhere. ὀπωροφύλαξ ("watcher of fruits, garden watcher,"
LSJ) is found in Aristotle in the fourth century B.C.E.:

82. Here I shall not include *Testament of Joseph* 19:11–12, where the occurrence
of ὀπωροφυλάκιον is clearly influenced by the biblical texts.

πολλὰς δὲ καὶ ἀτόπους φωνὰς ποιοῦσι τὰ σχήματα τῶν κοιλιῶν ἀνώμαλα ὄντα, ἐπεὶ καὶ ἀμφορέως τὸν πύνδακα ἐάν τις ἀφελὼν διὰ τοῦ πυθμένος τρίβῃ ἕλκων ἔσω καὶ ἔξω, εἰ τρίψει διὰ τοῦ καταδήματος, ψόφον ποιεῖ, ὥστε φεύγειν τὰ θηρία, ὅταν οἱ ὀπωροφύλακες κατασκευάσωσιν αὐτό.
(Aristotle, *[Prob.]* 938a 13–16)

Again, the historian Diodorus Siculus in the first century B.C.E. uses ὀπωροφύλαξ for a deity functioning as the protector of fields:

τοῦτον δὲ τὸν θεὸν τινὲς μὲν Ἰθύφαλλον ὀνομάζουσι, τινὲς δὲ Τύχωνα. τὰς δὲ τιμὰς οὐ μόνον κατὰ πόλιν ἀπονέμουσιν αὐτῷ [ἐν τοῖς ἱεροῖς], ἀλλὰ καὶ κατὰ τὰς ἀγροικίας ὀπωροφύλακα τῶν ἀμπελώνων ἀποδεικνύντες καὶ τῶν κήπων, ἔτι δὲ πρὸς τοὺς βασκαίνοντάς τι τῶν καλῶν τοῦτον κολαστὴν παρεισάγοντες. (*Bibliotheca historica* 4.6.4)

The word is also found in Documentary papyri. The following examples are a lease of a vineyard from 137 C.E. and a record of payment of a fruitwatcher (251–286 C.E.):

ὃν δὲ ἐὰν βούληται ὁ Σαραπίων <u>ὀπωροφύλακα</u> φυλάσσι<ν> τῷ τῆς ὀπώρας καιρῷ φύλακα πέμψει, τοῦ ὀψωνίου ὄντος πρὸς αὐτὸν ...
(*P.Oxy.* IV 729, line 11)

Ματρέᾳ ὀπωροφύλ(ακι) τοῦ χωρίου ὑπ(ὲρ) ἀρραβῶνος τῆς τηρ[ήσεως ?]
(PSI VIII 890: 1.35; transl. MNvdM)[83]

These occurrences give good enough reason to conclude that this word, in its different forms, had been a term in everyday use regardless of its infrequent occurrence in the LXX. Dines says that ὀπωροφυλάκιον "seems to have been coined by the LXX" and is unlikely to refer to "a shed for a garden watchman to spend the night in." Her view is based on the fact that φυλάκιον "is predominantly a military term, being used for a watchtower or fort, or a detachment of men on guard duty." She finds that the matching of ὀπώρα ("fruit") with φυλάκιον is an odd combination and is "more likely to mean a place or a person to protect fruit than the hut for the night-watchman to brew up his tea in."[84] However, ὀπωρο-φυλάκιον may simply be a rare word such as, according to Kaminka, the

---

83. I was alerted to these examples by Michaël N. van der Meer at the LXX-D conference in Wuppertal, Germany, in July 2008. For a complete list of attestations see his "The Question of the Literary Dependence of the Greek Isaiah upon the Greek Psalter Revisited," in *Die Septuaginta—Texte, Theologien, Einflüsse. 2. Internationale Fachtagung veranstaltet von Septaginta Deutsch (LXX.D), Wuppertal 23.–27.7.2008* (ed. Wolfgang Kraus and Martin Karrer; WUNT 252; Tübingen: Mohr Siebeck, 2010), 192–99.

84. Dines, "The Twelve Among the Prophets," 14–16.

Greek translator sometimes preferred.[85] We cannot conclude from the lack of evidence elsewhere that a form so closely related to ὀπωροφύλαξ did not exist.[86]

There is evidence that such a construction was commonly in use. Dalman notes that vineyards were protected (see Isa 27:3: "I, the LORD, am its keeper; every moment I water it. I guard it night and day so that no one can harm it" [NRSV]), and for the guard there was a tower or a hut (Isa 5:2: "He dug it and cleared it of stones, and planted it with choice vines; he built a watchtower in the midst of it, and hewed out a wine vat in it; he expected it to yield grapes, but it yielded wild grapes" [NRSV]; Job 27:18: "They build their houses like nests, like booths made by sentinels of the vineyard" [NRSV]).[87] The "tower" in the field is also mentioned in the NT in Matt 21:33 and Mark 12:1.

ὀπωροφυλάκιον in LXX Isaiah

In Isa 1:8, a guard's tower/hut in the middle of a field is most likely to have come to the mind of the translator when confronted by MT מלונה. The verse is clearly not referring to a night shelter for guests, for which מלון is used elsewhere.

מלונה ("hut, for watching field at night"[88]) is the feminine form of מלון ("lodging place"[89]). This feminine form does not occur anywhere else outside Isaiah (1:8; 24:20), but מלון is more common in the OT. In the Pentateuch it is translated by καταλύειν ("lodge") or the noun κατάλυμα ("lodging") (Gen 42:27; 43:21; Exod 4:24); in Joshua it acquires the meaning of camping or encampment (Josh 4:3, στρατοπεδεία; 4:8, παρεμβολή); in 4 Kgdms 19:23 it is probably not understood and therefore transliterated into μελον; in Jer 9:1 it is a lodging place in the desert (σταθμός). Isaiah's translator leaves מלון untranslated in 10:29 but renders the feminine form מלונה by ὀπωροφυλάκιον in both 1:8 and 24:20.

85. "Die Neigung zu seltenen und eleganten Ausdrücken zeigt sich hier bei ὀπωροφυλάκιον wie Ob₁₈ bei πυρφόρος"; Kaminka, *Studien*, 45.

86. Van der Meer concludes: "the word ὀπωροφυλάκιον is probably not a neologism invented by some Greek Bible translator, but derived from daily life in the vineyards of Egypt, where the precious fruit had to be protected against birds and other animals. The word refers to a shelter for common people performing that job"; Van der Meer, "The Question of the Literary Dependence," 198.

87. Figures 12 and 13 in the appendix are especially informative on such constructions. See Gustaf Hermann Dalman, *Arbeit und Sitte in Palästina* (1928; 7 vols.; Schriften des Deutschen Palästina-Instituts; repr., Hildesheim: Georg Olms, 1964), 2:61.

88. *DCH* 5:293.

89. *DCH* 5:292.

Despite the assortment of Greek equivalents for מלון, which could have served as options for translating the rarer מלונה, it would not have been difficult to arrive at this particular rendering in 1:8, since the context is clearly speaking about a guard's shed in a field. In 1:8, therefore, ὀπωροφυλάκιον for מלונה is a legitimate Greek equivalent. Not only is it contextually fitting for מקשה (LXX '[in] a cucumber field') but it also preserves the parallelism with סכה (LXX "[like] a booth") in that both elements represent basic structures for lodging. The Greek translator of Isaiah remains consistent in his rendering of מלונה in 24:20 where the element of *frailty* in this construction, which led him to the choice of this particular word, is even more evident.

Influence on LXX Isaiah

Despite this accurate rendering of מלונה and the contextual suitability of ὀπωροφυλάκιον to the verse as a whole, Seeligmann has argued that the translator was influenced by other texts in choosing this rendering. He believed that the Greek Psalter as well as the Greek TP preceded the translation of Isaiah into Greek and that, therefore, the influence comes from either LXX Micah or LXX Psalms.[90] Aejmelaeus agrees that LXX Isaiah has been influenced by other texts, namely the Greek text of Ps 78[MT79]:1, which itself had adopted the equivalence עי—ὀπωρο-φυλάκιον from Mic 1:6 and 3:12.[91] Williams, however, is undecided as to the direction of influence between the LXX Isaiah and LXX Psalms,[92] and Ziegler also recognizes the difficulty of determining where the priority lies.[93] Cécile Dogniez concludes that LXX Isaiah arrived at ὀπωρο-φυλάκιον independently of the other LXX books.[94] The view that the Greek Isaiah influenced other texts where ὀπωροφυλάκιον occurs will be discussed later.

ὀπωροφυλάκιον in LXX Jeremiah

Ziegler dismisses ὀπωροφυλάκιον in LXX Jer 33[MT26]:18 as a later harmonization to LXX Mic 3:12 (rel.: ex Mich.3₁₂ Ps.78₁) and adopts ἄβατον (B-S^c[-τος*]46CoAeth↓) as original. Ziegler's choice is supported by the fact that εἰς ἄβατον is a favourite phrase for Jeremiah's translator (12:10; 30:7, 11, 18; 31:9; 32:18, 38; 33:18; 49:18; 51:6, 22) and more

90. Seeligmann, *The Septuagint Version of Isaiah*, 227.
91. A. Aejmelaeus, "'Rejoice in the Lord!': A Lexical and Syntactical Study of the Semantic Field of Joy in the Greek Psalter," in Baasten and van Peursen, eds., *Hamlet on a Hill*, 512 n. 46.
92. Williams, "Towards a Date for the Old Greek Psalter," 268.
93. Ziegler, *Untersuchungen*, 104–5.
94. Dogniez, "L'indépendance du traducteur," 232–33.

likely to have been original in 33[MT26]:18. It is, therefore, possible that a copyist who was aware of Mic 3:12 replaced εἰς ἄβατον with ὡς ὀπωροφυλάκιον in order to harmonize the two texts.

However, in the same verse, the rendering of במה with ἄλσος should also have been a harmonization, since such identification does not occur anywhere else but Mic 3:12. There are no variants available for ἄλσος in Jeremiah or Micah, so this harmonization, if it is such, must have taken place very early, even at the initial translational stage. This rendering may suggest that the Greek translator of Jeremiah was aware of Greek Micah, or the other way round. Ziegler's adoption of ἄβατον as original leaves the question of a relationship between LXX Micah and LXX Jeremiah in the case of ἄλσος unexplained. If ἄλσος is original to both texts, then it is likely that Jeremiah's translator, and not a later harmonizer, was aware of Greek Micah.[95] However, we cannot be certain of the direction of influence since the Hebrew in the two texts is identical (except for עיים/עיין). It is likely, however, that the entire verse was *translated* in a way that matches the Greek text of the other, and that therefore ὀπωροφυλάκιον could have been original to LXX Jeremiah as well.

Dines thinks that εἰς ἄβατον is a much better match for עי (in its Aramaic or Hebrew plural forms) and was the original translation for Mic 3:12 and Jer 33[MT26]:18. εἰς ἄβατον was then changed by a reviser to ὀπωροφυλάκιον in both texts under the influence of LXX Isaiah.[96] According to HR, ἄβατος translates twelve different Hebrew words. In Jeremiah alone, ἄβατος is used 17 times (including 33[MT26]:18) for שוחה, שממה, ערבה, שמה, and אלה. In the Greek TP, however, ἄβατος occurs only once, translating איתן in Amos 5:24, but that was not a faithful rendering of the Hebrew consistent with his more informed rendering of the Hebrew at Mic 6:2. According to Muraoka, the reason the translator used ἄβατος in Amos 5:24 was that he had the related passage of LXX Ezek 47:5 in mind (see the case of Amos 5:24 in Chapter 5).[97] This shows that ἄβατος was not a favourite word of the translator of the Twelve, and we have no textual or other indication that this was the original reading for עיין in Mic 3:12. We can only speak of Jeremiah, where we are left with two possibilities: (a) the harmonization with Mic 3:12 was done at the initial translational stage and, subsequently, a scribe

95. Emanuel Tov thinks that ἄλσος for במה is a characteristic of the translator of Jer b' (chs. 29–52 of LXX Jeremiah) who is also behind LXX TP; *The Septuagint Translation of Jeremiah and Baruch*, 142. However, במה is usually translated by βωμός in Jer b' (39[MT 32]:35; 31[MT 48]:35).

96. Dines, "The Twelve Among the Prophets," 17.

97. Muraoka, "Literary Device," 22.

corrected ὀπωροφυλάκιον to the more common ἄβατος as being closer to עיים, but forgot to correct ἄλσος, and (b) ἄβατος was the original reading, which was then harmonized with Mic 3:12 through the adoption of ὀπωροφυλάκιον as well as ἄλσος. The cases are equally strong. Harmonizations are just as common as corrections towards a stricter representation of a proto-MT, and in this case I would tentatively adopt the first option. However, we shall return to Dines' contribution on this case later.

ὀπωροφυλάκιον in LXX Micah and the Meaning of עי

In Mic 3:12 the translator is faced with a rare word, עיין, which occurs only here and in 1:6 (עי) in the TP. It is obvious that the translator had to make a contextual guess or, according to one view, rely on his knowledge of Post-Biblical Hebrew.

Kaminka related עיין to its Post-Biblical Hebrew meaning ("observe, supervise")[98] or עיון [*sic*] from the Talmud ("to take care of, pay attention to").[99] Sokoloff gives the meaning "guard, watch" for עייני, with an example from the Palestinian Talmud: הוה מעייני תינין, "he was guarding fig trees" (*MQ* 81d[41]).[100] Jastrow gives the same meaning, "watch, guard," with an example of the *Pa'eli* form (עַיֵּינִי) from Targum Pseudo-Jonathan at Deut 32:10.[101] Influence from later Hebrew or Aramaic is also favoured by Lust, who thinks that ὀπωροφυλάκιον is a neologism of the LXX translator which can be paralleled in Syriac and Arabic.[102]

Is it possible that Micah's translator arrived at "guard's shed" on the basis of his knowledge of Post-Biblical Hebrew or Aramaic? Is the sense of "guarding" or "watching" sufficient to lead to the rendering of ὀπωροφυλάκιον when there is nothing in the context suggesting it? The context speaks of the levelling of Zion into a field. Nothing in the verse would suggest a construction like a "guard's shed," and it would also be very strange to go from the plural form of עי to the singular ὀπωροφυλάκιον. In Mic 1:6, עי is singular but the context is that of levelling Samaria's land to make it suitable only for vineyards. What would make the translator think of a "guard's shed"? Furthermore, what

---

98.   "*Feldwächterhütte* (wie מלונה Jes 1₈) ist eine Ableitung von Neuhebr. עיין *Ausschau halten, beobachten*"; Kaminka, *Studien*, 40.

99.   Ibid., 45.

100.   *Sokoloff*, 404.

101.   *Jastrow*, 1054.

102.   "- *ġayâya shed* -<>*ġyy* (Arab.) *to protect* or—*ʿay(y)en* (Syr.) guarded? for MT ל/עי *into a ruin, into a heap,* see also 3,12, Ps 78(79),1 neol."; LEH 442. Similarly, Schleusner, 2:577.

would make the translator of Ps 78[MT79]:1 render the plural עיים by ὀπωροφυλάκιον when there is no field or vineyard in the context at all? How can we explain this identification of ὀπωροφυλάκιον with עי in all three places?

ὀπωροφυλάκιον in LXX Psalms

Since the translator of Ps 78[MT79]:1 identifies עיים with ὀπωροφυλάκιον, it would be too great a coincidence for this difficult word to be "mistakenly" translated in the same way by two different translators.

Flashar,[103] Olofsson,[104] and van der Meer[105] support the view that LXX Psalms is dependent on LXX Isaiah. Mozley[106] considers the possibility of LXX Isa 1:8 exercising influence on both LXX Micah and LXX Psalms. Delitzsch seems more certain of the influence of LXX Isa 1:8 on the LXX Psalter.[107] But this would not account for the rendering of עיים also in LXX Micah.

We must in any case explore the possibility that the translator of Psalms was reminded of Mic 3:12. Tate observes that in the Hebrew text "a considerable amount of the psalm appears in other contexts." Among these, he includes Jer 26:18 and Mic 3:12 for v. 1c.[108] It is likely that the translator of Psalms was aware of Mic 3:12, especially in view of its highlighting in Jer 26:18.[109] Micah 3:12 is also noted repeatedly in rabbinic writings.[110] Psalm 78[MT79]:1 would have recalled either Micah's or Jeremiah's version of the prophecy through the connection of ירושלם and עיים. On the other hand, one could argue that the Hebrew wording of Ps 78[MT79]:1 reminded the translator of the use of שים in Mic 1:6:

---

103. Flashar, "Exegetische Studien," 181–82.

104. Staffan Olofsson, *The LXX Version: A Guide to the Translation Technique of the Septuagint* (ConBOT 30; Stockholm: Almqvist & Wiksell, 1990), 27.

105. Van der Meer, "The Question of the Literary Dependence," 199.

106. Mozley, *The Psalter of the Church*, 132.

107. "LXX übers. לעיים εἰς ὀπωροφυλάκιον, ein Schnörkel aus Jes. 1, 8." Franz Delitzsch, *Die Psalmen* (5th ed; Giessen: Brunnen, 1984), 532.

108. Marvin E. Tate, *Psalms 51–100* (WBC 20; Dallas: Word, 1990), 299.

109. Wilhelm Rudolph captures the intensity of the prophecy: "Dieses Wort mußte in den Ohren der Hörer blasphemisch klingen. Als er der Hauptstadt des Nordreiches mit ihren Götzenbildern dasselbe Schicksal verkündete (1,6f.), hatte er seine Landsleute ganz auf seiner Seite; aber daß er jetzt wagte, Samaria und Jerusalem gleichzustellen und so die wichtigsten Tabus zu durchbrechen, das war unerhört. Kein Wunder, daß dieses Wort noch mehr als ein Jahrhundert später nicht vergessen war und dem Propheten Jeremia das Leben rettete (Jer 26,18)"; *Micha–Nahum–Habakuk–Zephanja* (KAT 13/3; Gütersloh: Gerd Mohn, 1975), 74–75.

110. E.g. *Gen. Rab.* XXII.7; LXV.23; *Num. Rab.* VII.10; *b. Šabb.* 139a; *b. Yoma* 9b.

Mic 1:6   וְשַׂמְתִּי שֹׁמְרוֹן לְעִי

Ps 78[MT79]:1   שָׂמוּ אֶת־יְרוּשָׁלַם לְעִיִּים

Whether it was a recollection of one text or of a combination of texts from Micah, it is likely that Micah's Greek translation of עִי or עִיִּים informed the Greek Psalter. On the other hand, Ariane Cordes discusses the debate between Seeligmann and Flashar and highlights the difficulties of determining the direction of influence.[111] Is it possible, for example, that LXX Isa 1:8 has influenced the LXX Psalter and that the LXX Psalter has in turn influenced LXX Micah?

The psalm speaks about the destruction of the Jerusalem temple by the nations (v. 1), the massacre of the people (vv. 2–3), and the desolation of the land (v. 7). It is plausible that this psalm called to mind Isa 1 and, in the presence of an unknown word such as עִיִּים (a plural form), the translator, under the influence of Isa 1:8, brought in ὀπωροφυλάκιον (a singular form). Flashar sees this choice as pointing to the prophecy's fulfilment,[112] and van der Meer calls it an "actualising rendering" with reference to Antiochus IV Epiphanes' desecration of the temple in the middle of the second century B.C.E.[113] Seen from this angle, one could argue that Micah's translation of 1:6 and 3:12 was informed by the Greek rendering of עִיִּים in Ps 78[MT79]:1. This situation alerts us to the difficulty of treating cases of possible double intertextuality. When two different texts (LXX Psalms and LXX Micah) have been influenced by a common text (LXX Isa 1:8) and they are at the same time related to each other (the presence of עִי or עִיִּים), then it is difficult to determine which of the secondary texts preceded the other.

Was עִי Offensive?

Some problems with the word עִי had surfaced even before the Old Greek translation began to develop. McCarthy has noted the possibility of a very early emendation in 1 Kgs 9:8 where the Hebrew says that, as a result of sin, "this house will become lofty/exalted (עֶלְיוֹן)." Originally, this must have said that the house would become ruins (לְעִיִּין). This reading is contextually more fitting and is attested in the Old Latin and the Syriac versions. The Targum also presupposes it ("and this house

111.   Ariane Cordes, *Die Asafpsalmen in der Septuaginta: der griechische Psalter als Übersetzung und theologisches Zeugnis* (HBS 41; Freiburg: Herder, 2004), 163–65.

112.   "Man darf sagen, daß sich in der Herübernahme des Wortes ὀπωροφυλάκιον aus Jes I 8 das Streben zeigt, die Erfüllung dieser Weissagung nachzuweisen"; Flashar, "Exegetische Studien," 182.

113.   Van der Meer, "The Question of the Literary Dependence," 199.

which was lofty will become ruins"). Such a strong statement of complete destruction of the temple may have triggered this "euphemism." The LXX follows the MT and attests this change. 2 Chronicles 7:21 has incorporated this new reading in a more natural way by the use of a relative pronoun (והבית הזה אשר היה עליון) and the versions follow this. עליון is therefore original here.[114] This, however, was not a systematic correction, since Micah's strong prophecy (Mic 3:12 and Jer 26:18) was left untouched.

Is it possible that we have a similar tendency with עי in the LXX? Was Isaiah's ὀπωροφυλάκιον adopted as an equivalent for עי in order to avoid strong prophecies of *complete* ruin for Zion and the temple? B. Renaud thinks that ὀπωροφυλάκιον in LXX Mic 3:12 may be an attempt to attenuate the strong wording: "Cette traduction infidèle veut peut-être atténuer l'effet catastrophique de cette sentence: Jérusalem reste au moins une hutte (*cf.* Is 1,8 où ὀπωροφυλάκιον traduit *mlwnh*)."[115] Similarly, Wolff states: "Gk translates the questionable addition with εἰς ὀπωροφυλάκιον ἀγροῦ ('to the hut of the vinedresser in the field') and thus weakens the force of the threat after the manner of Isa. 1:8ab (cf. B. Renaud 14)."[116]

ὀπωροφυλάκιον is not adopted for every prophecy that speaks of Jerusalem's ruin. In Jer 9:10, where the MT reads וְנָתַתִּי אֶת־יְרוּשָׁלַ͏ִם לְגַלִּים ("I will make Jerusalem a heap of ruins" [NRSV]), the LXX has καὶ δώσω τὴν Ιερουσαλημ εἰς μετοικίαν, though it is possible that the translator read a form of גלה ("be exiled, go into exile, depart"[117]). Accordingly, as Seeligmann points out, "it is hard to see why, out of the numerous prophecies of disaster given out by the prophets, it should be precisely the phrase 'are like unto a ὀπωροφυλάκιον' that grew into a repeatedly quoted standard curse, and that only in those places where the Hebrew original gives either עי or עיים!"[118]

The best way, therefore, to explain this phenomenon is to conclude that, for one reason or another, it was some form of עי which triggered the adoption of ὀπωροφυλάκιον.

---

114. Carmel McCarthy, *The Tiqqune Sopherim and Other Theological Corrections in the Masoretic Text of the Old Testament* (OBO 36; Göttingen: Vandenhoeck & Ruprecht, 1981), 237–38.

115. B. Renaud, *La Formation du Livre de Michée: Tradition et Actualisation* (Études bibliques; Paris: J. Gabalda, 1977), 141. Bruce Waltke seems to agree with this: *A Commentary on Micah* (Grand Rapids: Eerdmans, 2007), 182–83.

116. Hans Walter Wolff, *Micah: A Commentary* (trans. Gary Stansell; Minneapolis: Augsburg Fortress, 1990), 42 n. 6a. Similarly, Rudolph, *Micha–Nahum–Habakuk–Zephanja*, 74–75.

117. *DCH* 2:349.

118. Seeligmann, *The Septuagint Version of Isaiah*, 227.

LXX Isaiah in Second-Temple Tradition
Jennifer Dines does not attempt to explain LXX Ps 78[MT79]:1, but her discussion of the scribal habits in the *Naḥal Ḥever* scroll of the Greek TP shows how, around 50 B.C.E., knowledge of LXX Isaiah had a role to play in the Kaige revision of the Twelve. In Mic 4:1–4 she notes that the scroll has been partially corrected towards LXX Isa 2:2–4, which is contrary to the general adjustment of this scroll to an emerging proto-MT. Dines notes that the motive for these alterations was clearly the assumption that they were Isaiah's words, and she suggests that Isaiah was emerging as a particularly authoritative prophet whose text was the "yardstick for correcting associated texts."[119] I agree with her conclusion that the *Naḥal Ḥever* reviser harmonized LXX Isa 2:2–4 and LXX Mic 4:1–4, since these two are clearly parallel and harmonizations would be expected. However, in the absence of external evidence, I hesitate to carry this solution over to the case of LXX Mic 3:12 where the connection to LXX Isa 1:8 and 24:20 is not so clear, and even less to LXX Mic 1:6 where the reference is to Samaria. Furthermore, the reviser's substitutions which Dines mentions are only between synonyms. In the case of עִי, however, it is not clear why a scribe would replace a *correct* rendering of עִי (ἄβατος) with a wrong one (ὀπωροφυλάκιον) where the passages are not even parallel to those in Isaiah. Moreover, accepting this solution for ὀπωροφυλάκιον in LXX Micah leaves LXX Ps 78[MT79]:1 unexplained, and the same questions are simply transposed from the translational stage to the revising stage.

Nevertheless, Dines' observations throw light on the authority which Greek Isaiah had acquired by the first century B.C.E. and on scribal familiarity with its language. This shows that Isaiah's translation had circulated by that time and was possibly well known orally. It is possible, then, that LXX Isaiah's identification of Zion with a guard's hut was well known and had acquired cliché status.

Possible Solutions and Conclusions
No scenario that we propose in explanation of these phenomena will be without its problems:

1. If it is intertextual influence that accounts for the adoption of ὀπωροφυλάκιον in the various verses that we have discussed, then we should have no way of knowing the directions of influence among the texts containing this Greek word. We should also have to ask why intertextuality occurs only where עִי is found, when it could have happened in other places such as Jer 9:10, for example.

---

119. Dines, "The Twelve Among the Prophets," 18.

2. If עי was interpreted under the influence of a post-biblical verb meaning "guard," then why do we have such a specific type of "guard shed" each time, even in LXX Psalms when the context says nothing about a field or a vineyard? Moreover, why is the plural form עיים/עיין ignored?

3. The third proposal, of a "euphemistic cliché," is the one that I would deem the most probable. As in the case of the euphemistic alteration of לעיין in 1 Kgs 9:8, as described by McCarthy, the word עי was possibly regarded as too "strong" and was replaced by the "milder" ὀπωροφυλάκιον (Renaud, Rudolph, Wolff), under the influence of the Greek Isaiah, whose language, as Dines notes, had become influential and authoritative by the first century B.C.E. It is not unlikely that Isaiah's description of the ὀπωροφυλάκιον had become a cliché so well known that it was evoked whenever the troublesome עי was encountered. It should be stressed that ὀπωροφυλάκιον does not seem to be a straight translation of עי, otherwise the plural would surely have been observed in at least one of its occurrences. Instead, עי would trigger the adoption of this cliché. Ziegler also allows for the possibility of circulating expressions: "Oftmals wird überhaupt keine Abhängigkeit von bestimmten Schriftstellen vorliegen, sondern der Übers. hat einfach in freier Weise Worte und Wendungen gebraucht, die ihm zwar auch aus der Hl. Schrift bekannt waren, aber alltägliche Redensarten darstellen, vgl. 30,14 (ὕδωρ μιχρόν); 32,4 (λαλεῖν εἰρήνην) u. ö."[120] However, in the case of ὀπωροφυλάκιον, it would not require a great leap to trace the origins of this cliché to Isaiah's translation, since it is a faithful rendering of the Hebrew.

---

120.   Ziegler, *Untersuchungen*, 105–6. Similarly, Mozley hinted at the possibility that "[t]he hut of the watcher of an orchard, compared as (1) lonely, (2) meanly built, perhaps come [*sic*] to be a proverb for solitary melancholy, unless Is. 1[8] was a pattern to the rest"; *The Psalter of the Church*, 132.

Chapter 4

CATCHWORD CONNECTIONS

It is widely recognized that catchwords have had an important function in the collection and arrangement of units such as "wisdom sayings, legal sayings, psalms, and prophetic logia."[1] The collection theory argues that "a compiler recognized the similar wording, and placed the completed works next to one another."[2]

Catchwords may be defined by their function, as Nogalski explains: "catchwords function as a type of allusion by using/reusing significant words to refer to another text(s)."[3] While Nogalski is looking at how catchwords have been *redactionally* implanted in texts in order to strengthen connections between them, the focus of this study is not on the formation of texts but on the reading of texts. My aim is to see how the Greek translator of the TP allowed certain significant words in his text to *function* as catchwords. In other words, certain words or phrases in the Hebrew *Vorlage* managed to generate for the translator a connection with other biblical texts where the same words or phrases are found, and this connection has left its traces in his translation.

This type of reading is similar to the rabbinic exegetical technique called *gezerah shavah*. *Gezerah shavah* or "Scriptural intertextuality," as Sarason calls it, has its roots in a fundamental conviction that

> Scripture interprets itself; that verses throughout the Tanakh, irrespective of their linear proximity, are intrinsically related to each other and shed mutual interpretive light on each other... God, as the author of Scripture, has left these interpretive "keys" within the text: any similarity among verses, however extrinsic it may appear to us at first, in fact is intrinsic and intentional.[4]

1. Nogalski, "Intertextuality and the Twelve," 112.
2. Nogalski, "The Redactional Shaping of Nahum 1," 196.
3. Nogalski, "Intertextuality and the Twelve," 112.
4. Richard S. Sarason, "Liturgy, Midrash In," *EOM* 1:478.

This exegetical technique was employed by both Hillel and Ishmael. In fact, Hillel stated that he had learned the *gezerah shavah* from his teachers, so it is possible that he did not "invent" this exegetical tool but simply transmitted it.[5] Indeed, some scholars think that exegetical methods identical to the rabbinic ones were already used in the Alexandrian schools,[6] and others have discerned patterns similar to the *gezerah shavah* in Jewish pre-rabbinic exegesis more generally.[7] On the other hand, it may be anachronistic and misleading to use the same terminology for pre-rabbinic exegesis, and so instead of *gezerah shavah*, Avemarie calls this tool "lexematic association"; I would prefer to use the term "catchword connections."

In this section, I present some examples where the LXX translator of the TP is reminded of other biblical passages by means of one or more "catchwords." In Amos 1:3 the catchphrase בחרצות הברזל, with pregnant women as the victims (הרות in the Hebrew *Vorlage* of the LXX), reminds the Greek translator of incidents of torture described in 1 Chr 20:3, where the similar phrase ובחריצי הברזל is found.

In Amos 1:11, the catchword שחת reminds the translator of Gen 38:9. He understands that sexual defilement is present in both passages and translates his text accordingly.

Amos 6:6 and Isa 25:6 share many contextual affinities in their descriptions of rich banquets, including the catchword שמנים. On the basis of this connection, the Greek translator of Amos reflects מזקק from Isa 25:6 in his translation of Amos 6:6.

In the above cases, the catchword or catchphrase activates the intertextual connection in the mind of the translator and directs his understanding of the passage that he is rendering.

However, not all cases that display apparent connections between two texts because of the presence of a catchword are necessarily intertextual. Although in many cases these apparent connections have been attributed to the initiative of the Greek translator by commentators, further examination of these in the section entitled "Apparent Intertextual Connections" (below) shows that the Greek renderings are to be accounted for differently.

---

5. Gary G. Porton, "Hermeneutics, A Critical Approach," *EOM* 1:255–60.

6. Saul Lieberman, *Hellenism in Jewish Palestine: Studies in the Literary Transmission, Beliefs and Manners of Palestine in the I Century B.C.E.—IV Century C. E.* (Texts and Studies of the Jewish Theological Seminary of America 18; New York: The Jewish Theological Seminary of America, 1950), 47–68.

7. Avemarie, "Interpreting Scripture Through Scripture," 84.

In LXX Hos 4:9, the presence of διαβούλια for מעללים triggered the suggestion that there is some connection to the Greek rendering διαβούλια for מעלות in Ezek 11:5. Such a connection was found wanting and other contextual reasons are given to account for the translational choice by both LXX texts independently.

The verb ἐνίσχυσεν in LXX Hos 12:4–5 suggests the influence of LXX Gen 32:29 upon the Greek translator of the TP, through the catchword שרה. Our study, however, shows that the Greek renderings in LXX Hos 12:4–5 can be explained from the influence of the Post-Biblical Hebrew/Aramaic שרר.

No fewer than three catchwords are noted as between Amos 1:15 and Jer 30:19[MT49:3], which could explain why the plus ἱερεῖς in LXX Amos 1:15 would have been borrowed from the Jeremiah text. A closer examination, however, shows that, while such an intertextual borrowing does exist, it was not the translator's doing. The assimilation of Amos 1:15 to Jer 30:19[MT49:3] goes back to the early stages of the Hebrew textual tradition.

In the case of LXX Amos 4:2, although the verse gives the impression that the Greek translator was reminded of LXX Jer 1:13 (possibly through סיר functioning as the catchword), no such relationship could be demonstrated. Instead, the Greek translator of the TP was using imagery which could better communicate the Hebrew metaphor of Amos 4:2 to his Greek audience.

Taken as a whole, the cases examined in this chapter demonstrate that the Greek translator sometimes understood his source text with the aid of catchwords and their related biblical passages. However, in some cases his renderings can be explained as arising from the employment of other tools, such as contextual exegesis, appeal to Post-Biblical Hebrew/Aramaic nuances for Classical Hebrew words, appropriation of imagery to Greek literary conventions, or from the existence of a different Hebrew *Vorlage*.

Amos 1:3

Amos 1:3

MT	LXX
כֹּה אָמַר יְהוָה עַל־שְׁלֹשָׁה פִּשְׁעֵי	καὶ εἶπε κύριος ἐπὶ ταῖς τρισὶν ἀσεβείαις
דַמֶּשֶׂק וְעַל־אַרְבָּעָה לֹא	Δαμασκοῦ καὶ ἐπὶ ταῖς τέσσαρσιν οὐκ
אֲשִׁיבֶנּוּ עַל־דּוּשָׁם בַּחֲרֻצוֹת	ἀποστραφήσομαι αὐτόν ἀνθ᾽ ὧν ἔπριζον πρίοσι
הַבַּרְזֶל אֶת־הַגִּלְעָד	σιδηροῖς τὰς ἐν γαστρὶ ἐχούσας τῶν ἐν Γαλααδ

Thus says the LORD: For three transgressions of Damascus, and for four, I will not revoke the punishment; because they have threshed Gilead with threshing sledges of iron. [NRSV]

And the Lord said: For three impious acts of Damascus, and for four, I will not turn away from him, because they were sawing pregnant women of those in Galaad asunder with iron saws. [NETS]

4 Kingdoms 8:12

MT	LXX
וַיֹּאמֶר חֲזָאֵל מַדּוּעַ אֲדֹנִי בֹּכֶה	καὶ εἶπεν Αζαηλ τί ὅτι ὁ κύριός μου κλαίει
וַיֹּאמֶר כִּי־יָדַעְתִּי אֵת אֲשֶׁר־תַּעֲשֶׂה	καὶ εἶπεν ὅτι οἶδα ὅσα ποιήσεις
לִבְנֵי יִשְׂרָאֵל רָעָה מִבְצְרֵיהֶם	τοῖς υἱοῖς Ισραηλ κακά τὰ ὀχυρώματα αὐτῶν
תְּשַׁלַּח בָּאֵשׁ וּבַחֻרֵיהֶם	ἐξαποστελεῖς ἐν πυρὶ καὶ τοὺς ἐκλεκτοὺς αὐτῶν
בַּחֶרֶב תַּהֲרֹג וְעֹלְלֵיהֶם	ἐν ῥομφαίᾳ ἀποκτενεῖς καὶ τὰ νήπια αὐτῶν
תְּרַטֵּשׁ וְהָרֹתֵיהֶם	ἐνσείσεις καὶ τὰς ἐν γαστρὶ ἐχούσας αὐτῶν
תְּבַקֵּעַ	ἀναρρήξεις

Hazael asked, "Why does my lord weep?" He answered, "Because I know the evil that you will do to the people of Israel; you will set their fortresses on fire, you will kill their young men with the sword, dash in pieces their little ones, and rip up their pregnant women." [NRSV]

And Hazael said, "Why is it that my lord weeps?" And he said, "Because I know what evil you will do to the sons of Israel; you will dispatch their fortresses by fire and kill their choice men by sword and drive into their infants and rip open their pregnant women." [NETS]

2 Kingdoms 12:31

MT	LXX
וְאֶת־הָעָם אֲשֶׁר־בָּהּ הוֹצִיא	καὶ τὸν λαὸν τὸν ὄντα ἐν αὐτῇ ἐξήγαγεν
וַיָּשֶׂם בַּמְּגֵרָה וּבַחֲרִצֵי	καὶ ἔθηκεν ἐν τῷ πρίονι καὶ ἐν τοῖς τριβόλοις
הַבַּרְזֶל וּבְמַגְזְרֹת הַבַּרְזֶל וְהֶעֱבִיר	τοῖς σιδηροῖς καὶ διήγαγεν
אוֹתָם [בַּמַּלְבֵּן] (בְּמַלְכֵּן) וְכֵן יַעֲשֶׂה	αὐτοὺς διὰ τοῦ πλινθείου καὶ οὕτως ἐποίησεν
לְכֹל עָרֵי בְנֵי־עַמּוֹן	πάσαις ταῖς πόλεσιν υἱῶν Αμμων
וַיָּשָׁב דָּוִד וְכָל־הָעָם	καὶ ἐπέστρεψεν Δαυιδ καὶ πᾶς ὁ λαὸς εἰς
יְרוּשָׁלָ͏ִם	Ιερουσαλημ

He brought out the people who were in it, and set them to work with saws and iron picks and iron axes, or sent them to the brickworks. Thus he did to all the cities of the Ammonites. Then David and all the people returned to Jerusalem. [NRSV]

And he brought out the people who were in it and set them at the saw and at the iron threshing machines and conducted them through the brickworks. And thus he did to all the cities of the sons of Ammon. And Dauid and all the people returned to Ierousalem. [NETS]

1 Chronicles 20:3

MT	LXX
וְאֶת־הָעָם אֲשֶׁר־בָּהּ הוֹצִיא	καὶ τὸν λαὸν τὸν ἐν αὐτῇ ἐξήγαγεν
וַיָּשַׂר בַּמְּגֵרָה וּבַחֲרִיצֵי הַבַּרְזֶל וּבַמְּגֵרוֹת	καὶ διέπρισεν πρίοσιν καὶ ἐν σκεπάρνοις σιδηροῖς
וְכֵן יַעֲשֶׂה דָוִיד לְכֹל עָרֵי	καὶ οὕτως ἐποίησεν Δαυιδ τοῖς πᾶσιν
בְנֵי־עַמּוֹן וַיָּשָׁב דָּוִיד	υἱοῖς Αμμων καὶ ἀνέστρεψεν Δαυιδ
וְכָל־הָעָם יְרוּשָׁלָ͏ם	καὶ πᾶς ὁ λαὸς αὐτοῦ εἰς Ιερουσαλημ
He brought out the people who were in it, and set them to work with saws and iron picks and axes. Thus David did to all the cities of the Ammonites. Then David and all the people returned to Jerusalem. [NRSV]	And he led out the people who were in it, and he sawed with saws and with iron adzes. And so Dauid did to all the sons of Ammon. And Dauid and all his people returned to Ierousalem. [NETS]

The oracle against Damascus in LXX Amos 1:3–5, with its reference to the ripping up of pregnant women, alludes to the predictions made by Elisha in 4 Kgdms 8:12 concerning Hazael's treatment of the people of Israel, after his ascension to the throne of Syria. Elisha predicts that Hazael will set Israel's strongholds on fire, kill their young men by the sword, dash their little ones into pieces, and, most importantly for our case, rip up their pregnant women. Generally, imagery similar to that in Elisha's prediction is used to describe the brutality of one nation against another (Hos 14:1; Nah 3:10; Isa 13:16, 18). However, our focus will be on the specific act of the "ripping up of pregnant women," which also describes Menahem's attack on Tiphsah in 4 Kgdms 15:16. This reference to brutality against pregnant women represents a plus in LXX Amos 1:3 *vis-à-vis* the MT.

LXX Amos 1:3

The Greek translator of Amos appears to have made the connection between the oracle against Damascus in 1:3 and Elisha's predictions concerning Hazael in 4 Kgms 8:12 more explicit through the plus of the "pregnant women." 4 Kingdoms 8:12, more than any other text, would have come to the mind of the translator since the immediate context clearly refers to the house of Hazael (cf. 1:4). Andersen and Freedman support the idea that the LXX wording, τὰς ἐν γαστρὶ ἐχούσας, is probably due to a connection with 4 Kgdms 8:12,[8] and so does Edward W. Glenny.[9]

8. Francis I. Andersen and David Noel Freedman, *Amos* (AB 24A; New York: Doubleday, 1989), 238–39.
9. "The LXX text makes the sin of Syria especially heinous and severe, and it shows that what they did fulfilled the prophecies of Elisha." Glenny, *Finding Meaning in the Text*, 157.

A closer look at the Greek text of Amos 1:3 reveals the following differences between the MT and the OG:

כֹּה	καὶ
אָמַר יְהוָה עַל־שְׁלֹשָׁה פִּשְׁעֵי	εἶπε κύριος ἐπὶ ταῖς τρισὶν ἀσεβείαις
דַמֶּשֶׂק	Δαμασκοῦ
וְעַל־אַרְבָּעָה לֹא אֲשִׁיבֶנּוּ	καὶ ἐπὶ ταῖς τέσσαρσιν οὐκ ἀποστραφήσομαι αὐτόν
עַל־דּוּשָׁם	ἀνθ᾽ ὧν ἔπριζον
בַּחֲרֻצוֹת הַבַּרְזֶל	πρίοσι σιδηροῖς
	τὰς ἐν γαστρὶ ἐχούσας τῶν ἐν
אֶת־הַגִּלְעָד	Γαλααδ

a. כה is rendered by καί. This is a peculiar rendering for the Greek translator of Amos since he usually renders כה by τάδε or οὕτως. One possibility is that the translator was influenced by the beginning of Amos 1:2, which has ויאמר, rendered by καὶ εἶπε. Another possibility is that the translator's *Vorlage* contained ויאמר instead of כה אמר.[10]

b. דושם is rendered by the third person plural imperfect verb ἔπριζον. A similar rendering of an infinitive construct with third person masculine plural suffix is found in 1:13 (ἀνέσχιζον for בקעם).

c. The object marker in את־הגלעד is ignored, and the "pregnant women" are added as the new object. The plus is made to fit well in the sentence by the addition of τῶν ἐν before Γαλααδ, thus generating the expression "the pregnant women of those in Galaad."

Possible Explanations

Before examining the rendering of דושם we must attempt to explain the plus in LXX Amos 1:3. There are three possible explanations:

a. The Greek translator is using a Hebrew *Vorlage* which contains this plus.

b. LXX Amos 1:3 is intertextually influenced by Amos 1:13 where the atrocities against Gilead's pregnant women are also mentioned.

c. LXX Amos 1:3 is intertextually influenced by 4 Kgdms 8:12.

---

10. The Achmimic version does not seem to follow the LXX and omits καί (W. Grossouw, *The Coptic Versions of the Minor Prophets* [Monumenta Biblica et Ecclesiastica 3; Rome: Pontifical Biblical Institute, 1938]). However, this could be attributed to the free style of the translator and cannot be used to argue for a different Greek *Vorlage* lacking καί. For the effect of this καί on the structural analysis of the passage, see Park, *The Book of Amos*, 144, 170.

Beginning with (a), it is actually the case that the discovery of a fragment containing Amos 1:3–5 (5QAmos or 5Q4) has shed some light on the LXX rendering. The text is transcribed as follows and appears to agree with the LXX rendering: הֹרֹ[ת] הגלֹעָ[ד].[11] The editors note the agreement with the LXX and explain the absence of הרות in the MT by homeoteleuton: א(רו)ת הרו)ת.[12] We should note that there is some degree of uncertainty concerning the letters marked with a circlet above them,[13] and also that this level of uncertainty appears to be slightly different in the transcription of *Biblia Qumranica*, published in 2005: הֹרֹוֹ[ת].[14] Despite the varying degrees of uncertainty, this fragment contains a reading that would naturally account for the corresponding plus in the LXX.

Other scholars, however, do not consider the possibility that הרות was in the Hebrew *Vorlage* of LXX Amos 1:3. George E. Howard, in his preface to the NETS translation of the Minor Prophets, says of the Greek translator's method that "he often uses what could be called tricks of the trade to make the text understandable."[15] Regarding Amos 1:3, he states the following:

> The general statement "threshed Gilead" is made into a more specific crime (i.e. "sawing pregnant women of those in Galaad asunder with iron saws"), perhaps more understandable to the translator and his readers, though the end result was basically the same. There is no way to predict when such variations will occur. The text is altered whenever the translator sees the need.[16]

Howard does not seem to consider the possibility of a different *Vorlage* behind this text, nor does he look for possible influences on the translator's decision to "alter" the text. Attributing these alterations to the freedom of the translator has its difficulties:

11. *DJD* 3:173, Pl. XXXVI, l. 3.
12. *DJD* 3:173.
13. "Letters are considered 'possible' if some ink is preserved and it conforms to the suggested letter but could also form any of several other letters sharing that feature; these are marked with a circlet above the letter (e.g., בֹּ). Claims made for letters so marked can be only as solid as the empirical basis supporting them." *DJD* 15:4.
14. ד, which used to be certain, now has a dot over it, indicating a damaged letter that can be safely identified, and וֹ, which previously could not be safely identified, now has a dot over it indicating some safety in identification. Beate Ego et al., eds., *Minor Prophets* (Biblia Qumranica 3B; Leiden: Brill, 2005), xvi, 49.
15. Howard, "To the Reader of the Twelve Prophets," 778.
16. Ibid.

a. the choice of τὰς ἐν γαστρὶ ἐχούσας is too specific to be simply epexegetical or clarifying of a difficult text. The translator could have said "the inhabitants of Gilead" in order to clarify, as the Targum does (as we shall see later);

b. if the plus τὰς ἐν γαστρὶ ἐχούσας originates with the Greek translator, then we need to explain how a Hebrew text like 5QAmos (or its ancestor) arose. Would a scribe change a Hebrew text on the basis of the LXX version, or did each add this plus independently of the other?

Prior to the Qumran discoveries, the LXX plus was viewed as borrowed from Amos 1:13,[17] but even after the publication of the DSS[18] some scholars continue to attribute this change to the influence of Amos 1:13 on the Greek translator.[19]

Another view has been proposed by Aaron W. Park, who states that "𝕲 reads הָרוֹת (pregnant women) instead of חרצות just as הָרוֹת...הגלעד in 1:13 (𝕲 τὰς ἐν γαστρὶ ἐχούσας τῶν Γαλααδιτῶν)."[20] This explanation creates more difficulties since, if τὰς ἐν γαστρὶ ἐχούσας represents a misreading of חרצות, this would mean that חרצות has been translated twice, the second time by πρίοσι. Again, הברזל would have had to be moved around for the translator to arrive at the reading הגלעד הרות. Rather, it seems more likely that חרצות הברזל stands behind πρίοσι σιδηροῖς.[21]

The simplest explanation for the plus in LXX Amos 1:3 appears to be that הרות was already present in the translator's *Vorlage* and the translator simply rendered הרות by the common Greek expression τὰς ἐν γαστρὶ ἐχούσας, used for "pregnant women." Therefore, I think that (a)

---

17. "Τὸ παρὰ τοῖς Ο´ «τὰς ἐν γαστρὶ ἐχούσας» προῆλθε προφανῶς ἐκ 1,13." V. Vellas, *Ἀμώς* (Athens: Astir, 1947), 25.

18. 5QAmos was published in 1962 in M. Baillet, J. T. Milik, and R. de Vaux, *Les "petites grottes" de Qumrân* (DJD 3; Oxford: Clarendon, 1962).

19. "The Septuagint has τὰς ἐν γαστρὶ ἐχούσας τῶν ἐν Γαλααδ, but compare 1.13." John Barton, *Amos's Oracles against the Nations: A Study of Amos 1.3–2.5* (SOTS Monograph Series 6; Cambridge: Cambridge University Press, 1980), 18 n. b. Also Sandro Paola Carbone and Giovanni Rizzi, *Il Libro di Amos: Lettura Ebraica, Greca e Aramaica* (Bologna: Dehoniane, 1993), 63 n. 9.

20. Park, *The Book of Amos*, 146.

21. So Tov and Polak, eds., *The Revised CATSS*. Johnson suggested that "the word חרוץ, 'sharp spike,' seems to have suggested the rendering." Moreover, he adds that "this freedom in treatment of the text points to a fairly early date." Sherman E. Johnson, "The Septuagint Translators of Amos" (Ph.D. diss., University of Chicago, 1936), 28.

is the best explanation for the presence of τὰς ἐν γαστρὶ ἐχούσας in LXX Amos 1:3.

In answer to the question of influence from 4 Kgdms 8:12 on LXX Amos 1:3, it must be admitted that there is no such indication. It is not possible to demonstrate that τὰς ἐν γαστρὶ ἐχούσας was meant to show that what Damascus did fulfilled the prophecies of Elisha (contra Andersen and Freedman, and Glenny)[22] since this expression is not exclusive to LXX 4 Kgdms 8:12 but common throughout LXX (see Exod 21:22; Judg 13:5, 7; Job 21:10; Hos 14:1; Isa 40:11). The reasons for the translator's peculiar choice of πρίζω and πρίων and the possibility of intertextuality behind these choices must be sought separately. Before examining the Greek translation we shall first look at the Hebrew reading of Amos 1:3 in 5QAmos.

5QAmos
At the Hebrew level, it is difficult to know whether the Amos 1:3 reading represented by 5QAmos (first century C.E.)[23] is secondary and inspired by Amos 1:13 or 2 Kgs 8:12, or whether the MT is secondary due to the loss of consonants through homeoteleuton. The MT reading is also present in 4QXII[g] (50–25 B.C.E.) where the object marker for Gilead is obvious: הגלעד [ת]א.[24]

A survey of the versional evidence reveals that the plus τὰς ἐν γαστρὶ ἐχούσας is preserved in all Greek manuscripts and in the daughter translations. The hexaplaric texts, however, follow the MT. Theodoret notes that Symmachus has την Γαλαάδ as direct object, and he also testifies to the agreement of the three: τὴν αὐτὴν δὲ διάνοιαν καὶ ὁ Ἀκ. καὶ ὁ Θεοδ. τεθείκασι.[25] The Peshiṭta follows the MT as well, as does the Targum, though it elaborates in typical fashion on the object of "threshing": "Thus says the Lord, For three transgressions of Damascus, and for four, I will not *forgive them*; because they threshed *the inhabitants of the land of Gilead* with threshing sledges of iron."[26] The Targumic addition of "the

---

22. "The LXX has the same gloss—*tas en gastri echousas*. This wording is probably due to connection with 2 Kgs 8:12 (Hazael!)." Andersen and Freedman, *Amos*, 238–39. Cf. Glenny, *Finding Meaning in the Text*, 157.

23. *DJD* 3:173.

24. *DJD* 15:294 frg. 41 l. 2.

25. F. Field, *Origenis Hexaplorum Quae Supersunt: Sive Veterum Interpretum Graecorum in Totum Vetus Testamentum Fragmenta* (2 vols.; Oxford: Clarendon, 1875), 2:967.

26. The explanation of a similar "threshing" idiom is also evident in the Targum of Isa 41:15 where the mountains and the hills to be threshed are paraphrased as the Gentiles and their kingdoms.

inhabitants of the land of" follows standard Targumic practice with such expressions as "they threshed *Gilead*" (e.g. Amos 2:5; 3:14; 5:5). A similar tendency may be observed in the LXX as well. LXX Micah 4:13 is one example of many[27] where an object (αὐτούς) is added when absent or unclear in the Hebrew:

קוּמִי וָדוֹשִׁי בַת־צִיּוֹן   ἀνάστηθι καὶ ἀλόα αὐτούς θύγατερ Σιων

The need to identify the object of the verb may have been the reason which triggered the addition of הרות in 5QAmos. But why "pregnant women" and not simply "inhabitants"? Our two options are again: (a) Amos 1:13, the only other place in Amos where Gilead is the victim, may have provided the desiderated element with which to fill the gap of 1:3, and (b) 2 Kgs 8:12, where the prediction concerning Hazael's harming of Israel's pregnant women is made, may have been the source of influence.

Since Amos 1:13 has the phrase הרות הגלעד, which is identical to the reading found in 5QAmos, הָרוֹ[ת] הגלע[ד], it is more likely that the copyist, wanting to identify the object of על־דושם in Amos 1:3, drew on the "parallel" text concerning Gilead's attack in Amos 1:13, thus internally harmonizing the two texts. The proximity of Amos 1:13 to Amos 1:3 and the mention of Gilead makes Amos 1:13 a more probable source of influence on the copyist of 5QAmos than 2 Kgs 8:12.[28]

Saws of Iron

LXX Amos 1:3 also has the peculiar picture of humans being "sawn asunder with iron saws," whereas the Hebrew text talks of "threshing." Comparable behaviour is described in only one other passage, where King David appears to be doing the same thing to Rabbah and all the

27. Examples of clarifying pluses: Amos 2:4 (LXX "*sons of* Judah" / MT "Judah"), 2:4 (LXX "the same lies *which they did*" / MT "the same lies"); 3:4, 5 (LXX "if it has captured *something*" / MT "if it has captured"); 4:1 (LXX "bring *us* that we may drink" / MT "bring that we may drink"); 5:6 (LXX "it will devour *him*" / MT "it will devour").

28. The view that הרות in 5QAmos was influenced by Amos 1:13 is shared by Alberto J. Soggin, *The Prophet Amos: A Translation and Commentary* (London: SCM, 1987), 32–33; Andersen and Freedman, *Amos*, 238–39; Shalom M. Paul, *A Commentary on the Book of Amos* (Hermeneia; Minneapolis: Fortress, 1991), 47 n. 32; Jan de Waard and William A. Smalley, *A Handbook on the Book of Amos* (UBS Handbook Series; New York: United Bible Societies, 1994), 218 n. 10; Billy K. Smith and Frank S. Page, *Amos, Obadiah, Jonah* (NAC 19B; Nashville: Broadman & Holman, 1995), 48–49; Gary V. Smith, *Amos* (rev. ed.; Fearn: Christian Focus, 1998), 62.

Ammonite cities.[29] This incident is described in 2 Sam 12:31 and 1 Chr 20:3 where in both cases the phrase ובחרצי הברזל or ובחריצי הברזל (cf. בחרצות in Amos 1:3) is present:

2 Sam 12:31a:

וְאֶת־הָעָם אֲשֶׁר־בָּהּ הוֹצִיא	καὶ τὸν λαὸν τὸν ὄντα ἐν αὐτῇ ἐξήγαγεν
וַיָּשֶׂם בַּמְּגֵרָה	καὶ ἔθηκεν ἐν τῷ πρίονι
וּבַחֲרִצֵי הַבַּרְזֶל וּבְמַגְזְרֹת הַבַּרְזֶל	καὶ ἐν τοῖς τριβόλοις τοῖς σιδηροῖς
וְהֶעֱבִיר אוֹתָם (בְּמַלְכֵּן) [בְּמַלְבֵּן]	καὶ διήγαγεν αὐτοὺς διὰ τοῦ πλινθείου
וְכֵן יַעֲשֶׂה לְכֹל עָרֵי	καὶ οὕτως ἐποίησεν πάσαις ταῖς πόλεσιν
בְנֵי־עַמּוֹן	υἱῶν Αμμων

1 Chr 20:3a:

וְאֶת־הָעָם אֲשֶׁר־בָּהּ הוֹצִיא	καὶ τὸν λαὸν τὸν ἐν αὐτῇ ἐξήγαγεν
וַיָּשַׂר בַּמְּגֵרָה	καὶ διέπρισεν πρίοσιν
וּבַחֲרִיצֵי הַבַּרְזֶל וּבַמְּגֵרוֹת	καὶ ἐν σκεπάρνοις σιδηροῖς
וְכֵן יַעֲשֶׂה דָוִיד לְכֹל	καὶ οὕτως ἐποίησεν Δαυιδ τοῖς πᾶσιν
עָרֵי בְנֵי־עַמּוֹן	υἱοῖς Αμμων

2 Samuel 12:31. 2 Samuel 12:31 has שׂים as the second verb, which allows one to interpret the verse as NRSV has done, that is, by avoiding any connotations of torture: "He brought out the people who were in it, and *set* (italics mine) them to work with saws and iron picks and iron axes, or sent them to the brickworks. Thus he did to all the cities of the Ammonites. Then David and all the people returned to Jerusalem."

The Targum translates the verse literally except for the rendering of והעביר אותם במלכן/במלבן by "and he dragged them in the streets." Saldarini and Harrington note that the Targum substitutes a more usual form of punishment.[30] The *Qere* מַלְבֵּן seems to have the meaning of a "brick-mould" or "quadrangle,"[31] which latter could have been connected with streets in the mind of the Targumist. Whatever the explanation, "dragging people in the streets" does not indicate clearly how the Targumist accounted for the expression. It could be either a vivid picture of forced labour or a humiliating parade of prisoners.[32] Likewise, in the

---

29. Judg 8:7, 16 refer to the "threshing" or "trampling" (דוש) of people, but no reference to "sawing" or "saws" is made.

30. Harrington and Saldarini, *Targum Jonathan*, 181 n. 18.

31. BDB 527.

32. In Roman Egypt this appears to have been a form of torture inflicted on Jewish families: "Outside this quarter individual Jews were set upon, some burned to death, others dragged through the cobbled streets until their bodies were

case of the LXX, it is probable that the verse was understood to describe certain forms of torture inflicted on the Ammonites (ἔθηκεν ἐν τῷ πρίονι). The phrase διήγαγεν αὐτοὺς διὰ τοῦ πλινθείου, however, is also unclear in meaning, and explanations vary. The feminine noun, πλινθεία, seems to refer to brick-making (LXX Exod 1:14; 5:8, 14, 18, 19), but the neuter noun could be a "brick factory" or "brickworks."[33] Walters gives it the meaning "big plate."[34]

Regardless of what was actually meant by the passage, it looks as if the actions of David in this particular instance have come to be understood in the light of tortures commonly inflicted on war prisoners. Josephus reflects such a tradition: τοὺς δ᾽ ἄνδρας αἰκισάμενος διέφθειρε ταῦτα δὲ καὶ τὰς ἄλλας τῶν Ἀμμανιτῶν πόλεις διέθηκεν ἐλὼν αὐτὰς κατὰ κράτος (Josephus, *Ant.* 7.161b).

This understanding seems to have developed early, as evidenced in 1 Chr 20:3 in both the Hebrew and the Greek.[35]

1 Chronicles 20:3. The parallel passage in 1 Chr 20:3 has the verb שׂור, which means "to saw."[36] The Targum reads MT וַיָּשַׂר with a causative sense, translating "he made them saw with saws."[37] In the LXX version, however, it is obvious that the Greek translator took the sons of Ammon to be the victims of the "sawing" (note also the omission of "cities" in the translation).

dismembered." John M. G. Barclay, *Jews in the Mediterranean Diaspora: From Alexander to Trajan (323 BCE–117 CE)* (Edinburgh: T. & T. Clark, 1996), 53.

33. LEH 499.

34. Walters, *The Text of the Septuagint*, 285.

35. Driver, on the basis of Hoffmann's views and the emendation of העביר to העביד, understands the passage to be referring to the employment of the Ammonites in different public works and וישׂר in 1 Chr 20:3 to be a textual corruption. He does, however, hold that Amos 1:3 is indeed referring to torture inflicted by the Syrians (S. R. Driver, *Notes on the Hebrew Text and the Topography of the Books of Samuel* [2d ed.; Oxford: Clarendon, 1913], 294–97). Similarly, McCarter holds that the object of שׂים is the city itself, not the people (P. Kyle McCarter, *II Samuel* [AB 9; New York: Doubleday, 1984], 311, 313). On the other hand, Gordon leaves the possibility of mistreatment open, especially in the light of David's similar behaviour towards the Moabites and Edomites (2 Sam 8:2; 1 Kgs 11:15–25). See Robert P. Gordon, *1 & 2 Samuel: A Commentary* (Exeter: Paternoster, 1986), 261.

36. BDB 965.

37. R. Le Déaut and J. Robert, *Targum des Chroniques.* Vol. 1, *Introduction et Traduction* (Analecta Biblica 51; Rome: Biblical Institute, 1971).

Sawing or Threshing?
The language of 1 Chr 20:3 suggests that this text influenced the Greek translator of Amos 1:3.[38] However, first we need to examine whether he could have come up with ἔπριζον πρίοσι apart from any such influence.

πρίζω/דוש. Looking at Amos 1:3 (על-דושם בחרצות הברזל), we note that the verb דוש means "thresh" or "tread," but never "saw."[39] In the LXX דוש is usually represented by ἀλοᾶν, καταπατεῖν, καταπάτησις and the like. Nowhere else in the Greek Bible does πρίζω represent דוש. The evidence within LXX TP is fairly consistent. In LXX Mic 4:13 the Greek translator seems to know the meaning of דוש, rendering the imperative דושי by ἀλόα, whereas in LXX Hab 3:12 and LXX Hos 10:11 he seems to be translating more freely. It is obvious that in Amos 1:3 the translator does not adopt a conventional term for דוש, but instead chooses the specific act of "sawing."[40] However, it is possible that, encountering הרות in his *Vorlage* and being aware of the "cutting" of הרות in 1:13, he decides to render דוש by a verb for "cutting." This is the meaning of πρίζω in Susanna (Th) 1:59, and it can apparently be done with a sword: εἶπεν δὲ αὐτῷ Δανιηλ ὀρθῶς ἔψευσαι καὶ σὺ εἰς τὴν σεαυτοῦ κεφαλήν μένει γὰρ ὁ ἄγγελος τοῦ θεοῦ τὴν ῥομφαίαν ἔχων πρίσαι σε μέσον ὅπως ἐξολεθρεύσῃ ὑμᾶς.

It is possible that πρίζω could have a general sense of "violent cutting," unless the instrument was specified. LXX 1 Chronicles 20:3 may indicate that one could saw/cut with either a πρίων or a σκέπαρνον, since the translator supplied no additional verb for the second tool.

πρίων/חרוץ. However, only where either מגרה[41] or משור[42] is present does πρίων appear (2 Kgdms 12:31; 1 Chr 20:3; Isa 10:15).[43] חרוץ or חריץ is

---

38. The similar construction in the two texts is also noted by Glenny (*Finding Meaning in the Text*, 156–57).
39. BDB 190.
40. Snaith thinks that the LXX, by translating "sawed with iron saws," is evidently guessing (Norman Snaith, *The Book of Amos*. Part 2, *Translation and Notes* [Study Notes on Bible Books; London: Epworth, 1946], 16), whereas Soggin holds that the LXX did not understand the verb דוש but caught the atrocity in question (*The Prophet Amos*, 32–33).
41. "[S]aw, used in cutting stone מְגֵרֹות בַּמְּגֵרָה 1 K 7[9]; used in torture (or as tools for enforced labour) of captives 2 S 12[31a] 1 Ch 20[3a]." BDB 176.
42. Noun from נשר "saw." BDB 673.
43. Aquila has πριστήρ and Symmachus πρίων for מגרה in 3 Kgdms 7:46[MT 9]. The word πρίων occurs in Jdt 3:9, but there is disagreement about what the underlying Hebrew word may have been. Some scholars have suggested a misreading of

never translated by πρίων apart from LXX Amos 1:3.[44] Elsewhere in the Minor Prophets the translator seems to adjust his renderings contextually whenever חרוץ shows up (Joel 4:14—δίκη; Zech 9:3—χρυσίον [= חָרוּץ]).[45]

The idea of "sawing" in LXX Amos 1:3, if taken on its own, could be explained in the light of Amos 1:13, if one accepts its general meaning of "cutting." But the specific instrument πρίων, accompanying the verb, seems to have been imported into the LXX translation of Amos 1:3, in rendering בחרצות. But is it possible that "threshing" instruments were referred to as "saws" in Greek? Perhaps the Greek translator had in mind certain saw-like threshing instruments. This could be supported by LXX Isa 41:15, where the LXX translator speaks of saw-shaped threshing cart wheels:

הִנֵּה שַׂמְתִּיךְ לְמוֹרַג	ἰδοὺ ἐποίησά σε ὡς τροχοὺς ἁμάξης
חָרוּץ חָדָשׁ בַּעַל פִּיפִיּוֹת	ἀλοῶντας καινοὺς πριστηροειδεῖς
תָּדוּשׁ הָרִים וְתָדֹק וּגְבָעוֹת	καὶ ἀλοήσεις ὄρη καὶ λεπτυνεῖς βουνοὺς
כַּמֹּץ תָּשִׂים	καὶ ὡς χνοῦν θήσεις

פִיפִיּוֹת, "mouths," is also used in Ps 149:6 with the sense of "edges," in describing a "two-edged" sword. Commenting on Isa 41:15, North says that "a threshing board was a heavy wooden board *studded with* metal *teeth* on its underside."[46] While metal is not explicitly stated in the verse, Dalman thinks that what is described in Isa 41:15 is most likely a threshing board with iron teeth instead of stone. He notes that the Targum renders this instrument as being "full of points" (מלי סמפורין), thus presenting an image of a "saw-like" instrument instead of a two-edged tool. Dalman also notes how the Targumist in Chronicles seems to relate the instrument mentioned in Isa 41:15 to that in 1 Chr 20:3 with his addition of "points" (סיפורין סמפורין) to his description of the harrows with which the sons of Ammon were made to "saw":[47]

---

mîšôr, "plain," as *maśśôr*, "saw." See Carey A. Moore, *Judith* (AB 40B; New York: Doubleday, 1985), 143. However, a Hebrew original for the book of Judith is by no means certain (see Toni Craven, *Artistry and Faith in the Book of Judith* [SBLDS 70; Chico: Scholars Press, 1983], 4–5).

44. In Isa 41:15, חרוץ is believed to stand behind ἀλοῶντας, not πριστηροειδεῖς. See Tov and Polak, *The Revised CATSS*.

45. The LXX knows (or invents) many meanings for חרוץ: χρυσίον (Ps 67[MT 68]:14; Prov 3:14; 8:10, 19; 16:16; Zech 9:3); γλωσσότμητος (Lev 22:22); ἀνδρεῖος (Prov 10:4; 13:4); ἐκλεκτός (Prov 12:24); καθαρός (Prov 12:27); δίκη (Joel 4:14); σκληρότης (Isa 28:27); ἀλοῶν (Isa 41:15); μῆκος (Dan 9:25).

46. Christopher R. North, *The Second Isaiah* (Oxford: Clarendon, 1964), 99 (italics original).

47. Dalman, *Arbeit und Sitte in Palästina*, 3:82.

MT 1 Chronicles 20:3	Targum 1 Chronicles 20:3[48]
וְאֶת־הָעָם אֲשֶׁר־בָּהּ הוֹצִיא וַיָּשַׂר	וְיָת עַמָּא דִיבַהּ אַגְלִי וּמְסָאַר יָתְהוֹן
בַּמְּגֵרָה וּבַחֲרִצֵי	סְמְפוֹרִין[50] בְּמַסָּארִין וּבְמוֹרִיגֵי סֵיפוֹרִין[49]
הַבַּרְזֶל וּבַמְּגֵרוֹת וְכֵן יַעֲשֶׂה דָוִיד לְכֹל	דְּפַרְזְלָא וְהַכְדֵין עֲבַד דָּוִד לְכָל
עָרֵי בְנֵי־עַמּוֹן	קִרְוֵי בְּנֵי עַמּוֹן
And the people who were in it, he brought out and sawed with the saw and with iron picks and with saws. Thus David did to all the cities of the sons of Ammon.	And the people who were in it, he deported and he made them saw with saws and with harrows with iron points. And thus did David to all the cities of the sons of Ammon.

For the Targumist, it is not the harrow (חריץ) that is made of iron, but the points on it. These harrows appear to be similar to saws, but not identical with saws. במגרה is rendered by בְּמַסָּארִין but ובחריצי by וּבְמוֹרִיגֵי ("an implement with grooves or indentations, esp. threshing sledge").[51] It is obvious that the Targumist is aware of threshing tools which look like saws due to their iron points, but an actual saw is something different and is used for different purposes.

So are there any indications of "sawing" and "threshing" functioning as synonyms in Greek? Is πρίζω ever used in the context of threshing elsewhere in Greek literature? Moulton and Milligan note that this rare Hellenistic verb is used for the sawing of date-palms in CP Herm. I, 28.11.[52] Apart from "sawing," the verb can be used for the "gnashing" or "grinding" of teeth (Symmachus on Ps 34[MT35]:16), for "biting," and also metaphorically for being "irritated" or "provoked."[53] An edict from Ephesus uses πρίζω for the cutting of stones.[54]

The noun πρίων shows up in the Duke Documentary Papyri database in various lists of building tools along with σκέπαρνον, τέρετρον,

48. Text taken from Le Déaut and Robert, *Targum des Chroniques*. Vol. 2, *Texte et Glossaire* (Analecta Biblica 51; Rome: Biblical Institute, 1971).

49. C = Manuscrit de Cambridge (*Ms. Or. Ee.* 5.9). Ibid., 2:58.

50. Supported by EL: E = Manuscrit d'Erfurt (maintenant Berlin MS. or. fol. 1210/1211) d'après l'édition de M. F. Beck (1680–1683); L = P. de Lagarde, *Hagiographa Chaldaice*, Leipzig, 1873. Le Déaut and Robert, *Targum des Chroniques*, 2:58.

51. *Jastrow*, 749–50.

52. J. H. Moulton and G. Milligan, *The Vocabulary of the Greek New Testament* (London: Hodder & Stoughton, 1930; repr., 1952), 536.

53. LSJ 1465.

54. G. H. R. Horsley, *New Documents Illustrating Early Christianity*. Vol. 4, *A Review of the Greek Inscriptions and Papyri Published in 1979* (North Ryde: The Ancient History Documentary Research Centre Macquarie University, 1987), 170.

τρυπάνιον, and others.⁵⁵ It appears that "saws" and "sawing" are mainly related to building, not threshing or ploughing.

Conclusion

If the Greek translator of Amos wanted to present humans as being "threshed" (דוש), literally or metaphorically, he could have used expressions appropriate to such activity: ἐγὼ ἀλοήσω τὰς σάρκας ὑμῶν; καταξανῶ τὰς σάρκας ὑμῶν (Judg 8:7[A]); ἔθεντο αὐτοὺς ὡς χοῦν εἰς καταπάτησιν (4 Kgdms 13:7); ἀλόα αὐτούς θύγατερ Σιων (Mic 4:13); καταπατηθήσεται ἡ Μωαβῖτις ὃν τρόπον πατοῦσιν ἅλωνα ἐν ἁμάξαις (Isa 25:10); ἐν θυμῷ κατάξεις ἔθνη (Hab 3:12). The fact that the translator portrays pregnant women being cut with saws is explained by his association of what is happening in Amos 1:3 with a specific type of torture with which he is familiar from 1 Chr 20:3.

The translator, upon encountering the catchphrase בחרצות הברזל used in connection with the "pregnant women" (הרות, present in his *Vorlage*), was immediately reminded of the other incident where various tools were used for cutting up people and where this exact catchphrase occurred. 2 Samuel 12:31 and 1 Chr 20:3 are the only candidates, with the latter being the more probable, since the verb matches the noun: וישר במגרה (διέπρισεν πρίοσιν). Already the act of "cutting" is associated with pregnant women in MT Amos 1:13, which explains the translator's emphasis on "cutting" by saws rather than "threshing." The translator is not borrowing the Greek translation of בחרצות הברזל. He is borrowing the brutal "sawing" scene of 1 Chr 20:3, of which this phrase reminds him. He replaces על־דושם בחרצות with וישר במגרה. It is possible that the Greek translator of Amos was aware of the Greek text of 1 Chr 20:3 and that he has borrowed and adjusted the Greek phrase διέπρισεν πρίοσιν, converting it into ἔπριζον πρίοσι, but this is difficult to prove. We can only observe the influence of what was perceived by the Greek translator of Amos to be a sawing torture scene in 1 Chr 20:3 on his translation of Amos 1:3.⁵⁶

55. *BGU* VI, 1295, 3; *P.Cair.Zen.* IV, 59782a, 5, 70; *P.Iand.* VIII, 148, v, 2.

56. Many commentators allow that a literal torture associated with the brutalities described in 2 Sam 12:31 and 1 Chr 20:3 is described in Amos 1:3: Ernest Arthur Edgill, *The Book of Amos* (2d ed.; London: Methuen, 1926), 6; Richard S. Cripps, *A Critical and Exegetical Commentary on the Book of Amos* (London: SPCK, 1929), 119; Harper, *A Critical and Exegetical Commentary on Amos and Hosea*, 17–18. Others allow for literal torture in Amos 1:3, but without any association with David's actions: S. R. Driver, *Joel and Amos* (Cambridge Bible; Cambridge: Cambridge University Press, 1897), 131; Page H. Kelley, *The Book of Amos: A Study Manual* (Shield Bible Study Outlines; Grand Rapids: Baker, 1966), 33; Barton,

Amos 1:11

Amos 1:11

MT	LXX
כֹּה אָמַר יְהוָה עַל־שְׁלֹשָׁה פִּשְׁעֵי	τάδε λέγει κύριος ἐπὶ ταῖς τρισὶν ἀσεβείαις
אֱדוֹם וְעַל־אַרְבָּעָה	τῆς Ιδουμαίας καὶ ἐπὶ ταῖς τέσσαρσιν
לֹא אֲשִׁיבֶנּוּ	οὐκ ἀποστραφήσομαι αὐτούς
עַל־רָדְפוֹ	ἕνεκα τοῦ διῶξαι αὐτοὺς
בַחֶרֶב אָחִיו	ἐν ῥομφαίᾳ τὸν ἀδελφὸν αὐτοῦ
וְשִׁחֵת רַחֲמָיו	καὶ ἐλυμήνατο μήτραν ἐπὶ γῆς
וַיִּטְרֹף לָעַד אַפּוֹ	καὶ ἥρπασεν εἰς μαρτύριον φρίκην αὐτοῦ
וְעֶבְרָתוֹ שְׁמָרָה נֶצַח	καὶ τὸ ὅρμημα αὐτοῦ ἐφύλαξεν εἰς νεῖκος

Thus says the LORD:
For three transgressions of
Edom, and for four, I will not
revoke the punishment;
because he pursued his brother
with the sword
and cast off all pity;
he maintained his anger
perpetually,
and kept his wrath forever.
[NRSV]

This is what the Lord says:
For three impious acts of Idumea
and for four, I will not turn away from
them;
because they pursued his brother with a
sword;
and he spoiled a womb upon the ground,
and seized his shivering fright for a
testimony,
and kept his onslaught unto victory.
[NETS]

Genesis 38:9

MT	LXX
וַיֵּדַע אוֹנָן כִּי לֹּא לוֹ	γνοὺς δὲ Αυναν ὅτι οὐκ αὐτῷ
יִהְיֶה הַזָּרַע	ἔσται τὸ σπέρμα
וְהָיָה אִם־בָּא אֶל־אֵשֶׁת	ἐγίνετο ὅταν εἰσήρχετο πρὸς τὴν γυναῖκα
אָחִיו וְשִׁחֵת אַרְצָה	τοῦ ἀδελφοῦ αὐτοῦ ἐξέχεεν ἐπὶ τὴν γῆν
לְבִלְתִּי נְתָן־זֶרַע לְאָחִיו	τοῦ μὴ δοῦναι σπέρμα τῷ ἀδελφῷ αὐτοῦ

Amos's Oracles, 19; Robert Martin-Achard and Paul S. Re'emi, *God's People in Crisis* (International Theological Commentary; Edinburgh: Handsel; Grand Rapids: Eerdmans, 1984), 17; Soggin, *The Prophet Amos*, 32–33; Smith and Page, *Amos, Obadiah, Jonah*, 48–49. Others view the language of Amos 1:3 as metaphorical, denoting general mistreatment or economic exploitation: Erling Hammershaimb, *The Book of Amos: A Commentary* (trans. John Sturdy; Oxford: Blackwell, 1970), 26; Wilhelm Rudolph, *Joel–Amos–Obadja–Jona* (KAT 13/2; Gütersloh: Gerd Mohn, 1971), 130; John H. Hayes, *Amos the Eighth Century Prophet: His Times and His Preaching* (Nashville: Abingdon, 1988), 71–72; Andersen and Freedman, *Amos*, 237; Harry Mowvley, *The Books of Amos & Hosea* (Epworth Commentaries; London: Epworth, 1991), 20; Paul, *Amos*, 47; Pietro Bovati and Roland Meynet, *Le livre du prophète Amos* (Paris: Cerf, 1994), 41; Waard and Smalley, *A Handbook on the Book of Amos*, 32; Smith, *Amos*, 74–75; Richard James Coggins, *Joel and Amos* (The New Century Bible Commentary; Sheffield: Sheffield Academic, 2000), 89.

But since Onan knew that the offspring would not be his, he spilled his semen on the ground whenever he went in to his brother's wife, so that he would not give offspring to his brother. [NRSV]	But because Aunan knew that the offspring would not be his, it would come about that he would pour out his semen upon the ground when he would go in to his brother's wife so that he would not give offspring to his brother. [NETS]

The LXX of Amos 1:11 contains certain hints which give the impression that the translator may have been reminded of Gen 38:9. A few commentators have suggested this, and with considerable confidence. Shalom Paul thinks that the presence of the plus ἐπὶ γῆς ("upon the ground") in the LXX is "*clearly* [emphasis added] influenced by the expression in Gen 38:9, וְשִׁחֵת אַרְצָה (G ἐξέχεεν ἐπὶ τὴν γῆν; 'he poured out on the ground')."[57] Daniel Sperber similarly states that "Ἐπί γῆς is *surely* [emphasis added] an interpretation based on a comparison with Gen. XXXVIII:9: ἐξέχεεν ἐπὶ τὴν γῆν—ושחת ארצה."[58] The connection with Gen 38:9 is also noted by John H. Hayes.[59] No explicit argumentation is offered to justify this certainty, and this invites an examination of LXX Amos 1:11 to see whether there are adequate grounds for holding this position. In order to clarify the issue we shall first examine whether the LXX translation of Amos 1:11 is plausible.[60]

First, we should note that the translator does not seem to be concerned about maintaining a consistency with the rendering of the נו- third masculine singular suffix. He shifts freely from plural to singular without worrying about how the context is affected. In 1:3 he renders אשיבנו using the third person masculine singular αὐτόν even though the following clause על־דושם takes him to the third person plural ἔπριζον. If he had been consciously referring to Damascus (a feminine name) he would have had to render the suffix in אשיבנו with the third person feminine singular, as in 1:9 where αὐτήν possibly refers to Tyre, a feminine name, regardless of the plural in the following clause על־הסגירם. In 1:11 אשיבנו is rendered by ἀποστραφήσομαι αὐτούς, using a third person

---

57. Paul, *A Commentary on the Book of Amos*, 65 n. 219.

58. Daniel Sperber, "Varia Midrashica IV. 1: Esau and His Mother's Womb—A Note on Amos 1:11," *REJ* 137 (1978): 151. See also Hayes, *Amos the Eighth Century Prophet*, 92.

59. Hayes, *Amos the Eighth Century Prophet*, 92.

60. The expression ἐπὶ γῆς is very common in the LXX: e.g. Deut 32:24; 1 Chr 29:15; 4 Macc. 15:15; Ps 109(MT 110):6; Job 19:25; Lam 4:21. See also *Letter of Aristeas* 147.6; Diodorus, *Bibliotheca historica* 20.93.3.

masculine plural. In the light of this inconsistency we shall not place much significance on the shift from plural (διῶξαι αὐτοὺς) to singular (ἀδελφὸν αὐτοῦ) in analyzing v. 11.

The usual interpretation of ושחת רחמיו reflected in English versions is "he stifled his mercy" (e.g. NIV, NASB). Others have "he cast off all pity" or something similar (e.g. KJV, JPS, ESV). In 1929, Cripps translated this phrase by "was (or kept) crushing down all pity" or "was destroying (or corrupting) his compassions,"[61] but many commentators since then have objected to this abstract rendering of the verse and have looked for a more solid object for שחת.

Shalom Paul criticizes the meaning "stifle/suppress" for שחת as a "makeshift" one, which is "totally unattested in connection with human emotions." He also expects that רחמיו, the object of שחת, would be parallel to אחיו and, therefore, would need to represent something more concrete than an abstract notion like "affection, mercy." He leans towards the meaning of "young women," as in Judg 5:30 (רחם רחמתים), a meaning for which there is cognate support in the Moabite Stele (*l.* 17).[62] Paul interprets the text as referring to the killing of women. He thinks the verse presents a merism: Edom persecuted both males (אחיו) and females (רחמיו), that is, he attacked the entire population. However, he does not completely disregard the meaning of "mercy" for רחמיו, being willing to see a double entendre or Janus-like construction.[63] Andersen and Freedman, after Fishbane, also lean towards a solid object for שחת rather than an abstraction ("compassion"). They prefer a concrete noun which describes either a person or a group in a unique kinship relationship, so they translate רחמיו as "his/their allies."[64]

Amos 1:11—The LXX and Other Greek Versions
When moving to the Greek versions, the ambiguity is still present. Apart from the LXX, which reads "womb," the Three have σπλάγχνα, which can mean both "inward parts, entrails" and "love, affection." The word

---

61. Cripps, *A Critical and Exegetical Commentary on the Book of Amos*, 130–31. Similarly, Robert B. Coote translates this as "covenant mercy." "Amos 1:11: RḤMYW," *JBL* 90 (1971): 208.

62. John C. L. Gibson, *Textbook of Syrian Semitic Inscriptions* (Oxford: Clarendon, 1971), 1:75.

63. Paul, *A Commentary on the Book of Amos*, 64–65.

64. Andersen and Freedman, *Amos*, 266–67; Michael Fishbane, "The Treaty Background of Amos 1[11] and Related Matters," *JBL* 89 (1970): 313–18. Others prefer to render "friends"; see S. David Sperling, "Biblical *rḥm* I and *rḥm* II," *JANES* 19 (1989): 159.

can therefore be used both literally (e.g. *4 Macc.* 11:19: καὶ ὀβελίσκους ὀξεῖς πυρώσαντες τοῖς νώτοις προσέφερον καὶ τὰ πλευρὰ διαπείραντες αὐτοῦ τὰ σπλάγχνα διέκαιον, "They heated sharp spits in the fire and applied them to his back, pierced his sides and burned his entrails" [NETS]) and metaphorically (e.g. Sir 33:5: τροχὸς ἁμάξης σπλάγχνα μωροῦ καὶ ὡς ἄξων στρεφόμενος ὁ διαλογισμὸς αὐτοῦ, "The emotions of a foolish person are like a wheel of a wagon and his argument is like a turning axle" [NETS]). However, Aquila tends to translate the plural noun רחמים with σπλάγχνα (Gen 43:30; Isa 63:15)[65] and the singular noun רחם with μήτρα (Ps 109[MT110]:3; Prov 30:16; Jer 20:17; Ezek 20:26).[66] We do not know whether Aquila and the rest intended σπλάγχνα to be abstract or concrete in Amos 1:11. Nevertheless, this is an indication that Aquila, and possibly the rest of the Three, read a plural Hebrew form, whether they had a plene reading רחמיו or defective רחמו in their *Vorlage*. The Aramaic Targum, the Peshitta and the Vulgate follow the MT in reading the plural רחמים :

Targum:
    and destroyed his *pity* (רַחֲמוֹהִי)

Peshitta:
    and did cast off all his *pity* (ܘܪܚܡܘܗܝ)

Vulgate:
    and he violated his mercy (misericordiam[67])

What is unique to the LXX translation is that the translator read the singular רחם instead of רחמים, and by his choice of μήτραν has left no room for an abstract meaning.[68] In the majority of cases, μήτρα translates רַחַם or רֶחֶם. In Amos 1:11, however, the translator seems to have ignored the third person suffix, possibly because he read the word literally and it

65. Joseph Reider, *An Index to Aquila: Greek–Hebrew, Hebrew–Greek, Latin–Hebrew with the Syriac and Armenian Evidence* (VTSup 12; Leiden: Brill, 1966), 220.
66. Ibid., 158.
67. Even though Jerome chooses "misericordiam," he does consider the interpretation of μήτρα (vulvam ejus) as valid. Field, *Origenis Hexaplorum*, 2:968.
68. Ziegler, as well as Rahlfs, adopted μήτραν "womb" instead of the variant μητερα "mother." μήτραν is supported by, among others of the Alexandrian group, W, a significant mid-third-century papyrus. Μητερα has the support of Vaticanus, some Lucianic witnesses and the Old Latin version, which indicates that the corruption MHTPA(N)/MHTEPA(N) took place very early in the transmission. Wolff notes that μητέρα, like the LXX divergence at Amos 1:3, is an interpretation based upon 1:13. Wolff, *Joel and Amos*, 130 n. s.

would not have made sense to translate "his womb(s)." Moreover, the absence of the suffix places distance between the object and the subject, so, unlike the Hebrew, the object defiled does not appear to be related to the aggressor in any way.

It is also very unlikely that the translator was ignorant of the alternative abstract meaning of "mercy" or "compassion" for רחמים since he repeatedly translates this root by "mercy" in Hosea (1:7; 2:3, 6, 21; 14:4). At the same time, he also seems to know when it is a "womb" that is in question (Hos 9:14—רחם):

תֶּן־לָהֶם יְהוָה מַה־תִּתֵּן תֶּן־לָהֶם   δὸς αὐτοῖς κύριε τί δώσεις αὐτοῖς δὸς αὐτοῖς
רֶחֶם מַשְׁכִּיל וְשָׁדַיִם צֹמְקִים   μήτραν ἀτεκνοῦσαν καὶ μαστοὺς ξηρούς

We have, therefore, a conscious choice by the translator between the two meanings. At the same time, it is possible that the LXX translator of Amos had the defective reading רחמו before him, which would make it easier, although not necessary, to read it as a singular. רחמו is attested in seven Hebrew Bible manuscripts cited by Kennicott (24, 82, 172, 173, 243, 269, 270)[69] and some rabbinic sources have both the defective and the plene reading side by side.[70] Sperber concludes that "it is clear that both readings were known in antiquity." He cites 2 Sam 24:14 where the *Kethib* is רְחֲמוֹ and the *Qere* is רַחֲמָיו. In the parallel passage, 1 Chr 21:13, only the plene reading is present in the text (כִּי־רַבִּים רַחֲמָיו). Similarly, Sperber thinks that LXX Amos 1:11 preserves, along with a few Hebrew manuscripts and some Midrashim, the ancient defective reading which the Masoretes replaced by the plene.[71] We cannot be certain which reading the LXX translator had before him but, regardless, since he seems to have dismissed the third person suffix, it is not unlikely that he took some freedom with the rest of the word as well.

It is rendering μήτραν combined with ἐλυμήνατο, his equivalent of שחת, that shifts the meaning of the verse to that of "sexual defilement" rather than "killing" or "destroying" as the Hebrew suggests.

LXX Amos 1:11 and "Sexual Defilement"

Three times λυμαίνομαι translates the *Piel* form of שחת (Prov 23:8; Amos 1:11; Jer 31[48MT]:18), three times the *Hiphil* form (Prov 18:9; Isa 65:8, 25), and once the *Hophal* (Prov 25:26). According to Muraoka,

---

69. Benjamin Kennicott, ed., *Vetus Testamentum Hebraicum: Cum Variis Lectionibus* (2 vols.; Oxford: Clarendon, 1776), 2:262.

70. For example, *Midrash Bereshit Rabbati* reads: ושחת רחמיו רחמו כתיב. For a full list of these rabbinic witnesses, see Sperber, "Varia Midrashica IV," 149–53.

71. Ibid., 152–53.

λυμαίνομαι followed by the accusative μήτραν would mean "to destroy."[72] Lust agrees with this meaning and compares Amos 1:11 with Jdt 9:2:

κύριε ὁ θεὸς τοῦ πατρός μου Συμεων ᾧ ἔδωκας ἐν χειρὶ ῥομφαίαν εἰς ἐκδίκησιν ἀλλογενῶν οἳ ἔλυσαν[73] μήτραν παρθένου εἰς μίασμα καὶ ἐγύμνωσαν μηρὸν εἰς αἰσχύνην καὶ ἐβεβήλωσαν μήτραν εἰς ὄνειδος εἶπας γάρ οὐχ οὕτως ἔσται καὶ ἐποίησαν.

He also cites *4 Macc.* 18:8: οὐδὲ ἔφθειρέν με λυμεὼν ἐρημίας φθορεὺς ἐν πεδίῳ οὐδὲ ἐλυμήνατό μου τὰ ἁγνὰ τῆς παρθενίας λυμεὼν ἀπάτης ὄφις.[74] LXX Ezek 16:25 may also be relevant: καὶ ἐπ᾽ ἀρχῆς πάσης ὁδοῦ ᾠκοδόμησας τὰ πορνεῖά σου καὶ ἐλυμήνω τό κάλλος σου καὶ διήγαγες τὰ σκέλη σου παντὶ παρόδῳ καὶ ἐπλήθυνας τὴν πορνείαν σου. It appears that λυμαίνομαι used in relation to female nakedness (μήτρα, ἁγνὰ τῆς παρθενίας, or κάλλος) has the sense of sexual defilement, and the choice of the translator has achieved this.[75]

Some manuscripts have μητέρα as the object of λυμαίνομαι in Amos 1:11, but this probably represents an inner-Greek corruption. If "mother" were indeed the object, then the idea could be of killing mothers on the ground.[76] However, since the object is μήτρα the verse is descriptive of an act of sexual defilement.

72. *Muraoka 2002*, 350. The word can also have the sense of "outrage," "maltreat," "dishonour," "murder," "harm," "spoil" or "injure" (LSJ 1065).

73. This is the first aorist active indicative third person plural form of λύω. Moore translates it as "violated" although, literally, it is "loosened." He also points out the uncertainty among scholars as to what the underlying Hebrew word was. Moore thinks that "the Greek word used here, *luō*, 'to loosen', can also mean 'to break' or 'to violate'." Moore, *Judith*, 189–91. Other meanings for this word would be "unfasten," "open," "release," "weaken," "destroy" (LSJ 1068–69). The resemblance of the two words and their closeness in meaning would justify the comparison between Amos 1:11 and Jdt 9:2.

74. LEH 377.

75. Perhaps a similar sense is found in the use of μολυνθήσονται ("be stained, defiled, soiled") in Zech 14:2 for the rape of women: καὶ διαρπαγήσονται αἱ οἰκίαι καὶ αἱ γυναῖκες μολυνθήσονται. However, in LXX Mal 2:8 διεφθείρατε is chosen for שחתם, where διαθήκη is the object.

76. The act of killing on the ground is found in Judg 20:21, καὶ διέφθειραν ἐν Ισραηλ ἐν τῇ ἡμέρᾳ ἐκείνη δύο καὶ εἴκοσι χιλιάδας ἀνδρῶν ἐπὶ τὴν γῆν for וישחיתו בישראל ביום ההוא שנים ועשרים אלף איש ארצה. See also Judg 20:25. Some rabbinic interpretations take "and he destroyed his womb" as a reference to the womb of Esau's mother. Sperber, "Varia Midrashica IV," 149–53.

The Plus ἐπὶ γῆς

The plus ἐπὶ γῆς which follows differentiates this sexual defilement from the texts we have mentioned above. If we had ἐλυμήνατο μήτραν on its own, the broad sense of the phrase would be "sexual defilement," which could imply either promiscuity or rape. The plus ἐπὶ γῆς, however, shows that something more is in mind. There is no manuscript or other versional evidence of a *Vorlage* which had ארצה ("to the ground"), which suggests that the LXX plus is interpretive. A possible example of a similar plus in the LXX TP is found in Hos 4:2:

אָלֹה וְכַחֵשׁ וְרָצֹחַ וְגָנֹב וְנָאֹף   ἀρὰ καὶ ψεῦδος καὶ φόνος καὶ κλοπὴ καὶ μοιχεία

פָּרָצוּ וְדָמִים בְּדָמִים נָגָעוּ   κέχυται ἐπὶ τῆς γῆς καὶ αἵματα ἐφ᾽ αἵμασιν μίσγουσιν

In this case, ἐπὶ τῆς γῆς follows the verb κέχυται, "poured," making more explicit the sense of the verb.[77] It would be quite natural for the translator to add "on the ground" when the verb "poured" is present, and the addition could be said to help render פרצו more successfully.[78] In Amos 1:11, however, the translator does not have the verb "pour" in his text. Why, then, would he attach ἐπὶ γῆς to ἐλυμήνατο? We have already established that the sense of the translation is not that of murdering on the ground (as in Judg 20:21, 25), but of sexual defilement. Adding ἐπὶ γῆς is unnatural unless the picture of "pouring something on the ground" is at the back of his mind, and there is good reason to think that Gen 38:9 has triggered the insertion of this plus.[79]

---

77. Muraoka suspects that the translator of Hos 4:2 may have had in his mind Onan's deed in Gen 38:9. He notes that "the same Heb. verb is also understood as bursting forth in sinful deeds, and that sexual (!), in Ho 4,10 ἐπόρνευσεν καὶ οὐ μὴ κατευθύνωσι." T. Muraoka, "Hosea IV in the Septuagint Version," *AJBL* 9 (1983): 28.

78. According to *Bible d'Alexandrie*, this could also be a case of homoioteleuton (*BA* 23.1:83). A. A. Macintosh, *A Critical and Exegetical Commentary on Hosea* (ICC; Edinburgh: T. & T. Clark, 1997), 129–31, suggests that בארץ stood originally in the Hebrew text but was lost by homoioteleuton following פרצו." However, he chooses to go with the possibility that ἐπὶ τῆς γῆς "may have been supplied ad sensum since it is difficult to render the verb satisfactorily without it."

79. Cf. Paul, *Amos*, 65 n. 219; Coote, "Amos 1:11," 208. Harper offers Hirscht's explanation for this plus: "אדם crept in after רחמיו by mistake from the previous line and was then read with the preceding י as באדם which then went over easily into באדמה." *A Critical and Exegetical Commentary on Amos and Hosea*, 31. This explanation is difficult because in the previous verse we have אדום, not אדם, and this was already rendered correctly by the translator with Ἰδουμαία. Four misreadings would have to take place to account for this view: (a) אדום creeping in from the previous line, (b) י read as ב, (c) ו in אדום deleted, and (d) a final ה added.

Genesis 38:9: Onan Defiles Tamar

ἐξέχεεν is not a common rendering of שחת: Gen 38:9 is the only text where שחת is translated by ἐξέχεεν. Moreover, there is no explicit object for שחת in Gen 38:9; the translator understands from the context that the object is "seed." His rendering ἐξέχεεν, therefore, helps make the meaning explicit to the reader. Furthermore, there is no other passage in the OT where the combination שחת ארצה ("ruin to the earth") occurs.[80] Only the context of sexual encounter would give rise to such a rendering. There are, then, no "rival" texts which could be influencing the Amos translator: if influence from another text is to be considered, Gen 38:9 is the only possible candidate.

Since the two words ושחת and אחיו are found in both texts, it is possible that the translator, who had already connected רחמיו with "womb," thought of the Onan text. Marguerite Harl says that divergencies in the Greek can often be explained as

> analogical ("intertextual") interpretations, due to the links with parallel passages elsewhere in the LXX. This method of interpreting a passage by reference to another one within the same work has been practiced in Antiquity for all great writings. We find it applied to the Bible by Christian exegetes as well as by the Rabbis (Torah explained through Torah).[81]

Could the Onan story be considered as a parallel passage to Amos 1:11 other than as regards the lexical parallels? It appears indeed that the two passages also share the common thematic link of "brotherhood betrayal."

Onan clearly acts in a way that betrays his brother in Gen 38. According to the law of Levirate marriage (as codified in Deut 25:5–10), when someone died without leaving male offspring, his brother was obliged to marry the widow. The first son to be born within this union was to be regarded as belonging to the dead brother.[82] Onan, however, breaks this brotherhood law by refusing to fulfil his duty to Tamar.

A similar theme is present in Amos 1. The judgment on Tyre in 1:9 is based on the accusation of failing to honour the covenant of brothers (οὐκ ἐμνήσθησαν διαθήκης ἀδελφῶν). The text moves on to the judgment against Edom in 1:11, with a similar accusation of strife against a brother (ἕνεκα τοῦ διῶξαι αὐτοὺς ἐν ῥομφαίᾳ τὸν ἀδελφὸν αὐτοῦ). The theme of "failure to honour brotherhood" is thus embedded in the context and the more likely to have suggested the Genesis parallel.

---

80. With accusative of place, the meaning would be "ruin, destroy, or annihilate" ("שחת," *HALAT* 4:1363–66).
81. Harl, "La Bible d'Alexandrie," 192.
82. Richard Kalmin, "Levirate Law," *ABD* 4:296–97.

Conclusion

In conclusion, the translator of Amos 1:11 appears to have been led to this particular rendering, which reflects Gen 38:9, for a variety of reasons: (a) the context of both texts talks about brotherhood betrayal; (b) the presence of אחיו ושחת in the two texts; (c) the act of "sexual defilement," which is clear in Gen 38:9 and also in Amos 1:11 on the basis of a certain way of reading רחמיו.

Finally, we have to consider the possibility of ארצה or על־האדמה being present in the LXX *Vorlage*. In that case, there would be no allusion to Gen 38:9 in the *Vorlage*, since the phrase ושחת רחמיו ארצה/על־האדמה would not carry any sexual connotations. The sexual connotations are only achieved through the Greek renderings, and allusion to Gen 38:9 is only demonstrable if ἐπὶ γῆς is the translator's plus.

Is it then justifiable to claim an intertextual connection between LXX Amos 1:11 and Gen 38:9? There are good grounds for one to argue in that direction, even if total certainty is not possible.

Amos 6:6 (and 6:4)[83]

Amos 6:6

MT	LXX
הַשֹּׁתִים בְּמִזְרְקֵי יַיִן וְרֵאשִׁית	οἱ πίνοντες τὸν διυλισμένον οἶνον καὶ τὰ πρῶτα
שְׁמָנִים יִמְשָׁחוּ וְלֹא נֶחְלוּ	μύρα χριόμενοι καὶ οὐκ ἔπασχον οὐδὲν
עַל־שֵׁבֶר יוֹסֵף	ἐπὶ τῇ συντριβῇ Ιωσηφ
who drink wine from bowls,	who drink thoroughly filtered wine and anoint
and anoint themselves with	themselves with the finest oils, they were not
the finest oils, but are not	even suffering anything over the ruin of
grieved over the ruin of	Ioseph [NETS]
Joseph [NRSV]	

Isaiah 25:6

MT	LXX
וְעָשָׂה יְהוָה צְבָאוֹת	καὶ ποιήσει κύριος σαβαωθ
לְכָל־הָעַמִּים בָּהָר הַזֶּה	πᾶσι τοῖς ἔθνεσιν ἐπὶ τὸ ὄρος τοῦτο πίονται
מִשְׁתֵּה שְׁמָנִים	εὐφροσύνην
מִשְׁתֵּה שְׁמָרִים שְׁמָנִים מְמֻחָיִם	πίονται οἶνον χρίσονται μύρον
שְׁמָרִים מְזֻקָּקִים	

---

83. After the conclusion of my study on LXX Amos 6:6, I became aware of Eberhard Bons' recent contribution on the same verse: "Le vin filtré: Quelques remarques concernant les textes hébreu et grec d'Amos 6,6a et les sens de la tournure οἱ πίνοντες τὸν διυλισμένον οἶνον," in Ausloos, Lemmelijn, and Vervenne, eds., *Florilegium Lovaniense*, 71–83. The two studies display many common elements and conclusions which have been arrived at independently.

On this mountain the LORD of hosts will make for all peoples a feast of rich food, a feast of well-aged wines, of rich food filled with marrow, of well-aged wines strained clear [NRSV]

On this mountain the Lord Sabaoth will make a feast for all nations: they will drink joy; they will drink wine; they will anoint themselves with perfume [NETS]

LXX Amos 6:6 is one of the verses to which LXX scholars point in order to argue for the dependence of LXX Isaiah on LXX Amos, or on LXX TP in general. Ziegler makes a passing reference to LXX Amos 6:6, "[d]ie verwandten Wiedergaben der Js-LXX mit verschiedenen Amosstellen (Am 6, 6; 6, 10; 9, 14, vgl. unten) lassen wohl auf eine Abhängigkeit der Js-LXX von der griech. übersetzung des Amos schließen,"[84] and Seeligmann discusses this connection further, allowing for the possibility that there is "in the clumsy and badly proportioned translation of 25.6, משתה שמרים שמנים ממחים מזקקים שמרים מזקקים שמנים משתה by πίονται εὐφροσύνην, πίονται οἶνον, χρίσονται μύρον, a reminiscence of Am. 6.6, where—also in the description of a drinking bout—ראשית שמנים ימשחו is translated by τὰ πρῶτα μύρα χριόμενοι."[85]

Dines shares this view, noting that "the Hebrew is difficult here and he [i.e. the LXX translator of Isaiah] might well have turned to a passage with similar ingredients to help him out."[86] If the above scholars are right, then the Isaiah translator had seen some connection between Isa 25:6 and Amos 6:6 and borrowed the concept of "anointing" with perfumes from Amos 6:6. Our purpose here is not to verify the correctness of these scholars' suggestions but to examine whether the reverse may also be true: that the Greek translator of Amos had noted some connections between the two verses.

The rendering of במזרקי by διυλισμένον in LXX Amos 6:6 raises the question whether the Amos translator had been influenced by מזקקים ("refined, purified")[87] in Isa 25:6. Among others, G. André is certain that "the LXX read *yayin mezuqqāq*, 'filtered wine',"[88] and Marti, in his commentary on Isaiah, had already hinted at this connection: "Mit מְזֻקָּקִים *geläutert, geseiht* vgl. Am 6₆ LXX und das 'Mückenseihen' Mt 23₂₄."[89]

84. Ziegler, *Untersuchungen*, 104.
85. Seeligmann, *The Septuagint Version of Isaiah*, 225–26.
86. Dines, "The Twelve Among the Prophets," 13.
87. BDB 279.
88. G. André, "זָרַק," *TDOT* 4:164.
89. Karl Marti, *Das Buch Jesaja* (KHC; Tübingen: J. C. B. Mohr, 1900), 189.

διυλισμένος/מזרקי

The main departure from the Hebrew in LXX Amos 6:6 is found in the rendering of במזרקי by διυλισμένον (perfect middle/passive masculine singular participle), so our main focus will be the study of this word.[90] Apart from the meaning of במזרקי ("from bowls [of]"), the translator appears to have ignored the preposition בּ as well as the plural ending. A correction to match the MT was deemed necessary, as shown by the reading found in Justin Martyr (εν φιαλαις—"in bowls").

The Targumist uses פיילי, which is a loan-word from Greek φιάλη ("They drink wine from *silver* bowls and anoint themselves with the choicest of *fine* oils; but they are not grieved over the ruin of *Israel*"). Bons notes that, like the LXX, the Targum deals with this difficult Hebrew text by introducing "wine" as the direct object, as well as the adjective "silver" for the bowls, and concludes that the Hebrew *Vorlage* of the Targum was very close to the MT.[91]

The Peshiṭta, however, follows the LXX with its rendering of "filtered, strained, purified" wine (ܚܡܪܐ ܡܨܠܠܐ).[92] Is it possible that both the LXX and the Peshiṭta shared a similar Hebrew *Vorlage* against the MT? Gelston cautions against jumping to such a conclusion before excluding all other possibilities.[93] In his study of the Peshiṭta of the TP, he found no agreements which point with any probability to the existence of a common Hebrew *Vorlage* distinct from the MT.[94] For Amos 6:6 he thinks that the Peshiṭta translators could have turned to the LXX for help in interpreting their Hebrew *Vorlage*.[95] However, it seems peculiar that the Peshiṭta would consult the LXX for rendering as familiar a word as מזרק.[96] In view of Gelston's caution, we may assume an MT *Vorlage* for the Peshiṭta as well, but we shall look later at what may have triggered the consultation of the LXX on this verse.

Bons does not discuss the Peshiṭta reading, but points to the Qumran fragment 4QXII[g] as an additional, although uncertain, witness to the MT:

90. Johnson thinks that, while τὰ πρῶτα μύρα χριόμενοι is "excellent Greek idiom," the so-called Greek accusative, τὸν διυλισμένον, may be "due to a corrupt or misunderstood Hebrew text." "The Septuagint Translators of Amos," 34.

91. Bons, "Le vin filtré," 75–76.

92. J. Payne Smith, *A Compendious Syriac Dictionary* (Oxford: Clarendon, 1903), 294.

93. Gelston, *The Peshiṭta*, 161.

94. Ibid., 177.

95. Ibid., 167–68.

96. In Zech 14:20 the Peshiṭta reads ܦܚܪ̈ܐ ("vials") for מזרקים.

ה.[שׁתׄיׄםׄ] במ[זׄרׄ]קׄי.[97] Bons concludes that the several textual witnesses, while demonstrating slight differences among them, confirm the MT, and thus sees no need to correct the MT against the LXX.[98] Instead, he suggests that we must distinguish between the Hebrew and Greek traditions and recognize that each alternative has its *raison d'être*.[99]

Theo A. W. van der Louw, observing how transformations happen from one language to another, concludes as follows: "Behind each transformation stands a literal rendering that has been rejected. Thus when we encounter a 'free rendering' we should not only categorize it as a transformation, but also investigate its rationale by studying the literal translation that was *not* chosen."[100]

Assuming that the Hebrew *Vorlage* of LXX Amos 6:6 is the same as the MT, we should compare the senses derived from both the Hebrew and the Greek in order to understand why the Greek translator of Amos would have chosen to deviate from a more "literal" rendering of the Hebrew.

MT Amos 6:6. Amos 6 introduces a "woe" oracle against those in comfort and security in Zion and Samaria (v. 1). In vv. 4 and 5 their luxurious comfort is further expounded through reference to their expensive furniture ("beds of ivory"), their food ("lambs from the flock, and calves from the stall") and their musical entertainment ("[they] sing idle songs to the sound of the harp").

Verse 6 comments on their "wine drinking" and "perfume anointing." The perfumes are described as the "finest" (וראשית שמנים), which shows that the accusation is against the high cost of this luxury. According to Lentin, the imagery of the drunkards of Amos 6:6 functions as a metaphor for the "unjust" and is grouped together with verses such as Prov 31:4–7; Isa 5:11–13, 22–23 and Amos 4:1.[101] However, Amos' accusation concerning the wine-drinking is not clear. The first impression is that what is condemned is the utensils used: השתים במזרקי יין. It

---

97. Bons, "Le vin filtré," 74–75. Transcription of 4QXII[g] taken from Ego et al., eds., *Minor Prophets*, 59.

98. Bons, "Le vin filtré," 76.

99. Ibid., 78. This is contra Dahmen, who supports the existence of a different underlying Hebrew text for the LXX which is earlier than what the MT reflects. Ulrich Dahmen, "Zur Text- und Literarkritik von Am 6,6a," *BN* 32 (1986): 7–10.

100. Van der Louw, *Transformations in the Septuagint*, 57.

101. Rachel Lentin, "Seeing Double: Strategies for Understanding Imagery with Reference to the Wine-Related Images of the Hebrew Bible" (Ph.D. diss., University of Cambridge, 2008), fig. 6 (opp. 68).

seems that מזרק signified some kind of vessel, bowl, or basin.[102] מזרק, however, seems to be a specialized word never used outside a cultic context. Bons points out that this is a temple item used particularly for sacrifices (e.g. Num 7:13; Zech 9:15), and no use outside such a context is attested, except for Amos 6:6.[103] In Qumran מזרק occurs mainly in the Temple Scroll and it is always cultic, used in connection with blood (11QT 23:12; 26:6; 33:13; 34:7).[104] It is probable, therefore, that this "cultic" term is deliberately chosen in order to add a sense of "blasphemy."[105]

"Blasphemy" could, then, be part of the accusation against the "drinkers," but Bons points to the rhetorical function of במזרקי, which he sees as a type of "metonymy." The large quantity of consumption is indirectly attacked through the reference to the "large cups": "la large coupe à vin, à savoir le récipient, symbolise le contenu, en l'occurrence la grande quantité de vin… Toujours est-il que l'accent est mis non sur la boisson elle-même, mais sur la quantité ainsi que sur la manière dont on la consomme."[106]

(a) *Rabbinic Tradition on Amos 6:6.* However, the Rabbis do not recognize the "blasphemous" connotation of מזרק being used for wine consumption. They understand Amos' attack to be against a certain type of wine rather than the utensils or the implied quantity. The question of the type of wine that Amos is condemning in 6:6 is raised in some of their discussions: "Rab, R. Joḥanan, and the Rabbis discussed this: Rab said: What is meant is a hot drink of wine and water."[107] Concerning the origins of this wine, "R. Abbahu said in the name of R. Ḥanina: From Pethugta, seeing that their wine seduced (*pittah*) their body (*guf*) to immorality. The Rabbis said in the name of R. Ḥanina: [They obtained their wine] from Pelugta [or 'separation'], since through their wine, the Ten Tribes were seduced [from God], and were exiled."[108]

It is possible that this later rabbinic discussion of the wine in Amos 6:6 reflects a much earlier interest dating back to the time of the Greek translator of Amos.

102. BDB 284.
103. Bons, "Le vin filtré," 73.
104. See *DCH* 5:212–13.
105. Bons, "Le vin filtré," 73.
106. Ibid.
107. *Lev. Rab.* V.3.
108. Ibid.

(b) *Targum Amos 6:6*. While the Rabbis connected Amos' accusation to the wine, the targumist draws attention to the vessels. He holds that these are not just *any* bowls, but they are "silver" bowls (בְּפֵילָוָן דִּכְסַף), whereas in Zech 9:15 and 14:20, where מזרק occurs again, the targumic rendering is simply "bowls."

It is not clear what the addition of "silver" was meant to achieve. We know of "silver" bowls used for worship (Num 7:13, 84), as well as "golden" bowls (3 Kgdms 7:36[MT7:50]; 2 Chr 4:8), so perhaps the addition of "silver" shows that the targumist understood these to be cultic vessels and the banquet to be particularly "blasphemous" in nature. In *Num. Rab.* XIII.15–16, as Cathcart and Gordon point out, מזרק is described as a "silver bowl" or a "silver basin."[109] Here Amos 6:6 is connected to Num 7:19 where Nethanel presents his offering of fine flour mixed with oil in a silver bowl (כסף מזרק אחד): "ONE SILVER BASIN (MIZRAK) was brought as a symbol of the Torah which has been likened to wine... Now because it is customary to drink wine in a *mizrak*, as you may gather from the text, *They drink wine in bowls-*mizreke (Amos VI, 6), he on that account brought a MIZRAK."[110]

Perhaps by specifying the material of which the bowls were made, the targumist aimed at making the connection between Amos 6:6 and the silver מזרקות of the cult (e.g. Num 4:14; 7:13). Otherwise, he could simply be drawing attention to their high value. Silver utensils also appear at pagan royal tables for the consumption of wine (Est 1:7). Rachel Lentin illustrates the difficulty of interpreting such descriptions as follows:

> For example, modern translators of Jer. 51:7 find in the word זהב a reference to the riches of Babylon (seen to be represented through synecdoche as a single piece of its own vast wealth), but Kimchi's interpretation is that it 'does not refer to the metal of which the cup is made but signifies the purity of the wine it contains, "a cup of golden wine"' [*sic*], thereby indicating that its contents have not been diluted with water and are dangerously potent. Significantly, however, the specific 'cognitive content' of the whole metaphor seems to be equally available to both medieval and modern translators; a change in the sense of one word alters only one of the range of weak implicatures made available through and governed by this metaphor.[111]

---

109. Cathcart and Gordon, *The Targum*, 88 n. 8.
110. *Num. Rab.* XIII.15–16.
111. Lentin, "Seeing Double," 11–12.

(c) *Amos 6:6 in 1 Enoch*. As part of a list of "woes" for the wicked in ch. 96, the author of 1 Enoch condemns the riches of the sinners because, as he says, "[they] make you appear like the righteous" (96:4). The following "woe" alludes to Amos 6:6: "Woe to you who devour the finest of the wheat, and drink wine in large bowls, and tread under foot the lowly with your might." Charles notes that drinking in "large bowls" serves as the opposite of drinking in ordinary wine-cups.[112] In other words, the author of 1 Enoch seems to have understood the accusation of Amos to be against the large quantity of wine consumed, but also holds that such luxuries were meant to be enjoyed by the righteous, not the wicked.

LXX Amos 6:6. The possible steps by which the Greek translator of the TP understood and rendered השתים במזרקי יין are as follows:

a. He understands מזרק as having an exclusively cultic use. Thus a literal translation would be: "those who drink from sacrificial wine bowls." The following contradiction would then occur: if מזרק is always a "sacrificial" bowl, then it cannot be used in the expression מזרקי יין. How could the same bowls be associated with worship and also serve as "wine" bowls (i.e. table utensils)?[113] This may have been the dilemma in the mind of the translator. Apparently, he has taken יין as the object of the participle [ה]שתים, in the same manner as the targumist has done. Likewise, Edghill proposes that the LXX rendering attempts to make up for the omission of the object of "drinking" by making "wine" into the object (rather than "you drink in wine-bowls").[114] These difficulties are very likely to have caused the Peshiṭta translators to consult the LXX for the rendering of this verse.

b. Now, the Greek translator is left with "those who drink wine from 'sacrificial' bowls" and he would have used the Greek word φιάλη as he does elsewhere for מזרק (Zech 9:15; 14:20). His rendering would thus be: οἱ πίνοντες οἶνον ἐν φιάλαις. The problem with this translation is that Amos' accusation would not have been very clear, unless drinking from bowls (φιάλαι) was deemed inappropriate or symbolized something contemptible.

112.　R. H. Charles, ed., *The Apocrypha and Pseudepigrapha of the Old Testament*. Vol. 2, *Pseudepigrapha* (Oxford: Clarendon, 1913; repr., Berkeley: The Apocryphile, 2004), 267 n. 5.

113.　Although there were drink-offerings of wine (e.g. Lev 23:13; Num 28:14).

114.　Edgill, *The Book of Amos*, 63.

(a) φιάλη. While it may not have been appropriate to drink wine from a מזרק ("sacrificial bowl") in the Hebrew Bible, it would not have been inappropriate to drink wine from a φιάλη. φιάλη has a broader usage than does מזרק. It is not restricted to cultic contexts as מזרק is, even though it functions as the standard equivalent for מזרק in the LXX.[115] In the LXX Pentateuch, φιάλη is the stereotype for מזרק (Exod 27:3; 38:23[MT3]; Num 4:14; 7:13, 19, 25, 31, 37, 43, 49, 55, 61, 67, 73, 79, 84, 85, 86), while for מנקית ("sacrificial bowl")[116] the stereotype κύαθος ("cup")[117] is used. κόνδυ is another word for "cup" used for Joseph's silver cup (גביע—Gen 44:2, 5, 9, 10, 12, 16, 17) and the cup of God's wrath (כוס— Isa 51:17, 22). A synonym of κόνδυ is ποτήριον, usually rendering either כוס or כיס (e.g. Ps 115:4[MT116:13]; Hab 2:16; Jer 16:7). One instance where φιάλη and ποτήριον may have been used synonymously is LXX Prov 23:31:

> μὴ μεθύσκεσθε οἴνῳ ἀλλὰ ὁμιλεῖτε ἀνθρώποις δικαίοις καὶ ὁμιλεῖτε ἐν περιπάτοις ἐὰν γὰρ εἰς τὰς φιάλας καὶ τὰ ποτήρια δῷς τοὺς ὀφθαλμούς σου ὕστερον περιπατήσεις γυμνότερος ὑπέρου.

The Three seem to understand φιάλη as "cup" and they use it in places where the LXX has κύαθος (Θ and Σ—Exod 25:29 [מנקית]; A—Jer 52:19 [מנקית]) or κόνδυ (Σ—Gen 44:2 [גביע]). To clarify things further, it is necessary to see how φιάλη was used in Greek literature.

Just as in LXX Song (5:13; 6:2), Xenophanes (*Fragmenta* B1.3) shows that φιάλη could be used to store perfumes, and from Herodotus we see that a φιάλη was used for libations in worship:

> ἐκέχρητό σφι κατ᾽ ἀρχὰς αὐτίκα ἐνισταμένοισι ἐς τὰς τυραννίδας τὸν χαλκέη φιάλη σπείσαντα αὐτῶν ἐν τῷ ἱρῷ τοῦ Ἡφαίστου, τοῦτον ἁπάσης βασιλεύσειν Αἰγύπτου. (*Hist.* 2.147.13–16)

Aristophanes speaks of "sacred" bowls: φιάλην ἐπητιῶντο κλέψαι τοῦ θεοῦ (*Vespae* 1447).

However, the most informative texts are the ones describing rich banquets, such as Xenophon's *Symposium*. Xenophon describes a banquet which is in many ways reminiscent of Amos 6:6, including the practice of "perfume anointing." At this symposium, Socrates praises Callias for his faultless feast. Callias then asks whether he can add to their enjoyment of the occasion by bringing some perfume to them: Τί

---

115. Non-Pentateuch examples: 3 Kgdms 7[MT40]:26; 4 Kgdms 12:14; Zech 9:15; 14:20; Jer 52:18.
116. BDB 667.
117. LEH 358.

οὖν εἰ καὶ μύρον τις ἡμῖν ἐνέγκαι, ἵνα καὶ εὐωδίᾳ ἑστιώμεθα (*Symposium* 2.3). Socrates finds this unnecessary. He thinks that no additional perfume is needed for the wives of Niceratus and Critobulus who are present at the banquet. However, as regards men, Socrates states that no man uses perfume for a man's sake: καὶ γὰρ ἀνδρὸς μὲν δήπου ἕνεκα ἀνὴρ οὐδεὶς μύρῳ χρίεται (*Symposium* 2.3). This comment may be necessary because perfumes were normally used at weddings by both bride and groom.[118] Socrates prefers the odour of the olive oil used in the gymnasium, and thinks that anointing with perfume would make the slave and the free indistinguishable in odour. For Socrates, the "odours that result from the exertions of freemen demand primarily noble pursuits engaged in for many years if they are to be sweet and suggestive of freedom."[119]

Apart from the "perfume anointing" practice, we are informed of the wine vessels. After Philip performs his dance and is thirsty, he asks to be served in the large "bowl": ἐγὼ γοῦν διψῶ· καὶ ὁ παῖς ἐγχεάτω μοι τὴν μεγάλην φιάλην (*Symposium* 2.23). Callias jokes that the rest of the guests would need the same quantity since they became thirsty from laughing at Philip's dance. Socrates interposes again to offer his insights on wine-drinking. He suggests that instead of taking in large quantities of wine at once, which would weaken both their bodies and minds, they should instead have the servants frequently bring them "small cups," to avoid intoxication but achieve a more "sportive" mood:

> ἂν δὲ ἡμῖν οἱ παῖδες μικραῖς κύλιξι πυκνὰ ἐπιψακάζωσιν, ἵνα καὶ ἐγὼ ἐν Γοργιείοις ῥήμασιν εἴπω, οὕτως οὐ βιαζόμενοι μεθύειν ὑπὸ τοῦ οἴνου ἀλλ' ἀναπειθόμενοι πρὸς τὸ παιγνιωδέστερον ἀφιξόμεθα. (*Symposium* 2.26)

The quantity of wine does not seem to be lessened with Socrates' suggestion, but is simply spread out over the course of the evening. However, the discussion shows that a large φιάλη was possibly a utensil available at banquets. In Xenophon's *Cyropaedia*, a φιάλη was the vessel in which wine was served to a guest:

> οἱ δὲ τῶν βασιλέων τούτων οἰνοχόοι κομψῶς τε οἰνοχοοῦσι καὶ καθαρείως ἐγχέουσι καὶ διδόασι τοῖς τρισὶ δακτύλοις ὀχοῦντες τὴν φιάλην καὶ προσφέρουσιν ὡς ἂν ἐνδοῖεν τὸ ἔκπωμα εὐληπτότατα τῷ μέλλοντι πίνειν. (*Cyropaedia* 1.3.8)

φιάλη is also used for wine-drinking in Plato's *Symposium*, in the midst of a discussion with Socrates, where perhaps the bowl was passed from one to the other: Ἀγάθωνα δὲ καὶ Ἀριστοφάνη καὶ Σωκράτη ἔτι μόνους

---

118.   Xenophon, *Symposium* 2.3 (O. J. Todd, LCL, 542 n. 2).
119.   Xenophon, *Symposium* 2.4 (O. J. Todd, LCL).

ἐγρηγορέναι καὶ πίνειν ἐκ φιάλης μεγάλης ἐπὶ δεξιά. τὸν οὖν Σωκράτη αὐτοῖς διαλέγεσθαι (*Symposium* 223.c).

It is clear, therefore, that φιάλη, unlike מזרק, does not occur exclusively in cultic contexts. It is a vessel commonly used for drinking wine, and it is possibly bigger than a regular cup (κυλίκιον), although when size is significant it can be specified (τὴν μεγάλην φιάλην). It therefore remains uncertain whether Amos' accusation would have been obvious had the Greek translator rendered οἱ πίνοντες οἶνον ἐν φιάλαις. We must, then, explore whether τὸν διυλισμένον οἶνον was effective in communicating what the translator thought was Amos' condemnation.

(b) *τὸν διυλισμένον οἶνον*. Except for LXX Amos 6:6, διυλίζω ("to strain, filter thoroughly")[120] does not occur in the LXX, but is found frequently outside the LXX for the filtering of wine and other liquids (cf. Matt 23:24).

Muraoka notes that διυλισμένος with reference to wine speaks of its good quality.[121] A variant of διυλισμένος referring to olive oil[122] is διυλιστόν, found in *P.Ryl.* II, 97,3 functioning as a synonym to "good," "clean," "unblemished":

ἐλαίου ἀρεστοῦ
[νέο]υ καθαροῦ ἀδόλου [δι]υλιστοῦ

Among the various types, "clear/pure wine" was one of the wine categories in antiquity.[123] "Filtered" wine should not be confused with "diluted" wine. It was common practice in antiquity to dilute wine with water so that one would retain the enjoyment but refrain from getting drunk too easily. There were different measurements for the wine and the water, but in most cases the water was proportionately more than the wine.[124] Wine filtering, however, was similar to oil separation and was done by skimming or decantation.[125]

120. *Muraoka 2009*, 172.
121. Ibid.
122. "Wine and olive oil are both derived from liquids expressed from fruit and, as a result, the basic processes of production were very similar." Rafael Frankel, *Wine and Oil Production in Antiquity in Israel and Other Mediterranean Countries* (JSOT/ASOR Monograph Series 10; Sheffield: Sheffield Academic, 1999), 41.
123. Shalom M. Paul, "Classifications of Wine in Mesopotamian and Rabbinic Sources," *IEJ* 25 (1975): 43. Paul expands on the wine classification suggested by Aaron Demsky in "Dark Wine from Judah," *IEJ* 22 (1972): 233–34.
124. Everett Ferguson, "Wine as a Table-drink in the Ancient World," *ResQ* 13 (1970): 141–53.
125. *Skimming*: skimming the floating oil off the lees using a ladle or similar utensil while the lees sit at the bottom. *Decantation*: an opening just below the rim of a vessel or vat [overflow decantation] allowed the floating oil to flow out, while the water lees remained. In "underflow decantation" the separated liquids were

The Rabbis describe two ways of straining the wine from the lees: through cloths and through baskets made of palm twigs.[126] That clarified wine was of the choicest quality is also evident in the discussion on tithes and offerings in the Tosefta (*t. Ter.* 4:3).

Among various texts concerning wine-filtering that Bons examines (e.g. Galen, *De naturalibus facultatibus* I.15; *P.Oxy.* III, 413, 154),[127] he finds Plutarch's *Symposiaka*, in the first century C.E., to be one of the most relevant texts for LXX Amos 6:6. The question discussed in this table-talk is whether it is right to strain wine (εἰ δεῖ τὸν οἶνον ἐνδιηθεῖν). The main speakers are Niger and Aristion, and they defend opposite views. Niger was finding everything at the dinner too costly and elaborate (ἑστιῶντος οὖν ἡμᾶς Ἀριστίωνος, τήν τ' ἄλλην χορηγίαν ὡς πολυτελῆ καὶ περίεργον ἐμέμφετο…[692b]). His criticism of filtering was that the whole purifying process was too costly, luxurious, vain, over-refined. He regards the whole practice as a trick that enables those who do it to drink more, since the wine becomes smoother. Apart from the fact that this was an elaborate and costly procedure, he regards unfiltered wine as better since the lees help maintain the high quality of the wine: ὅ τι γὰρ στόμωμα τοῦ οἴνου καὶ κράτος ἐστίν, τοῦτ' ἐν τῷ διυλίζειν ἐξαιροῦσι καὶ ἀποκρίνουσι (Plutarch, *Moralia* 692d).

Aristion, on the other hand, defends the opposite view. For him the purification brings the wine into a better, healthier state: οὕτω δὴ καὶ ἡ κάθαρσις τοῦ οἴνου τὸ πληκτικὸν ἀφαιροῦσα καὶ μανικόν, εἰς πραεῖαν ἕξιν καὶ ὑγιαίνουσαν καθίστησι (Plutarch, *Moralia* 693b). Bons points out that Niger's argument about the quality of the wine is actually a criticism aimed at its consumers and their excesses.[128] From the general debate between Niger and Aristion we gather that only the elite class could afford the product of this elaborate filtering process. It is not clear that this would have been the situation at the time of the LXX translator of the TP. However, before the technological innovations of the Romans, wine-filtering may have been even more costly, and the consumption of filtered wine would have been a privilege reserved for the upper class. Bons says that, in the absence of other sources to shed light on LXX Amos 6:6, it is legitimate to draw information from Greek and Latin texts available to us.[129] And for the same idea that filtered wine enables

---

allowed to flow out in turn through an opening at the bottom of the separating vessel. Frankel, *Wine and Oil Production*, 174–75.
126. *b. Shabb.* 139b (cf. 109a).
127. Bons, "Le vin filtré," 79–80.
128. Ibid., 81.
129. Ibid., 82.

one to drink more, he quotes Pliny the Elder (first century C.E.), *Natural History* (Book XIV), as well as Theodore of Mopsuestia, who interprets LXX Amos 6:6 in this manner.[130]

We may conclude that, by using διυλισμένον οἶνον, the Greek translator meant to suggest that an elite group of people indulged in the best quality of wine, a kind which encouraged more consumption than would unfiltered wine.[131] By employing διυλισμένον οἶνον, the LXX translator is presenting Amos as attacking such excessive luxuries.

Moreover, οἱ πίνοντες τὸν διυλισμένον οἶνον thus understood parallels the anointing with first quality perfumes (τὰ πρῶτα μύρα χριόμενοι) also mentioned in 6:6.[132] Indeed, the parallelism would have been a strong stylistic concern of the translator, and scholars have noted this characteristic of the Greek verse.[133]

Amos 6:4

In LXX Amos 6:4, we observe what might be another case of "clarification" of what seems to be an "unclear" criticism by the prophet. The last word in the Greek verse, γαλαθηνά ("sucking, young, tender"),[134] has no representative in the Hebrew:

הַשֹּׁכְבִים עַל־מִטּוֹת שֵׁן	οἱ καθεύδοντες ἐπὶ κλινῶν ἐλεφαντίνων
וּסְרֻחִים עַל־עַרְשׂוֹתָם	καὶ κατασπαταλῶντες ἐπὶ ταῖς στρωμναῖς αὐτῶν
וְאֹכְלִים כָּרִים מִצֹּאן וַעֲגָלִים	καὶ ἔσθοντες ἐρίφους ἐκ ποιμνίων καὶ μοσχάρια
מִתּוֹךְ מַרְבֵּק	ἐκ μέσου βουκολίων γαλαθηνά

In the Hebrew Bible, עֵגֶל־מַרְבֵּק (lit. "calf out of the stall") seems to be an idiom for "fattened" or "well-fed" (cf. 1 Kgdms 28:24; Mal 3:20; Jer 26[MT46]:21). In Amos 6:4, the idiom is interrupted by מִתּוֹך, which the Greek translator renders by ἐκ μέσου. He seems to have read מרבק as מבקר; the prefixed *mem* was probably taken as מִן (parallel to מִצֹּאן), and was left untranslated since its function was already served by מִתּוֹך.[135] Assuming the translator's *Vorlage* was similar to the MT, we have a "manipulation" here on the part of the translator, aimed at preserving the verse's parallelism:

---

130. Ibid., 81–83.
131. Also ibid., 83.
132. The article τὸν seems necessary for the parallelism with (τὰ) πρῶτα μύρα.
133. E.g. Nowack, *Die kleinen Propheten*, 156; Sellin, *Das Zwölfprophetenbuch*, 200; Snaith, *The Book of Amos*, 113.
134. LSJ 336.
135. Perhaps the Greek translator of the TP did not know the exact meaning of מרבק since he does not represent it accurately in Mal 3:20 either.

ἐρίφους ἐκ ποιμνίων
καὶ μοσχάρια ἐκ μέσου βουκολίων

The parallelism is achieved in the Greek, but at the expense of communicating the sense of the expression "calves out of the stall" (= "fattened, well-fed"). γαλαθηνά, however, does not appear to be an accurate interpretation of the expression, since it refers to a tender suckling, the opposite of "fattened."

ἄρνα γαλαθηνὸν translates טלה חלב in 1 Kgdms 7:9, and this is also believed to be the Hebrew reading behind ἀρνὸς γαλαθηνοῦ in Sir 46:16,[136] since both texts refer to Samuel's offering which helped rescue Israel from the Philistines (cf. Josephus, *Ant.* 6.25). The superior quality of the γαλαθηνά is attested in Herodotus' description of what may be sacrificed on the golden altar of the Babylonian temple, as opposed to the larger altar where the full-grown of the flock (τὰ τέλεα τῶν προβάτων) may be sacrificed: ἐπὶ γὰρ τοῦ χρυσέου βωμοῦ οὐκ ἔξεστι θύειν ὅτι μὴ γαλαθηνὰ μοῦνα (*Historiae* 1.183).

It is possible that, through the plus γαλαθηνά, the Greek translator is once more emphasizing the superior quality of products enjoyed by the upper class.

Manipulation or Misreading?

At Amos 6:6 we have seen the translator turning יין into an object, ignoring both the preposition בְּ and the plural ending in במזרקי and taking it as an adjective fitting for "wine." We have also seen how the translator in LXX Amos 6:4 may have used *metathesis* of consonants to read בקר, in order to produce perfect parallelism, and may have added γαλαθηνά in order to bring out the sense of Amos' accusation. All these elements point to some degree of intentionality on the part of the translator, who tried to communicate the sense of the verses without drifting far from the consonantal text.

This LXX phenomenon has been observed by others as well, not just for the Greek TP, but for other LXX books also. Among many types of "manipulation" on the part of the Greek translators, Emanuel Tov speaks of the "maneuvering" of the Hebrew consonantal text:

> The maneuvering of the translators may be paralleled by the principles that underlie some midrashim which, as it were, play with the consonants of the words of MT. Often such midrashim are based on Hebrew words

136. See Israel Lévi, *The Hebrew Text of the Book of Ecclesiasticus* (SSS 3; Leiden: Brill, 1904), 64; Pancratius C. Beentjes, *The Book of Ben Sira in Hebrew* (VTSup 68; Leiden: Brill, 1997), 83.

which were created in this way through maneuvering with the elements of MT. In a sense, these Hebrew words are variants that were created in the minds of the Rabbis.[137]

זקק

In the light of the above, it is unlikely that what we have in LXX Amos 6:6 arises from a mere confusion of consonants, as Kaminka argues (ר–ק).[138] He suggests that instead of במזרקי the translator read some form of זקק ("refine" or "purify"), either by mistake or because his *Vorlage* actually had such a reading. Indeed, Kennicott's Ms 4 lacks the letter ר,[139] but the reading במזקי does not align with either the LXX or the MT.

זקק has the general sense "refine"[140] and the *Pual* of זקק always occurs as a participle, mostly with reference to the refining of metals.[141] The only place where this participle refers to wine, however, is Isa 25:6 (שמרים מזקקים), and the wine-refining meant there is believed to be done by decanting (cf. Jer 31[MT48]:11).[142] Others explain it by way of "straining":

> NRSV's translation of the second half of the v. 'of well-aged wines strained clear' should be preferred to NIV's 'the finest of wine,' since it actually expresses the process (as indicated by the MT) of straining after a long period of resting undisturbed (Young, *The Book of Isaiah*, 2:193), which makes these wines so expensive and fine.[143]

Similarly, Barker notes the difference between the wine in Isa 25:6 and that in Jer 48:11: "The fact that the שְׁמָרִים have undergone filtering in Isa. 25:6 suggests that the wine is dregs-free. Thus, the unfiltered, bitter lees-wine found in Jer. 48:11 is, ostensibly, a contrast to the well-strained wine of the Isaiah 25 banquet."[144]

---

137. Tov, *The Text-critical Use of the Septuagint*, 164. See also Baer, *When We All Go Home*, 29; Glenny, *Finding Meaning in the Text*, 85–86; Palmer, "'Not Made with Tracing Paper,'" 55. Palmer says that "the large number of examples of contextual manipulation show that this method was most frequently the recourse of the translator." His conclusions may be extended to the other books of the LXX TP, given that the same translator is behind them all.

138. Kaminka, *Studien*, 29. Van Hoonacker has allowed for the same possibility (*Les Douze Petits Prophètes Traduits et Commentés* [Études Bibliques; Paris: Gabalda, 1908], 257).

139. Kennicott, *Vetus Testamentum Hebraicum*, 2:266.

140. *DCH* 3:133.

141. Used of gold in 1 Chr 28:18 and of silver in 1 Chr 29:4 (cf. Ps 11[MT 12]:7).

142. Leon J. Wood, "זָקַק," *TWOT* 1:575.

143. Gerald A. Klingbeil, "זָקַק," *NIDOTTE* 1:1141.

144. William D. Barker, "Isaiah 24–27: Studies in a Cosmic Polemic" (Ph.D. diss.; University of Cambridge, 2006), 78.

However, in Isa 25:6 מזקקים was left untranslated in the LXX. The familiarity of the Greek translator of the TP with the זקק root is difficult to ascertain since its only occurrence is in Mal 3:3. There, the translator renders זקק by χεεῖ ("pour") since the illustration used is that of purifying metals. Elsewhere in the LXX זקק is translated by δόκιμος, διηθέω, ἐπιχέω, καθαρίζω. διυλίζω, however, is a *hapax legomenon* in the LXX, though not in the hexaplaric texts of Aquila and Theodotion.

Aquila (Ps 11[MT12]:7) and Theodotion (Isa 25:6) use διυλίζω to translate זקק. Theodotion's use of διυλισμένων for מזקקים in Isa 25:6 (an asterisked Hexaplaric reading) supports the possibility that מזקק lies behind the Greek rendering in Amos 6:6.[145] If a Hebrew word had been in the translator's mind when he rendered the middle/passive form of διυλισμένον in LXX Amos 6:6, this would have been the *Pual* participle מְזֻקָּק. Although we can never exclude the possibility that מזקק was in the translator's *Vorlage*, on the basis of the common practice of consonantal "manoeuvring" by the Greek translator of Amos it is more likely that he "manipulated" במזרקי into מזקק. He would also have transposed the words into יין מזקק in order to produce διυλισμένος modifying οἶνος (his treatment of the adjective-noun order is consistent; cf. Amos 5:12; 6:2; 8:3).[146]

Dines observes that the Greek translator of Amos manages somehow to utilize the consonantal text to offer an idiomatic translation:

> One gets the impression however that respect for his Hebrew text sometimes prevented the translator from translating as idiomatically as he was capable of doing. When faced with difficulties (e.g., 3:11, 12; 4:2f), he normally prefers to struggle with the individual items of the text (sometimes adding a verb for clarity) rather than to paraphrase (an exception may be 6:5).[147]

Since he was unable to translate במזרקי without losing the sense of "accusation" in the prophet's words, Isa 25:6, being a "parallel" text and the only one where מזקק refers to wine, provides him with a convenient alternative very close in form to מזרק. An examination of Isa 25:6 will reveal its connections with Amos 6:6, and why it would readily come to mind.

145. Field, *Origenis Hexaplorum*, 2:472 n. 7. The connection of the participial form of διυλίζω in LXX Amos 6:6 and Theodotion's reading in Isa 25:6 is also noted by Carbone and Rizzi, *Il Libro di Amos*, 117.

146. Nowack, *Die kleinen Propheten*, 156; Sellin, *Das Zwölfprophetenbuch*, 200; Edgill, *The Book of Amos*, 63; Paul, *A Commentary on the Book of Amos*, 208 n. 76.

147. Dines, "The Septuagint of Amos," 308.

Isaiah 25:6

Lexically as well as thematically, Isa 25:6 is an unparalleled passage in the Hebrew Bible, and, according to Barker, in ancient Near Eastern literature as well.[148] Isaiah 25:6 describes a lavish banquet prepared by the Lord himself for all the peoples. Wine will be present (שמרים מזקקים)[149] and there will be all kinds of rich "oily" (שמנים) foods. The wines of this banquet are "described with rare vocabulary and are contrasted with the absence of wine in chapter 24."[150] The passage is characterized by a cluster of rare words, and, according to Barker, "the most likely purposes for the use of rare terminology are the maintaining of alliterative effect and the need to use uncommon vocabulary in order to describe a most uncommon event."[151]

שמנים occurs only five times in the Hebrew Bible, twice in 25:6 and once each in Isa 28:1 and 4. In 28:1–4 it functions as a name for the Valley of Ephraim, namely, the "valley of fatness" (גיא שמנים), in the context of an oracle against the drunkards of Ephraim. The fifth occurrence of שמנים is in Amos 6:6. Barker notes that "Amos 6:6 employs שמנים substantivally as 'oils,' and at first glance seems unrelated. However, in addition to this rare lexical parallel, Amos 6:6 also contains thematic parallels to Isa. 25:6–8. In both passages, there is the drinking of wine and an impending future divine judgement."[152]

However, in Isa 25:6, this feast of "fatness" is a positive celebration for the nations, the exact opposite of the condemned banquet of Amos 6:6. Most commentators view the banquet of Isa 25:6 in this positive light.[153] The Targum, however, stands as an exception, reading the passage negatively: "On this mountain the LORD of hosts will make for all peoples a feast *and a festival; they think that it is of glory, but it will*

148. Barker, "Isaiah 24–27," 74.
149. "Wine that has acquired strength and flavour by remaining on its lees (cp. Jer 48[11]) after the first fermentation, and has been rendered clear by being filtered before use." George Buchanan Gray, *A Critical and Exegetical Commentary on the Book of Isaiah: I–XXXIX*, vol. 1 (Edinburgh: T. & T. Clark, 1928), 430.
150. Barker, "Isaiah 24–27," 64.
151. Ibid., 69.
152. Ibid., 72.
153. Gary V. Smith, *Isaiah 1–39* (NAC 15A; Nashville: Broadman & Holman, 2007), 431–33; Joseph Blenkinsopp, *Isaiah 1–39* (AB 19; New York: Doubleday, 2000), 359–60; J. Alec Motyer, *The Prophecy of Isaiah: An Introduction and Commentary* (Downers Grove: IVP, 1993), 209; Gray, *A Critical and Exegetical Commentary on the Book of Isaiah*, 429–30.

be to them for shame, strokes[154] *from which they will not be rescued, strokes by which they will come to an end.*"[155]

This interpretation does not view the Lord's banquet as a blessing for the nations, but as God's judgment on them. It is possible that other judgment feasts of Yahweh were read into this passage by the targumist (e.g. Jer 32[MT25]:15; 51:39; Ps 74[MT75]:9). The way the imagery of wine-drinking functions in these "negative" texts may have dominated the targumist's understanding of the feast of Isa 25. Lentin accounts for this as follows: "Another factor which makes it difficult to paraphrase any imagery is the extent to which the interpretation is reliant upon the input of each individual reader. This goes beyond variations in senses of words caused by shifts over time or location."[156]

For the Greek translator of the TP, however, Amos 6:6 is conversely connected to Isa 25:6. Amos 6:6 shows the unjust elite group enjoying the finest, most luxurious products available, in a way that hubristically imitates the Lord's table of Isa 25:6 (cf. *1 En.* 96:4).

Conclusion

Several factors seem to have been at work in bringing about the Greek rendering of the difficult Hebrew of Amos 6:6: the peculiar connection of מזרק with יין, the inadequacy of ἐν φιάλαις to communicate Amos' accusation, the stylistic concerns of the Greek translator of Amos to achieve parallelism in the verse, and the obvious correspondences between Amos 6:6 and Isa 25:6 (the drinking of wine and especially the rare link-word, שמנים) which suggested מזקק to him.

It has been observed in the Dead Sea Scrolls, the New Testament and Rabbinic works that lexical associations served as a basis for linking texts together: "the rabbis could combine scriptural passages which treated cognate subject matter even if they occurred at rather distant places"; "they could fill the informational lacunae they perceived in the wording of a given passage by recourse to the other, sufficiently explicit biblical formulations."[157] Moreover, "as regards the Dead Sea scrolls and

---

154. "'[S]trokes' (*mḥn*) is distantly related to "full of marrow" (*mmḥym*) in the MT, which the meturgeman has taken as derived from the Hebrew *mḥh* in the sense, 'strike'." Bruce D. Chilton, *The Isaiah Targum: Introduction, Translation, Apparatus and Notes* (ArBib 11; Edinburgh: T. & T. Clark, 1987), 48.

155. According to Chilton, there are anti-Roman allusions in this passage (25:1–12): "It is part of the national confidence that the LORD will make a festival of '*strokes*' on Mount Zion for all peoples, especially their chief '*master*' and '*king*,' the Roman Emperor (vv. 6, 7)." *The Isaiah Targum*, 49 n. 25:1–25:12.

156. Lentin, "Seeing Double," 12.

157. Avemarie, "Interpreting Scripture Through Scripture," 86.

the New Testament, the combination of different scriptural passages on the basis of lexematic overlaps is found in both bodies of literature, and occasionally, conspicuous changes in the wording of a passage show very clearly that the lexematic association was made consciously."[158]

It is not unlikely that the Greek translator adopts a similar practice. It appears that lexematic, as well as thematic, associations between Amos 6:6 and Isa 25:6 encouraged the borrowing of מזקק by the LXX translator of Amos, to help in clarifying the meaning of his difficult Hebrew *Vorlage*.

* * *

Apparent Intertextual Connections

Hosea 4:9 (5:4 and 7:2)

Hosea 4:9

MT	LXX
וְהָיָה כָעָם כַּכֹּהֵן	καὶ ἔσται καθὼς ὁ λαὸς οὕτως καὶ ὁ ἱερεύς
וּפָקַדְתִּי עָלָיו דְּרָכָיו	καὶ ἐκδικήσω ἐπ' αὐτὸν τὰς ὁδοὺς αὐτοῦ
וּמַעֲלָלָיו אָשִׁיב לוֹ	καὶ τὰ διαβούλια αὐτοῦ ἀνταποδώσω αὐτῷ
And it shall be like people, like priest; I will punish them for their ways, and repay them for their deeds. [NRSV]	And it shall be as the people, so also the priest, and I will avenge on him his ways and repay him for his designs. [NETS]

Ezekiel 11:5

MT	LXX
וַתִּפֹּל עָלַי רוּחַ יְהוָה	καὶ ἔπεσεν ἐπ' ἐμὲ πνεῦμα
וַיֹּאמֶר אֵלַי אֱמֹר כֹּה־אָמַר יְהוָה	καὶ εἶπε πρός με τάδε λέγει κύριος
כֵּן אֲמַרְתֶּם בֵּית יִשְׂרָאֵל וּמַעֲלוֹת	οὕτως εἴπατε οἶκος Ισραηλ καὶ τὰ διαβούλια
רוּחֲכֶם אֲנִי יְדַעְתִּיהָ	τοῦ πνεύματος ὑμῶν ἐγὼ ἐπίσταμαι
Then the spirit of the LORD fell upon me, and he said to me, "Say, Thus says the LORD: This is what you think, O house of Israel; I know the things that come into your mind." [NRSV]	And a spirit fell upon me and said to me, "This is what the Lord says: Speak thus, O house of Israel, I understand even the deliberation of your spirit." [NETS]

After the Lord's condemnation of the inhabitants of the earth (Hos 4:1–4a), the prophetic word is turned against the people of Israel who are likened to their priests (4:9; cf. 4:4).[159] The Lord's punishment will come

---

158. Ibid.

159. This is a common idiom in the Hebrew Bible (Gen 18:25; Lev 7:7; Num 15:15; Judg 8:18; 3 Kgdms 22:4; Ps 138[MT 139]:12; Isa 24:2). Muraoka thinks

against their ways (דרכיו) and their deeds (ומעלליו).[160] It is possible to understand LXX Hos 4:9b as referring either to the priests' punishment, or to that of the λαός.[161] However, the references to λαός tend to be formed in the third person plural (LXX Hos 4:7–8, נפשו = τὰς ψυχὰς αὐτῶν; 4:12, ישאל = ἐπηρώτων, יגיד = ἀπήγγελλον, התעה = ἐπλανήθησαν), so it is not unlikely that 4:9b was understood to be against the priesthood. What is of particular interest in this verse, though, is the translator's choice of διαβούλια for the plural form of מעלל.

מעלל

מעלל, always found in the plural, refers to "deeds," both good and bad,[162] that is, outward expressions (action or speech [Isa 3:8]), not inner thoughts or plans. Its most frequent synonym in the OT is מעשה (Ps 105[MT106]:39), followed by פעל (Ps 27[MT28]:4; Prov 20:11), and דרך (e.g. Judg 2:19; Jer 17:10).[163] מעלל is mostly used in the prophets: seventeen times in Jeremiah, five in Hosea, three in Isaiah, three in Micah, two in Zechariah and one in Ezekiel.

The usual Greek stereotype for מעלל is ἐπιτήδευμα,[164] but one can also find it translated by ἔργον,[165] πονηρία,[166] ἀνομία[167] or πράγμα.[168] The Greek translator of the TP is consistent in rendering מעלל as ἐπιτήδευμα (Hos 9:15; 12:3; Mic 2:7; 3:4; 7:13; Zech 1:4, 6), except for the first three occurrences in Hosea (4:9; 5:4; 7:2) where he prefers διαβούλια ("counsels, deliberations"). In the light of the Hebrew meaning of מעללים, διαβούλια is not an accurate translation, thus raising a question as to what has caused the translator to deviate from his usual practice.

---

that in this type of idiom it is wrong to assume that one term is the subject while the other term is the standard of comparison: "the idiom means that one and the same standard applies to both, which otherwise would belong to two different categories." "Hosea IV," 39.

160. Another form of מעלל is מעליל, which is also parallel to דרך in Zech 1:4. דרך ("way, i.e. behaviour") is listed as a synonym of מעלל in *DCH* 5:406–7. In Jer 39[MT32]:19 the plural form of מעלל is translated by ὁδός in the LXX suggesting that they were understood as synonymous.

161. This problem was solved in various mss by pluralizing the αὐτόν/αὐτοῦ/αὐτῷ into αὐτούς/αὐτῶν/αὐτοῖς (V La[S] Ach Aeth[P] Cyr.[F] Th.).

162. *HALAT* 2:580–81; BDB 760; *DCH* 5:406–7.

163. *TDOT* 11:143.

164. Deut 28:20; Judg 2:19; 1 Kgdms 25:3; Neh 9:35; Pss 27:4; 105[MT 106]:29, 39, etc.

165. Pss 76[MT 77]:12; 77[MT 78]:7; Isa 3:10; Jer 33[MT 26]:13; 39[MT 32]:19.

166. Isa 1:16.

167. Isa 3:8.

168. Jer 51[MT 44]:22.

Muraoka's View

Muraoka attempts to explain two striking peculiarities which he identifies: (1) the distribution of the Greek equivalents for מעלל in the TP, given that they all come from a single translator, and (2) the correspondence of διαβούλιον ("debate, counsel, deliberations") and מעלל ("[most bad] practices, deeds").[169] The first difficulty is not as serious as the second one for him. He attributes the distribution of the Greek equivalents for מעלל to a mere inconsistency on the part of the translator.[170] Muraoka's solution to the second peculiarity is that the identification of מעלל with διαβούλια in LXX Hos 4:9, and consequently 5:4 and 7:2, arose under the influence of the Greek translation of Ezek 11:5, τὰ διαβούλια τοῦ πνεύματος ὑμῶν ἐγὼ ἐπίσταμαι for MT וּמַעֲלוֹת רוּחֲכֶם אֲנִי יְדַעְתִּיהָ.[171]

Muraoka works with the hypothesis of a single translator for the TP and Thackeray's Ezekiel α' (chs. 1–27), and he thinks that

> such influence becomes only possible under the assumption of a single translator for the two corpora in question, since no inner relation or even midrashic one is apparent between them. It is also important to remark that such influence can work only in one direction viz. from Ez to Ho, which implies the earlier date of the former translation.[172]

He also notes that the formally and semantically related עלילה is rendered ἐνθύμημα in 14:22, 23; 24:14 (and nowhere else in the LXX). Muraoka is not very clear on how the influence from Ezek 11:5 on Hos 4:9 (and 5:4; 7:2) came about. He seems to be suggesting that the Greek translator of Ezekiel α' and the TP uses two Greek equivalents for מעלל, ἐπιτήδευμα and διαβούλιον. He also uses at least two equivalents for עלילה, ἐπιτήδευμα (Ezek 20:43, 44; 21:29) and ἐνθύμημα (14:22, 23; 24:14). Moreover, Muraoka seems to be suggesting that, in Ezek 11:5, the translator mistook וּמַעֲלוֹת as including the plural of מעלל, thus rendering καὶ τὰ διαβούλια. In Hosea, the Greek translator simply uses διαβούλια and ἐπιτηδεύματα, the two meanings he knows for the plural of מעלל, interchangeably.

Regardless of whether one translator is involved in both the TP and Ezekiel α', we shall argue that the rendering διαβούλια in both LXX Ezekiel and LXX Hosea may be explained independently. First, we shall attempt to account for how LXX Ezek 11:5 may have come about. Second, we shall examine the sense of ἐπιτήδευμα, the translator's stereotype,

---

169. Muraoka, "Hosea IV," 40.
170. Ibid., 41.
171. Ibid., 40. Also adopted by *BA* 23.1:13.
172. Muraoka, "Hosea IV," 40–41.

and then compare it with διαβούλιον in order to establish what the difference is between the two. If the two can be used interchangeably, then the
correspondence between διαβούλιον and מעלל may not be as striking as
Muraoka suggests.

LXX Ezekiel 11:5

MT Ezekiel 11:5 has its own problems. ידעתיה has a feminine singular
suffix while its antecedent is plural. *BHS* suggests that ומעלות should be
read as ומעלת, and ידעתיה should be read as ידעתי. However, there is a
precedent for such incongruence, and no amendment of the text is
required.[173]

The noun מעלה is derived from the verb עלה ("to go up"). It is commonly used for "steps" or "stairs," as well as for "pilgrimage" or "ascent"
to Jerusalem.[174] It is found in titles of Psalms to be sung on the way up to
Jerusalem.[175] The phrase "the things that come up in your spirit" has the
sense of "that which you have in mind" (cf. 20:31[MT32]), but the more
usual phrase has "heart" instead of "spirit."[176] One example with a
negative sense, similar to Hos 4:9, is the "things" (i.e. evil schemes)
which go up in Gog's heart (Ezek 38:10; cf. LXX Ezek 14:3, 7). At the
same time, "things coming up to one's heart" may mean "to remember"
(Isa 65:16; Jer 3:16; 28[MT51]:50; 51[MT44]:21). Ezekiel 11:5 is the only
place where the noun מעלה is used metaphorically for the "evil thoughts"
that arise within. διαβούλια does mean "thoughts" or "deliberations," so,
in that sense, the Greek translator of Ezek 11:5 has grasped the contextual meaning of ומעלות accurately, and has translated "dynamically."
Elsewhere, he keeps to the common meaning ("steps," "stairs," "ascent")
for מעלה (40:6, 22, 26, 31, 34, 37, 49; 43:17). We find the same understanding of ומעלות in the Targum as well: "Then the spirit of *prophecy*
from before the Lord rested upon me, and He said to me, 'Say, Thus says
the Lord: So you have said, O House of Israel, but *what you are planning*
and what comes to your mind *are revealed before Me.*'"

The targumist has included the epexegetical gloss "what you are
planning" next to "what comes to your mind" in order to clarify this rare
use of מעלה. Similarly, the Peshitta has ܘܕܚܘܫܒܝ ܪܘܚܟܘܢ ("and the
thoughts of your spirit").

173. GKC § 135*p*.
174. Aquila and Theodotion render τους αναβαθμους, while Symmachus renders
το ωρολογιον in Ezek 11:5.
175. BDB 752.
176. Other examples meaning "to cross one's mind" are found in 4 Kgdms 12:5
and Jer 39[MT32]:35.

To conclude, in Ezek 11:5 we have a unique use of מעלה which called for an interpretive translation equivalent in order to preserve the sense. LXX, Peshiṭta and Targum have managed to give accurate renderings. It is, therefore, not necessary to assume that the translator read a form of מעלל, if this is indeed what Muraoka had in mind. However, the question in relation to Hosea still remains: Is διαβούλιον an appropriate equivalent for מעלל in 4:9; 5:4 and 7:2?

ἐπιτηδεύματα

ἐπιτήδευμα translates nine different Hebrew terms (מעשה; מועצה; גלולים; תועבה; שרירות; צעד; מעלל; מעליל; עלילה).[177] Muraoka's first definition (for the plural form) is "that in which one usually engages with devotion and eagerness," and his second is "that which one intends to do."[178] Similarly, Lust offers "pursuit, business, habits, ways of living, practices."[179] Muraoka's definitions, especially, show that the word can refer to both outward expressions (actions) and internal thoughts or plans, and is thus much broader than מעלל.

ἐπιτηδεύματα in Ezekiel. ἐπιτήδευμα is used in its "internal" sense in LXX Ezekiel also. Although ten out of 39 occurrences of גלולים are rendered by εἴδωλα in LXX Ezekiel, the Greek translator mostly prefers other lexicographical choices such as ἐπιτηδεύματα, ἐνθυμήματα and διανοήματα. Lust notes that, when LXX Ezekiel uses these terms, the context, both in Hebrew and in Greek, refers to the "inner life" of a person or to his/her "wrong doings."[180] However, Lust concludes that the scattering of the Greek translation equivalents is not random, nor can it be explained by a compound translation theory. He thinks that ἐπιτηδεύματα, ἐνθυμήματα or διανοήματα is used when גלולים has no direct ritual connotation, and denotes mental images or desires, or the objects of these desires, often involving foreign cultural influences.[181] From these data we can see the refusal, on the translator's part, to render terms stereotypically without sensitivity to the different contexts of the word. It is obvious that the problem of a sinful "inner life," and not just idolatrous cultic acts, is brought to the foreground by the Greek translator. If indeed the same translator was involved in both Ezekiel α' and the TP, we could perhaps expect him to be just as sensitive to the different contexts of the word in Hosea when choosing his translation equivalents.

---

177. HR 535.
178. *Muraoka 2009*, 284.
179. LEH 236.
180. Lust, "Idols?," 319 n. 14, 323.
181. Ibid., 332–33.

ἐπιτηδεύματα in *Other Biblical and Extra-Biblical Texts.* ἐπιτηδεύματα may refer to the "inner person" as well as to his/her deeds in the book of Psalms (Ps 80[MT81]:13): καὶ ἐξαπέστειλα αὐτοὺς κατὰ τὰ ἐπιτηδεύματα τῶν καρδιῶν αὐτῶν πορεύσονται ἐν τοῖς ἐπιτηδεύμασιν αὐτῶν. In Jdt 13:5 (cf. Jdt 10:8; 11:6) ἐπιτήδευμα is exclusively used in the "mental" sense: ὅτι νῦν καιρὸς ἀντιλαβέσθαι τῆς κληρονομίας σου καὶ ποιῆσαι τὸ ἐπιτήδευμά μου εἰς θραῦσμα ἐχθρῶν οἳ ἐπανέστησαν ἡμῖν. The same is observed in extra-biblical Greek literature. The word ἐπιτήδευμα is used in reference to the "customs" of a city:

> βασιλεὺς δέ, ὡς λέγεται, ἐθαύμασέ τε αὐτοῦ τὴν διάνοιαν καὶ ἐκέλευε ποιεῖν οὕτως. ὁ δ' ἐν τῷ χρόνῳ ὃν ἐπέσχε τῆς τε Περσίδος γλώσσης ὅσα ἐδύνατο κατενόησε καὶ τῶν ἐπιτηδευμάτων τῆς χώρας. (Thucydides, *Historiae* 1.138.1–2)

It is also used of "habits" or "way of life":

> φίλων παρόντων καὶ ἀπόντων μεμνῆσθαί φησι· μὴ τὴν ὄψιν καλλωπίζεσθαι, ἀλλὰ τοῖς ἐπιτηδεύμασιν εἶναι καλόν. (Thales, *Testimonia* 1.141–43)

> αἰσχρὸν μὲν μηδὲν μήτε ὁρῶντες μήτε ἀκούοντες, ἐν δὲ καλοῖς κἀγαθοῖς ἐπιτηδεύμασι διημερεύοντες. (Xenophon, *Cyropaedia* 7.5.86.5–6)

And it is also used for "thoughts": καὶ γὰρ οἶμαι δεῖν, ὦ βουλή, τὰ τοῦ σώματος δυστυχήματα τοῖς τῆς ψυχῆς ἐπιτηδεύμασιν ἰᾶσθαι, εἰκότως (Lysias, Ὑπὲρ τοῦ ἀδυνάτου [*On the Refusal of a Pension*] 24.3). An "inner" sense of ἐπιτηδεύματα may also be present in Philo (*Agr.* 1.56; *Virt.* 1.87) and Josephus (*Ant.* 4.46).

All the above suggest that the translation of מעלל by ἐπιτήδευμα has, as a result, broadened its meaning, unless the meaning of מעלל was broader for the Greek translators than we may think.

διαβούλια
We must now establish how closely related διαβούλια is to ἐπιτηδεύματα. διαβούλια with the sense of "plans" or "schemes" is found in Polybius, *Hist.* 1.3.9:

> ἵνα μηδεὶς ἐπιστὰς ἐπ'αὐτὴν τὴν τῶν πραγμάτων ἐξήγησιν τότε διαπορῇ καὶ ζητῇ ποίοις διαβουλίοις ἢ ποίαις δυνάμεσι καὶ χορηγίαις χρησάμενοι Ῥωμαῖοι πρὸς ταύτας ὥρμησαν τὰς ἐπιβολάς

but the most common use of the word refers to "councils" (e.g. Polybius, *Hist.* 2.39.6): πρῶτον μὲν ἀπέδειξαν Διὸς Ὁμαρίου κοινὸν ἱερὸν καὶ τόπον, ἐν ᾧ τάς τε συνόδους καὶ τὰ διαβούλια συνετέλουν.

In the LXX, διαβούλιον is much rarer than ἐπιτήδευμα, and it mainly carries negative connotations. As Theodore of Mopsuestia explains, the plural διαβούλια denotes precisely the inner evil plans and not simply the actions: Τιμωρήσομαι γὰρ αὐτοὺς ἀνάλογα οἷς τε ἐβουλεύοντο ἐπιτελεῖν καὶ προῄρηντο (*Commentarius in XII Prophetas* 4, 9b). Likewise, Cyril of Alexandria comments: Ὁδοὺς μὲν, ὡς ἔοικε, τὰς ὡς ἐν ἔργοις πορείας λέγει· διαβούλια δὲ αὖ, τὰ ἐκ λογισμῶν ἀτόπων πταίσματα (*Commentarius in XII Prophetas Minores* 1.103.24–25).

Apart from the three cases of διαβούλια under examination (Hos 4:9; 5:4; 7:2), there is just one other occurrence of διαβούλια, in Hos 11:6, where the Hebrew equivalent is not מעללים, the plural of מעלל, but מעצות from מוֹעֵצָה.[182] מוֹעֵצָה has the meaning "counsel, plan, principle, device,"[183] and it is also translated by βουλή, a more neutral term, in Mic 6:16. In Wis 1:9, the sense of διαβούλια is also negative, meaning "evil schemes," and in LXX Ezek 11:5 it refers to "evil thoughts" (מעלות).

διαβούλια translates מעצות in Ps 5:11, but in Ps 80[MT81]:13 מעצות is rendered as ἐπιτηδεύματα, a hint that the two terms could be treated as synonymous. In Ps 9:23[MT10:2], it is clear that διαβούλια (מזמות, "purposes, devices")[184] are "evil schemes": ἐν τῷ ὑπερηφανεύεσθαι τὸν ἀσεβῆ ἐμπυρίζεται ὁ πτωχός συλλαμβάνονται ἐν διαβουλίοις οἷς διαλογίζονται.

From the above data we conclude that διαβούλια is never used to mean "deeds," but refers mainly to "mental" acts and is always negative in the LXX, except for Sirach (see below). At least for the Greek translator of the Psalms, we can say that διαβούλια and ἐπιτηδεύματα are interchangeable because of their semantic overlap. In other words, διαβούλια makes up a very large subset of ἐπιτηδεύματα, which allows the two words to be used interchangeably in certain contexts. This suggests that the treatment of the two words as synonymous may have not been unique to the Greek translator of Psalms, but could also hold for the Greek translator of the TP and Ezekiel α´.

---

182. Hedley discusses the ambiguity of the plural διαβουλιων and concludes that there is no evidence to suppose that a feminine διαβουλία existed, only διαβούλιον, and he recommends its removal from the lexica and concordances. P. L. Hedley, "ΔΙΑΒΟΥΛΙΑ," *JTS* 34 (1933): 270.

183. BDB 420.

184. BDB 273.

διαβούλιον/צר in *Sirach and Qumran*

In Sirach the situation is slightly different. The word occurs three times, twice in the singular and once in the plural (15:14 [singular]; 17:6 [singular]; 44:4 [plural]) with neutral or even *positive* connotations. In 44:4, διαβούλια are the wise counsels which characterize the leaders of the people (ἡγούμενοι λαοῦ ἐν διαβουλίοις καὶ συνέσει γραμματείας λαοῦ σοφοὶ λόγοι ἐν παιδείᾳ αὐτῶν). In 17:6, διαβούλιον is given by God in creation (διαβούλιον καὶ γλῶσσαν καὶ ὀφθαλμοὺς ὦτα καὶ καρδίαν ἔδωκεν διανοεῖσθαι αὐτοῖς), and in 15:14 it refers to the responsibility or freedom of choice given to Adam (αὐτὸς ἐξ ἀρχῆς ἐποίησεν ἄνθρωπον καὶ ἀφῆκεν αὐτὸν ἐν χειρὶ διαβουλίου αὐτοῦ).

Sirach 15:14 is in the context of a debate with respect to the origin of sin in a person's life, where the author argues against blaming God for inciting one to sin. Hadot discusses the development of this notion, observed already in the Chronicler's reaction to 2 Sam 24:1.[185] The agency bringing sin about is attributed to Satan in 1 Chr 21:1, thus protecting God's morality. The idea of human responsibility becomes dominant in Jewish writings. However, Hadot raises the question whether διαβούλιον (צר)[186] in Sir 15:14 refers to freedom of choice or to the evil inclination towards sin. Various scholars argue that Sirach could only have had the "evil inclination" in mind, as the "good inclination" is a later concept, but Hadot prefers to see a neutrality in צר, as well as διαβούλιον, since the context (15:15–17) demands the sense of "free will" or "ability to choose between good and evil."[187] The knowledge of good and evil is not something catastrophic in Sirach, as it is portrayed in Genesis, but is the gift of Wisdom (17:7).[188] The meaning of διαβούλιον in Sirach is thus very different from the rest of the LXX.

Stuart is in agreement with taking διαβούλιον as something neutral or positive in Sirach, but he argues that 15:14 may have been the first stage in the development of the rabbinic teaching of the good and evil inclinations.[189] In Qumran, he finds a very different picture for צר (Sirach's διαβούλιον). His study of the Dead Sea Scrolls reveals that the term was understood in a strikingly different way from what we find in Sirach:

185. Jean Hadot, *Penchant Mauvais et Volonté Libre dans la Sagesse de Ben Sira* (Brussels: University of Brussels Press, 1970), 92–93.

186. Beentjes, *The Book of Ben Sira in Hebrew*, 44.

187. Hadot, *Penchant Mauvais*, 98–99, 107.

188. Ibid., 109.

189. G. H. Cohen Stuart, *The Struggle in Man Between Good and Evil: An Inquiry into the Origin of the Rabbinic Concept of Yeṣer Haraʾ* (Kampen: Kok, 1984), 89, 91, 93.

Man seems to be much more powerless against the powers of evil, Belial and the spirits of deceit. The natural helplessness of man in confrontation with evil becomes clear from expressions like 'creature of clay'...in nearly all cases the *yeṣer* seems to be governed by external powers. Decisions on human life seem to be made outside of man.[190]

The Frequency of διαβούλια in Hosea

The existence of this notion in Qumran is important for our study of Hos 4:9, 5:4 and 7:2, where the evil διαβούλια and a "spirit of prostitution" (4:12; 5:4) prevent the people from knowing God. Although יצר is not present in the book of Hosea, it is interesting to look at parallel concepts in the passages where διαβούλια is preferred, instead of ἐπιτηδεύματα. Roth notes that "[u]nique to Hosea is language that gives the deeds a life of their own: 'they surround him' and 'do not permit him to return to Yahweh' (7:2; 5:4)."[191]

The fact that Hosea is the "home" of διαβούλια in the LXX may suggest something about the translator's understanding of the book (or at least its initial chapters). While both διαβούλια and ἐπιτηδεύματα could have been used to refer to mental deliberations, the choice of διαβούλια instead of ἐπιτηδεύματα eliminates the ambiguity in מעלליהם. While ἐπιτηδεύματα may refer to both thoughts and actions, διαβούλια limits the reference to the evil deliberations of the inner man as opposed to one's external actions, and it appears that the Greek translator began translating Hosea with this understanding in mind. But why διαβούλια for only the first three occurrences of מעללים?

Wolff notices something unique about these three verses (4:9; 5:4; 7:2). He notes on Hos 7:2:

> As in 4:9; 5:4, 5b, man is pictured as captive to the principle of that fateful sphere which he creates for himself by his own actions. Yet this does not work itself out independently, but "before Yahweh's face." Appearing before him are not those who in their distress seek communion with him (5:15; 6:6), but those who are caught in and circumscribed by their own deeds. They make necessary the further chastisement announced by the prophet (5:9, 14).[192]

Similarly, Macintosh notes that,

> the very wickedness to which the nation is given seems to prevent its repudiation of it.[193]

---

190. Ibid., 100.
191. W. Roth, "עלל," *TDOT* 11:145.
192. Wolff, *Hosea*, 124.
193. E.g. Macintosh, *A Critical and Exegetical Commentary on Hosea*, 183.

The wickedness of the nation has become so compulsive that the possibility of repentance and return to the God of truth and justice is virtually precluded.[194]

[T]he truth is that their wicked deeds are noted by Yahweh and at the same time they have brought about inexorably the confinement of their perpetrators.[195]

The διαβούλια have trapped the people because of the prevailing deception of the רוח זנונים in their midst. Stuart interprets this spirit to be an "orientation" among the people, rather than something which possesses each one individually.[196] Wolff agrees that this spirit is not something that possesses them, but it prevails in their midst just as Israel's leaders are working among the people.[197] However, this is not the only way to interpret רוח זנונים, and indeed Harper has understood this spirit to be "in their constitution."[198]

Hamori examines the "spirit of falsehood" in various OT texts, including Hos 4:12; 5:4; 9:7 and 12:2, and suggests that in Hosea the "spirit of falsehood" probably refers to something more than a feeling or inclination.[199] She says: "These three references (i.e. Hos 4:12–5:4; 9:7; 12:1–2) taken together imply that Hosea, whether intending these references as allusion or as wordplay based on knowledge of the tradition, does know the tradition of the רוח who misleads."[200]

Whatever the intention of the author, it appears that this spirit deceives the mind of the people with the result that they are entangled by their "evil thoughts" (διαβούλια).

Spiritual Deception

The "deceiving spirit" appears in LXX Jer 4:11 (ἐν τῷ καιρῷ ἐκείνῳ ἐροῦσιν τῷ λαῷ τούτῳ καὶ τῇ Ιερουσαλημ πνεῦμα πλανήσεως ἐν τῇ ἐρήμῳ ὁδὸς τῆς θυγατρὸς τοῦ λαοῦ μου οὐκ εἰς καθαρὸν οὐδ᾽ εἰς ἅγιον), while *absent* from the MT, and it is also found in *Pss. Sol.* 8:14 (διὰ τοῦτο ἐκέρασεν αὐτοῖς ὁ θεὸς πνεῦμα πλανήσεως ἐπότισεν αὐτοὺς ποτήριον οἴνου ἀκράτου εἰς μέθην).[201] The deception of the mind may also be present in

194. Ibid., 184.
195. Ibid., 253.
196. Douglas Stuart, *Hosea–Jonah* (WBC 31; Waco: Word, 1987), 93.
197. Wolff, *Hosea*, 99–100.
198. Harper, *A Critical and Exegetical Commentary on Amos and Hosea*, 270.
199. Esther J. Hamori, "The Spirit of Falsehood," *CBQ* 72 (2010): 26.
200. Ibid., 27.
201. Deception is introduced in LXX Hos 8:6 (διότι πλανῶν ἦν ὁ μόσχος σου Σαμάρεια) where the MT reads differently: כִּי־שְׁבָבִים יִהְיֶה עֵגֶל שֹׁמְרוֹן.

the *pesher* of Hosea. In 4QpHos[a] the unfaithful ones are those who are led astray, and Horgan thinks that they may be the followers of the Man of the Lie or the One who Spouts the Lie (1QpHab 10:9; 4QpPs[a] 1–10 I 26–27).[202] The Pesher of Hos 2:8 suggests that the author understood this verse to be about mental deception: "[SHE CANNOT FIND] HER PATHS. [...The interpretation of it is...that...with madness] and with blindness and bewilderment [of mind..." (Col. 1, *ll.* 8–9)[203]

Instruction on the two spirits, the spirit of light and the spirit of deceit, is found in the Community Rule (1QS 3:13–4:26), among other texts, and shares similarities with ideas found in Philo.[204] The above texts attest to the widespread dissemination of ideas on spiritual deception in Second Temple Judaism.

Conclusion

Back in Hosea, while Aquila is faithful to his stereotype ἐπιτηδεύματα, Symmachus reads βουλας and Theodotion reads γνωμην in Hos 5:4. Both these renderings of מעלליס show that the verse was understood as referring to the "mind" instead of actual deeds.[205]

Similarly, the LXX translator may have understood Hos 1–7 as having to do with the people's evil minds or the deception of their minds, rather than their actions, possibly owing to the presence of the deceiving "spirit of prostitution." The focus on the "mind" was better communicated by the Greek translator through διαβούλια, rather than through ἐπιτηδεύματα, and may possibly explain the distribution of the Greek equivalents of מעלליס in the corpus of the TP. Of course, the possibility of random choice of Greek equivalents is equally strong, and we must allow room for that option. However, I see no indication of influence coming from LXX Ezek 11:5.

To summarize: the choice of διαβούλια is not an accurate equivalent of מעלליס in LXX Hos 4:9; 5:4 and 7:2, but it is a narrower term than its normal stereotype ἐπιτηδεύματα. However, we have seen the two terms

202. Maurya P. Horgan, *Pesharim: Qumran Interpretations of Biblical Books* (CBQMS 8; Washington: Catholic Biblical Association of America, 1979), 139.

203. Ibid., 140.

204. Jutta Leonhardt-Balzer, "A Case of Psychological Dualism: Philo of Alexandria and the Instruction on the Two Spirits," in *Early Christian Literature and Intertextuality.* Vol. 2, *Exegetical Studies* (ed. Craig A. Evans and H. Daniel Zacharias; Library of New Testament Studies 392; London: T&T Clark International, 2009), 27–45.

205. No hexaplaric readings are preserved for Hos 4:9, but for 7:2 we have ἐπιτηδεύματα for both Aquila and Symmachus.

used interchangeably, especially in LXX Psalms. Because ἐπιτηδεύματα can mean both "thoughts" and "actions," we suggested the possibility that διαβούλια was chosen in order to limit the reference to the "mind" because of the idea of deception by the "spirit of prostitution" in the wider context. On the other hand, the Greek translator of the TP may be using the two terms διαβούλια and ἐπιτηδεύματα interchangeably, without any apparent consistency in the pattern. What was difficult to demonstrate, however, was that the use of διαβούλια in LXX Hosea is explained by means of a connection with the rendering of מעלות in LXX Ezek 11:5. Instead, the two renderings were able to be accounted for independently.

Hosea 12:4–5

Hosea 12:4–5a

MT	LXX
בַּבֶּטֶן עָקַב אֶת־אָחִיו	ἐν τῇ κοιλίᾳ ἐπτέρνισεν τὸν ἀδελφὸν αὐτοῦ
וּבְאוֹנוֹ שָׂרָה אֶת־אֱלֹהִים	καὶ ἐν κόποις αὐτοῦ ἐνίσχυσεν πρὸς θεὸν
וַיָּשַׂר אֶל־מַלְאָךְ וַיֻּכָל	καὶ ἐνίσχυσεν μετὰ ἀγγέλου καὶ ἠδυνάσθη
בָּכָה וַיִּתְחַנֶּן־לוֹ בֵּית־אֵל	ἔκλαυσαν καὶ ἐδεήθησάν μου ἐν τῷ οἴκῳ Ων
יִמְצָאֶנּוּ וְשָׁם יְדַבֵּר עִמָּנוּ	εὕροσάν με καὶ ἐκεῖ ἐλαλήθη πρὸς αὐτόν
In the womb he tried to supplant his brother, and in his manhood he strove with God. He strove with the angel and prevailed, he wept and sought his favor; he met him at Bethel, and there he spoke with him. [NRSV]	In the womb he kicked his brother with the heel and in his struggles prevailed against God. And he prevailed with an angel and predominated. They wept and implored me; they found me in the house of On, and there [a word] was spoken to him. [NETS]

Genesis 32:29

MT	LXX
וַיֹּאמֶר לֹא יַעֲקֹב יֵאָמֵר עוֹד	εἶπεν δὲ αὐτῷ οὐ κληθήσεται ἔτι τὸ ὄνομά σου
שִׁמְךָ כִּי אִם־יִשְׂרָאֵל	Ιακωβ ἀλλὰ Ισραηλ ἔσται τὸ ὄνομά σου
כִּי־שָׂרִיתָ עִם־אֱלֹהִים	ὅτι ἐνίσχυσας μετὰ θεοῦ
וְעִם־אֲנָשִׁים וַתּוּכָל	καὶ μετὰ ἀνθρώπων δυνατός
Then the man said, "You shall no longer be called Jacob, but Israel, for you have striven with God and with humans, and have prevailed." [NRSV]	Then he said to him, "Your name shall no longer be called Iakob, but Israel shall be your name, because you have prevailed with a god, and with humans you are powerful." [NETS]

This passage features in Tov's discussion in the category of "Quotations and Allusions."[206] He claims that "allusions to passages in the Hebrew

---

206. Tov, "The Impact of the LXX," 589.

Pent. occurring in the later books of the Bible were often phrased in the Greek in a manner identical with the translation of the Pentateuchal passages in the LXX of the Pent."[207]

In Hos 12:4 (אֶת־אֱלֹהִים שָׂרָה, ἐνίσχυσεν πρὸς θεὸν) and 12:5 (וַיָּשַׂר אֶל־מַלְאָךְ, καὶ ἐνίσχυσεν μετὰ ἀγγέλου), it appears that the phraseology is borrowed from LXX Gen 32:29: שָׂרִיתָ עִם־אֱלֹהִים, ἐνίσχυσας μετὰ θεοῦ.

An Ambiguous Story

Before analyzing the texts, we must note that the story of Jacob wrestling with a mysterious individual at Jabbok has troubled many of its readers. The identity of the "man" (אִישׁ) is not explicit in Gen 32:25, but his refusal to disclose his name and the authority he exercises by naming Jacob as "Israel" suggest that he is a heavenly being. Hosea is the one who identifies him as an "angel" (מלאך), though the word is regarded as a gloss by many writers.[208] Hosea's allusion to the struggle at the Jabbok, and to other events in Jacob's life, is not particularly helpful in illuminating the story. Hosea is either following a different tradition unknown to us, or he is reinterpreting Gen 32 in an innovative way in order to catch the attention of his hearers/readers.[209]

The weeping in Hos 12:5 creates further problems for scholars who try to reconcile Jacob as a victor in this struggle with his "weeping" and "begging" for a favour. The ambiguity of the text and the uncertainty in interpretation are also reflected in rabbinic discussion:

> Yea, he strove with an angel, and prevailed; he wept, and made supplication unto him. I know not who prevailed over whom. But when it says, For thou hast striven with God and with men and hast prevailed, I know that Jacob became master over the angel. He wept and made supplication unto him! I know not who wept unto whom. But when it says, And he said, Let me go, I know that the angel wept unto Jacob. (*b. Ḥul.* 92a)

No weeping is mentioned in the Genesis account, and Holladay suggests that Jacob weeps for Esau's favour, not the angel's.[210] This ambiguity has led some commentators, following Nyberg's suggestion, to solve the apparent problem by revocalizing אֶל as אֵל, making God the victor

---

207.   Ibid., 588.
208.   E.g. M. Gertner, "The Masora and the Levites: Appendix on Hosea XII," *VT* 10 (1960): 281; W. L. Holladay, "Chiasmus, the Key to Hosea XII 3–6," *VT* 16 (1966): 56; Wolff, *Hosea*, 212; Steven L. McKenzie, "The Jacob Tradition in Hosea XII 4–5," *VT* 36 (1986): 313.
209.   See E. M. Good, "Hosea and the Jacob Tradition," *VT* 16 (1966): 137–51.
210.   Holladay, "Chiasmus," 56.

over Jacob.[211] Harper notes that, for whatever reason, the LXX presents both Jacob and the angel weeping together: ἔκλαυσαν καὶ ἐδεήθησάν μου.[212]

Reception-history of the Story of the Struggle at the Jabbok
The conflation of the Genesis account and Hosea's version is attested as early as Demetrius the Chronographer, around the third century B.C.E.[213] In Fragment 2:7, Demetrius mentions that an angel of the Lord wrestled with Jacob and touched the hollow of his thigh. The angel then renames Jacob as Israel.[214] Since no angel is mentioned in the Genesis story, we may assume that the Genesis and Hosea references were already mutually interpreted.[215]

Philo understands that Israel is the name of the greatest of angels, the firstborn Logos, a tradition taken over by Justin Martyr regarding Christ:[216]

κἀνκαί μηδέπω μέντοι τυγχάνῃ τις ἀξιόχρεως ὢν υἱὸς θεοῦ προσαγορεύεσθαι σπουδαζέτω κοσμεῖσθαι κατὰ τὸν πρωτόγονον αὐτοῦ λόγον, τὸν ἀγγέλων πρεσβύτατον, ὡς ἂν ἀρχάγγελον, πολυώνυμον ὑπάρχοντα· καὶ γὰρ ἀρχὴ καὶ ὄνομα θεοῦ καὶ λόγος καὶ ὁ κατ' εἰκόνα ἄνθρωπος καὶ ὁ ὁρῶν, Ἰσραήλ, προσαγορεύεται. (*De confusione linguarum* 1:146)

A similar understanding is found in the Prayer of Joseph, a first-century C.E. text. In Fragment A, Israel is the archangel and the chief captain of the sons of God, the minister before God's face, who had descended on earth and had been called Jacob. The angel Uriel, the eighth in a list

---

211. Gertner, "The Masora and the Levites," 277; Holladay, "Chiasmus," 56; Wolff, *Hosea*, 212–13; L. M. Eslinger, "Hosea 12:5a and Genesis 32:39: A Study in Inner Biblical Exegesis," *JSOT* 18 (1980): 94; Andersen and Freedman, *Hosea*, 593, 608; McKenzie, "The Jacob Tradition," 313; Macintosh, *A Critical and Exegetical Commentary on Hosea*, 484.

212. Harper, *A Critical and Exegetical Commentary on Amos and Hosea*, 381. Also *BA* 1:243.

213. *OTP* 2:843–44.

214. *OTP* 2:849.

215. The "man" in Gen 32:25 may have been understood to be an angel independently of Hosea, given the prominence of the angelic presence in the beginning of ch. 32. Robert Hayward, *Interpretations of the Name Israel in Ancient Judaism and Some Early Christian Writings: From Victorious Athlete to Heavenly Champion* (Oxford: Oxford University Press, 2005), 50–51, 66–67.

216. The Christian tradition regarding Christ, the Logos, who is called Israel from the beginning and who wrestled with Jacob, bestowing his name on the patriarch, may be dependent on this (Justin, *Dial.* 125.5).

headed by Israel, envied him and fought him for first rank.²¹⁷ Perhaps this tradition arose in order to provide a motivation for the struggle.

Moreover, the interpretation of שׂרה (v. 4) and וישׂר (v. 5) has been just as varied. The verbs allude to Israel's name, which Josephus interpets as "the one who opposes the angel of God": ἐκέλευσέ τε καλεῖν αὐτὸν Ἰσραῆλον σημαίνει δὲ τοῦτο κατὰ τὴν Ἑβραίων γλῶτταν τὸν ἀντιστάτην ἀγγέλῳ θεοῦ (*Ant.* 1.333). Philo, on the other hand, does not offer any insight on שׂרה but understands the name Israel to be derived from אישׁ ראה אל ("a man seeing God"). Philo uses ὁ ὁρῶν,²¹⁸ which is also employed by various Church Fathers.²¹⁹ Our question, however, is how the LXX translator of the TP understood שׂרה and וישׂר in Hos 12:4–5, and whether he consulted LXX Gen 32:29 in order to render them.

שׂרה *and Related Terms*

The word שׂרה ("persist, persevere")²²⁰ occurs only in Hos 12:4–5 and Gen 32:29. While many writers distinguish between the verbs in vv. 4 and 5,²²¹ the Greek translator assumed the same root in both instances. However, the meaning of שׂרה seems not to correspond to the Greek ἐνισχύω (intr. "prevail,"²²² "be strong"²²³). ἐνισχύειν is also used in LXX Joel 4:16 for מעוז ("place or means of safety, protection"),²²⁴ which can be explained if the translator read a form of עזז ("be strong").²²⁵ The root עזז may also have been read in LXX Jer 6:1 (ἐνισχύσατε for העזו).

Another occurrence of ἐνισχύω in the TP, which could illumine the verse under discussion, comes in Hos 10:11 for the verb שׂדד (*Piel*,

217. *OTP* 2:713.
218. For the references in Philo, see *OTP* 2:703 n. 20.
219. *OTP* 2:703 n. 19.
220. BDB 975.
221. Some scholars who distinguish between the verbs of v. 4 and v. 5 are: Gertner, "The Masora and the Levites," 277; P. R. Ackroyd, "Hosea and Jacob," *VT* 13 (1963): 248; R. B. Coote, "Hosea XII," *VT* 21 (1971): 395; Wolff, *Hosea*, 206; Barthélemy, *Critique Textuelle*, 602; Macintosh, *A Critical and Exegetical Commentary on Hosea*, 483. Some scholars who take the verb to be the same in both vv. 4 and 5 are: H. L. Ginsberg, "Hosea's Ephraim, More Fool Than Knave: A New Interpretation of Hosea XII: 1–14," *JBL* 80 (1961): 342; Good, "Hosea and the Jacob Tradition," 141; Holladay, "Chiasmus," 56; Andersen and Freedman, *Hosea*, 593; McKenzie, "The Jacob Tradition," 313; Stuart, *Hosea-Jonah*, 185.
222. LSJ 569.
223. LEH 204.
224. BDB 731.
225. BDB 738. מעוז is treated differently every time it occurs in the TP (Nah 1:7; 3:11).

"harrow"). It is possible that the verb here was read as שׂרר ("rule") owing to a ר–ד confusion.[226] So did the Greek translator of Hos 10:11 read שׂרר rather than שׂדד, and also connect the verbs in 12:4 and 5 with שׂרר? A survey of roots with the consonants שׂ and ר shows that in the LXX they are rendered as ἄρχειν (שׂור Qal—Judg 9:22; Hiphil—Hos 8:4; שׂרר—Isa 32:1; שׂרה—Judg 5:29; 3 Kgdms 11:1[MT3]; Isa 49:23; Lam 1:1; שׂר—3 Kgdms 21[MT20]:19),[227] μεγαλύνειν (Prov 8:16)[228] or κατάρχειν (Num 16:13),[229] but never as ἐνισχύειν. The main Hebrew root behind ἐνισχύειν is חזק, so if the Greek translator read the שׂרר root in Hos 10:11 and 12:4–5, he should have chosen at least ἄρχειν. However, as the editors of BA suggest, the Greek translator of Hos 10:11, and consequently 12:4–5, must have read not שׂרר but the Aramaic/late Hebrew שׂרר (Pael "to make strong, hard"; Ithpaal "to become hard"):[230] "confusion de la racine *śdd*, 'herser,' et de la racine araméenne *shrr* 'être fort' (confusion du *daleth* et du *resh*). L'image agricole du TM a été abandonnée par le traducteur en faveur d'une allusion historique anticipant ce qui sera dit en Os 12 (en particulier aux v. 3–4)."[231]

While the allusion to Gen 32:29 is there in Hos 12:4–5 and could justify the borrowing of ἐνισχύειν from the LXX Pentateuch, it is difficult to see how this explanation could also account for the use of ἐνισχύειν for שׂדד in Hos 10:11.[232] A connection with the Aramaic שׂרר could, on the other hand, account for ἐνισχύειν in all cases (Gen 32:29; Hos 10:11 [ר for ד]; 12:4, 5).[233]

At the same time, a question remains as to why the verbs in Hos 10:11 and 12:4, 5 were not connected with the known שׂרר[234] ("rule") in Hos 8:4:[235]

226. BDB 979.
227. *HR* 163.
228. *HR* 902.
229. *HR* 743.
230. See *Jastrow*, 1634.
231. *BA* 23.1:138.
232. The root שׂדד is rare, occurring twice more in Job 39:10 and Isa 28:24.
233. Wevers notes that the Targum, the Peshiṭta and the Vulgate all agree with the LXX on ἐνισχύειν for שׂרה in Gen 32:29. Aquila and Symmachus have forms of ἄρχω reflecting שׂרר, "rule, govern." Wevers, *Notes on the Greek Text of Genesis*, 543.
234. HR has הַשִּׂירוּ under the root שׂור (163). However, Joüon and Muraoka note that there are some geminate forms with *i* in the *Hiphil* with contamination from the hollow verbs. The root, therefore, in Hos 8:4 is שׂרר (§ 82*n*). See also GKC § 67*v*.
235. Barthélemy, with many others, regards this root as being behind Hos 12:5 and translates: "il fut prince à l'égard de l'ange." Barthélemy, *Critique Textuelle*, 602.

הֵם הִמְלִיכוּ וְלֹא מִמֶּנִּי   ἑαυτοῖς ἐβασίλευσαν καὶ οὐ δι' ἐμοῦ
הֵשִׂירוּ וְלֹא יָדָעְתִּי   ἦρξαν καὶ οὐκ ἐγνώρισάν μοι

Prepositions אֶל *and* אֶת

The peculiar preposition μετά for אל in LXX Hos 12:5 raises further suspicion. אל is never translated by μετά in the entire corpus of the TP.[236] Moreover, although ἐνισχύω is found with πρός in Theophrastus (*De sensu et sensibilibus* 67.9 [fourth to third century B.C.E.]: τοῦτο μάλιστα ἐνισχύειν πρός τε τὴν αἴσθησιν καὶ τὴν δύναμιν), it is never accompanied by μετά in Greek extra-biblical literature. Could, then, this peculiar construction with μετά have been borrowed from LXX Gen 32:29?

Harl examines the preposition in LXX Gen 32:29 and notes that the text demands that we interpret שׂרית עם ("you fought with") as "you fought against." In Greek, however, the preposition μετά does not mean "against"; it simply follows the Hebrew עם literally in this case. πρός would have been the expected preposition (for πρός meaning "against" see LXX Num 21:5; Job 1:5; Hos 14:1); instead, the use of μετά confused some interpreters of this text, for example Origen, who thought that Jacob prevailed over his adversary with the help of an angel.[237] Harl argues that a similar sense is given by LXX Hos 12:4–5: he was strong *against* God (πρὸς θεὸν), he was strong *with* the angel (μετὰ ἀγγέλου), and he won (ἠδυνάσθη).[238] There is no reason why the Greek translator would have used μετά in Hos 12:5 unless (a) he had a different *Vorlage* with עם; (b) the Hebrew prepositions אל and אֶת were transposed, thus reading אל־אלהים in v. 4 and אֶת־מלאך in v. 5; (c) he was influenced by Gen 32:29, which has עם. This last case would not require an awareness of the Greek version of Gen 32. The translator could just as easily have been reminded of the Hebrew text and translated עם by μετά as his normal practice is.

To examine the first and second possibilities we should look at what the other Greek versions have done with this verse:

236.   The Hebrew prepositions behind μετά are: עַם (Hos 2:20; 4:5, 14; 5:5; 9:8; 12:2; 14:3; Amos 2:3; 4:10; Mic 2:7; 6:2, 8; Joel 2:26; Jon 1:3; Zech 8:23; 10:5; 14:5); בְּ (Hos 5:6; 6:2; Amos 1:14; 2:2; Mic 3:11; Jon 2:10; Zeph 1:12); אַחַר (Hos 3:5; Amos 8:10; Joel 2:2; 3:1); אֶת (Hos 7:5; Amos 4:2; 5:14; Hag 1:13; 2:4; Mal 2:5, 6); עַל (Hab 3:1).

237.   Hayward thinks that Jacob's "victory and the new name Israel consequent upon it are achieved by his strengthening himself along with God, like an angel, to overcome his opponent (whoever it might be) and to be strong with men." He connects this understanding with the strengthening of the angels in LXX Deut 32:43. *Interpretations of the Name Israel*, 66.

238.   *BA* 1:77, 243.

	MT	LXX	A	Σ	Θ
Hos 12:4	שָׂרָה אֶת־אֱלֹהִים	ἐνίσχυσεν πρὸς θεὸν	κατωρθωσε προς αγγελον (Syh)		
Hos 12:5	וַיָּשַׂר אֶל־מַלְאָךְ	καὶ ἐνίσχυσεν μετὰ ἀγγέλου	και κατωρθωσε μετα θεου	\<και\> κατεδυναστευσε τον αγγελον (Syh)	και κατωρθωσε μετα θεου

Notable features are evident in these two verses. Aquila, who interprets שרה as κατορθόω ("keep straight, set right, accomplish successfully"),[239] was inspired by the root ישׁר,[240] and transposed the objects in vv. 4 and 5, which may be paralleled in Theodotion. In the case of Symmachus, it is possible that his *Vorlage* had את־מלאך and that he read את as the object marker.[241] Other versions read:

> *Targum*:
> And by his might he contended (אתרב) with *the angel*. Thus he contended (אתרב) with the angel and prevailed.

> *Peshiṭta*:
> By his might he became great (ܐܬܘܪܒ) before God. And he prevailed (ܘܐܬܚܝܠ) over the angel.

> *Vulgate*:
> And by his strength he had success (*directus est*)[242] with an angel. And he prevailed (*invaluit*) over the angel.

The verb of v. 4 was identified with that of v. 5 by the LXX, Aquila and the Targum. The Peshiṭta distinguishes between the two verbs; similarly the Vulgate, which agrees with Aquila on the first verb and with the LXX or Symmachus on the second. אלהים and מלאך are both translated by "angel" in the Targum and the Vulgate. It is possible that this reflects an interpretation, or even translates a *Vorlage*, which does not want to present God as having been prevailed upon.

The variation in the Greek versions suggests that a Hebrew *Vorlage* with an arrangement of the prepositions different from that of the MT was known to the LXX translator.[243] In this case, his text would have read as

239. Used for battle in Lysias. See LSJ 930.

240. Barthélemy, *Critique Textuelle*, 602.

241. The confusion of the preposition אֶת ("with") and the accusative particle אֵת is an ancient one. GKC §103*j*.

242. Jerome may have followed the interpretation of Aquila, inspired by the root ישׁר. Barthélemy, *Critique Textuelle*, 602.

243. The oldest witness to this text is 4QXII[g] [4Q82] (ca. 50–25 B.C.E.), which follows the MT:]בָּאֹ[נו שרה] את א[לוהים וי]שׁר אל] (*DJD* 15:286 [f.30α *l.*11]).

that supposed for Symmachus: אֶל־אֱלֹהִים in v. 4 and אֶת־מַלְאָךְ in v. 5. In fact, two Kennicott manuscripts, 76 and 126, have אֶת instead of אֶל in v. 5.[244] The LXX version would, therefore, be an accurate translation of its Hebrew text if it had אֶל behind πρός and אֵת behind μετά.

The variation in order within the Greek tradition, as seen above, gives weight to the transposition theory in explaining the preposition μετά in LXX Hos 12:5. There is no ground for assuming עַם in the *Vorlage*, as theory (a) proposes, and no reason to suppose an influence from עַם in Gen 32:29, as theory (c) proposes.

Conclusion

We conclude that a connection with the Aramaic/late Hebrew שׁרר could account for ἐνισχύειν in all cases (Gen 32:29; Hos 10:11 [ר for ד]; Hos 12:4, 5). Moreover, in the light of the textual variations in Aquila and Theodotion, the prepositions πρός and μετά may be explained by a transposition of אֵת and אֶל in the Hebrew *Vorlage* of the LXX, this also possibly shared by Symmachus. However, the story of Jacob's struggle with the angel and the origins of Israel's name were of wide interest in antiquity, and do not allow the dismissal of the possibility that the Greek translator of Hosea was aware of how Gen 32:29 was rendered in Greek.

Amos 1:15

Amos 1:15

MT	LXX
וְהָלַךְ מַלְכָּם	καὶ πορεύσονται οἱ βασιλεῖς αὐτῆς
בַּגּוֹלָה הוּא	ἐν αἰχμαλωσίᾳ οἱ ἱερεῖς αὐτῶν
וְשָׂרָיו יַחְדָּו	καὶ οἱ ἄρχοντες αὐτῶν ἐπὶ τὸ αὐτό
אָמַר יְהוָה	λέγει κύριος.
Then their king shall go into exile, he and his officials together, says the LORD. [NRSV]	And its kings shall go into captivity, their priests and their rulers together, says the Lord. [NETS]

Jeremiah 30:19[MT49:3]

MT	LXX
הֵילִילִי חֶשְׁבּוֹן כִּי שֻׁדְּדָה־עַי	ἀλάλαξον Εσεβων ὅτι ὤλετο Γαι
צְעַקְנָה בְּנוֹת רַבָּה	κεκράξατε θυγατέρες Ραββαθ
חֲגֹרְנָה שַׂקִּים סְפֹדְנָה וְהִתְשׁוֹטַטְנָה בַּגְּדֵרוֹת	περιζώσασθε σάκκους καὶ κόψασθε ὅτι
כִּי מַלְכָּם בַּגּוֹלָה יֵלֵךְ	Μελχολ ἐν ἀποικίᾳ βαδιεῖται
כֹּהֲנָיו וְשָׂרָיו יַחְדָּיו	οἱ ἱερεῖς αὐτοῦ καὶ οἱ ἄρχοντες αὐτοῦ ἅμα.

244.　Kennicott, *Vetus Testamentum Hebraicum*, 2:256.

Wail, O Heshbon, for Ai is laid waste! Cry out, O daughters of Rabbah! Put on sackcloth, lament, and slash yourselves with whips! For Milcom shall go into exile, with his priests and his attendants. [NRSV]	Shout, O Hesebon, because Gai perished! Cry out, O daughters of Rabbath! Put on sackcloth, and lament, because Melchol shall go in exile, his priests and his rulers together. [NETS]

The resemblance between Amos 1:15 and Jer 30:19[MT49:3] is striking. According to S. R. Driver and many others, Jer 49:3 is a reminiscence or an adaptation of Amos 1:15.[245] The context of both texts is the judgment against Ammon, and includes such elements in common as the mention of Rabbah and its destruction by fire (Amos 1:14/Jer 49:2).

The plus of οἱ ἱερεῖς αὐτῶν in LXX Amos 1:15 raises the question whether the Greek translator of Amos recognized this resemblance between the two texts and inserted this plus under the influence of Jeremiah.

Scholars have answered this question in a variety of ways:

a. The LXX attests a different *Vorlage* including כהניו. Nowack states the possibility that the LXX translator read כהניו instead of הוא, and then moves on to say that this text (assuming he means this different Hebrew text) was probably dependent on Jer 48:7 or 49:3 because of a wrong interpretation of מַלְכָּם.[246] In this he follows Wellhausen, who states: "Für הוא hat die Septuaginta οἱ ἱερεῖς αὐτῶν vgl. Hier. 49,3... Es scheint dass die Lesart כהניו dem falschen Verständnis von מלכם als Milkom ihre Entstehung verdankt."[247] Harper also seems to hold to the existence of a different reading which had כהניו instead of הוא,[248] and so do Andersen and Freedman.[249]

b. The LXX translator was influenced by Jeremiah's parallel text and inserted οἱ ἱερεῖς αὐτῶν. Following van Hoonacker, who suggested the possibility of the Jeremiah text influencing the

245. Driver, *Joel and Amos*, 142. Others include: van Hoonacker, *Les Douze Petits Prophètes*, 216; Andersen and Freedman, *Amos*, 285; Thomas Edward McComiskey, ed., *The Minor Prophets: An Exegetical and Expository Commentary. Hosea, Joel, and Amos*, vol. 1 (Grand Rapids: Baker, 1992), 355–56.

246. Nowack, *Die kleinen Propheten*, 132.

247. Wellhausen, *Die Kleinen Propheten*, 71.

248. Harper, *A Critical and Exegetical Commentary on Amos and Hosea*, 35.

249. "The Greek translation is based on a Hebrew text that varied from MT (four of the six words being different), though the wording in Hebrew or Greek may have been influenced by the corresponding passages in Jeremiah, such as the reference to 'the priests.'" *Amos*, 285.

Greek version, the focus has shifted to the LXX translator, and this has become a popular view among more recent scholars.[250]

c. The pair οἱ ἱερεῖς αὐτῶν καὶ οἱ ἄρχοντες αὐτῶν for one Hebrew equivalent, וְשָׂרָיו, was not dependent on any intertextual influence, but was the result of the Greek translator's technique.[251]

An examination of the textual evidence for Amos 1:15 will show that, while the LXX translator demonstrates some freedom in his renderings, nevertheless, the existence of a different Hebrew *Vorlage* used by the LXX translator, as well as by other Greek versions, is the most probable explanation that accounts for the difference between the Hebrew and the Greek.

Amos 1:15
An analysis of the verse gives us the following differences between the Greek and the Hebrew:

MT		LXX	
וְהָלַךְ	and he will go	καὶ πορεύσονται	and they will go
מַלְכָּם	their king	οἱ βασιλεῖς αὐτῆς	her kings
בַּגּוֹלָה	into exile	ἐν αἰχμαλωσίᾳ	into exile
הוּא	he		
		οἱ ἱερεῖς αὐτῶν	their priests
וְשָׂרָיו	and his officials	καὶ οἱ ἄρχοντες αὐτῶν	and their officials
יַחְדָּו	together	ἐπὶ τὸ αὐτό	together
אָמַר	says	λέγει	says
יְהוָה	the Lord	κύριος	the Lord

It is normal practice for the translator to shift from plural to singular or masculine to feminine and vice versa wherever he thinks that context or style is served. Some examples are: היה–ἐγένοντο (1:1); בריח–μοχλούς (1:5); יושב–κατοικοῦντας (1:5); אשיבנו–ἀποστραφήσομαι αὐτήν (1:9);

---

250. Van Hoonacker, *Les Douze Petits Prophètes*, 216; Wolff, *Joel and Amos*, 132–33; Johan Lust, "The Cult of Molek/Milchom: Some Remarks on G. H. Heider's Monograph," *ETL* 63 (1987): 364; Petra Verwijs, "The Septuagint in the Peshiṭta and Syro-Hexapla Translations of Amos 1:3–2:16," *BIOSCS* 38 (2005): 29.

251. This is Jan de Waard's view, "A Greek Translation-Technical Treatment of Amos 1:15," in *On Language, Culture and Religion: In Honor of Eugene A. Nida, Approaches to Semiotics*, LVI (ed. Matthew Black and William A. Smalley; The Hague: Mouton, 1974), 115–16, which is also adopted by Hayes, *Amos the Eighth Century Prophet*, 96–97. The initiator of this idea was Jerome. In his comments on Amos 1:15 he regards the LXX plus as epexegetical. Field, *Origenis Hexaplorum*, 2:969. Dines thinks that the LXX translator uses ἱερεῖς as a veiled attack against the Hasmonean dynasty. "The Septuagint of Amos," 80–81.

רדפו–διῶξαι αὐτοὺς (1:11). Therefore, these variations would not neces-sarily demand a different *Vorlage* but could be attributed to a "context-sensitive" translation. For example, it is expected that הלך would be turned into the plural πορεύσονται, since the choice of the plural βασιλεῖς has been made. Again, in 1:15, the pronoun αὐτῆς refers to Ραββα, as with the two previous occurrences of αὐτῆς in v. 14.[252]

The Rendering βασιλεῖς for מלכם. The translator's choice of the plural βασιλεῖς, however, is puzzling. In antiquity מלכם in Amos 1:15 was rendered as follows by the ancient versions:

MT:
> Their *king* will go into exile, he and his princes together, says the Lord.

LXX:
> And her *kings* will go into captivity, their *priests* and their rulers together, says the Lord.

Targum:
> Their *king* will go into exile, he and his princes together, says the Lord.

ΑΣΘ:
> And *Melchom* [ΑΣ] will go into captivity, her(Syh)/his(Q) *priests* [ΑΣΘ], and his princes together, says the Lord.

Syrohexapla:
> And her *kings* will go into captivity, her *priests* and their rulers together, says the Lord.

Peshitta:
> And *Malcom* will go into captivity, he and his *priests* and his princes together, says the Lord.

Vulgate:
> And *Melchom* will go into captivity, both he and his princes together, says the Lord.

Wolff says that the LXX βασιλεῖς was derived from a "faulty" text which read מְלָכֶיהָ,[253] but no such variant is extant. Moreover, this explanation would also require that the "faulty" Hebrew text had והלכו instead of והלך. De Waard rejects Wolff's view as "highly unlikely,"[254] but does not attempt to explain the presence of βασιλεῖς. He only gives the

---

252. Moreover, Jan de Waard argues convincingly that the pronoun αὐτῆς can be explained as the result of a translation-technical operation rather than through the assumption of a different *Vorlage*: "A Greek Translation-Technical Treatment," 112–13.

253. Wolff, *Joel and Amos*, 132–33.

254. De Waard, "A Greek Translation-Technical Treatment," 112.

translational rationale behind αὐτῆς and notes the correction of αὐτῆς into αὐτῶν in some Greek manuscripts. He presents a table of the available Greek witnesses, taken from Ziegler's critical apparatus:[255]

Amos 1:15a

	καὶ	πορεύσονται	οἱ	βασιλεῖς	αὐτῆς	ἐν	αἰχμαλωσίᾳ
130′ 407[txt]	x	x	x	x	αυτων	x	x
86[mg 2]	x	πορευθησονται	x	x	αυτων	x	x
86[txt]	x	πορευθησονται	x	x	x	x	x
86[mg 1] L′–407[mg]	x	πορευσεται	μελχομ		ø	x	x
46′ C–68	x	x	ø	x	x	x	x
36[c]	x	x	x	x	ø	x	x
α′ σ′		πορευσεται	μελχομ				

Amos 1:15b

		οἱ	ἱερεῖς	αὐτῶν	καὶ	οἱ	ἄρχοντες	αὐτῶν	ἐπὶ	τὸ	αὐτό
106	και	x	x	x	x	x	x	x	x	x	x
68		x	x	x	x	x	x	ø	x	x	x
Q[c] L–86[c]		x	x	αυτου	x	x	x	αυτου	x	x	x
1 II		x	x	x	x	x	x	x εν αιχμαλωσια	x	x	x

α′ σ′ θ′ pro αυτων 1°: ωσαυτως αυτης; pro αυτων 2°: αυτου

The alteration of αὐτῆς into αὐτῶν in some manuscripts was probably meant to achieve homogeneity with the following two occurrences of αὐτῶν and was not necessarily influenced by the Hebrew text. If so, this would explain why βασιλεῖς—as well as ἱερεῖς—was left untouched.

Lust, on the other hand, tries to explain why the LXX adds "his priests" by saying that

> the mention of these priests is very well understandable when it follows upon an original *mlkm* meaning Milkom. This suggests that the original text must have read: 'Milkom shall go into exile with his priests and his princes'. This is exactly what can be found in the Lucianic manuscripts, as well as in Theodorus, Theodoretus and the Syrohexapla. They transliterate *mlkm* and read the name of the Ammonite god Milkom adding *oi iereis autou*.[256]

Lust, therefore, is assuming a Greek copyist who, faced with Milkom, corrected it into "her kings." This correction could have happened either on the basis of his *memory* of the Hebrew text (otherwise a correction towards the Hebrew text would require the more literal "their king[s]"),

255. Ibid.
256. Lust, "The Cult of Molek/Milchom," 364 (*pace* Lust, the Syrohexapla appears to follow the LXX reading "kings" rather than "Milkom").

or on the basis of his awareness of another Greek witness which had "her kings." However, this view does not offer the most satisfactory explanation of the textual data. A move from "her kings" to "Milkom" is more likely to have happened, especially in the light of LXX Jer 30:19[MT49:3].[257]

A better explanation, based on the translational freedom that we can observe in the first part of the verse, is that βασιλεῖς αὐτῆς is original and lies with the translator, not with his *Vorlage* or a later corrector. The translator may have wanted to generalize this judgment against kingship. There is an instance of this in LXX Hos 7:3 where the singular מלך is rendered in the plural: ἐν ταῖς κακίαις αὐτῶν εὔφραναν βασιλεῖς καὶ ἐν τοῖς ψεύδεσιν αὐτῶν ἄρχοντας (ברעתם ישמחו־מלך ובכחשיהם שרים). Also, such generalization occurs in LXX Hos 7:5 for both "king" and "day": αἱ ἡμέραι τῶν βασιλέων ὑμῶν (יום מלכנו).[258]

The Peshiṭta and the Vulgate agree with the reading of Aquila and Symmachus (Μελχομ), which gives us a possible indication that the connection to LXX Jer 30:19[MT49:3] was recognized by these translators,[259] or that they attest a separate reading tradition for מלכם in Amos 1:15. Most commentators accept "king" as original to Amos and think that Melchom is an erroneous vocalization,[260] or that it has been influenced by LXX Jer 30:19[MT49:3].[261] Usually, the reasons given for the

257.   Similarly, Jennifer Dines accepts βασιλεῖς as original and as the result of an anti-Milcom stance. She says that "we are being told that we are precisely *not* to think in terms of Milcom. The sustained plural forms could make sense as a reaction against this obvious interpretation, and the chief *raison d'être* of the plural βασιλεῖς is to exclude the identification." "The Septuagint of Amos," 77. One wonders, however, why such a stance towards a pagan deity was not also taken in LXX Amos 5:26 where Μολοχ occurs against מַלְכְּכֶם of the MT. Puech holds that the translator may have read מלכם as the plural מלכים written defectively, and then added αὐτῆς to refer to Rabbah. Émile Puech, "Milkom, le Dieu Ammonite, en Amos I 15," *VT* 27 (1977): 118, 120.

258.   John H. Hayes also sees the differences in the LXX as reflecting a translation technique rather than a different reading in the source text: *Amos the Eighth Century Prophet*, 96–97.

259.   The only two places in the LXX where the specific form of this Greek name occurs are in LXX Jer 30:17 and 19.

260.   E.g. Carl Friedrich Keil, *The Twelve Minor Prophets* (Clark's Foreign Theological Library 17–18; 4th series; Edinburgh: T. & T. Clark, 1871), 249; Sellin, *Das Zwölfprophetenbuch*, 169; Cripps, *A Critical and Exegetical Commentary on the Book of Amos*, 132.

261.   E.g. Nowack, *Die kleinen Propheten*, 132; Snaith, *The Book of Amos*, 29; Wolff, *Joel and Amos*, 132–33. For the view that the MT is not the original reading, see Puech, "Milkom," 117–25.

preference of "king" are: (a) the support of the LXX and the Targum; (b) the accompanying "and his princes," as usually a king has his own officials (as in 2:3);[262] (c) the parallelism with 1:5, 8 ("the one who holds the sceptre");[263] (d) the absence of any reference to idolatry in the preceding passages;[264] (e) the tendency of the oracles against the nations to speak against the nations themselves, and not their gods.[265] In fact, we might just as well be facing a case of *double entendre* since the object of judgment is Ammon, and it would be natural to hear echoes of its chief deity's name in מלכם.[266]

In Zeph 1:5 we encounter a similar division between MT בְּמַלְכָּם, supported by the LXX (κατὰ τοῦ βασιλέως αὐτῶν), and οἱ λ', which have the proper name μολοχ, in agreement with the Targum which avoids naming the idol but has instead "and swear by *the name of their idols*." Another theory proposed is that these variations מִלְכֹּם/מַלְכָּם (2 Sam 12:30; 1 Kgs 11:7; 2 Chr 20:2; Jer 49:1, 3; Zeph 1:5, and possibly also Amos 1:15) show that the MT vocalization involves a euphemism.[267]

This uncertainty as to how certain occurrences of מלך should be vocalized is not limited to the Greek translation of the Twelve but is also evident in other parts of the LXX. In Lev 18:21 the MT has לַמֹּלֶךְ while the LXX translates ἄρχοντι, and this same difference continues in 20:2–5. In 1 Kgs 11:7 the MT has וּלְמֹלֶךְ while the LXX (3 Kgdms 11:5) has καὶ τῷ βασιλεῖ αὐτῶν, and in 1 Kgs 11:33 the MT has וּלְמִלְכֹּם while the LXX (3 Kgdms 11:33) has καὶ τῷ βασιλεῖ αὐτῶν. In 4 Kgdms 23:13, however, the LXX translates Μολχολ where the MT (2 Kgs 23:13) reads וּלְמִלְכֹּם. These examples show that the vocalization of מלך would in each case depend on such considerations as the contextual understanding of the translator or his familiarity with a particular reading tradition. Therefore, faced with מלכם in Amos 1:15, the Greek translator decided that the verse speaks against the king/kings, which, according to the majority of commentators, happens to be the intended reading.

Finally, in the next phrase there is a shift to αὐτῶν (2°), which could have two possible referents, the kings or the "sons of Ammon." In 1:13 αὐτῶν refers to the "sons of Ammon," and it is very likely that αὐτῶν in 1:15 does as well. Just as the βασιλεῖς are the authorities of the *city*, the

262.   E.g. Keil, *The Twelve Minor Prophets*, 249. However, there are "princes of god" in 1 Chr 24:5 and Jer 48:7; see Marti, *Das Dodekapropheton*, 164.

263.   Van Hoonacker, *Les Douze Petits Prophètes*, 216.

264.   Harper, *A Critical and Exegetical Commentary on Amos and Hosea*, 37.

265.   Paul, *A Commentary on the Book of Amos*, 70–71.

266.   See ibid.

267.   McCarthy, *The Tiqqune Sopherim*, 243 n. 256. Also Dines, "The Septuagint of Amos," 77.

ἱερεῖς and the ἄρχοντες are the authorities of the *inhabitants* in general. So, αὐτῶν either refers to three separate groups (βασιλεῖς, ἱερεῖς, ἄρχοντες) of the Ammonite nation,[268] or it refers to the kings under whom are the priests and rulers.

The Plus ἱερεῖς. The major issue in Amos 1:15 is the plus ἱερεῖς which is found in all extant Greek manuscripts. Jerome explains this plus as epexegetical for שָׂרָיו.[269] Just like the MT and the Targum, the Vulgate lacks this plus, but the Peshiṭta includes it, along with other witnesses (Q[c] L–86[c] Th. Tht.). Aquila, Symmachus and Theodotion, together with the Syrohexapla, include this plus but read αὐτῆς (or αὐτοῦ according to Q) instead of αὐτῶν.[270]

Hexaplaric Versions
According to the Syrohexapla, Aquila and Symmachus would have read as follows: πορεύσεται Μελχόμ εν αἰχμαλωσίᾳ, οἱ ἱερεῖς αὐτῆς (αὐτοῦ Q) καὶ οἱ ἄρχοντες αὐτοῦ ἐπὶ τὸ αὐτό λέγει κύριος. It seems that, in the case of OG αὐτῶν 1°, the hexaplaric information preserved by Q is more appropriate than that of the Syrohexapla. It would be strange to switch from the pronoun αὐτῆς for the "priests" to αὐτοῦ for the "rulers." The hexaplaric versions in this verse are almost identical with the Peshiṭta, which reads: "And Malcom shall go into captivity, he and his priests and his princes together, says the Lord." The fact that Aquila preserves ἱερεῖς is significant, since he is guided by the principle of providing one-for-one correspondences with the Hebrew text.[271] The agreement between Aquila, Symmachus, Theodotion and the Peshiṭta is congruent with their sharing a Hebrew text including כהניו.[272]

268.   It is possible that this is the way in which it was understood in the manuscripts containing the amendment from αὐτῆς to αὐτῶν (130′, 407[txt], and 86[mg 2]), as this change levels all three groups and turns them into a list.
269.   "Idolum Ammonitarum, quod vocatur *Melchom*, id est, *rex eorum*, feretur in Assyrios; et *principes ejus*, id est, *sacerdotes ejus*, pariter abducentur. *Sacerdotes* in Hebraeo non habetur, sed *principes*. Addiderunt itaque LXX *sacerdotes*, ut si velis scire qui sint illi principes, audias sacerdotes." Field, *Origenis Hexaplorum*, 2:969.
270.   Since two pronouns are attested for Aquila, Symmachus and Theodotion, we assume that the first corresponded to ἱερεῖς and the second to ἄρχοντες.
271.   Jellicoe states: "The extraordinary feature of Aquila's version is its extreme literalness, which renders it of inestimable value to the textual critic in determining the Hebrew which underlies it." Sidney Jellicoe, *The Septuagint and Modern Study* (Oxford: Clarendon, 1968), 80. See also the section on Aquila in Jobes and Silva, *Invitation to the Septuagint*, 38–40.
272.   John F. A. Sawyer suggested that ἱερεῖς is a plus which could reflect a "belligerent comment about the 'Damascus' sect." "'Those Priests in Damascus': A

The Peshiṭta

There are many possible explanations for the agreements between the Peshiṭta and the LXX against the MT. According to Gelston, three explanations must be ruled out:

   a.   the Peshiṭta was translated directly from the LXX and not from the MT or any other Hebrew *Vorlage*;

   b.   the Peshiṭta translators were Christians and, having a higher regard for the LXX, occasionally preferred its readings to those of the MT;

   c.   the exclusive agreements between the LXX and the Peshiṭta arose from pure coincidence.[273]

According to Gelston, some explanations we ought to consider are:

   a.   a common Hebrew *Vorlage* for the LXX and the Peshiṭta which is distinct from the MT. Gelston warns that "caution must however be exercised in inferring the existence of a common distinctive Hebrew *Vorlage* on the basis of LXX and the Peshitta alone";[274]

   b.   independent reliance on common exegetical traditions;

   c.   the Peshiṭta translators' direct use of the LXX.[275]

If Septuagintal influence on the Peshiṭta is to be considered, this could only have come from a Lucianic Greek text, seeing that only "priests" is adopted and not "kings."[276] On the other hand, seeing that the Peshiṭta is close to Aquila and Symmachus, since they all render מלכם as a proper name, the influence could have come from either of these versions, assuming their availability to the Peshiṭta translator.

Possible Example of Anti-Sectarian Polemic in the Septuagint Version of Amos 3:12," *ASTI* 8 (1970–71): 130 n. 34.

   273.   Gelston, *The Peshiṭta*, 160–61. Weitzman, on the other hand, gives serious consideration to the phenomenon of polygenesis: *The Syriac Version*, 68–70. Polygenesis seems to be the preferred view of Petra Verwijs for Amos 1:15: "I suggest that the LXX and/or the P translators referred to the almost-identical Jer 49:3 (30:19 LXX) which in H does include כהניו." Petra Verwijs, "The Septuagint in the Peshitta and Syro-Hexapla," 29.

   274.   Gelston, *The Peshiṭta*, 161.

   275.   Ibid., 161–62.

   276.   Jellicoe notes that "Lucianic readings are widely attested in the Old Latin and Peshitta versions of the Old Testament." *The Septuagint and Modern Study*, 346–47.

Assimilation

Assimilation is not a characteristic practice of Aquila. In view of the presence of ἱερεῖς in Aquila, Symmachus, and Theodotion, we have enough indication to consider that there existed a Hebrew *Vorlage*, different from the MT, which included כהניו.[277] Had there been an assimilation of LXX Amos 1:15 to LXX Jer 30:19 we should have expected Aquila, at least, to differ. We should also have expected more of the wording of LXX Jer 30:19 to have been adopted by the translator of Amos, if such an assimilation were done consciously.[278] In fact, there is no indication that there was Greek to Greek assimilation. The only Greek words shared by both texts are ἱερεῖς and ἄρχοντες, which are extremely common throughout the LXX. There is no term other than ἱερεῖς to translate כהניו, had this been in the *Vorlage*, and ἄρχων is a standard equivalent of שר. It is theoretically possible that the LXX translator of Amos assimilated only on the basis of his knowledge of Hebrew Jeremiah, but this would be impossible to prove. This forces us to push the assimilation, if such there was, back to the source text, which would have been shared by both the LXX and Aquila. This Hebrew text of Amos 1:15, which was assimilated to Jer 49:3 through the addition of כהניו and formed the basis of both the LXX and Aquila, was immediately connected to the deity by Aquila (unless the *mater lectionis* was present—מלכום),[279] but not by the LXX translator. Nevertheless, they both translated כֹּהֲנָיו: Aquila, faithful to his style, is literal in his treatment of the pronominal suffix (αυτου Q), while the LXX translator displays some freedom (αὐτῶν).

De Waard's Theory

De Waard, however, rejects the assimilation theory at both the Hebrew and Greek levels, and he also rejects the theory of a different *Vorlage*. His answer to the problem is in two parts: (a) "the LXX translator of Amos simply divided this broad group of authorities into two more

---

277. This suggestion is similar to that proposed by some commentators (Wellhausen, Nowack, Sellin, Wolff), viz. that the LXX translator read כהניו instead of הוא. It is not necessary, however, to dismiss הוא. De Waard notes: "One should not forget that the use of the pronoun in the source text may have been conditioned in more than one way... However, the same conditioning does not exist in the receptor language." De Waard, "A Greek Translation-Technical Treatment," 114.

278. Also ibid., 115.

279. Graetz emends as follows: "מלכם | מַלְכּוֹם= nomen idoli P. Aq. Sym." Heinrich Graetz, *Emendationes in Plerosque Sacrae Scripturae Veteris Testamenti Libros* (ed. G. Bacher; 3 vols in 1; Breslau: 1892–94), 16.

specific subgroups, one religious (οἱ ἱερεῖς), the other secular (οἱ ἄρχον-τες)";[280] (b) the reason this word-pair escaped "corrections" in other Greek manuscripts was because it existed in Greek parallel texts.[281] By "parallel texts," De Waard must be referring to Jeremiah's parallel passages where this Greek word-pair occurs (LXX Jer 30:19; 31:7).

De Waard's conclusions, while they take account of the translator and place translation technique at the centre, raise more questions than they actually answer. His proposal that the LXX divides שר into two groups is not supported anywhere else in the LXX. There is, however, an instance where the LXX translator appears to be interpreting כהנים as "chiefs of court" in LXX 2 Kgdms 8:18, but this may actually be influenced by 1 Chr 18:17.[282] Again, in LXX Zech 6:13, the translator seems to be distinguishing between the priest and the one sitting on the throne, but this distinction may have arisen because of בין שניהם at the end of the verse, which phrase may be taken as requiring two individuals. There are approximately forty different equivalents of שר in the LXX, and ἱερεῖς is not one of them. Every time the word-pair of ἱερεῖς and ἄρχοντες occurs they always represent either ראש and כהן (e.g. Ezra 1:5; Neh 8:13; 11:3; 12:12) or שר and כהן (e.g. Ezra 9:1; Neh 9:34; 10:1; Jer 2:26; 33:16; 39:32), but never do the two Greek words represent a single Hebrew word. ἱερεύς always translates כהן in the LXX, and in Aquila, as far as the evidence goes.[283] It is possible that the LXX translator wanted to include both groups of authorities (religious and secular) in his rendering of ושריו, but this solution leaves the versional evidence unaccounted for.

De Waard's next argument asserts that other Greek manuscripts let this plus stand because it was also found in Jeremiah. This is possible, especially if these manuscripts exhibit assimilation tendencies. However, this lack of correction may also indicate that they had no access to a Hebrew text and were unaware that "priests" was lacking in the Hebrew. We have already accounted for the corrections of αὐτῆς into αὐτῶν in some Greek manuscripts without them necessarily depending upon a Hebrew text. The real question, however, is why the three minor Greek versions, Aquila, Symmachus and Theodotion let this plus stand. Why would Aquila, who is guided by the strictest principles of word-for-word representation, fail to correct the LXX while Jerome did correct it? The most logical conclusion would be that Aquila's Hebrew and the LXX *Vorlage* contained the plus כהניו.

280.   De Waard, "A Greek Translation-Technical Treatment," 116.
281.   Ibid.
282.   See, Gordon, *1 & 2 Samuel*, 247.
283.   Reider, *An Index to Aquila*, 116.

Conclusion

In the case of οἱ βασιλεῖς αὐτῆς we have concluded that the translator, faced with מלכם in Amos 1:15, decided that the verse speaks against the king/kings, which, according to the majority of commentators, happens to be the intended reading. He also chose the pronoun αὐτῆς with reference to Ραββα (as in v. 14). The supposition, therefore, of a different Hebrew *Vorlage* containing מלביה is unnecessary.

In the case of ἱερεῖς, the evidence points to the existence of a plus in the Hebrew *Vorlage* which was shared by the Greek versions, although conclusive proof is impossible. As far as Aquila is concerned, it is more likely that he translated word-for-word rather than that he assimilated or failed to correct the assimilation of the LXX. Nevertheless, given the scarcity of Aquilanic readings, we must always allow for the possibility that this reading is mistakenly attributed to him or corrupted in the copying process.[284]

The most likely explanation for the majority of the phenomena observed is that there existed a different *Vorlage* which included כהניו, shared by the LXX, Aquila, Symmachus, Theodotion and possibly the Peshiṭta. It is most probable that assimilation to Jer 30:19[MT49:3] had taken place in the Hebrew manuscript tradition at an early stage, prior to the making of the various translations.

Amos 4:2

Amos 4:2

MT	LXX
נִשְׁבַּע אֲדֹנָי יְהוִה בְּקָדְשׁוֹ כִּי הִנֵּה	ὀμνύει κύριος κατὰ τῶν ἁγίων αὐτοῦ διότι ἰδοὺ
יָמִים בָּאִים עֲלֵיכֶם וְנִשָּׂא אֶתְכֶם	ἡμέραι ἔρχονται ἐφ' ὑμᾶς καὶ λήμψονται ὑμᾶς
בְּצִנּוֹת וְאַחֲרִיתְכֶן בְּסִירוֹת	ἐν ὅπλοις καὶ τοὺς μεθ' ὑμῶν εἰς λέβητας
דּוּגָה	ὑποκαιομένους ἐμβαλοῦσιν ἔμπυροι λοιμοί

284. "…es ist ziemlich leicht ein Minimum von solchen Fällen, wo die Übersetzung Aquilas einen anders lautenden hebräischen Text notwendigerweise voraussetzt, festzustellen. Aber auch in einer buchstäblichen Übertragung gibt es Wiedergaben—um so mehr weil das Material so lückenhaft ist—, bei denen es sehr mühevoll ist, zu entscheiden, ob es um einen abweichenden Grundtext geht, oder etwa um eine Veränderung der Kopiierung [*sic*], oder aber um Unfolgerichtigkeit des Übersetzers selbst, z. B. die Präpositionen bilden eine Gruppe, bei der man oft alle drei Möglichkeiten offen lassen muss." Kyösti Hyvärinen, *Die Übersetzung von Aquila* (ConBOT 10; Uppsala: Almqvist & Wiksell, 1977), 108.

The Lord GOD has sworn by his holiness: The time is surely coming upon you, when they shall take you away with hooks, even the last of you with fishhooks. [NRSV]

The Lord swears by his holy ones: For behold, days are coming upon you, and they shall take you with weapons, and fiery pests shall cast those with you into cauldrons heated from underneath. [NETS]

Jeremiah 1:13

MT	LXX
וַיְהִי דְבַר־יְהוָה אֵלַי שֵׁנִית	καὶ ἐγένετο λόγος κυρίου πρός με ἐκ δευτέρου
לֵאמֹר מָה אַתָּה רֹאֶה וָאֹמַר	λέγων τί σὺ ὁρᾷς καὶ εἶπα
סִיר נָפוּחַ אֲנִי רֹאֶה	λέβητα ὑποκαιόμενον
וּפָנָיו מִפְּנֵי צָפוֹנָה	καὶ τὸ πρόσωπον αὐτοῦ ἀπὸ προσώπου βορρᾶ

The word of the LORD came to me a second time, saying, "What do you see?" And I said, "I see a boiling pot, tilted away from the north." [NRSV]

And a word of the Lord came to me a second time, saying, "What do you see?" And I said, "A cauldron being heated, and its face is from the north." [NETS]

The Old Greek translation of Amos 4:2 has a peculiar rendering of בסירות דוגה: εἰς λέβητας ὑποκαιομένους ἐμβαλοῦσιν ἔμπυροι λοιμοί. Explanations for this rendering vary from "erroneous translation" to "intentional interpretation." Harper, agreeing with Vollers, states: "εἰς λέβητας is the translation of בסירות, ὑποκαιομένους an explanatory addition, ἐμβαλοῦσιν a vb. supplied from the context, and ἔμπυροι λοιμοί (= burning plagues) an erroneous translation of דוגה."[285]

Tov notes that the LXX of Amos 4:2 manifestly depends on the LXX of Jer 1:13.[286] Similarly, Carbone and Rizzi, find this *midrash haggadah*, as they call it, to be an allusion to MT/LXX Jer 1:13.[287] Dines believes that the focus of the LXX on Amos 4:2 betrays a very different understanding from the "traditional" one: "The commentators have the destruction of Samaria by the Assyrians specifically in mind, but we cannot tell whether this was the primary focus of LXX. From what follows, it is perhaps not so likely."[288]

An examination of the elements in MT/LXX Amos 4:2 may shed some light on the nature of the Greek rendering.

---

285. Harper, *A Critical and Exegetical Commentary on Amos and Hosea*, 85.
286. Tov, *The Septuagint Translation of Jeremiah and Baruch*, 149.
287. Carbone and Rizzi, *Il Libro di Amos*, 89. The connection is also noted by Wolff (*Joel and Amos*, 204 n. j).
288. Dines, "The Septuagint of Amos," 122–23.

Amos 4:2

ὀμνύει. The present active of ὀμνύει gives the sense of the Lord's action being carried out as the prophet speaks. The referent in the oath is God's "holy ones" or "holy things" (κατὰ τῶν ἀγίων αὐτοῦ). ἅγια (plural) is normally used for God's sanctuary (e.g. Exod 26:33; Lev 10:4; Num 3:28; 3 Kgdms 8:8).[289] Carbone and Rizzi suggest that this is a reference to the Temple of Jerusalem by which God swears, as opposed to "the atonement (ἱλασμός) of Samaria" (LXX Amos 8:14) by which those condemned by the prophet swear.[290] Dines suggests that ἀγίων may be masculine, referring to prophets (Wis 11:1) or angels (Zech 14:5), or even the guilty "cows of Bashan" themselves: "the 'heifers' who are the implicit objects of disapproval in v.1 and are now the recipients of an oracle of judgment, are defined none the less as the people of God (especially if ἀγίων is personal)."[291]

λήμψονται. The third person plural λήμψονται ("take" or "capture") for the third person singular נשא[ו] is clearly not referring to the "days," but is either indefinite or anticipates a subject which will be introduced later by the translator: ἔμπυροι λοιμοί.

ὅπλοις. ὅπλοις seems to refer broadly to an individual's military equipment.[292] In the LXX ὅπλον translates eight Hebrew words: מגן, כלי, חנית, שלט, שלח, צנה, סריון, נשק. It can be something carried or put on for protection (καὶ ἐπέθεντο ἐπ᾽ αὐτὸν—3 Kgdms 14:27), and it can be made of either bronze (3 Kgdms 14:27) or even gold (3 Kgdms 10:17). ὅπλον is found five times in the Greek TP (Amos 4:2 [צנה]; Joel 2:8 [plus]; Nah 2:4 [מגן]; 3:3 [חנית]; Hab 3:11 [חנית]). Symmachus agrees with the rendering of the LXX, Aquila has ἐν θυρεοῖς ("with shields") and Theodotion has ἐν δόρασι ("with spears"), all found within the category ὅπλον.[293]

289. For Johnson, κατὰ τῶν ἀγίων αὐτοῦ is "a mistranslation which apparently discloses an ignorance of Hebrew idiom." "The Septuagint Translators of Amos," 32.
290. Carbone and Rizzi, *Il Libro di Amos*, 89.
291. Dines, "The Septuagint of Amos," 121.
292. See Andersen and Freedman, *Amos*, 423. They think that the LXX translation is very loose and interpretive at this point and that it is impossible to recover any viable Hebrew variants from its wording (ibid.).
293. Jan de Waard thinks that the translator was unsure of a more specific meaning and therefore "he decided to give the generic information ἐν ὅπλοις, knowing that a word on a higher level of the taxonomy would automatically include all items on lower levels" ("Translation Techniques," 344). The unlikely suggestion of "ropes" for ὅπλα is made by Siegfried J. Schwantes on the basis of a Delphi inscription ("Note on Amos 4:2b," *ZAW* 79 [1967]: 82–83).

The Peshiṭta agrees with the LXX (ܪܘܡܚܐ, "arms, armour, weapons"),[294] but the Targum, while agreeing with Aquila, understands the verse extremely literally, thus giving a picture of people being carried on shields: *"The Lord God has sworn by his holiness that, behold, the days are coming upon you and the nations shall carry you off upon their shields, and your daughters in fishermen's boats."*[295]

καὶ τοὺς μεθ' ὑμῶν. For ואחריתכן the LXX has καὶ τοὺς μεθ' ὑμῶν. George Howard explains this rendering as follows:

> When the translator came to it (the word אחריתכן), he was at a loss. First he divided it into the two words אחרית and כן. This he rendered as Τοὺς μεθ' ὑμῶν. His reasoning for the translation seems to be the following: In Greek μετά may mean either "after" or "with." Here the word was employed because of its correspondence to אחר "after." But then it was taken with its second meaning, "with." The genitive ὑμῶν stands for כן. The plural Τοὺς was taken because of a mistaken understanding of ית as a form of the plural. (Such ית forms were possibly confused with plural forms also in i 8 and v 15).[296]

According to codex 86, Theodotion understands אחריתכן as τὰ ἔκγονα (ὑμῶν) ("your descendants"). The Targum understands this as the next generation as well, and translates specifically "your daughters." This rendering could have been influenced by the next verse and its reference to women, but the Targumist seems to have understood 4:3 to be referring to men who would be deported *like* "women."[297] Regardless of the reason for "daughters" in the Targum, the idea, as in Theodotion, is that of "posterity," whereas the rendering of LXX (καὶ τοὺς μεθ' ὑμῶν) allows for a more general understanding. אחרית occurs on four other occasions in the TP and the Greek translator adapts his renderings according to each context: Hos 3:5, באחרית הימים—ἐπ' ἐσχάτων τῶν ἡμερῶν; Amos 8:10, ואחריתה—καὶ τοὺς μετ' αὐτοῦ;[298] Amos 9:1, ואחריתם—καὶ τοὺς καταλοίπους αὐτῶν; Mic 4:1, באחרית הימים—ἐπ' ἐσχάτων τῶν ἡμερῶν.

---

294.   Gelston thinks that the Peshiṭta translators turned to the LXX for help in interpreting their Hebrew *Vorlage* (*The Peshiṭta*, 167–68).

295.   Cathcart and Gordon note that the connection to "fishing boats" is made in the Talmud (*b. B. Bat.* 73a) (*The Targum*, 82 n. 4).

296.   Howard, "Some Notes on the Septuagint of Amos," 109–10. The Greek translator behaved in the same way in Amos 8:10: ואחריתה - καὶ τοὺς μετ' αὐτοῦ.

297.   On the gender ambiguities of this verse, see Andersen and Freedman, *Amos*, 420–21. A similar oracle by Isaiah against rich women mentions the punishment of the *daughters* of Zion (Isa 3:16; 32:9).

298.   μετά with genitive is a Hebraism used in both the OT and the NT. Conybeare §93. Dines's treatment is especially instructive: "μετά with genitive expresses

εἰς λέβητας. εἰς λέβητας can be considered an accurate translation of בסירות. The word סיר is a homonym which can mean either "pot" or "thorn, hook" (see Eccl 7:6).[299] Usually, the less clear the context, the more ambiguous a homonym would be, thus generating a variety of understandings for the reader. In this case, something in the context must have been lacking or was unclear to the Greek translator. Glenny thinks that the translator "could have used the flexibility allowed by a homonym to make sense of a difficult context."[300] A reading from 4QXII^c has בסופוד[301] instead of בסירות, which may also be indicative of Amos 4:2 being a difficult verse in need of some interpretive manipulation. 4QXII^c may also show that its scribe realized the brutality of the scene described and attempted to make it less graphic.

ὑποκαιομένους. ὑποκαιομένους accompanies λέβητας and specifies the type of pot which the translator has in mind, since several kinds of pots could be signified by סיר (large water-jar, washing pot, pots used in the sanctuary).[302] Both words (λέβητας and ὑποκαιομένους) could be translating סירות, and the combination of the two words makes it clear that a "cooking" pot is in mind.[303] The phrase λέβης ὑποκαιόμενος is found only in LXX Jer 1:13, but Dines sees an association of λέβης and ὑποκαίειν in Ezek 24 as well (vv. 3 and 5 respectively): "It is to be noted that in v. 5 the verb דור is translated by ὑποκαίειν; thus, although λέβης and ὑποκαίειν do not actually appear together, they are associated."[304]

either 'with' or 'among'. The latter would imply a group within a larger body (Moulton 1963:269); the former implies 'together with', 'alongside', perhaps here no more than an expansion of ὑμᾶς (i.e. ὑμᾶς, and τοὺς μεθ᾽ ὑμῶν refer to the same people). Or possibly μετά implies 'on your side' (see LSJ, s.v. μετά AII for examples of μετά τινος εἶναι, 'to be on someone's side'; cf. 'I am with you' as a divine promise, e.g., Is. 41:10 μετὰ σοῦ γάρ εἰμι. So also Is. 43:2,5; Amos 5:14). In this case, a new group is envisaged, 'those who support you'." "The Septuagint of Amos," 123.

299. BDB 696. Paul argues for the meaning of "baskets." For a thorough treatment of both צנות and סירות, see Paul, *A Commentary on the Book of Amos*, 130–34. See also his "Fishing Imagery in Amos 4:2," *JBL* 97 (1978): 183–90. Driver argues for the meaning "fish-pots" (G. R. Driver, "Babylonian and Hebrew Notes," *WO* 2 [1954]: 20–21).

300. Glenny, *Finding Meaning in the Text*, 119.

301. *DJD* 15:247, Pl. XLIV–XLVI, f. 29 l. 10. The meaning is "in wailing, lament, mourning." BDB 704.

302. BDB 696.

303. In LXX Dan 3:25 we find ὑποκαιόμενη κάμινος. Forms of ὑποκαίω are found in LXX Dan 3:46 and *4 Macc.* 11:18.

304. Dines, "The Septuagint of Amos," 125.

Outside the LXX, the phrase λέβης ὑποκαιόμενος is present in various forms in Greek writers, such as Strato (third century B.C.E.):

οἱ γὰρ ἐκ τῶν ὑποκαιομένων λεβήτων ἀτμοὶ οὐκ ἄλλο τί εἰσιν ἢ αἱ τοῦ ὑγροῦ λεπτύνσεις εἰς ἀέρα χωροῦσαι. (*Fragmenta* 88.8–9)

Heron of Alexandria (around first century C.E.):

Λέβητος ὑποκαιομένου σφαιρίον πρὸς κνώδακα κινεῖσθαι. Ἔστω λέβης ὑποκαιόμενος ἔχων ὕδωρ ὁ ΑΒ καὶ ἐπιπεφράχθω τὸ στόμιον τῷ ΓΔ πώματι. (*Pneumatica* 2.11.1–3)

Athenaeus (second–third century C.E.):

εἰ γὰρ οἱ κρατῆρες ἀπὸ τοῦ συμβεβηκότος τῆς ὀνομασίας ἔτυχον οὗτοί τε κερασθέντες παρέκειντο πλήρεις, οὐ ζέον τὸ ποτὸν παρεῖχον, λεβήτων τρόπον ὑποκαιόμενοι. (*Deipnosophistae* 3.96.5–8)

Dines notes similar language in sacrificial contexts in Herodotus (4,61—both λέβης and ὑποκαίειν are present) and Aeschylus (*Agamemnon* 69—only ὑποκαίειν is present); also in contexts relating to torture in Diodorus Siculus (19,108,1—only ὑποκαιόμενος is present; 20,71,3—only ὑποκαίειν is present), and Lucian (*Phalaris* 1,11—only ὑποκαίειν is present).[305] The combination of the two words is therefore fairly well represented. However, what triggered the rendering ὑποκαιόμενος in LXX Amos 4:2 is a matter of debate.

דוגה is a *hapax legomenon*, but its relationship to "fish" would have been easily recognizable (Hos 4:3; Jon 2:1, 11; Hab 1:14; Zeph 1:3). Nevertheless, it seems to have been ignored or, according to Wolff, read as דלקה ([*sic*] "set fire to").[306]

Dines entertains two perspectives. One option is that דוד, translated by ὑποκαίειν in LXX Ezek 24:5, was read instead of דוגה in Amos 4:2.[307] She also thinks it possible that an association of דוגה with "fire" might have given rise to both ὑποκαιομένους and ἔμπυροι.[308] The other option arises from her examination of accounts of Christian martyrdoms (Conon of Nazareth and St. Theodotus of Ancyra). She notes: "It looks as though, in Christian literature, λέβης ὑποκαιόμενος may have been a stock phrase. If so, the question arises whether this has in retrospect influenced the text of Amos 4:2 (i.e. an original εἰς λέβητας was expanded by the addition of ὑποκαιομένους)."[309]

305. Ibid.
306. Wolff, *Joel and Amos*, 204 n. j.
307. Dines, "The Septuagint of Amos," 125.
308. Ibid., 124.
309. Ibid., 130.

If the latter was the case, then an association of דוגה with "fire" would only have given rise to ἔμπυροι, and a Christian scribe would have inserted ὑποκαιομένους under the influence of this stock phrase.

Glenny accepts ὑποκαιομένους as original and argues that דוגה was read as מדורה ("pile of wood") in order to fit with the translator's choice of λέβης for סיר:

> The interchange of these two homonyms [סִיר = "hook" and "pot"] may explain why דּוּגָה, a fish word, was translated as though it were מְדוּרָה, "pile [of wood]" (2x in MT: Isa. 30:33; Ezek. 24:9), resulting in the translation ὑποκαιομένους, "to heat [*sic*] from underneath," which I have translated "boiling." The connection the translator makes with דּוּגָה to come up with ὑποκαιομένους is the verb דּוּר, the cognate of the noun מְדוּרָה, meaning "heap up, pile." This Hebrew verb only occurs once in the MT in Ezek. 24:5 where ὑποκαίω translates דּוּר.[310]

It is obvious that דוגה was somehow associated with "fire," and Dines' explanation of דוגה giving rise to both fire-related Greek words (ὑπο-καιομένους and ἔμπυροι) is very plausible. At the same time, we cannot rule out the possibility that ὑποκαιομένους entered the text by a later hand. Arieti would confirm such an explanation as congenial to the nature of LXX Amos:

> The additions came from paraphrasing, supplying the object or subject where it is vague in the Hebrew, verbal expressions inserted to clarify the sense, and double translations.[311]

Arieti goes on to say,

> There are also additions to the text in the form of double translations, translations of one Hebrew word by two in Greek. Some of these may result from the transmission of the text—when the marginal note of one copyist was incorporated into the text of the next.[312]

ἐμβαλοῦσιν ἔμπυροι[313] λοιμοί. This phrase is a significant departure from the Hebrew. This is partly why Johnson thinks that "a more confused translation than this verse presents could hardly be imagined."[314] λοιμοί most probably stands for the word ופרצים from the following verse. The translator would have read פְּרִיצִים, "violent ones" (see LXX Ezek 18:10),

---

310. Glenny, *Finding Meaning in the Text*, 104.
311. Arieti, *A Study in the Septuagint of Amos*, 30.
312. Ibid., 44.
313. The variant ἔμπoροι is probably not original. See Dines, "The Septuagint of Amos," 137.
314. Johnson, "The Septuagint Translators of Amos," 32.

but he seems to be aware of the sense of פֶּרֶץ in Mic 2:13 (διακοπή). λοιμός/λοιμοί is sometimes used as an adjective (e.g. 1 Kgdms 25:25; 29:10; 2 Chr 13:7; 1 Macc 10:61) and sometimes as a noun (e.g. 1 Macc 15:21; Ps 1:1; Isa 5:14; Ezek 7:21), but in the Prophets it is mostly associated with enemies from other nations (LXX Ezek 7:21; 28:7; 30:11; 31:12; 32:12). ἔμπυροι, which seems to be a plus[315] or a rendering arising from a certain reading of דוגה, modifies λοιμοί and has the sense of "fiery" when used metaphorically of people.[316] It is used only one other time in the Greek version, in LXX Ezek 23:37 (...καὶ τὰ τέκνα αὐτῶν ἃ ἐγέννησάν μοι διήγαγον αὐτοῖς δι’ ἐμπύρων), but the sense of the word in this context seems to be related to that of "divination by fire."[317] The association of λοιμοί with "fire," even metaphorical fire, is observable in Prov 29:8: ἄνδρες λοιμοὶ ἐξέκαυσαν πόλιν σοφοὶ δὲ ἀπέστρεψαν ὀργήν. Moreover, LXX Nah 2:3–4 describes destruction by men with ὅπλα who are "sporting with fire" (NETS): ...διέφθειραν ὅπλα δυναστείας αὐτῶν ἐξ ἀνθρώπων ἄνδρας δυνατοὺς ἐμπαίζοντας ἐν πυρί. Carbone and Rizzi view these figures eschatologically by connecting the verse to other similar passages (LXX Hos 7:5; Joel 2:3; 3:3),[318] but Glenny examines and defends this position much more thoroughly,[319] concluding that these "destroyers," as he calls them, "would be good prospects to represent Syrians, but they could also be taken to be supernatural agents, probably angels."[320]

An interesting explanation is given by Vellas, who proposes that for the first word of the following verse (Amos 4:3) the Greek translator read שְׂרָפִים = ἔμπυροι, while a corrector read פְּרָצִים = λοιμοί, thus leaving us with the peculiar phrasing in the Greek.[321] At least for ἔμπυροι, Dines assures us that "the word is so unusual and difficult that it is certainly original."[322]

The verb ἐμβαλοῦσιν seems to fill out the Hebrew verbless clause בסירות ואחריתכן, and, according to Dines, obscure Hebrew resulting in an expansion in the LXX is a characteristic of the Greek translator of

---

315.   Glenny favours the option of ἔμπυροι being a plus (*Finding Meaning in the Text*, 165 n. 66, 209).

316.   LSJ 549.

317.   LSJ 549.

318.   Carbone and Rizzi, *Il Libro di Amos*, 89.

319.   Glenny, *Finding Meaning in the Text*, 207–10.

320.   Ibid., 165 n. 66.

321.   Vellas, *Ἀμώς*, 53.

322.   Dines, "The Septuagint of Amos," 132. She includes a thorough survey of the word uses (pp. 131–32).

Amos.[323] Dines focuses on the use of this verb in contexts of persecution and martyrdom,[324] though the verb is perhaps too common (meaning "to throw in" or "to put in") to be associated with a specific theme, and it is difficult to imagine what other alternatives the translator would have chosen when a pot was in mind.

In the Greek, therefore, the verse has generally moved away from the imagery of people dragged with fishing hooks (MT) or carried away in fishing boats (Targum) and has been transformed into a picture of people captured with weapons and thrown into boiling pots.[325] This could even have cannibalistic connotations, since boiling pots were used to boil meat for food (LXX Exod 16:3; 1 Kgdms 2:14; 4 Kgdms 4:38), but this view will be examined later. First, we shall see how Dines, Park and Glenny have perceived the sense of LXX Amos 4:2.

Dines' View

Dines has explored various occurrences of λέβης in the Greek Bible,[326] and has focused especially on the tortures inflicted on faithful Jews in 2 Macc 7:3, *4 Macc.* 8:13 and 12:1. From these texts she concludes that "two objects (λέβης and τήγανον) were sometimes taken as representative of all such horrors."[327] She also observes that ὑποκαίειν turns up in LXX Dan 3:25 where Daniel and his friends are persecuted, as well as in the martyrdom of the sixth brother in *4 Macc.* 11:18. From the above she concludes: "In the light of all this, it is not impossible that the strange expansion in the text at Amos 4:2 could have come from the hand of the translator, and that he intended to convey a 'martyrdom' scene."[328]

Dines narrows down the image that the translator was trying to convey to two possibilities: "Perhaps the controlling image is that of the punishment scenes in Ezekiel (especially chs. 11 and 24), where the cauldron is the doomed city. But it is possible also that the scene is of the horrific

323. Ibid., 124.
324. Ibid., 130–31.
325. The fish metaphor is also found in Hab 1:14–15; cf. Eccl 9:12; Jer 16:16; Ezek 29:4. Any hint of deportation is done away with in the Greek version of Amos 4:2–3, and the emphasis changes to torture, death and disposal. Hayes does not see any reference to deportation in the Hebrew text either (Hayes, *Amos the Eighth Century Prophet*, 140–42).
326. Dines, "The Septuagint of Amos," 125–26.
327. Ibid., 129.
328. Ibid., 130: She further suggests: "If λέβητας ὑποκαιομένους already had these overtones in Amos, it is possible that the same nuances are there in LXX Jer. 1:13, especially if the same translator was at work" (p. 130 n. 15).

tortures of faithful adherents to the Law, such as are described in 1 and 2 Maccabees."[329]

While one may agree with Dines that an image of torture is communicated, it is difficult to see an intention on the part of the translator to communicate a scene of persecution or martyrdom. His language may have been influenced by persecution and martyrdom incidents, but that does not tell us how precisely he deployed this language. Persecution and martyrdom imply undeserved torture or death, and this is not the case in LXX Amos 4:2. The context, as the translator seems to perceive it, is that of deserved punishment/judgment. It is possible, however, that the language used here by the translator may have influenced later descriptions in martyrdom accounts.[330]

Park's View

Park comments very briefly on LXX Amos 4:2, but without any attempt to substantiate his bold claims:

> The 𝔊 translation reflects socio-historical circumstance during the Second Temple period. Linguistic analysis displays...the persecution of Jews by Antiochus IV Epiphanes (λέβητας ἐκπυροῦν "heated caldrons" in 2 Macc 7:3 // Amos 4:2). Thackeray's contention that the TP were translated by the end of the second century B.C.E. may be correct.[331]

According to Park, what is described in LXX Amos 4:2 has one historical referent, Antiochus' persecution of the Jews, and the basis for that conclusion is purely linguistic. Park is referring specifically to the martyrdom of the seven sons and their mother by Antiochus IV Epiphanes (175–163 B.C.E.), when the Seleucid king ordered frying-pans and cauldrons to be heated (ἔκθυμος δὲ γενόμενος ὁ βασιλεὺς προσέταξεν τήγανα καὶ λέβητας ἐκπυροῦν [2 Macc 7:3]), and the family to be tortured and fried. While Dines has opened the possibility of allusion to Antiochus' tortures, Park seems to have adopted it with absolute certainty.

Glenny's View

Glenny combines the above two views and also builds on them. He agrees with Dines in that, "with the descriptions of people being taken away 'with weapons' and being thrown 'into burning caldrons' the translator intended to communicate a scene of persecution or torture in v. 2b, perhaps even a scene of martyrdom."[332]

329. Ibid., 136–37.
330. See ibid., 129–30, where she mentions some examples of these.
331. Park, *The Book of Amos*, 171; cf. 149.
332. Glenny, *Finding Meaning in the Text*, 103.

Like Dines, he observes linguistic sharing between LXX Amos 4:2 and other cases of persecution in the Greek version, based on the three words λέβης, ὑποκαίω and βάλλω.[333] Glenny focuses on the incident of the three young men in the fiery furnace from the book of Daniel, as well as on the tortures inflicted on Jews by Antiochus IV Epiphanes. The following table shows how the texts selected by Glenny share occurrences of the three above-mentioned words:

Texts containing a form of:	λέβης	ὑποκαίω	βάλλω
LXX Dan 3:25		x	
LXX Dan 3:46		x	x
2 Macc 7:3	x		
4 Macc. 8:13	x		
4 Macc. 11:18		x	
4 Macc. 12:1	x		x
4 Macc. 18:20	x		

However, one or more of these key words may be found in Greek texts which do not communicate persecution or martyrdom, but rightful judgment (Jer 1:13; Ezek 11:3, 7, 11; 24:3, 5, 6), or even "cannibalistic" behaviour (Mic 3:3).

At times, Glenny seems to side with Park's views, sharing his certainty concerning allusions to Antiochus:

> What is important here is the possibility that in the LXX this verse may refer to enemies of the Jews, perhaps even Antiochus Epiphanes.[334]

He goes on to say,

> Perhaps the clearest allusion to Antiochus Epiphanes in LXX-Amos is in 4:2, and there he is seen not as an end time oppressor (Gog), but rather as one in the role of the enemy who takes the people into captivity and punishes them for their sins. Thus, in LXX-Amos the actualization of prophecy is seen most often in the judgment and oppression of Israel that was predicted in Amos because of their sins and is realized by the readers of LXX-Amos in their experience of exile and foreign domination.[335]

Unlike Dines, Glenny here preserves the sense of deserved judgment for sins prevalent in the context of Amos 4:2 and proposes that the translator understands this prophesied judgment as actualized/fulfilled in the experiences of faithful Jews under Antiochus Epiphanes. Whether this

---

333. Ibid., 163–65.
334. Ibid., 163.
335. Ibid., 255–56.

was the LXX translator's intention or the way the readers of LXX-Amos would understand 4:2 is uncertain. Nevertheless, Glenny seems to hold to both.

Other passages (such as Jer 1:13; Ezek 24:5; Mic 3:3 and Ezek 11 [esp. v. 3]) are also brought in as having played a role in influencing LXX Amos 4:2b.[336] Upon examining these other texts, Glenny, drawing on Dines' views, generalizes that: "'caldrons' were used metaphorically as images of 'divine punishment on the elite of the land through the arrival of powerful enemies.' They certainly convey the images of punishment and suffering."[337]

Reluctant to leave any possible explanation out, Glenny concludes that the language in LXX Amos 4:2, "probably draws on imagery from the punishment of Jerusalem, which is pictured like a cauldron in Ezek. 11 and 24, from the torture of the seven brothers in Maccabees, and from the foreign nations (λοιμοί) that are sent to judge wicked Tyre and Egypt in Ezek. 28–32."[338]

Glenny's hesitation to single out one particular passage as having preeminence in the mind of the Greek translator of Amos 4:2 points to the likelihood that what we have here is a literary *topos* (which will be explained later) and not an exclusive intertextual relationship. Nevertheless, we should examine these passages to see the extent of their correspondence to LXX Amos 4:2.

Jeremiah 1:13
Since Jer 1:13 has the Hebrew word נפוח standing behind ὑποκαιόμενον, while Amos 4:2 has the possibly "manipulated" or otherwise "ignored" דוגה, the question arises whether it is possible to argue for intertextual borrowing by LXX Amos 4:2 from LXX Jer 1:13. At the same time, because ὑποκαιόμενος λέβης is attested elsewhere one cannot argue for an exclusive relationship between the two texts, unless additional elements are shared (e.g. thematic context).

Amos 4:2: Threat on Samaria's Women. Amos 4:2 is part of an oracle against Samaria, especially against the wealthy women who abuse the poor (Amos 4:1). The translator understands these women to be the recipients of the judgment as far as 4:3, where he has them brought out naked opposite one another: καὶ ἐξενεχθήσεσθε γυμναὶ κατέναντι ἀλλήλων

336.   Ibid., 163.
337.   Ibid., 104.
338.   Ibid., 210.

(MT: "you will go out through breaches [in the walls], one in front of the other").[339] This image of women being stripped naked is found in Isaiah's oracle against the rich women (3:16–24; LXX 32:11b: ἐκδύσασθε γυμναὶ γένεσθε περιζώσασθε σάκκους τὰς ὀσφύας), which could have influenced the translator's understanding of Amos 4:3.[340] In the Hebrew, the focus on Hermon suggests the attackers are coming from the north, whether they are Assyria or Aram.[341] However, it is not clear who the Greek translator envisaged as the enemy or where he regarded as the enemy's place of origin, given his puzzling rendering of Ρεμμαν. The Greek manuscript evidence and the other Greek versions also have variants on this name.

Jeremiah 1:13: Threat Against Jerusalem. Jeremiah 1:13 is part of an oracle against Jerusalem. The "boiling pot," in this case, features in a vision about the enemy preparing to come forth from the north against all the inhabitants of the land of Judah (1:14). While the phrase and the context of impending advances from the north are common to both texts, there are some differences. In LXX Amos 4:2 the "boiling pot" is an instrument *used* by the enemy for torture or killing of their victims, while in Jer 1:13 the pot is merely a symbol of the enemies themselves. No comment is made about the evil acts of the enemies in Jer 1:13, other than the fact that they will set their thrones against Jerusalem's walls. Therefore, we do not have sufficiently strong thematic links to claim that the phrase εἰς λέβητας ὑποκαιομένους was exclusively influenced by LXX Jer 1:13.

Other Possible Parallels: Ezekiel 11 and 24
In Ezek 11 and 24, the image of the pot is present again. In 11:3, Yahweh is using the people's own words ("The time is not near to build houses; this city is the pot, and we are the meat" [NRSV])[342] and borrows their

---

339.   Harper thinks that γυμναὶ κατέναντι "is probably a corruption of γυναῖκες ἔναντι" (*A Critical and Exegetical Commentary on Amos and Hosea*, 85).
340.   Dines thinks γυμναὶ entered the text at a later stage ("The Septuagint of Amos," 137–39). Johnson suggests that "perhaps the translator wrote γυνή, a literalism for אשה, or misread פרצים as ערמים (defective writing for ערומים)." "The Septuagint Translators of Amos," 32.
341.   Sweeney, *The Twelve Prophets*, 1:226.
342.   This proverbial phrase is ambiguous and there is no unanimity on whether it was intended to be negative (i.e. "this is no time to build houses; we are shut up in the city and are lost unless we do something soon" [J. Blenkinsopp, *Ezekiel* (Interpretation; Louisville: John Knox, 1990), 61]), or positive (i.e. "intended to suggest both the high worth of Jerusalem's present rulers and also their security from all external dangers" [W. Eichrodt, *Ezekiel: A Commentary* (trans. Cosslett Quin of

"pot" image to turn it against them (11:7, 11). In ch. 24 the "pot" metaphor is employed again to communicate a variety of messages, one of which is that the stains of the city's corruptions are irremovable. Despite the fact that humans are portrayed like meat in a pot, as in LXX Amos 4:2, the thrust of this parable is not about an enemy's violent attack on the inhabitants. Ezekiel's "pot" has Jerusalem as its referent, which is very different from both Jer 1:13 and LXX Amos 4:2.

In LXX Amos 4:2, the "pot" does not function as a symbol having a specified referent (the enemy from the north or Jerusalem). The "pot" is part of the description of a brutal "military" (ἐν ὅπλοις) attack, and the agents of this brutality are described as "fiery pests/destroyers." We observe that while the above passages make use of the cooking pot imagery, they do not use it in the same way, thus making it inappropriate to transfer the meaning communicated by it from one passage to another. The cooking pot may be a neutral symbol until given a specific function in a specific context. We must therefore examine the function of the cooking pot in LXX Amos 4:2 in its own context. In LXX Amos the cooking pot is not the enemy; nor is it Jerusalem. Instead, it symbolizes what the attackers will do to the "cows of Bashan." We shall examine the possibility that here we have a cannibalistic description communicated by the translator.[343]

Cannibalistic Imagery in the Bible and Surrounding Cultures
Cannibalistic imagery was not foreign to the Greek translator of the TP. It is found in Zech 11:9, but especially in Mic 3:3 where people are described as meat in a pot (סִיר/λέβης):

MT	LXX
וַאֲשֶׁר אָכְלוּ שְׁאֵר עַמִּי	ὃν τρόπον κατέφαγον τὰς σάρκας τοῦ λαοῦ μου
וְעוֹרָם מֵעֲלֵיהֶם	καὶ τὰ δέρματα αὐτῶν ἀπὸ τῶν ὀστέων αὐτῶν
הִפְשִׁיטוּ וְאֶת־עַצְמֹתֵיהֶם פִּצֵּחוּ	ἐξέδειραν καὶ τὰ ὀστέα αὐτῶν συνέθλασαν
וּפָרְשׂוּ כַּאֲשֶׁר בַּסִּיר וּכְבָשָׂר	καὶ ἐμέλισαν ὡς σάρκας εἰς λέβητα καὶ ὡς κρέα
בְּתוֹךְ קַלָּחַת	εἰς χύτραν

Cannibalism in the Hebrew Bible is also presented as a consequence of disobedience to God (Jer 19:9), usually under conditions of famine during siege (4 Kgdms 6:25–30). Walton notes that

Der Prophet Hesekiel [Das Alte Testament Deutsch 22/1–2; Göttingen: Vandenhoeck & Ruprecht, 1965–66]; OTL; London: SCM, 1970), 136–37]).

343.   By "cannibalistic" I mean not just the actual consumption of humans but more generally the savage treatment of humans as if they were food. While "eating" humans is not explicit in LXX Amos 4:2, their savage treatment as meat that is boiled in a cooking pot is clearly intended.

cannibalism is a standard element of curses in Assyrian treaties of the seventh century. It was the last resort in times of impending starvation. This level of desperation could occur in times of severe famine (as illustrated in the Atrahasis Epic) or could be the result of siege (as during Ashurbanipal's siege of Babylon, about 650 B.C.) when the food supply had become depleted, as mentioned in this text [2 Kgs 6:29] and anticipated in the treaty texts. Siege warfare was common in the ancient world, so this may not have been as rare an occasion as might be presumed.[344]

This practice has been difficult to corroborate in archaeological discoveries, but there are strong indications of its existence: "[C]utmarks on bone that relate to de-fleshing a corpse, the splitting of long bones, and the systematic opening of the skull to extract the brain are usually taken as strong indicators."[345]

However, cannibalistic imagery in literature seems to serve specific goals.

Cannibalistic Imagery in Greek Literature

Harril has explored cannibalistic language in Greco-Roman culture in order to understand Jesus' sayings in John 6:52–66. He explores how this imagery served in Greek and Roman culture to express social threat. Beginning with Homeric epic he notes how the Iliad, "increasingly compares warriors to bestial, blood-hungry predators. Simile and narrative correspond as *fighting* and *eating* become indistinguishable on the level of diction, the war descending into factionalism, an essentially cannibalistic enterprise."[346]

According to Harril, this language removes any sense of heroism in war and communicates its pointless savagery and destruction.[347]

Euripides describes the Cyclops as throwing Odysseus' companions into a pot (λέβης) to boil them (Euripides, *Cyclops* 395–405), and Aristotle speaks of tyrants who would punish people by throwing them into burning pots (λέβητας) (Aristotle, *Fragmenta Varia* 8.45 frg. 611 l. 340). According to Tamara Neal, "displacement of normative social

344. John H. Walton, Victor H. Matthews and Mark W. Chavalas, *The IVP Bible Background Commentary: Old Testament* (Downers Grove: IVP, 2000), 393.

345. Timothy Darvill, "Cannibalism," in *The Concise Oxford Dictionary of Archaeology* (Oxford: Oxford University Press, 2008), n.p. Online: http://www. oxfordreference.com/views/ENTRY.html?subview=Main&entry=t102.e645. Cited July 31, 2009.

346. J. Albert Harrill, "Cannibalistic Language in the Fourth Gospel and Greco-Roman Polemics of Factionalism (John 6:52–66)," *JBL* 127 (2008): 137 (italics original).

347. Ibid., 138.

rituals such as meal taking compound the increasingly bestial aspects of warrior behavior."[348]

From Thucydides we hear that cannibalism "tends to relate to sieges and is usually something the enemy does, not your own side."[349] Thus, given the common cannibalistic language in warfare, it appears that such a description of the enemy by the LXX translator of Amos would be an effective communicator of the morbid threat and would be better able to excite fear in the reader than would a strange "fishing" metaphor.

Cannibalistic Descriptions in the Greek Bible

In Ps 26[MT27]:2, enemies are portrayed as brutal eaters of humans, at least in the LXX. Kings are often portrayed as acting with similar brutality. The plus in LXX Prov 24:22 employs "cannibalistic" language for this purpose:

> ...μάχαιρα γλῶσσα βασιλέως καὶ οὐ σαρκίνη ὃς δ' ἂν παραδοθῇ συντρι-
> βήσεται ἐὰν γὰρ ὀξυνθῇ ὁ θυμὸς αὐτοῦ σὺν νεύροις ἀνθρώπους ἀναλίσκει καὶ
> ὀστᾶ ἀνθρώπων κατατρώγει καὶ συγκαίει ὥσπερ φλὸξ ὥστε ἄβρωτα εἶναι
> νεοσσοῖς ἀετῶν.[350]

Similar language is used to describe the Canaanites in Wis 12:5, a first-century B.C.E. text: τέκνων τε φονὰς ἀνελεήμονας καὶ σπλαγχνοφάγον ἀνθρωπίνων σαρκῶν θοῖναν καὶ αἵματος ἐκ μέσου μύστας θιάσου.[351]

Cannibalistic Descriptions in Josephus

When Josephus tells the story of Ptolemy Lathyrus' invasion of Judaea, he does not hold back from giving the full vivid brutality of the

348.   Tamara Neal, "Blood and Hunger in the *Iliad*," *CP* 101 (2006): 26.

349.   Simon Hornblower and Antony J. S. Spawforth, "Cannibalism," in *The Oxford Classical Dictionary* (Oxford: Oxford University Press, 2009), n.p. Online: http://www.oxfordreference.com/views/ENTRY.html?subview=Main&entry=t111. e1341. Cited July 31, 2009.

350.   This could also represent a different Hebrew *Vorlage*. See Tessa Rajak, *Translation and Survival: The Greek Bible of the Ancient Jewish Diaspora* (Oxford: Oxford University Press, 2009), 178–79.

351.   Cameron Boyd-Taylor notes that the charge of cannibalism in this text is a known motif from current philosophical discourse. "Robbers, Pirates and Licentious Women," in *Die Septuaginta—Texte, Kontexte, Lebenswelten: Internationale Fachtagung veranstaltet von Septuaginta Deutsch (LXX.D), Wuppertal 20.–23. Juli 2006* (ed. Martin Karrer and Wolfgang Kraus; WUNT 219; Tübingen: Mohr Siebeck, 2008), 560. James M. Reese notes that the Bible never accuses the Canaanites of cannibalism, but this charge was a common feature in Greek writers who attacked ancient myths. *Hellenistic Influence on the Book of Wisdom and Its Consequences* (Analecta Biblica 41; Rome: Biblical Institute, 1970), 8–9.

cannibalistic acts of Ptolemy's soldiers. When his armies came to some Judaean villages full of women and infants, Ptolemy Lathyrus commanded that their bodies be cut up and their parts be thrown into boiling cauldrons: ἐκέλευσεν τοὺς στρατιώτας ἀποσφάττοντας αὐτοὺς καὶ κρεουργοῦντας ἔπειτα εἰς λέβητας ζέοντας ἐνιέντας τὰ μέλη ἀπάρχεσθαι (Josephus, *Ant.* 13.345).

Josephus thinks that this order, confirmed by Strabo and Nicolas, was given specifically so that Ptolemy and his armies would create the image of being σαρκοφάγοι ("eaters of human flesh") and thus spread this terrifying reputation of themselves among their enemies (Josephus, *Ant.* 13.346–47). The description of this type of militaristic attack by various historians of the period, gives us, if not fully accurate facts, at least the idea of how the worst of war villains would be perceived. Tessa Rajak explores the use of archetypes of persecution and martyrdom in Jewish–Greek literature and notes that the figure of the "tyrant" was a common archetype employed in 2 Maccabees and *4 Maccabees*.[352]

The "Boiling Pot" as Literary Topos
The use of such cannibalistic descriptions of enemies in the Hebrew Bible, in the Greek version and in other Greek texts points to its successful rhetorical effect. The translator may have employed this language in order to communicate more effectively to a Greek audience what he thought the Hebrew passage was saying with less effect. Some commentators, however, prefer to go beyond this and find specific allusions to historical events.[353] At the same time, one should be careful when mapping a literary *topos*[354] on to specific historical circumstances. Richard Soulen considers how literary *topoi* should be read:

> The topos has been likened to a vessel sometimes filled with water, sometimes with wine, i.e., a form possessing different functions at different times depending on what is deemed appropriate to the rhetorical situation. The reader, who because of ignorance of the topos considers a specific formulation of an author to be a completely original creation of the

---

352. Tessa Rajak, "Dying for the Law: The Martyr's Portrait in Jewish-Greek Literature," in *The Jewish Dialogue with Greece and Rome: Studies in Cultural and Social Interaction* (Leiden: Brill, 2001), 114–15.

353. See the views of Park and Glenny above. Dines, following Musurillo, mentions the influence of the Hellenistic "novel" on "martyrdom" literature ("The Septuagint of Amos," 130). However, as already discussed, the context does not compel us to see LXX Amos 4:2 as a "martyrdom" scene.

354. Richard N. Soulen, *Handbook of Biblical Criticism* (3d ed.; Louisville: Westminster John Knox, 2001), 198.

moment, overestimates its meaning and errs just as the reader who, filled with knowledge of the topos, considers the passage nothing but a semantically empty filler.[355]

In the case of LXX Amos 4:2 the cannibalistic language employed has to be contextually read in order to understand its function. We cannot import the function that this language has had in other contexts.[356] In Daniel and Maccabees, the language is indeed employed to describe the persecution and the martyrdom of God's people. In other texts it highlights the savage nature of certain rulers or it presents in a graphic way the beastly abuse of one class of people by another (Mic 3:3). The same literary *topos* can express undeserved brutality (Daniel, Maccabees) but it can also express what appears to be a *lex talionis* punishment for the crime, as when those of a higher class have been "eating" the poor (Mic 3:3). Their own "cannibalism" would thus be deserving an appropriate judgment. Throwing the guilty into a "meat pot" would be appropriate to the "fattened cows" metaphor of Amos 4:1. The variety of uses for which the "cooking pot" is employed in different texts suggests that the language may have been borrowed from anywhere and its meaning adapted to the context of LXX Amos 4:2, which is that of rightful punishment. I do not, therefore, see the translator envisaging a scene of martyrdom or persecution in this text (contra Dines and Glenny).

Conclusion
The cannibalistic language creates a typical literary portrayal of the savage inhuman enemy. Moreover, the introduction of "nakedness" in the following verse (LXX Amos 4:3) adds to the brutal image of a "humiliating" enemy. The reference to the naked women (γυμναὶ) introduced in the LXX serves a successful rhetorical function of intensifying the judgment on these women, underlining their loss of power and control, not only of others but also of themselves.[357] Therefore, we conclude

---

355. Ibid., 197–98.

356. James Barr alerts us to similar types of fallacies: "The identity of the object to which different designations are given does not imply that these designations have the same semantic value. The mistake of supposing that it does we may for convenience call 'illegitimate identity transfer'... The error that arises, when the 'meaning' of a word (understood as the total series of relations in which it is used in the literature) is read into a particular case as its sense and implication there, may be called 'illegitimate totality transfer'." *The Semantics of Biblical Language*, 217–18.

357. For language on women and war, see Claudia V. Camp and Carole R. Fontaine, eds., *Women, War, and Metaphor: Language and Society in the Study of the Hebrew Bible* (Semeia 61; Atlanta: Scholars Press, 1993).

that the picture of humans being arrested in war and thrown into boiling pots is not necessarily rooted in another specific text or event but serves the literary function of turning an otherwise peculiar judgment threat into a scene of familiar brutality in war.

Chapter 5

NON-CATCHWORD ALLUSIONS

In this chapter, the intertextual phenomenon under consideration takes the form of allusions to specific biblical stories, events and characters. While we have already observed such allusions in the previous chapter, they were usually triggered by shared, often rare, catchwords. Even where translational freedom is apparent, the Greek translator tends to utilize the textual elements of his *Vorlage*, but in these cases the intertext exerts a stronger pull than does the Hebrew text being translated.

This appears to be the case in LXX Hos 6:9. The killing of Shechem, Dinah's rapist, in Gen 34 appears to lie behind the translational shifts in LXX Hos 6:9, in a context condemning the sinful priests of Israel. Around the same time, the *Testament of Levi* 2:1–2 and 6:3–6 (second century B.C.E.) makes reference to Levi's evil act in regard to Shechem. This is why both brothers, Simeon and Levi, were passed over in the blessings of Gen 49 (*T. Levi* 6:6). It is clear that there is a living tradition linking Gen 34 and 49:5–7. The condemnation of the Levitical priestly line (Gen 49:5–7) was based on the Gen 34 incident, and the translator is probably aware of this tradition.

In Amos 4:5, through some textual "manipulation," the Greek translator presents northern Israelite worship in extravagant terms reminiscent of the national outdoor worship of Ezra's time. The translator draws on the story of the famous national act of worship in the days of Ezra, where the Israelites gathered outside, read the law, and called for confession of sins. This event from the Jewish past appears to stand out as the epitome of bold community cultic expression of loyalty and seriousness about purity, and it is still so at the time of Josephus, who vividly records it with emphases similar to those alluded to by the LXX translator.

A significant aspect of intertextuality as presented in this section is that it brings to the surface the future expectations of the Greek translator. His translational choices as he engages with prophetic oracles betray an attitude to prophecy which is far from disinterested. It is similar to that observed in Jewish writings, especially in Qumran documents (see "Judeo-Hellenistic Milieu" in Chapter 1).

In LXX Amos 5:24, "righteousness" and "justice" describe states which are expected to be achieved through divine action, not human effort. This is also the case in other LXX passages (e.g. Amos 5:7), as well as various Qumran documents where this word pair occurs. The exhortation to the people to let justice and righteousness roll like water, in MT Amos 5:24, is instead attributed to divine agency by the Greek translator. The passage is understood as referring to the eschatological divine initiative in the light of the vision of the impassable waters of Ezek 47.

Israel's peaceful and undisturbed life in the land is a hope very much alive in the time of the translator. Expectations of the defeat of all evil are evident in the wide-ranging attention the eschatological enemy of Israel, Ezekiel's Gog, receives in early Judaism (see the Appendix). The Greek translator is not immune to contemporary traditions concerning this figure. In Amos 7:1, he seems to make explicit what he perceives to be the "apocalyptic" message of Amos' locust vision: the coming locusts equal Gog's armies. Various important intertexts are drawn in to illumine Amos' vision: Balaam's oracle on Gog, Joel's foe from the north presented as an army of locusts, and Ezekiel's enemy Gog, also from the north.

Hosea 6:9

Hosea 6:9

MT	LXX
וּכְחַכֵּי אִישׁ גְּדוּדִים	καὶ ἡ ἰσχύς σου ἀνδρὸς πειρατοῦ
חֶבֶר כֹּהֲנִים דֶּרֶךְ	ἔκρυψαν ἱερεῖς ὁδὸν
יְרַצְּחוּ־שֶׁכְמָה כִּי זִמָּה עָשׂוּ:	ἐφόνευσαν Σικιμα ὅτι ἀνομίαν ἐποίησαν
As robbers lie in wait for someone, so the priests are banded together; they murder on the road to Shechem, they commit a monstrous crime. [NRSV]	And your strength is that of a man, a brigand; priests have hidden the way; they have murdered Sikima, because they did lawlessness. [NETS]

Genesis 34:26

MT	LXX
וְאֶת־חֲמוֹר וְאֶת־שְׁכֶם בְּנוֹ	τόν τε Εμμωρ καὶ Συχεμ τὸν υἱὸν αὐτοῦ
הָרְגוּ לְפִי־חָרֶב	ἀπέκτειναν ἐν στόματι μαχαίρας
וַיִּקְחוּ אֶת־דִּינָה	καὶ ἔλαβον τὴν Διναν
מִבֵּית שְׁכֶם וַיֵּצֵאוּ	ἐκ τοῦ οἴκου τοῦ Συχεμ καὶ ἐξῆλθον
They killed Hamor and his son Shechem with the sword, and took Dinah out of Shechem's house, and went away. [NRSV]	They killed both Hemmor and his son Sychem with a dagger's edge and took Dina out of Sychem's house and went away. [NETS]

Hosea 6:9

In its LXX form, Hos 6:9 appears to be referring to the murder of an individual called Σικιμα, which is a possible allusion to the killing of Shechem, the defiler of Dinah, in Gen 34:26. The connection of this verse with Shechem, the individual of Gen 34:26, was first made by Theodore of Mopsuestia (350–428 C.E.),[1] an Antiochean Church Father, and by Cyril of Alexandria (378–444 C.E.).[2] This case is a good example of how ambiguity in the translation has affected early Christian Patristic interpretation. It raises the question whether the allusion was introduced by the translator or, in this case, by the Christian interpreters.[3]

Σικιμα usually occurs as a city name with a neuter plural form and here the name functions as the direct object of ἐφόνευσαν. Had this name always been treated as a plural then it could not have referred to an individual. Since different treatments of the name are attested in the LXX, as we shall see, we are free to consider the possibility that the referent in the Greek Hos 6:9 is a person.

Various Treatments of Σικιμα

In Gen 48:22 the name Σικιμα, which translates שכם, is treated as a singular feminine form: ἐγὼ δὲ δίδωμί σοι Σικιμα ἐξαίρετον ὑπὲρ τοὺς ἀδελφούς σου ἣν ἔλαβον ἐκ χειρὸς Ἀμορραίων. Here ἐξαίρετον, even though it is a two-termination adjective, has to be taken as a feminine accusative singular describing Σικιμα, since the following ἣν is also referring back to Σικιμα. Therefore, Σικιμα is treated as a feminine

---

1. "He intends by the comparison to demonstrate their wickedness: Your ancestors (he is saying, meaning Jacob's sons, Levi and Simeon) on seeing their sister subjected to indecent violence felt such indignation at the deed as to converse deceitfully and with guile with the Shechemites on pretence of friendship (the meaning of *concealed the way*), and took the opportunity to slay them all at the one time for the crime committed." Theodore, Bishop of Mopsuestia, *Commentary on the Twelve Prophets* (trans. Robert C. Hill; The Fathers of the Church 108; Washington: The Catholic University of America, 2004), 67.

2. "Now, observe how God reminds us of the ancient story, and mentions the former crimes of Levi... Such is the story he now reminds us of, saying with some delicacy, *they murdered Shechem because they did wrong in the house of Israel.* He says this to charge them with sinning at that time against the house of Jacob, or Israel, by robbing the girl of her virginity. Consequently, we in turn killed Shechem." Saint Cyril, Patriarch of Alexandria, *Commentary on the Twelve Prophets*, vol. 1 (trans. Robert C. Hill; The Fathers of the Church 115; Washington: Catholic University Press of America, 2007), 148–49.

3. Hos 6:9 is also quoted in 4QpIsᶜ 23, ii, 14–14a against the Seekers-After-Smooth-Things who are in Jerusalem. See Horgan, *Pesharim*, 120–21.

singular name instead of a neuter plural one. Likewise in 3 Kgdms 12:24, 25, Σικιμα (את־שׁכם) is clearly taken as a feminine name, as the article τὴν shows twice, and as also does αὐτῇ: καὶ ἐπορεύθη Ιεροβοαμ εἰς Σικιμα τὴν ἐν ὄρει Εφραιμ…καὶ ᾠκοδόμησεν Ιεροβοαμ τὴν Σικιμα τὴν ἐν ὄρει Εφραιμ καὶ κατῴκει ἐν αὐτῇ.

Σικιμα is also often treated as a neuter plural name. Some examples are: Gen 33:18: πόλιν Σικιμων (עיר שׁכם); Josh 24:32: ἐν Σικιμοις (בשׁכם); Judg 9:6: ἄνδρες Σικιμων (בעלי שׁכם).

Other occurrences of שׁכם are simply transliterated into Συχεμ (e.g. Gen 12:6; Josh 20:7; Judg 9:34) by the translator. Sometimes the context requires the word to be translated as "shoulders" or "back" (Gen 9:23; 21:14, etc.). We should also note that whenever שׁכמה appears with reference to Shechem, the directional ה is always translated with εἰς (Gen 37:14; Josh 24:1; Judg 9:1, 31; 21:19; 2 Chr 10:1).

שׁכם *as a Personal Name*

The question, now, is whether Σικιμα could be used as a personal name. The translator of the story of Shechem in Genesis is consistent in his translation of the individual's name as Συχεμ (Gen 33:19; 34:2, 18; 34:4, 6, 8, 11, 13, 24, 26). Naturally, in such a short space we would not expect the translator to use different versions of the name. Otherwise, we do not have many other references to the personal name Shechem in other OT books. The only instances (transliterated as Συχεμ) are in LXX Num 26:35(MT26:31); Josh 17:2; Judg 9:28 and 1 Chr 7:19. The evidence is not enough to tell us whether Σικιμα was ever used as a masculine personal name. We cannot make a decision based on this evidence since the flexibility with which the name was treated in the OT (Σικιμα/Συχεμ— feminine singular/neuter plural) allows for a small possibility that Σικιμα could have been used as a masculine personal name.

The Verb ἐφόνευσαν

ἐφόνευσαν usually translates רצח, and the translator remains consistent in his rendering of this root (see also 4:2). In 6:9 ירצחו is noticeably rendered in the aorist, thus making the action appear to be an event of the past. The reason is probably that the translator understands the verse to be part of a pair of past evil actions, or one past evil action in two stages: "priests have hidden the way, they have murdered Sikima" (NETS).[4] It is possible by metonymy to use a city's name as the object of ἐφόνευσαν,

---

4.   In the majority of cases in Hosea the Hebrew imperfect forms are translated by Greek imperfect forms. Some exceptions are 4:11, 7:7, 15, 16, 8:3 and 9:11.

meaning "the citizens of that city" (Josh 10:28, 30, 32, 35). We are then left with two choices: the translator, by this particular rendering, departs from the MT which has the sense of a repetitive evil action *on the way to Shechem*, and creates the meaning of either the city of Sikima or Sikima the person having been murdered.

The Translator's View of 6:9

Before we explore our two options we shall take a look at the rendering of the verse as a whole. We suspect that כחך[5] was read instead of כחבי (possibly *Piel* infinitive construct of חכה, "wait") and gave rise to ἡ ἰσχύς σου as in Judg 16:6, 15 and Prov 5:10 (cf. Hos 7:9). A similar reading is attested in the Peshiṭta: "Your strength is that of a robber," possibly influenced by the LXX.[6] The LXX links this first line with the previous verse by καί, and this line is also rendered in the second person singular, possibly referring us back to the direct address to Ephraim and Judah in v. 4.

Following this word, the translator could have read בְּ before אִישׁ, which is possible for the Peshiṭta as well, but we have no such indication since he usually renders בְּ by ὡς. It is more likely that the Peshiṭta is influenced by the LXX than that both versions independently misread in the same way or that both worked with a *Vorlage* containing בְּ.

πειρατοῦ has the meaning of "[of a] raider"[7] or "[of a] brigand,"[8] while the underlying noun גדוד is found in Gen 49:19 with the sense of a band[9] or troop of robbers, as most English translations recognize. The word occurs in Hos 7:1 again, where (probably for the sake of variety) it is translated by λῃστής. According to Philo, a behaviour is pirate-like when it involves deceitful plotting, trickery, sophistry, pretense or hypocrisy:

---

5. Allegro (*DJD* 5, 25, note on Hos 6:9) suggests that the LXX *Vorlage* had כיחכה as 4Q163 (frg. 23 l. 14) and that the translator misread the י as ו (כוחכה instead of כיחכה). However, this explanation is unnecessary since the translator does not need the middle ו to understand כח as "strength" (see Hos 7:9). Muraoka suggests that "כחבי has been broken down into כח + an archaic, dialectal 2fem. sg. possessive pronoun כי." T. Muraoka, "Hosea 6 in the Septuagint," in Ausloos, Lemmelijn, and Vervenne, eds., *Florilegium Lovaniense*, 347.

6. A. Gelston considers the possibility that "some of these apparent differences in reading or vocalization may be due to the translator's interpretative licence or to the influence of another ancient version (especially the LXX) rather than to an actual divergence of the *Vorlage* from MT." *The Peshiṭta*, 123–25.

7. LEH 477–78.

8. *Muraoka 2009*, 543.

9. "גְּדוּד," *HALAT* 1:170.

ὁ δὲ πειρατικώτερον ἐνεδρεύων τοὺς ἀντιλοχῶντας ἀπάτης, φενακισμοῦ,
γοητείας, σοφισμάτων, προσποιήσεως, ὑποκρίσεως, ἅπερ ἐξ ἑαυτῶν ψεκτὰ
ὄντα κατ' ἐχθρῶν γινόμενα ἐπαινεῖται· ὁ δὲ πλουτεῖν τὸν φύσεως πλοῦτον
ἐπιτηδεύων ἐγκρατείας, ὀλιγοδεΐας· ὁ δὲ εἰρήνης ἐρῶν εὐνομίας, εὐδικίας,
ἀτυφίας, ἰσότητος. (*Somn.* 2.40)

The LXX translator chooses the singular in 6:9: (a) to match the preceding singular pronoun σου, (b) because of the influence of the singular
איש, or (c) owing to the absence of ים from the *Vorlage*, which was
possibly similar to 4Q163, if indeed it had the singular.[10] The real question, however, is whether the translator could render the plural in a way
that would seem consistent with the rest of the phrase. Since πειρατοῦ
was understood to be descriptive of ἀνδρὸς, the only way to translate it
naturally would be in the singular.

חבר ("company, association")[11] is rendered by ἔκρυψαν, which could
have been read as חֶבְאוּ (*BHS*; cf. Job 24.4) or חֶבָּאוּ.[12] Another possibility
is that the ם of the previous word was read as ס at the beginning of the
following word, that is, מחבר was read as סתרו. One could come up with
various proposals, but we do know that the translator was familiar with
the חבר root from his rendering of 4:17 (μέτοχος εἰδώλων for חבור עצבים).
However, the translator's tendency to confuse similar letters would offer
the best explanation for this case, as van Hoonacker argues.[13] The
translator then renders כי by ὅτι, making the following dependent clause
a causal (adverbial) one.[14]

In order to understand the translator's flow of thought we shall break
down the verse into parts:

(1) καὶ ἡ ἰσχύς σου ἀνδρὸς πειρατοῦ
(2) ἔκρυψαν ἱερεῖς ὁδὸν
(3) ἐφόνευσαν Σικιμα
(4) ὅτι ἀνομίαν ἐποίησαν.

---

10. Allegro (*DJD* 5, 25, note on Hos 6:9) suggests that [ ]גדוד in 4Q163 may
indicate a singular reading (or interpretation) of גדודים.
11. BDB 288.
12. Macintosh, *A Critical and Exegetical Commentary on Hosea*, 244. Also
Muraoka, "Hosea 6," 348.
13. "Pour חבר les LXX donnent ἔκρυψαν; il ne faut pas s'empresser d'en conclure
qu'ils ont eu dans leur texte חבאו; ils pourraient simplement avoir lu חבו et rattaché
cette forme, pour lui donner un sens quelconque à חבא; cette même confusion entre
ר (ou ד) et ו (ou י) s'observe en d'autres passages, comme tout à l'heure au v.8 מים
pour מדם; x, 12: ועת, LXX: γνώσεως (=דעת); xii, 1: רד עם, LXX: ἔγνω αὐτοὺς (=ידעם),
etc." Van Hoonacker, *Les Douze Petits Prophètes*, 66.
14. On this category, see Daniel B. Wallace, *Greek Grammar Beyond the Basics*
(Grand Rapids: Zondervan, 1995), 460.

The accusation 1 is made in the form of a metaphor. It states a quality that characterizes the guilty party: his strength is like a pirate's. This could mean that his power is misused in a sinful, deceptive way for the purposes of stealing and destruction. The statement is parallel in form to another simile in 6:7, which states another negative quality of the guilty party, the tendency to break agreements: αὐτοὶ δέ εἰσιν ὡς ἄνθρωπος παραβαίνων διαθήκην. Following this accusation (1), there follows what appears to be an example from the past—statements (2), (3) and (4)—which supports the accusation (1). The priests hid the way (2), a treacherous, pirate-like action, and they (the priests) murdered Sikima (3), a second pirate-like action in the sequence. Finally, statement 4 is the ground of (2) and (3).

The Lexical Choices
Commentators have seen this verse as part of a thematic unity describing treachery and treason.[15] Moreover, the language used in this verse by the LXX translator is found in other places in the OT, especially the Psalter. In Ps 141:4(MT142:3) we find the combination of "road," "hiding," and the element of malicious intent: ἐν ὁδῷ ταύτῃ ᾗ ἐπορευόμην ἔκρυψαν παγίδα μοι. Similarly in Ps 139:6(MT140:5) we read: ἔκρυψαν ὑπερήφανοι παγίδα μοι καὶ σχοινία διέτειναν παγίδας τοῖς ποσίν μου ἐχόμενα τρίβου σκάνδαλον ἔθεντό μοι.

Kruger thinks that the description of Israel in Hos 6:9 is after the typical pattern of the "evildoer" used to describe people's evil acts in the Psalter (e.g. Pss 9:29–30[MT10:8–9]; 16:12[MT17:12]; 63:5[MT64:4]). This "evildoer" image is enhanced in the Greek through the rendering of חבה by ἔκρυψαν, because the element of secrecy is usually present in the portraying of this image.[16] This language is also very prominent in Abimelech's story in Judg 9. The men of Shechem are hiding in order to rob those passing along the way:

καὶ ἔθηκαν αὐτῷ οἱ ἄνδρες Σικιμων ἐνεδρεύοντας ἐπὶ τὰς κεφαλὰς τῶν ὀρέων καὶ διήρπαζον πάντα ὃς παρεπορεύετο ἐπ' αὐτοὺς ἐν τῇ ὁδῷ καὶ ἀπηγγέλη τῷ βασιλεῖ Αβιμελεχ. (Judg 9:25)

Abimelech is later described in similar fashion (9:43–44). Thus the victim of these evildoers can be either an individual (Psalms) or an entire city (Abimelech's case). Is it possible to know which of the two choices

---

15. See the titles for section 6:7–7:2 by Macintosh, *A Critical and Exegetical Commentary on Hosea*, 236, and Mays, *Hosea*, 99.
16. Paul A. Kruger, "The Evildoer in Hosea 6:8–9," *JNSL* 17 (1991): 17–22.

(individual or city) was intended by the Greek translator to be the victim named Sikima or which historical referent he could have had in mind?

The Murdering of a City

The city of Shechem has a long history of murders and murderers. We read in Josh 21:21: καὶ ἔδωκαν αὐτοῖς τὴν πόλιν τοῦ φυγαδευτηρίου τὴν τοῦ φονεύσαντος τὴν Συχεμ καὶ τὰ ἀφωρισμένα αὐτῇ... Shechem was one of the cities allotted to the Levites by the tribe of Ephraim (Josh 21:20). This was a city of refuge for those who had committed unintentional homicide (Josh 20:7). Had the translator meant that they murdered the city of Sikima, this would have served as a poetic reversal of the city's function. The priests would now be the murderers of those dwelling in Sikima.[17] The priests, like pirates, have hidden the way, possibly the way taken by the homicides who were escaping to Sikima to save their lives. In a spiritual sense, then, the way to finding life, mercy, and deliverance was hindered by the priests. The priests were now the murderers of the inhabitants of Sikima. This is a possibility, but, since LXX Hos 6:9 puts the action in the past tense, it appears to be referring to a past incident in Israel's history, not a repetitive action as the MT implies. The following are the two candidate cases to be considered:

a. The story of Abimelech in Judg 9 links Shechem with treachery and murder and could be considered as a possible referent of LXX Hos 6:9. Abimelech's troops burned and looted the city, and massacred the people.

b. The other reference to the murder of inhabitants of Shechem is Gen 34. It was not just the man Shechem who was murdered for Dinah's rape, but every male of that city. This operation too was carried out in a treacherous manner. The inhabitants had made an agreement with Jacob's sons to intermarry on the condition that every male would be circumcised. However, Simeon and Levi took advantage of the situation when every male was in pain on the third day after their circumcision; they slipped in, killed all the males, and looted the place.

To which event, then, is LXX Hos 6:9 alluding? The image of the "evildoer" is present on both of these occasions. Abimelech, however, is not a priest nor has he any connection to the priesthood, whereas the killing of Shechem in Gen 34 was carried out by Simeon and Levi, the latter being representative of the Levitical priestly line.

---

17. A similar meaning can be derived from the MT as well. See Macintosh, *A Critical and Exegetical Commentary on Hosea*, 243–44.

What could possibly tilt the scale further in favour of Gen 34 is the condemnation of Simeon and Levi in Gen 49:5–7, in a clear allusion to the Gen 34 incident,[18] for the misuse of their sword, their violence, their assemblies, and their slaying of people in their wrath:

> Συμεων καὶ Λευι ἀδελφοί συνετέλεσαν ἀδικίαν ἐξ αἱρέσεως αὐτῶν εἰς βουλὴν αὐτῶν μὴ ἔλθοι ἡ ψυχή μου καὶ ἐπὶ τῇ συστάσει αὐτῶν μὴ ἐρείσαι τὰ ἥπατά μου ὅτι ἐν τῷ θυμῷ αὐτῶν ἀπέκτειναν ἀνθρώπους καὶ ἐν τῇ ἐπιθυμίᾳ αὐτῶν ἐνευροκόπησαν ταῦρον ἐπικατάρατος ὁ θυμὸς αὐτῶν ὅτι αὐθάδης καὶ ἡ μῆνις αὐτῶν ὅτι ἐσκληρύνθη διαμεριῶ αὐτοὺς ἐν Ιακωβ καὶ διασπερῶ αὐτοὺς ἐν Ισραηλ.

This is the only passage which shows the "striking contrast between Levi here as a tribe in disfavor and the consistent concept of the other Torah sources, such as Num 3:12f., 8:14–18, and 16:19f., that the Levites were God's elect who enjoyed a privileged status."[19]

The prophecies of Gen 49 relating to the twelve sons of Jacob must have been among the best known passages in Judaism, as the *Testament of Levi* shows. The *T. Levi* 2:1–2 and 6:3–6 (second century B.C.E.) makes reference to Levi's evil act regarding Shechem, as a response to the abominable thing they had done to Dinah. This is the reason both brothers were passed by in the blessings of Gen 49 (*T. Levi* 6:6). It is clear that there is a living tradition linking Gen 34 and 49:5–7.

The condemnation of the Levitical priestly line (Gen 49:5–7) was based on the Gen 34 incident, and the translator is probably aware of this tradition about Simeon and Levi, so that it is not impossible that the first statement in Hos 6:9, καὶ ἡ ἰσχύς σου ἀνδρὸς πειρατοῦ, in connection with "priests," reminded him of the two brothers and their warlike qualities.[20]

---

18. Supported by the majority of commentators. See, for example, Hermann Gunkel, *Genesis* (trans. Mark E. Biddle, 1901; Macon: Mercer University Press, 1997), 359, 455, and Nahum M. Sarna, *The JPS Torah Commentary, Genesis: The Traditional Hebrew Text with the New JPS Translation* (Philadelphia: Jewish Publication Society, 1989), 334.

19. Sarna, *Genesis*, 334.

20. The failure of the line of Levi is prominent in the TP, especially in Malachi where one sees the priests turning from the way and failing to honour the covenant of Levi: ὑμεῖς δὲ ἐξεκλίνατε ἐκ τῆς ὁδοῦ καὶ πολλοὺς ἠσθενήσατε ἐν νόμῳ διεφθείρατε τὴν διαθήκην τοῦ Λευι λέγει κύριος παντοκράτωρ (2:8). However, the cleansing of the sons of Levi is promised in Mal 3:3. Certain scholars have argued that the LXX of the TP presents a more negative view of the priesthood than the MT. See Jack R. Lundbom, "Contentious Priests and Contentious People in Hosea IV 1–10," *VT* 36 (1986): 54, and Sawyer, "'Those Priests in Damascus'," 123–30.

The Murdering of the Individual
The only possible referent of ἐφόνευσαν Σικιμα, if a specific individual is indicated, would be Shechem the son of Hamor of Gen 34. The name alone cannot tell us whether the reference is to the son of Hamor or to the entire city. The language of the "evildoers" can be equally applied to robbers attacking either an individual or a whole town (Judg 9). Therefore, again, it is difficult to determine whether the son of Hamor or the whole town of Shechem is in view.

Conclusion
Our conclusion can only narrow down to one incident in Israel's past, Gen 34, as the text most likely to have influenced the Greek translation of Hos 6:9. This story, as interpreted in Gen 49 and on into the Christian era, portrays the representative of Israel's priesthood in the role of the "evildoer," whose power is misused for piracy and murder. While the MT has "they murder on the way to Shechem," the LXX translator, by his rendering, manages to pin down Sikima as the direct object of murder, that is, as the victim, and he thus "historicizes" the act as an incident in Israel's past for which the priesthood is condemned.

Amos 4:5

Amos 4:5

MT	LXX
וְקַטֵּר מֵחָמֵץ תּוֹדָה	καὶ ἀνέγνωσαν ἔξω νόμον
וְקִרְאוּ נְדָבוֹת	καὶ ἐπεκαλέσαντο ὁμολογίας
הַשְׁמִיעוּ כִּי כֵן אֲהַבְתֶּם	ἀπαγγείλατε ὅτι ταῦτα ἠγάπησαν
בְּנֵי יִשְׂרָאֵל	οἱ υἱοὶ Ισραηλ
נְאֻם אֲדֹנָי יְהוִה	λέγει κύριος ὁ θεός
[B]ring a thank offering of leavened bread, and proclaim freewill offerings, publish them; for so you love to do, O people of Israel! says the Lord GOD. [NRSV]	They read the law outside and called for confessions. Announce that the sons of Israel have loved these things, says the Lord God. [NETS]

Nehemiah 8:8/2 Esdras 18:8

וַיִּקְרְאוּ בַסֵּפֶר בְּתוֹרַת	καὶ ἀνέγνωσαν ἐν βιβλίῳ νόμου
הָאֱלֹהִים מְפֹרָשׁ וְשׂוֹם שֶׂכֶל	τοῦ θεοῦ καὶ ἐδίδασκεν Εσδρας καὶ
וַיָּבִינוּ בַּמִּקְרָא	διέστελλεν ἐν ἐπιστήμη κυρίου
	καὶ συνῆκεν ὁ λαὸς ἐν τῇ ἀναγνώσει
So they read from the book, from the law of God, with interpretation. They gave the sense, so that the people understood the reading. [NRSV]	And they read from the book of the law of God, and Esdras was teaching and expanding on the knowledge of the Lord, and the people understood during the reading. [NETS]

Nehemiah 9:3/2 Esdras 19:3

וַיָּקוּמוּ עַל־עָמְדָם   καὶ ἔστησαν ἐπὶ τῇ στάσει αὐτῶν

וַיִּקְרְאוּ בְּסֵפֶר תּוֹרַת   καὶ ἀνέγνωσαν ἐν βιβλίῳ νόμου

יְהוָה אֱלֹהֵיהֶם   κυρίου θεοῦ αὐτῶν

רְבִעִית הַיּוֹם וּרְבִעִית מִתְוַדִּים   καὶ ἦσαν ἐξαγορεύοντες τῷ κυρίῳ

וּמִשְׁתַּחֲוִים לַיהוָה אֱלֹהֵיהֶם   καὶ προσκυνοῦντες τῷ κυρίῳ θεῷ αὐτῶν

They stood up in their place and read
from the book of the law of the LORD
their God for a fourth part of the day,
and for another fourth they made
confession and worshiped the LORD
their God. [NRSV]

And they kept their stance and read in
the book of the law of the Lord, their
God, and they were declaring to the
Lord and doing obeisance to the Lord,
their God. [NETS]

Torah Reading in the Square and Confession

The picture of the people of Israel gathering outside to read the law is found in the book of 2 Esdras (MT Nehemiah). In ch. 18, the people gather together in the square and ask Ezra the scribe to read the Torah to them:

καὶ συνήχθησαν πᾶς ὁ λαὸς ὡς ἀνὴρ εἷς εἰς τὸ πλάτος τὸ ἔμπροσθεν πύλης τοῦ ὕδατος καὶ εἶπαν τῷ Εσδρα τῷ γραμματεῖ ἐνέγκαι τὸ βιβλίον νόμου Μωυσῆ ὃν ἐνετείλατο κύριος τῷ Ισραηλ. (2 Esd 18:1[MTNeh 8:1])

This reading is followed by the celebration of the feast of booths. Everyone gathered branches for the building of booths and stayed outside their homes, even on their roofs, reading the law outside for seven days (2 Esd 18:16–18[MTNeh 8:16–18]).

Not only was the Torah read in the squares, but the whole scene is characterized by confession. The people are described as prostrating with their faces to the ground (καὶ ἔκυψαν καὶ προσεκύνησαν τῷ κυρίῳ ἐπὶ πρόσωπον ἐπὶ τὴν γῆν [2 Esd 18:6(MTNeh 8:6)]), and weeping at the hearing of the Torah (καὶ εἶπαν παντὶ τῷ λαῷ ἡμέρα ἁγία ἐστὶν τῷ κυρίῳ θεῷ ἡμῶν μὴ πενθεῖτε μηδὲ κλαίετε ὅτι ἔκλαιεν πᾶς ὁ λαὸς ὡς ἤκουσεν τοὺς λόγους τοῦ νόμου [2 Esd 18:9(MTNeh 8:9)]). Then the whole of 2 Esd 19 is concerned with the people's confession of their sin. They are presented as fasting in sackcloth and dirt, confessing not only their own but their fathers' iniquities as well (2 Esd 19:1–2[MTNeh 9:1–2]). The two acts (Torah reading and reciting of sins) were done in combination (2 Esd 19:3[MTNeh 9:3]).

The gathering of the people outside and the collective confession of sin is also narrated in 2 Esd 8–10(MTEzra 8–10)[21] and 1 Esd 9:37–55.[22]

---

21. Williamson holds that the reading of the Torah described in Neh 8 must have preceded the public confession in Ezra 9: "The view is adopted here that places

Our examination will not be concerned with the sequence of the events described or with the question whether these chapters refer to a single "covenant renewal" ceremony.[23] Our purpose is to understand the tradition surrounding this/these event(s) of collective worship and to determine whether this tradition has influenced the LXX translator's reading of Amos 4:5. In this examination we shall be treating all the records of these events as a single tradition. The following table shows where the story is found, including Josephus' narration:

Gathering and recognition of sin	1 Esd 9:5–17	2 Esd. 10:9–17 (MTEzra 10:9–17)	Josephus, *Ant.* 11:148–53
Public reading of the Torah	1 Esd 9:37–55	2 Esd. 17:73–18:12 (MTNeh 7:73–8:12)	Josephus, *Ant.* 11:154–58

LXX Rendering of Amos 4:5

καὶ ἀνέγνωσαν. καὶ ἀνέγνωσαν corresponds to MT וְקַטֵּר. There is more than one possible explanation for this change: (1) The translator read וקראו, which is also the second verb in the verse, instead of וקטר, but he gave different renderings for the two occurrences of the verb.[24] It is not the case that he was ignorant of קטר (Hos 2:15; 4:13; 11:2; Hab 1:16). (2) The translator, thinking that Torah was the object of this verb, was influenced towards his rendering. Both van Hoonacker and Gelston think that it was the misreading of תורה for תודה that was influential in the rendering of the previous two words.[25] (3) The third explanation is given

Ezra's reading of the law between Ezra 8 and Ezra 9. Thus within the original Ezra narrative it was the community's understanding and acceptance of that law which pricked their leaders' consciences into bringing their confession to Ezra." H. G. M. Williamson, *Ezra, Nehemiah* (WBC 16; Waco: Word, 1985), 127.

22. Opinions vary as to whether this book is a portion of an earlier and larger form of the biblical accounts or is dependent on the biblical record. See the chapter on the composition of 1 Esdras by Zipora Talshir, *I Esdras: From Origin to Translation* (SBLSCS 47; Atlanta: SBL, 1999).

23. For different views, see Williamson, *Ezra, Nehemiah*, 279–86.

24. So Max L. Margolis, "Notes on Some Passages in Amos," *AJSL* 17 (1901): 171. Margolis does not see a problem with the repetition of the same word, comparing it with the repetition of פשע in v. 4.

25. "Le traducteur grec qui a lu par méprise תורה au lieu de תודה comprend le passage de la lecture de la Loi; pour וקטר il donne καὶ ἀνέγνωσαν; ce qui suppose au lieu de וקטר le verbe וְקָרְאוּ (comp. *Néh.* VIII, 8)." Van Hoonacker, *Les Douze Petits Prophètes*, 236. Gelston thinks that "the misreading of תודה seems to have influenced his misreading or misinterpretation of the two previous words as well. Whether he actually misread these as וְקָרָא מֵחָמֵץ or merely guessed at these words as a substitute for a *Vorlage* he could not decipher or could not understand remains

by Glenny who thinks that there are too many changes in this verse and the preceding one, and that this makes it unlikely that all the differences were triggered by the misreading of the *daleth* in תודה as a *resh*.[26]

Glenny is right to claim that the misreading of the *daleth* as *resh* in תודה would be an unlikely explanation for the various misreadings in the Greek, since, as we have noted, the translator is familiar with קטר (Hos 2:15; 4:13; 11:2; Hab 1:16). Option (1) could account for the rendering of קטר. However, if that were the case one would expect the translator to render וקראו in the future tense or even as an imperative, but he does not do this for either of the verbs. He continues as he had been doing in the immediately preceding context, that is, listing past actions (Amos 4:4): εἰσήλθατε εἰς Βαιθηλ καὶ ἠνομήσατε καὶ εἰς Γαλγαλα ἐπληθύνατε τοῦ ἀσεβῆσαι καὶ ἠνέγκατε εἰς τὸ πρωὶ θυσίας ὑμῶν εἰς τὴν τριημερίαν τὰ ἐπιδέκατα ὑμῶν. It is, therefore, more likely that his translation by καὶ ἀνέγνωσαν was intentional.

Amos 4:4 is manipulated into the past tense, but in the second person plural. It is likely that the translator had read the imperative correctly (hence the second person plural) but was reluctant to translate an invitation to sin as coming from the lips of God. He therefore turns the invitations into accusations by shifting all the verbs to the past tense.[27] Although he keeps to the past tense "accusatory" form, he shifts to the third person plural in v. 5: καὶ ἀνέγνωσαν. This verb, with νόμον for its object, is found only once in 1 Esd 9:48, and twice in 2 Esdras with νόμον as indirect object (18:8 and 19:3).[28] In the light of the translator's "historicizing" of v. 4, and in the light of his "misreading" of תודה as תורה, another historical communal act of worship, under Ezra the scribe, appears to have suggested itself to him.[29]

---

uncertain. It is likely, however, that the misreading of *daleth* as *resh* in the third word was a significant factor in his rendering of the clause." "Some Hebrew Misreadings," 494.

26. W. E. Glenny, "Hebrew Misreadings or Free Translation in the Septuagint of Amos?," *VT* 57 (2007): 538–39.

27. The Targum reads similarly: "*they came to Bethel and rebelled,* in Gilgal *they increased sinning, bringing* your sacrifices every morning, your tithes every three days." It is suggested that the Targumist also "probably wanted to avoid Yahweh's involvement in a summons to evil." Cathcart and Gordon, *Targum*, 86 n. 6.

28. Also noted by van Hoonacker, *Les Douze Petits Prophètes*, 236.

29. Glenny also concludes that it "appears that there is evidence of historicizing interpretation in this passage, in which the translator manipulates the text, trying to make it relevant to his audience." Glenny, "Hebrew Misreadings," 539. However, Glenny does not suggest a specific historical event as the background for this

ἔξω. The word ἔξω ("outside") is also hard to account for. The corresponding word in the MT is מֵחָיץ, which could have been read as מחוץ.[30] It is unlikely that the word חמץ ("leaven") was unknown to a Jewish translator or anyone acquainted with Jewish culture (see Hos 7:4).[31] However, this lexical choice would have made no sense in the context of Torah reading. It is possible that the translator made an adaptation to fit the rest of the clause.

Reading outside, in the open space, is stressed in 1 Esdras. Three times (1 Esd 9:6, 38, 41) the noun εὐρύχωρον[32] ("open space") is used. While 2 Esd 18:1 has πλάτος ("breadth, width, plane surface"), the Peshiṭta has "street" and Josephus ὑπαίθρῳ ("under the sky, in the open air") when describing this gathering (*Ant.* 11.149). He later uses ἀνειμένον τοῦ ναοῦ ("the open court of the temple"; *Ant.* 11.154).

A significant aspect of being gathered outside, stressed by Josephus (*Ant.* 11.149) and 1 Esdras, was the cold weather that the people had to endure: τρέμοντες διὰ τὸν ἐνεστῶτα χειμῶνα (1 Esd 9:6). This element is also found in 2 Esd 10:9, ἀπὸ τοῦ θορύβου αὐτῶν περὶ τοῦ ῥήματος καὶ ἀπὸ τοῦ χειμῶνος, and 10:13, καὶ ὁ καιρὸς χειμερινός καὶ οὐκ ἔστιν δύναμις στῆναι ἔξω. In other words, for these sources, the fact that people gathered ἔξω was not simply geographical information: it served to underline the seriousness of the situation and the urgency of repentance and action. By being there, the people demonstrated how determined they were to stay together as a group of former exiles, purify their nation from any foreign influence, and follow the Mosaic law.[33] This aspect of the story is

rendering. He thinks that "the first two clauses describe a group, apparently priests outside of the Temple in the past, reading the law and calling for public confessions." Ibid., 538.

30. A not widely shared view is that of Margolis who suggests that 4:5 read: וְקִרְאוּ בַחוּץ תּוֹדָה ("Call out in the streets, Thanksgiving!"), thus getting rid of the mention of leaven. Margolis, "Notes on Some Passages in Amos," 171.

31. This would be contrary to Glenny's view that the translator possibly would not have recognized the word for leaven and that he recognized it in Hos 7:4 only because it is in the context of making bread. Glenny, "Hebrew Misreadings," 538.

32. Talshir offers a reconstruction of 1 Esdras' *Vorlage* and states that "εὐρύχωρος is the usual equivalent for רחוב in 1 Esd…compared with πλατεῖα in the LXX." Talshir, *I Esdras*, 293.

33. "The ninth month, Kislev, approximates our December. This is the season of the early winter rains in Palestine, and they can be very heavy. For those who had had to travel some distance, this would have made the occasion uncomfortable enough. However, the solemnity of the occasion, perhaps heightened by the fact that they were meeting in the same square as that where two months previously they had gathered to hear Ezra read the Law (cf. Neh 8:1) was the overriding factor that led to their apprehension." Williamson, *Ezra, Nehemiah*, 155.

likely to have been known to the Amos translator. Therefore, the choice of מחוֹץ instead of מֵחָמָץ historicizes the clause further.

ἐπεκαλέσαντο ὁμολογίας. ἐπεκαλέσαντο for וְקִרְאוּ, as in Amos 4:12, has the meaning "call on, appeal for help, invoke" and continues the past tense. However, when this verb is used with the accusative ὁμολογίας, "confessions," it has the meaning of "call for some action."[34] The NETS translators render this first part of the verse as, "They read the law outside and called for confessions." A call to confession regarding the sin of intermarriage was central to Ezra's speech in 1 Esd 9:8: καὶ νῦν δότε ὁμολογίαν δόξαν τῷ κυρίῳ θεῷ τῶν πατέρων ἡμῶν. ὁμολογία here must have the sense of confession or acknowledgment, and not offering, as in 5:58: καὶ ἐφώνησαν δι᾽ ὕμνων ὁμολογοῦντες τῷ κυρίῳ ὅτι ἡ χρηστότης αὐτοῦ καὶ ἡ δόξα εἰς τοὺς αἰῶνας ἐν παντὶ Ισραηλ.[35] In 2 Esd 10:11, the text has αἴνεσιν ("praise") instead of ὁμολογίαν: καὶ νῦν δότε αἴνεσιν κυρίῳ τῷ θεῷ τῶν πατέρων ὑμῶν. However, the L-text expands αἴνεσιν by καὶ ἐξομολόγησιν ("and confession") and the Old Latin has *confessionem* instead of αἴνεσιν, possibly to bring it into line with the parallel text of 1 Esd 9:8, which contains ὁμολογίαν.

The plural accusative noun ὁμολογίας is translating נְדָבוֹת. נדבה occurs in Hos 14:5 where it is translated adverbially as ὁμολόγως meaning "confessedly, openly"[36] or "willingly."[37] *HALAT* gives two meanings for נְדָבָה, "free motivation" and "voluntary offering,"[38] which both can be translated by ὁμολογία in the LXX (e.g. Lev 22:18; Deut 12:17).[39] In Hos 14:5 the translator shows familiarity with the first meaning of נדבה but that does not prove that he is ignorant of the second. What, then, is

---

34. *Muraoka 2009*, 273.

35. Tov thinks that the meaning of the word in these passages is "to give thanks." Tov, "Greek Words and Hebrew Meanings," 101–2. Muraoka disagrees on the meaning of ὁμολογίαν in 1 Esd 9:8, which he places, together with Amos 4:5, under the definition of "acknowledgement, confession of sin or error." *Muraoka 2009*, 497. Even if the meaning "to give thanks" was intended, it does not guarantee that it was understood as such by its readers, since the verb ὁμολογέω is used for both "confess" and "give thanks." In the context, where the people had been confronted by Ezra about their sin of intermarriage, it would be natural to understand Ezra's invitation as a call to confession rather than thanksgiving (cf. Josh 7:19).

36. LSJ 1226.

37. *Muraoka 2009*, 497.

38. *HALAT* 3:634–35.

39. However, ὁμολογία is never used with the meaning of "voluntary offering" outside the LXX. Only a person familiar with the Greek Pentateuch might have understood such a meaning.

the meaning intended by ἐπεκαλέσαντο ὁμολογίας in Amos 4:5? There are three options: (a) they called on their offerings, that is, depended on them; (b) they called for offerings, that is, invited people to bring in their offerings; (c) they called for confessions, that is, exhorted people to confess their sins.

We have to rule out option (a) because ἐπικαλεῖσθαι is never used with something inanimate as its direct object. Usually God or God's name are the direct objects. It seems that "people" is the implied direct object of the clause and ὁμολογίας is the indirect object. This leaves us to decide between the two last options.

In Lev 22:18, ὁμολογία seems to mean "agreement" or "promise," like its Hebrew equivalent נדר (cf. Jer 51:25). In the same verse, נדבה ("free motivation, voluntary offering") is rendered as αἵρεσις. In Lev 22:18 ὁμολογία and αἵρεσις are, then, descriptive of offerings. In Deut 12:17, however, נדר is translated by εὐχάς while נדבה is rendered by ὁμολογία. Here the words are not descriptive of the offerings but are replacing them (cf. Ezek 46:12). Arieti thinks that נדבה was unknown to the translators of the Prophets but was better understood in other books where it is translated by ἑκούσιος (Lev 7:16; Num 15:3; Ps 67:10).[40] Glenny agrees with Arieti, and goes further to suggest that the translator "misses or changes the sacrificial vocabulary in 4:5."[41] However, it seems that the word ὁμολογία was established as a legitimate equivalent of נדבה in the Pentateuch, and the translators of the Prophets must have recognized that ὁμολογία could be used to translate a Hebrew word for offerings (see Ezek 46:12). Deuteronomy 12:17 would not have made sense when forbidding people to eat τὰς ὁμολογίας unless this word had acquired the meaning of "voluntary offerings" in this cultic context.

On the other hand, it is most likely that the translators were aware of the various meanings of the term. ὁμολογεῖν commonly means "confess" (e.g. 2 Macc 6:6; Sir 4:26), and in the light of this common use many scholars (Lust,[42] Muraoka,[43] Glenny,[44] NETS translators) have taken ὁμολογίας in Amos 4:5 to mean "confessions." It is difficult to make a decision as to which one of the two last options the Amos translator had in mind, but it seems more likely, since he also used ἐπεκαλέσαντο, that the translator wanted to convey the sense of a call to confession. The MT has the sense of "proclaiming" and "making known" these offerings. But

---

40. Arieti, "The Vocabulary of Septuagint Amos," 347.
41. Glenny, *Finding Meaning in the Text*, 88.
42. *LEH* 437.
43. *Muraoka 2009*, 497.
44. Glenny, "Hebrew Misreadings," 538.

the LXX ἐπεκαλέσαντο turns the clause into an exhortation to confession. This is also achieved by the fact that the LXX translator treats השמיעו as the beginning of a new clause. The object of ἀπαγγείλατε in the LXX is not the "freewill offerings" but what follows ὅτι.

Through the acts of "reading the law outside" and "calling for confessions" introduced by the LXX translator, he was able to allude to this historical national worship event. However, his word choices do not necessitate that he is dependent on a Greek version of the story. He could have been equally influenced by a Hebrew version of the story (Neh 8:1–3; 9:1–3).

Conclusion

While the MT has the Lord calling people to go on performing their cultic worship, sacrifice, tithe, and make known their freewill offerings, the LXX presents a different picture. It narrates these communal acts of worship as acts of the past, in an ironic accusatory manner. The translator is reminded of the famous national act of worship in the days of Ezra, where they gathered outside, read the law, and called for confession of sins, all these being bold cultic expressions of the people's loyalty and seriousness about purity. The translator states ironically: "Announce that the sons of Israel have loved these things." In other words, the translator sees Amos condemning the northern worshippers for a sort of national outdoors pseudo-confession which wants to mimic the one in Ezra's time. It seems that a communal expression of public confession and Torah reading becomes the object of ridicule for the LXX translator when it is performed in the wrong context.

Amos 5:24

Amos 5:24

MT	LXX
וְיִגַּל כַּמַּיִם מִשְׁפָּט וּצְדָקָה כְּנַחַל אֵיתָן	καὶ κυλισθήσεται ὡς ὕδωρ κρίμα καὶ δικαιοσύνη ὡς χειμάρρους ἄβατος
But let justice roll down like waters, and righteousness like an ever-flowing stream. [NRSV]	And judgment will roll down like water, and justice like an unfordable wadi. [NETS]

Ezekiel 47:5

MT	LXX
וַיָּמָד אֶלֶף נַחַל אֲשֶׁר לֹא־אוּכַל לַעֲבֹר כִּי־גָאוּ הַמַּיִם מֵי שָׂחוּ נַחַל אֲשֶׁר לֹא־יֵעָבֵר	καὶ διεμέτρησε χιλίους καὶ οὐκ ἠδύνατο διελθεῖν ὅτι ἐξύβριζε τὸ ὕδωρ ὡς ῥοῖζος χειμάρρου ὃν οὐ διαβήσονται

Again he measured one thousand, and it was a river that I could not cross, for the water had risen; it was deep enough to swim in, a river that could not be crossed. [NRSV]	And he measured a thousand, and he could not pass through, because the water was violently rushing as the rush of a wadi, which they shall not cross. [NETS]

The apparent discrepancy in the Hebrew–Greek equivalence of אֵיתָן– ἄβατος[45] is explained, according to Muraoka, by the influence of a parallel passage (Ezek 47:5) on the translator. Muraoka believes that "the probability of such influence must be fairly high when the passages concerned are believed, on other grounds, to be ascribable to a single translator."[46]

איתן can function as an adjective or a noun with the meaning of "continuous" or "continuous (one), continuity, perennial (one), eternal (one), eternity, reliable (one), reliability."[47] It can also mean "enduring" or "firm."[48] However, this meaning may not have been known by ancient translators. A survey of ancient witnesses may shed some light on how this Hebrew word was understood in antiquity.

איתן *in the LXX*
The LXX Pentateuch exhibits a variety of renderings for this word. It seems to be associated with "strength" or "power," taking the form of a noun in Gen 49:24 (μετὰ κράτους–באיתן) and of an adjective in Num 24:21 (ἰσχυρὰ ἡ κατοικία σου–מושבך איתן). In Exod 14:27 the translator seems to offer a simplified interpretive translation with ἐπὶ χώρας for לאיתנו in order to communicate that the water had returned to "its place."[49] We have no indication as to whether he knew the meaning of the Hebrew word, which in this case would have the sense of "[its] normal state" ("normal depth" [NRSV]; "normal state" [NET]; "normal course" [ESV]; *but* "its strength" [KJV and JPS]), or whether he translated on the basis of the context. The only other occurrence of איתן in the Pentateuch is in Deut 21:4, where the same phrase as that in Amos 5:24

45. "das ἄβατος 'unpassierbar' von 𝔊 meint wohl dasselbe—trifft den Sinn nicht genau." Rudolph, *Joel–Amos–Obadja–Jona*, 206.
46. Muraoka, "Literary Device," 21. Muraoka follows Thackeray's theory of a common translator for Ezekiel α and the Greek TP. See Thackeray, "The Greek Translators of Ezekiel," 398–411.
47. *DCH* 1:238.
48. BDB 450.
49. It is not unlikely that the translator had made some connection between איתן and נתן ("to put"/"place").

(נחל|אֵיתָן) occurs. LXX Deuteronomy 21:4 has φάραγγα τραχεῖα, with אֵיתָן rendered by an adjective meaning "rough" or "uneven."[50] The Greek translator of Deuteronomy usually lets the context decide whether נחל refers to a brook/wadi (χείμαρρος) or a ravine/valley (φάραγξ).[51] The adjective τραχεῖα must also have been gathered from the context, which describes the נחל as not having been ploughed or sown. It is clear, at the least, from this overview that the Greek translator of Amos did not resort to the Greek Pentateuch for help in rendering אֵיתָן.

In many places אֵיתָן functions as a proper name, or is understood as such (3 Kgdms 5:11; 8:2; 1 Chr 2:6, 8; 6:27, 29; 15:17, 19; Pss 73[MT74]:15; 88[MT89]:1; Jer 30:13[MT49:19]; 27[MT50]:44). In LXX Job 12:19 we seem to have an interpretive move in the rendering of אֵתָנִים by δυνάστας. It is possible that Job's translator was influenced by the Greek Pentateuchal association of the word with "strength" or "power," but it could also have been a mere guess aiming at preserving the parallelism of the verse (i.e. religious and governmental authorities: ἐξαποστέλλων ἱερεῖς αἰχμαλώτους δυνάστας δὲ γῆς κατέστρεψεν). Guessing may also have been behind the Greek translation of the only other occurrence of אֵיתָן in Job (33:19), this time by the verb ἐνάρκησεν ("grew stiff, or numb"). The above data suggest that the Greek translator of Job was uncertain of the meaning of this word.

In Prov 13:15 אֵיתָן is translated by ἐν ἀπωλείᾳ, suggesting the translator's unfamiliarity with the Hebrew word, while in Jer 5:15 אֵיתָן remains untranslated, probably due to homoeoarkton, given that there are four phrases in the verse beginning with גוי.

אֵיתָן in LXX Micah 6:2

In the TP the situation is similar. There is no indication that the translator was aware of the meaning of this word. Apart from Amos 5:24, the only other place where a form of אֵיתָן occurs is Mic 6:2, where it is rendered by φάραγγες ("ravines"):

MT	LXX
שִׁמְעוּ הָרִים אֶת־רִיב יְהוָה	ἀκούσατε λαοί[52] τὴν κρίσιν τοῦ κυρίου
וְהָאֵתָנִים מֹסְדֵי אָרֶץ כִּי רִיב	καὶ αἱ φάραγγες θεμέλια τῆς γῆς ὅτι κρίσις
לַיהוָה עִם־עַמּוֹ	τῷ κυρίῳ πρὸς τὸν λαὸν αὐτοῦ
וְעִם־יִשְׂרָאֵל יִתְוַכָּח	καὶ μετὰ τοῦ Ισραηλ διελεγχθήσεται

50. The rabbis also understand אֵיתָן to mean "rough" (*m. Sotah* 9:5).
51. See Deut 2:36 where both renderings are found.
52. Rahlfs has βουνοί as original but Ziegler showed preference for λαοί (supported by witnesses such as W' and B).

Muraoka explains the choice of φάραγγες as deriving from the parallel passage of LXX Ezek 6:3 where mountains and ravines (אפיקים) are summoned to hear God:[53]

MT	LXX
וְאָמַרְתָּ הָרֵי יִשְׂרָאֵל שִׁמְעוּ	καὶ ἐρεῖς τὰ ὄρη Ισραηλ ἀκούσατε
דְּבַר־אֲדֹנָי יְהוִה כֹּה־אָמַר אֲדֹנָי	λόγον κυρίου τάδε λέγει κύριος
יְהוִה לֶהָרִים וְלַגְּבָעוֹת לָאֲפִיקִים	τοῖς ὄρεσι καὶ τοῖς βουνοῖς καὶ ταῖς φάραγξι
וְלַגֵּאָיֹת] (וְלַגֵּאָיָא) הִנְנִי אֲנִי מֵבִיא	καὶ ταῖς νάπαις ἰδοὺ ἐγὼ ἐπάγω
עֲלֵיכֶם חָרֶב	ἐφ᾽ ὑμᾶς ῥομφαίαν
וְאִבַּדְתִּי בָּמוֹתֵיכֶם	καὶ ἐξολεθρευθήσεται τὰ ὑψηλὰ ὑμῶν

The summons to mountains to hear God occurs once more in Ezek 36:4, where φάραγγες is present as well:

MT	LXX
לָכֵן הָרֵי יִשְׂרָאֵל שִׁמְעוּ דְּבַר־אֲדֹנָי יְהוִה	διὰ τοῦτο ὄρη Ισραηλ ἀκούσατε λόγον κυρίου
כֹּה־אָמַר אֲדֹנָי יְהוִה לֶהָרִים	τάδε λέγει κύριος τοῖς ὄρεσι
וְלַגְּבָעוֹת לָאֲפִיקִים	καὶ τοῖς βουνοῖς καὶ ταῖς φάραγξι
וְלַגֵּאָיוֹת וְלֶחֳרָבוֹת	καὶ τοῖς χειμάρροις καὶ τοῖς ἐξηρημωμένοις
הַשֹּׁמֲמוֹת וְלֶעָרִים	καὶ ἠφανισμένοις καὶ ταῖς πόλεσι
הַנֶּעֱזָבוֹת אֲשֶׁר הָיוּ	ταῖς ἐγκαταλελειμμέναις αἳ ἐγένοντο
לְבַז וּלְלַעַג	εἰς προνομὴν καὶ εἰς καταπάτημα
לִשְׁאֵרִית הַגּוֹיִם אֲשֶׁר מִסָּבִיב	τοῖς καταλειφθεῖσιν ἔθνεσι περικύκλῳ

If the Greek translator of the TP was aware of these parallel passages, then when encountering the invitation to the mountains to hear God's word in Mic 6:1–2 he may have supplied φάραγγες for the unknown אתנים. For the Greek translator of Micah, φάραγξ corresponds to the Hebrew גיא (Zech 14:5), so he may just as easily have been reminded of גיא in Ezek 6:3.

However, there seems to be a certain monocularity in Muraoka's approach, in that he tends to show preference for LXX Ezekiel, partly on the basis of his assumption of a common translator for Ezekiel and the Twelve. One may consider other valid explanations for the rendering of אתנים in Mic 6:2. It is obvious that אתנים was not understood as an adjective here, but as a plural noun in apposition to מסדי ארץ (θεμέλια τῆς γῆς).[54] It is possible that the translator was aware of some sort of

53. Muraoka, "Literary Device," 22.
54. θεμέλια is used for the foundations, the roots or lowest points of human constructions (e.g. 3 Kgdms 7:9; 4 Kgdms 16:18; 1 Esd 6:19; Ezra 5:16; Sir 3:9; 50:16; Hos 8:14; Amos 1:4, 7, 10, 12, 14; 2:2, 5), but it is also used for the lowest points of natural places like the sea (e.g. 2 Kgdms 22:16; Ps 17[MT 18]:16) and the mountains (e.g. Deut 32:22; Ps 17[MT 18]:8; Job 18:4; Jdt 16:15).

connection between נחל and איתן, not only through Amos 5:24 but especially through the expiation law for murdered individuals by unknown
agents in Deut 21:4, where נחל is rendered by φάραγξ. He seems to have
supplemented his lack of knowledge of איתן by introducing its accom-
paniment, נחל. φάραγξ is a common equivalent for נחל, but its connection to איתן could have been suggested to the translator by LXX
Deut 21:4.

Whatever the case might be, LXX Mic 6:2 confirms that the translator
did not know אתנים and possibly had to draw on corresponding passages.

איתן *in the Minor Greek Versions*
Not much is known about other Greek versions of Amos 5:24, except for
Symmachus' reading of ἀρχαῖος or παλαιός ("ancient," "old"). This
appears to be the typical rendering that Symmachus gives for איתן, while
Aquila seems to prefer στερεός ("strong" or "firm"):[55]

	Σ	A
Exod 14:27	εἰς το ἀρχαῖον αὐτῆς	εἰς το ἀρχαῖον αὐτοῦ[56]
Deut 21:4		πρὸς χείμαρρον στερεόν
Ps 73[MT74]:15	σὺ ἐξήρανας ποταμοὺς ἀρχαίους	ποταμοὺς στερεούς
Jer 5:15	ἰσχυρόν	στερεόν
Jer 30:13[MT49:19]	ἀπὸ δόξης...ἐπὶ τὸ κατοικητήριον τῶν ἀρχῶν[57]	ἐπὶ τὸ κατοικητήριον τὸ ἀρχαῖον[58]
Jer 27[MT50]:44	ἐπὶ τὸ κατοικητήριον τὸ ἀρχαῖον	ἐπὶ τὸ κατοικητήριον Αἰθάμ
Mic 6:2	καὶ τὰ παλαιὰ θεμέλια τῆς γῆς	καὶ τὰ στερεά

LXX Isaiah 23:17 has τὸ ἀρχαῖον for אתננה ("wages of a harlot"), which
looks like איתן, but in LXX Isa 22:11 τῆς ἀρχαίας correctly translates a
form of [ה]ישנה ("old").[59] It appears as if the two Hebrew words were
confused or substituted, and it is an indicator that perhaps Symmachus
was reading איתן forms as ישן forms (ש corresponding to ת). Under יָשֵׁן

55. The meaning of "strong" for איתן is found in *b. Roš. Haš.* 11a and *Gen.
Rab.* XCVIII (*Jastrow*, 62).
56. "Nobil. Lectio suspecta, tum propter pronomen masculinum αὐτοῦ, tum quia
אֵיתָן Aquilae στερεὸς, Symmacho autem ἀρχαῖος constanter sonat." Field, *Origenis
Hexaplorum*, 1:106 n. 29.
57. ἀρχαῖαν according to Eusebius (ibid., 2:720 n. 71).
58. "Aliter: Aquila πρὸς εὐπρέπειαν στερεάν." This is supported by Syh and Vulg.
and Eusebius (ibid.).
59. ישן is also translated by παλαιός elsewhere (Lev 25:22; 26:10; Song 7:14).

Jastrow gives the meanings "to be strong, hard, old," and he also makes the connection of יָשֵׁן with אִיתָן.[60] Thus, while the meaning "strong" for אִיתָן is attested in LXX Pentateuch and Aquila, the meaning "ancient" is absent from the LXX (except for LXX Isaiah's possible misreading in 23:17).

The data from the minor Greek versions provide further indication that the meaning of "continuous" or "perennial" for אִיתָן was unknown in antiquity.

אִיתָן *in Other Versions*

Targum:
But let justice *be revealed* like water, and righteousness like a *mighty* stream.

Peshitta:
But let justice be revealed (ܘܢܶܬ݂ܓ݁ܠܶܐ) like waters, and righteousness as a mighty (ܥܰܫܺܝܢܳܐ) stream.

Vulgate:
Et revelabitur quasi aqua iudicium et iustitia quasi torrens fortis.

All three versions read גלה ("to reveal") instead of גלל, and they all agree in rendering אִיתָן with "strong" or "mighty." As we have already seen, this is the meaning which seems to prevail in the LXX Pentateuch and in Aquila's version, a meaning which was apparently unknown to the Greek translator of the TP.[61]

ἄβατος

Since "continuous" or "perennial" are meanings which are not attested for אִיתָן in these ancient witnesses, the most likely rendering to be expected for אִיתָן in LXX Amos 5:24 would be a word with the meaning "strong" or "mighty." Instead, we have ἄβατος, a word the Greek translator of the TP never otherwise uses.

Meanings for ἄβατος elsewhere in the LXX are: "impassable" (e.g. Lev 16:22; Ps 62[MT63]:2), "[tract of land] not amenable to easy and regular passage" (e.g. Job 38:27; Jer 39[MT32]:43) and "deserted and

---

60. *Jastrow*, 601. However, Jastrow tends to link roots without necessarily demonstrating any etymological basis for doing so.

61. "The phrase used in this verse contains the word *ʾeytan*, the meaning of which was lost until the modern systematic study of Arabic. The ancient Versions guessed at the meaning from the context, and so the medieval Jewish commentators; hence the meaning 'strong, mighty, rough'. But the word beyond question means 'ever-flowing'; cf. Arabic *watana* (to be constant)." Snaith, *The Book of Amos*, 106.

waste" (Jer 30:18[MT49:2]).[62] These meanings are uniform throughout Greek literature. When used specifically for a river, ἄβατος means "unfordable," as in Xenophon (*Anabasis* 5.6.9):

τρίτον δὲ Ἅλυν, οὐ μεῖον δυοῖν σταδίοιν, ὃν οὐκ ἂν δύναισθε ἄνευ πλοίων διαβῆναι· πλοῖα δὲ τίς ἔσται ὁ παρέχων; ὡς δ' αὕτως καὶ ὁ Παρθένιος ἄβατος· ἐφ' ὃν ἔλθοιτε ἄν, εἰ τὸν Ἅλυν διαβαίητε.

The Greek translator of Amos is clearly interpreting 5:24 in relation to such an unfordable wadi, and, as we shall see, it is possible that he was reading this verse through an eschatological lens.

LXX Eschatological Reading of Amos 5:24

MT Amos 5:23 begins with the *Hiphil* imperative (הָסֵר rendered by μετάστησον in the LXX), commanding Israel to remove their superficial worship, and ends with God's declaration that he will not listen (לֹא אֶשְׁמָע). Amos 5:24 follows with the prefixed conjugation וְיִגַּל[63] (*Niphal* imperfect of גלל),[64] which is generally understood as jussive ("But let justice roll"—NRSV, JPS, NJB, NIV, KJV, ESV; NET has "justice must flow"), with the *waw* being adversative.[65] The LXX translates ויגל with the indicative future passive κυλισθήσεται ("will roll"),[66] which suggests that this event is the future consequence of the ceasing of the false worship of Israel. Moreover, there is no hint of the *waw* being understood as adversative.[67] Hyatt thinks that the LXX (as well as the Vulgate) understood the *waw* correctly.[68] In that case, 5:24 would not be understood as further exhortation to make up for false worship, but as a statement of God's future/eschatological action. The text was not read as if it was the responsibility of the addressee, but is stating a divine initiative. This is further supported by a parallel LXX reading a few verses earlier, where the pair משפט and צדקה also occurs (Amos 5:7):

62. *Muraoka 2009*, 1.
63. See Joüon § 82*m*.
64. *Holladay* 61; BDB 164.
65. Paul, *A Commentary on the Book of Amos*, 192 n. 47.
66. See NETS, and Dines, "The Septuagint of Amos," 165. Sherman E. Johnson regards the "future passive" in LXX Amos 5:24 as one of the renderings which are "as poor as they can be." *The Septuagint Translators of Amos*, 12–13.
67. One would have expected ἀλλά (Mal 2:9) or δέ (e.g. Amos 2:9; 4:7; 7:13).
68. Speaking of how Amos 5:24 is usually translated, Hyatt says that "following vs. 23, one would normally expect here a stronger adversative conjunction and continuation of the imperative, to express the idea which is contained in the customary translation." He translates the *waw* with "in order that." Philip J. Hyatt, "The Translation and Meaning of Amos 5,23.24," *ZAW* 68 (1956): 17–18.

הַהֹפְכִים לְלַעֲנָה מִשְׁפָּט   κύριος ὁ ποιῶν εἰς ὕψος κρίμα
וּצְדָקָה לָאָרֶץ הִנִּיחוּ   καὶ δικαιοσύνην εἰς γῆν ἔθηκεν

The Greek translator has read 5:7 as continuing the reference to "the Lord" in the preceding verse, possibly through some degree of contextual manipulation.[69] While this word pair always refers to people and not to God in the Hebrew of Amos (e.g. 6:12),[70] in 5:7 the Greek translator relates them to divine action.

According to Hyatt, this word pair in various Qumran documents has the significance of "salvation" or "redemption" when referring to God's expected acts, and does not refer to social justice.[71] Applying this to Amos 5:24 he comments:

> If our interpretation of Amos 5₂₃₋₂₄ is correct, the prophet is saying to the Israelites that they must cease their preoccupation with feasts, festal gatherings, offerings, etc., in order that Yahweh may cause to flow down upon them His deliverance and salvation… When they do these things and turn to Yahweh in genuine repentance, He will send His salvation upon them, and it will be as constant and dependable as an everflowing stream of water.[72]

This is probably the way the LXX translator of Amos understood 5:24, with Isa 48:18 offering a close parallel: καὶ εἰ ἤκουσας τῶν ἐντολῶν μου ἐγένετο ἂν ὡσεὶ ποταμὸς ἡ εἰρήνη σου καὶ ἡ δικαιοσύνη σου ὡς κῦμα θαλάσσης. LXX Psalm 35[MT36]:7–9 is also cast in a future (eschato-logical) dimension (contra MT), with salvific connotations for δικαιοσύνη and the river of God. Moreover, *1 En.* 39:5, through what seems to be an allusion to Amos 5:24,[73] understands the flowing of the waters of justice as the result of intercessory prayer:

> Here mine eyes saw their dwellings with His righteous angels,
> And their resting-places with the holy.
> And they petitioned and interceded and prayed for the children of men,
> And righteousness flowed before them as water,
> And mercy like dew upon the earth: Thus it is amongst them for ever and ever.

---

69. See Glenny, *Finding Meaning in the Text*, 80. Also Wolff, *Joel and Amos*, 229 n. s, and Dines, "The Septuagint of Amos," 159. See also Park, *The Book of Amos*, 151–52.

70. Wolff, *Joel and Amos*, 264.

71. Hyatt, "The Translation and Meaning," 20–21.

72. Ibid., 24.

73. Charles, *The Apocrypha and Pseudepigrapha of the Old Testament*, 2:210 n. 5.

Contrary to the other ancient versions which read a form of גלה ("to uncover, reveal"),[74] the LXX has recognized גלל and preserved the vivid picture of water flowing. The sense of the verse, therefore, is that if Israel would get rid of their false worship the eschatological righteousness and justice (or deliverance and salvation, according to Hyatt) will flow like an "impassable winter-torrent."[75]

Flowing Waters
The vision of flowing waters is found in various eschatological texts. Isaiah 33:21 expresses the idea of the Lord being a place of rivers and wide canals:

כִּי אִם־שָׁם אַדִּיר יְהוָה לָנוּ	ὅτι τὸ ὄνομα κυρίου μέγα ὑμῖν
מְקוֹם־נְהָרִים יְאֹרִים	τόπος ὑμῖν ἔσται ποταμοὶ καὶ διώρυγες
רַחֲבֵי יָדָיִם בַּל־תֵּלֶךְ בּוֹ	πλατεῖς καὶ εὐρύχωροι οὐ πορεύσῃ ταύτην
אֳנִי־שַׁיִט וְצִי אַדִּיר לֹא יַעַבְרֶנּוּ	τὴν ὁδόν οὐδὲ πορεύσεται πλοῖον ἐλαῦνον

We should note that these streams and rivers are impassable (לֹא יעברנו) to ships or boats, communicating a sense of protection from foreign invasion.[76] The context is about Jerusalem becoming an undisturbed habitation, shielded from outside threats. The impassable waters have a protective function, which is very different from the way in which the image is used in our passage. Moreover, neither נחל nor איתן is present in Isa 33:21.

In the TP there are a few passages picturing flowing waters. One of them is Mic 1:4 where the mountains are described as melting like water when the Lord comes down to step on the high places:

וְנָמַסּוּ הֶהָרִים תַּחְתָּיו	καὶ σαλευθήσεται τὰ ὄρη ὑποκάτωθεν αὐτοῦ
וְהָעֲמָקִים יִתְבַּקָּעוּ כַּדּוֹנַג	καὶ αἱ κοιλάδες τακήσονται ὡς κηρὸς
מִפְּנֵי הָאֵשׁ כְּמַיִם	ἀπὸ προσώπου πυρὸς καὶ ὡς ὕδωρ
מֻגָּרִים בְּמוֹרָד	καταφερόμενον ἐν καταβάσει

Although the flowing of the water is mentioned, there is no reference to rivers or wadis and no emphasis on the waters being impassable. The function of the image here is simply to stress the instability of creation and the dissolution which God's coming in judgment brings. It is a negative metaphor very different from that in our passage. The translator also uses water negatively in Mic 7:12 by rendering וְיָם מִיָּם וְהַר הָהָר as

---

74. Symmachus read κεκυλισται γαρ ("for it has rolled") and Theodotion read και αποικισθησεται ("and it will be exiled").

75. Dines' translation ("The Septuagint of Amos," 165).

76. The water imagery was used to portray a military attack in Isa 8:6–8.

ἡμέρα ὕδατος καὶ θορύβου, so creating the image of a judgment day which involves water.

A positive image of flowing waters, however, is found in Joel 4:18:

וְהָיָה בַיּוֹם הַהוּא יִטְּפוּ הֶהָרִים	καὶ ἔσται ἐν τῇ ἡμέρᾳ ἐκείνῃ ἀποσταλάξει τὰ ὄρη
עָסִיס וְהַגְּבָעוֹת תֵּלַכְנָה חָלָב	γλυκασμόν καὶ οἱ βουνοὶ ῥυήσονται γάλα
וְכָל־אֲפִיקֵי יְהוּדָה יֵלְכוּ מָיִם	καὶ πᾶσαι αἱ ἀφέσεις Ιουδα ῥυήσονται ὕδατα
וּמַעְיָן מִבֵּית יְהוָה יֵצֵא וְהִשְׁקָה	καὶ πηγὴ ἐξ οἴκου κυρίου ἐξελεύσεται καὶ ποτιεῖ
אֶת־נַחַל הַשִּׁטִּים	τὸν χειμάρρουν τῶν σχοίνων

This passage mentions a winter torrent (נחל–χειμάρρουν) which is filled from the flowing waters coming from the Lord's house, and it gives an optimistic eschatological vision, much like LXX Amos 5:24. The emphasis is on the abundant blessing of renewed fertility in the land. However, an emphasis on the volume or intensity of the torrent is absent.

Zechariah 14:8 also utilizes the "flowing water" imagery eschatologically:

וְהָיָה בַיּוֹם הַהוּא יֵצְאוּ מַיִם־חַיִּים	καὶ ἐν τῇ ἡμέρᾳ ἐκείνῃ ἐξελεύσεται ὕδωρ ζῶν
מִירוּשָׁלַ͏ִם חֶצְיָם אֶל־הַיָּם	ἐξ Ιερουσαλημ τὸ ἥμισυ αὐτοῦ εἰς τὴν θάλασσαν
הַקַּדְמוֹנִי וְחֶצְיָם	τὴν πρώτην καὶ τὸ ἥμισυ αὐτοῦ
אֶל־הַיָּם הָאַחֲרוֹן בַּקַּיִץ	εἰς τὴν θάλασσαν τὴν ἐσχάτην καὶ ἐν θέρει
וּבָחֹרֶף יִהְיֶה	καὶ ἐν ἔαρι ἔσται οὕτως

Zechariah 14 begins negatively by portraying the eschatological vision of the Lord doing battle and then coming with his holy ones (vv. 1–5). After the "light" metaphor in vv. 6–7, the vision describes the "living waters" flowing out of Jerusalem, but without a wadi (נחל) being mentioned. The emphasis is on the perennial nature of the flow, which idea could have been thwarted by the mention of a "winter-torrent." At the same time, there is no suggestion of the impassable nature of the waters.

χειμάρρους in LXX Ezekiel 47

The most extended use of the "flowing water" imagery is found in Ezek 47:1–12, where the visionary account of the stream that flows from the new temple is given in elaborate form. Nowhere else in Ezekiel is נחל found except in this chapter, where we have seven occurrences in the following verses: 5, 6, 7, 9, 12. According to Allen, the explanation "functions as a means of communicating the miraculous effects of the river."[77] The central focus of the description is the "test of the passability of the stream."[78] In vv. 3 to 5 the increasing depth of the water is

77. Leslie C. Allen, *Ezekiel 20–48* (WBC 29; Dallas: Word, 1990), 277.

78. Expression used by Walther Zimmerli (*Ezekiel. Vol. 2, A Commentary on the Book of the Prophet Ezekiel, Chapters 25–48* [trans. James D. Martin;

established as the prophet is led through it and becomes gradually aware of it. Zimmerli notes that "the text of Ezek 47 breaks off after the four measurements and leaves to the reader to imagine for himself the corresponding further increase of the stream to a river and to a large river."[79]

The conclusion of the prophet's experience of this river in v. 5 is its impassable nature, which is emphasized through the repetitive statements of one's inability to cross it:

| לֹא־אוּכַל לַעֲבֹר | οὐκ ἠδύνατο διελθεῖν |
| אֲשֶׁר לֹא־יֵעָבֵר | ὃν οὐ διαβήσονται |

Impassability is thus the key characteristic of Ezekiel's eschatological river which sets it apart as the main candidate of influence on LXX Amos 5:24. The entire description of this river communicates the expected reversal of a cursed or defiled state through a divine initiative. The fantastic elements of the river and its effects "suggest an impressionistic literary cartoon with an intentional ideological aim."[80] However, it may not have been perceived ideologically by everyone. Ezekiel 47 was so influential in biblical interpretation in antiquity that it may have helped determine the location of the Qumran community:

> Geographically, the Qumran community's choice of the Dead Sea seems influenced, at least in part, by Ezekiel's vision of the last days when a mighty river would flow from the Temple in Jerusalem to the Dead Sea (Ezek 47:1–12). This lifeless body of water would one day become the location of an apocalyptic outpouring of divine blessing, and the people at Qumran were perfectly situated to participate in its abundance.[81]

In the NT, this river and its healing properties are universalized (Rev 22:2) and the waters' origin is no longer the temple, which is replaced by God and the Lamb (Rev 21:22; 22:1).

Conclusion
Ezekiel's torrent vision of ch. 47, with its expectation of eschatological blessing and the lifting of the curse, was an influential text and very likely to have been known by the Greek translator of Amos. While many

Neukirchen–Vluyn: Neukirchener Verlag, 1969; Hermeneia; Philadelphia: Fortress, 1983], 505 n. 5).

79. Zimmerli, *Ezekiel*, 2:512.

80. Daniel I. Block, *The Book of Ezekiel: Chapters 25–48* (NICOT; Grand Rapids: Eerdmans, 1997), 701.

81. David Noel Freedman and Jeffrey G. Geochegan, "Another Stab at the Wicked Priest," in *The Bible and the Dead Sea Scrolls: The Princeton Symposium of the Dead Sea Scrolls* (ed. James H. Charlesworth; Waco: Baylor University, 2006), 18.

biblical texts speak of eschatological waters and could have been familiar to the Greek translator of Amos, they seem to converge in the vision of Ezek 47, with its focus on the impassable nature of these waters. It is this impassable character which is the common element between LXX Amos 5:24 and Ezek 47:3–5. The Greek translator of Amos compares or equates the expected justice, or salvation (δικαιοσύνη), with Ezekiel's unfordable winter-torrent.

Amos 7:1

Amos 7:1

MT	LXX
כֹּה הִרְאַנִי אֲדֹנָי יְהוִה וְהִנֵּה יוֹצֵר	οὕτως ἔδειξέν μοι κύριος καὶ ἰδοὺ ἐπιγονὴ
גֹּבַי בִּתְחִלַּת עֲלוֹת הַלָּקֶשׁ	ἀκρίδων ἐρχομένη ἑωθινή
וְהִנֵּה־לֶקֶשׁ אַחַר גִּזֵּי הַמֶּלֶךְ:	καὶ ἰδοὺ βροῦχος εἷς Γωγ ὁ βασιλεύς
This is what the Lord GOD showed me: he was forming locusts at the time the latter growth began to sprout (it was the latter growth after the king's mowings). [NRSV]	Thus the Lord showed me and behold, an early offspring of grasshoppers coming, and behold, one locust larva, Gog the king. [NETS]

Amos 7 introduces a series of visions granted to the prophet (7:1, 4, 7). Shalom Paul has compared these visions to Joseph's two dreams (Gen 37:5–9) and the two dreams of Pharaoh (Gen 41:1–7), where the same divine message is reiterated by means of different symbols. Paul says that, as in other ancient Near Eastern cultures, "the repetition underlies their importance as well as authenticates their veracity."[82] In the words of Joseph himself, the repetition confirms the certainty of the future divine action (Gen 41:32): "And the doubling of Pharaoh's dream means that the thing is fixed by God, and God will shortly bring it about" (NRSV).

The first vision shown to Amos (7:1–3) involves an attack of locusts on the late-sown crops. The MT presents God as the agent forming the swarm of locusts before the prophet's eyes at a time when such an attack would have been catastrophic for the economy of the land. Paul explains that,

> At the time when the late sowing (nongrain crops such as vegetables and onions) is beginning to sprout, the earlier sowing, the grain crop, is already well advanced. Thus, the locusts would devastate not only the late crop but also the more developed, but as yet unreaped, earlier, crop— spelling a total agricultural catastrophe. If the locust invasion were a bit

---

82. Paul, *A Commentary on the Book of Amos*, 224.

earlier, when the late crop had not yet sprouted, this future harvest would remain untouched and unharmed and subsequently could be reaped; if the locusts came a bit later, the first crop would already have been harvested. Either way, earlier or later, at least one crop could have been saved. However, an attack precisely at this late-spring season of the year would consume both crops and culminate in a disastrous year of famine.[83]

The *hapax legomenon* לקש is the reason many commentators view the words which conclude 7:1 as a later explanatory addition: "it was the latter growth after the king's mowings."[84] Paul, however, takes this as "an additional description of the exacerbating situation, relating that whatever there was to reap before the locust assault had already been harvested for the king."[85]

This part of the verse takes on a very different meaning in the LXX, which treats the locust assault as a symbolic image in need of "interpretation." The LXX communicates the sense that the locust attack is a symbol of a foreign army led by the eschatological king Gog. An examination of the various elements of Amos 7:1 will show how the Greek translator may have arrived at this conclusion.

κύριος

The phrase אדני יהוה is common in Amos where it is sometimes abbreviated by the Greek translator to κύριος (1:8; 4:2; 5:3 [cf. Rahlfs]; 6:8; 7:4, 6; 8:1, 3, 9 [cf. Rahlfs], 11), fully translated by κύριος ὁ θεός (3:7, 8, 11, 13; 4:5; 9:8 [κυρίου τοῦ θεοῦ]), or represented by the vocative κύριε κύριε (7:2, 5). The varied treatment of אדני יהוה by the Greek translator of Amos offers us no basis for arguing for a Hebrew *Vorlage* different from the MT.

ἐπιγονὴ ἀκρίδων

The feminine singular noun ἐπιγονή shows that the participle יֹצֵר was read as the noun יֵצֶר ("form, framing, purpose"),[86] whereas in Amos 4:13 and Hab 2:18 (where it is written *defective*), the Hebrew participle יֹצֵר is represented as such in the Greek. It is not unlikely that the *defective* form יצר existed in Hebrew manuscripts of Amos 7:1 that were also used by the Targum and the Peshitta,[87] since both versions translate this as a noun. ἐπιγονή is used twice more in the LXX (2 Chr 31:16, 18) with the

---

83. Ibid., 227.
84. Rudolph, *Joel–Amos–Obadja–Jona*, 229; Wolff, *Joel and Amos*, 291–92.
85. Paul, *A Commentary on the Book of Amos*, 227.
86. BDB 428.
87. See Gelston, *The Peshitta*, 122.

sense of "offspring."[88] For ἐπιγονή in LXX Amos, Dines suggests the nuance "plentiful."[89] ἀκρίδων translates גֹּבַי correctly, and its two other occurrences are both found in Nah 3:17 (MT כְּגוֹב גֹּבָי).

ἐρχομένη ἑωθινή

Both ἐρχομένη ("coming") and ἑωθινή ("early [in the morning]"), standing in apposition, modify ἐπιγονή. The Hebrew behind these Greek words is בתחלת עלות, which is not accurately represented by the Greek. It should have been translated as "in the beginning of the rising [of]."

First, ἑωθινή is used to translate בקר (Exod 14:24) and שחר (Ps 21[MT22]:1). However, in Jon 4:7 ἑωθινή translates the word-pair בעלות השחר. A form of עלה accompanying שחר is very common in the Hebrew Bible (Gen 19:15; 32:25, 27; Josh 6:15; Judg 19:25; 1 Kgdms 9:26; Neh 4:15), which makes it highly probable that the Greek translator of Amos, upon seeing the infinitive construct of עלה in Amos 7:1, mentally supplied its common pair שחר and translated ἑωθινή.[90] For the translator, the entire phrase בתחלת עלות [השחר] would have the sense of "early in the beginning of the day," which he manages to summarize in a single word, ἑωθινή. It is unlikely that the translator had השחר in place of הלקש in his *Vorlage*, but it is possible that הלקש had dropped out from his *Vorlage* due to haplography.[91] "Deliverance at dawn" is a common motif, as Dines points out, but "judgment at dawn" is reminiscent of Jonah's story. Dines notes:

> The 'deliverance at dawn' motif is also found in Jud. 12:5 and 1 Mac. 5:30. In the latter passage, the size of the Seleucid force is described in terms reminiscent of the locust invasion of Joel 2:2; cf. 2:5; while in Jud. 2:20 the army of Holofernes is ὡς ἀκρίς...οὐ γὰρ ἦν ἀριθμὸς ἀπὸ πλήθους αὐτῶν; cf. also Ezek. 38; 1 Macc. 11:1; Rev. 20:8. It seems reasonable to suppose that locusts arriving at dawn in Amos 7:1 belong to

88. LEH 226.
89. Dines, "The Septuagint of Amos," 213.
90. Also ibid.
91. That לקש is probably omitted in its first occurrence is supported by Tov and Polak, eds., *The Revised CATSS*, and by Glenny, *Finding Meaning in the Text*, 47, and Dines, "The Septuagint of Amos," 214 n. 4. Park thinks that the first לֶקֶשׁ is translated by ἑωθινή: *The Book of Amos*, 157. Gelston agrees, stating that "the fact that the same word is rendered quite differently within the same verse suggests that, while lexical ignorance or uncertainty may have been a factor, the principal difficulty for the translator lay in deciphering the Hebrew word." He follows Rudolph's proposal that the first rendering ἑωθινή may have been occasioned by a confusion with נשף: "Some Hebrew Misreadings," 497.

the same range of ideas. But, as with Jonah's early-morning worm, the implication is sinister: at the very time when deliverance is most to be expected, disaster strikes.[92]

Second, forms of ἔρχομαι usually represent some form of בוא (Amos 4:2; 8:11; 9:13). A difficult case is the occurrence of the participle ἐρχόμενοι in LXX Amos 6:3 (Rahlfs), which is probably an inner-Greek corruption of εὐχόμενοι (chosen by Ziegler) and resulted from a confusion of נדה, a rare verb in the Old Testament which is found only here and in Isa 66:5, for נדר. It is also possible that the Greek translator of Amos had a form of נדר in his *Vorlage*. The MT form occurring in Amos 6:3, הַמְנַדִּים ("the ones who expel/put away"), may have arisen by the dropping of a *resh*.[93] Nevertheless, I agree with Ziegler that εὐχόμενοι is original and that it would be difficult to get ἐρχόμενοι out of either נדר or נדה. In the light of this, we cannot use LXX Amos 6:3 to see how the Greek translator uses ἐρχόμενοι.

In LXX Song 7:1, the participle ἡ ἐρχομένη may have been used to fill in the gap left by the Hebrew text. Something similar may have happened in Amos 7:1, since the description of the vision is elliptical. From the translator's perspective, the prophet sees the early morning locusts and in 7:2 the grass of the earth has been devoured. He may have made up for the lack of a verbal element with a form of ἔρχομαι in order to complete the image and to clarify that the danger concerning this "early offspring of locusts" is in the imminent future. ἐρχομένη may also carry eschatological connotations (Amos 4:2; 8:11; 9:13; Hab 2:3; Zech 14:1; cf. Heb 10:37–38), which would fit well with the rest of the Greek renderings in the verse.

καὶ ἰδοὺ βροῦχος εἷς

As already noted, הלקש may have dropped out of the translator's *Vorlage*, due to haplography, since it remains unrepresented in the Greek. It is more probable, however, that it was regarded as redundant and thus abbreviated (cf. ילי omitted in LXX Nah 3:15).[94] The translator picks up from והנה with καὶ ἰδοὺ.

βροῦχος, a type of locust, translates three different Hebrew words in the LXX: ארבה (Lev 11:22; 3 Kgdms 8:37; Nah 3:15), חסיל (2 Chr 6:28)

---

92. Dines, "The Septuagint of Amos," 214.
93. Arieti thinks that "making a vow" about the day (i.e. wishing that it should stay away) makes more sense in the context. Arieti, "A Study in the Septuagint of Amos," 14–15.
94. So Glenny, "Hebrew Misreadings," 539–40.

and ילק (Ps 104[MT105]:34; Joel 1:4; 2:25; Nah 3:15, 16).[95] It appears that the closest word that הלקש could have been confused with is ילק.[96] βροῦχος, however, is not common in Greek literature; it occurs as βροῦκος in Theophrastus (*Fragmenta* 174.4.1).[97]

לקש as a noun ("after-growth, after-math, i.e. spring-crop"[98]) occurs only in Amos 7:1.[99] In Job 24:6 we have the *Piel* imperfect third masculine plural form יְלַקֵּשׁוּ, usually translated "they glean." The rarity of לקש may have thrown the translator off, and he then had to make sense of the word from the context. However, rather than connecting לקש with מלקוש ("latter rain"[100]), which he renders by ὄψιμος in Hos 6:3; Joel 2:23 and Zech 10:1, he chose a different direction. The "locust" theme (גבי) must have triggered the "correction" of הלקש into ילק.

Had ילק already been in the Hebrew *Vorlage*, then the presence of two types of locusts (גבי and ילק) in the same verse would have strengthened the correspondence of this passage to Joel 1:4 and 2:25 in the eyes of the Greek translator. The connection of Amos' locusts to Joel's locusts will be discussed later. In this verse, there is no evidence for the existence of a different Hebrew *Vorlage* containing ילק; the correction may therefore have come from the translator.

The other Greek versions demonstrate some sense of the meaning of לקש (α´ σ´ θ´—ὄψιμος ["late"]), and both the Targum and the Peshiṭta have "latter growth." As we assume to be the case here, the Greek translator tends to render ילק by βροῦχος (Joel 1:4; 2:25; Nah 3:15, 16), whose form is "conveniently" masculine for what follows in our text. Once the translator realized that the text finally focuses upon one individual, the "correction" of the following words, especially גזי, took its course.

The main factor which may have steered the translator to understand the text as referring to an individual is found in the verse following. The *Piel* third masculine singular perfect כלה (LXX—συντελέσῃ)[101] in

95. For the various names of locusts denoting developmental stages, see Ovid R. Sellers, "Stages of Locust in Joel," *AJSL* 52 (1935–36): 81–85.

96. Also *BHS*.

97. Also in Philo, *Leg.* 2.105. See Lee, *A Lexical Study*, 42.

98. BDB 545. According to Edmond Power, לֶקֶשׁ denotes the late corn crop. "Note to Amos 7,1," *Biblica* 8 (1927): 90.

99. The word is found in the Gezer Calendar, among various agricultural terms. In view of the meaning of the stem *lqs* in modern Syrian-Arabic, and the general agricultural situation, Albright thinks "late planting" would be the only possible translation. W. F. Albright, "The Gezer Calendar," *BASOR* 92 (1943): 22 n. 31.

100. BDB 545.

101. In LXX Amos, the related noun συντέλεια (כלה) is an eschatological term (8:8; 9:5). Aaron Schart connects this word to LXX Dan 9:26, where συντέλεια

Amos 7:2 would demand a masculine singular subject. The translator understood הַמֶּלֶךְ, the closest antecedent, as the subject of this verb. Moreover, the passage immediately preceding Amos 7:1 speaks of a foreign nation which the Lord would bring up against Israel (6:14: διότι ἰδοὺ ἐγὼ ἐπεγείρω ἐφ᾽ ὑμᾶς οἶκος τοῦ Ισραηλ ἔθνος). It would not have been difficult for the translator to equate the locusts (גֹּבַי) in Amos' vision with this foreign nation and thus interpret all the difficult elements in v. 1 in the light of the context. εἷς is therefore אַחֻר, (mis)read as אַחַד.[102] One need not think of the translator's changes as manipulative. He may simply be "correcting" what he supposed to be corruptions in his *Vorlage*.[103]

Γωγ ὁ βασιλεύς

The name Γωγ is a peculiar mapping of גִּזַּי to a well-known royal figure of the Hebrew Bible. גִּזַּי is the plural construct form of גֵּז ("shearing, mowing").[104] In Deut 18:4 and Job 31:20, the word is used for the sheared wool of sheep and is understood as such by the Greek translators of those texts (κουρά).[105] The word גֵּז occurs once more in Ps 71[MT72]:6 where the reference is to mown grass. However, the Greek translator renders גֵּז as πόκον ("wool, fleece"),[106] an indication that perhaps גֵּז was identified only with the shearing of wool. In LXX 2 Esd 13[MT Neh 3]:15, κουρά ("shearing") is used to translate גַּן ("enclosure, garden"), but this is not an indication that κουρά had come to mean "garden." On the contrary, we seem to have a גֵּז–גַּן confusion which made the translator think of "fleeces at the shearing of the king" (NETS).

---

denotes the end of history; thus the meaning may also be inferred for LXX Amos' uses of συντέλεια (except Amos 1:14). Schart thinks that "the Septuagint perceived Amos as someone speaking of the end time." "The Jewish and the Christian Greek Versions of Amos," 168.

102. It is more natural for εἷς to refer to βροῦχος than to Γωγ. εἷς is placed after the noun in order to conform with the Hebrew text. As Bøe notes, in Greek it would have been more natural to express this in the genitive ("one of the locusts"), but it seems that the translator struggled to remain as faithful to the Hebrew text as possible. Sverre Bøe, *Gog and Magog* (WUNT 2/135; Tübingen: Mohr Siebeck, 2001), 64.

103. While Gelston ("Some Hebrew Misreadings," 494–95) suggests a mere ד-ר confusion, Glenny ("Hebrew Misreadings," 540) recognizes that "if the translator was having problems with the verse, he would manipulate the radicals in this word to make sense of the verse."

104. BDB 159.

105. Lee confirms the meaning of "fleece" for κουρά in *P.Cair.Zen.* 433.26 (third century B.C.E.): ἔχουσιν τά τε πρόβατα καὶ τὰς κουράς. Lee, *A Lexical Study*, 58.

106. LEH 503.

Symmachus and Theodotion use κουρά for גזי in Amos 7:1, but it is unclear whether they use it to refer to the king's "shearing," or more generally to "that which is cut." It seems that the connection with "the grass of the earth" would have been clear to them from Amos 7:2.

Aquila transliterates גזי into γάζης.[107] However, γάζα, a Persian loan word, means "treasure, treasury"[108] (see 2 Esd[MT Ezra] 5:17; 7:20). Therefore, Aquila's translation, ὀπίσω τῆς γάζης τοῦ βασιλέως, signifies a raid after the king's treasures, perhaps a picture of looting. If γάζα signifies a sort of monetary treasure (cf. LXX Isa 39:2), this would indicate that, for Aquila also, the locusts were not literal, but a symbol of intruding armies.[109]

Although גז is rare, its identification with a sense of "shearing" in Greek Deuteronomy, Job and Psalms would suggest that the meaning was probably available to the Greek translator of Amos. His choice of Γωγ ὁ βασιλεύς therefore calls for an explanation.

It is possible that גזי was simply read as גוג.[110] Kaminka notes two examples where ג and ז are confused (*Kethib* [לְבֵג] and *Qere* [לְבַז] of Ezek 25:7; גֶה read as זֶה in Ezek 47:13 LXX, Targum and Vulgate).[111] However, we cannot be certain whether גוג was in the Greek translator's *Vorlage* or whether he produced it himself. Dines thinks that the military reference at the end of the previous chapter may have influenced the Greek translator to find "Gog" in the place of גזי.[112] Likewise, Gelston, after attempting to explain the differences between MT and LXX Amos 7:1 by attributing them to "difficulty in deciphering some of the Hebrew letters," recognizes that "the eschatological expectations associated with

---

107. Like Jerome, Bøe thinks that Aquila probably did not find any clear meaning in the word. *Gog and Magog*, 62.

108. LEH 115.

109. Jerome did not think that Aquila's γάζης had anything to do with the meaning "treasure" or the region of Gaza. Field, *Origenis Hexaplorum*, 2:976–77.

110. Dines thinks that there is a confusion between *waw* and *zayin*. She also notes that the translator, influenced by the "locust" theme, could have connected גזי with גזם (κάμπη in Amos 4:9), albeit the military sense of the oracle still dominated. "The Septuagint of Amos," 214–15. Bøe thinks that the shift from גזי to גוג presupposes a certain similarity between the letters *gimmel* and *yod* and refers to Cross's and Naveh's table of Jewish scripts. *Gog and Magog*, 63. Schart thinks that the Greek translator's *Vorlage* may have had גג ("roof"). However, גג is a very common word and was probably known to the translator (Zeph 1:5). Therefore, if גג was in the *Vorlage*, some active imagination would still be required to connect this with Gog instead of "roof." "The Jewish and the Christian Greek Versions of Amos," 168.

111. Kaminka, *Studien*, 27.

112. Dines, "The Septuagint of Amos," 215.

Gog were strong at the time when the LXX translation was being made" and may have had some influence on this rendering.[113] The same expectations may be apparent in LXX Ezekiel as well, as Wong concludes in his examination of LXX Ezek 39:21–29. Wong says that the Greek translator of Ezek 39 "saw the Gog-event as something near to his time, and it was no longer seen as belonging to the distant indefinite future."[114]

The Name Gog. The Greek name Γωγ is found only once in LXX Pentateuch (LXX Num 24:7) and twelve times in LXX Ezekiel (chs. 38 and 39).[115] In LXX Num 24:7, it translates the name אגג and in LXX Ezek 38–39 it translates the Hebrew גוג.[116] Agag/Αγαγ is the name of the king of the Amalekites (1 Kgdms 15) whom Saul failed to slaughter, but who was then killed by Samuel. Agag, however, is a specific king who lived at the time of Saul, whereas Ezekiel's Gog "is the archetypal enemy from the N, the head of the forces of evil that rise against God and his people."[117] The choice of Γωγ in LXX Amos 7:1 could only be connected with Ezekiel's Γωγ (cf. Γουγ in 1 Chr 5:4).

As far as the origins of the name Gog are concerned, no consensus has been reached, and various proposals have not been demonstrated with certainty.[118] Eichrodt concludes that it is "impossible to say any more than that the name of Gog is derived from legendary accounts of campaigns by northern nations and may in some way unknown to us have come to be the name given to their commander-in-chief."[119]

---

113. Gelston, "Some Hebrew Misreadings," 498.

114. Ka Leung Wong, "The Masoretic and Septuagint Texts of Ezekiel 39,21–29," *ETL* 78 (2002): 135.

115. It is also found in some variant readings in Deut 3:1, 13, 4:47, and Sir 48:17: Εζεκιας ὠχύρωσεν τὴν πόλιν αὐτοῦ καὶ εἰσήγαγεν εἰς μέσον αὐτῆς ὕδωρ (B: τον Γωγ) ὤρυξεν σιδήρῳ ἀκρότομον καὶ ᾠκοδόμησεν κρήνας εἰς ὕδατα. This latter text associates Hezekiah with Gog, but scholars consider this to be a corruption of an original γειων (= Gihon) or ἀγωγόν (= water course). The connection between Gog and Hezekiah is most likely secondary. Dines, "The Septuagint of Amos," 217; Bøe, *Gog and Magog*, 73–74.

116. BH גג ("roof") is well known in the LXX (incl. the LXX TP [Zeph 1:5]) as δῶμα ("roof") and is never transliterated as Γωγ.

117. Kenneth H. Cuffey, "Gog," *ABD* 2:1056.

118. "Attempts to identify Gog have included proposals of connections with (a) Gyges, King of Lydia (*Gugu* of Ashurbanipal's records); (b) *Gaga*, a name in the Amarna correspondence for the nations of the North; (c) Gaga, a god from Ras Shamra writings; (d) a historical figure, especially Alexander; and (e) mythological sources, with Gog being a representation of the evil forces of darkness which range themselves against Yahweh and his people." Ibid.

119. Eichrodt, *Ezekiel*, 522.

Gog Prophecies. It is difficult to know whether the Gog tradition originated with Ezekiel or whether he drew from existing traditions, since no
extra-biblical records of an independent Gog tradition exist. Moreover,
there is no consensus as to whether Ezek 38 and 39 are organically
related to their context or whether they are later insertions.[120] Reddish
sees Ezekiel "eschatologizing" existing prophecies:

> Ezekiel has likely combined earlier traditions which spoke of an enemy
> from the north who would bring destruction to the Israelites (cf. Jer 1:13–
> 15; 4:6) with the prophecy of Isaiah that God would destroy the enemies
> of Israel upon the mountains (Isa 14:24). These prophecies, which for
> Ezekiel are still unfulfilled, will take place "in the latter days" when
> God's salvation of Israel will become evident to all the nations… In the
> Ezekiel oracles the figure of Gog has assumed mythical proportions.[121]

Do we have any indications of which earlier Gog traditions Ezekiel
might have made use? A hint may be given in Ezek 38:17 where God
asks: "Are you he of whom I spoke in former days by my servants the
prophets of Israel, who in those days prophesied for years that I would
bring you against them?" [NRSV].

The problem with this verse, as Block points out, is that "In the MT
(followed by the Targum) the principal clause is cast in the form of a
rhetorical question: 'Are you the one of whom the prophets spoke?'
However, many recent translations and most scholars follow the LXX, the
Vulgate and the Peshiṭta in rendering this clause affirmatively."[122]

Block outlines the question noting that "the present emphasis on an
apparently continuous tradition of prophecy combined with the absence
of any reference to Gog elsewhere in the Old Testament raises the
question of which prophecies those might have been."[123] Block, then,
examines three possibilities offered to solve this problem: (a) the existence of an unattested strand of prophetic tradition to which Ezek 38:17
is referring; (b) Ezek 38:17 as not being a reference to any specific
oracle(s), but to general pronouncements concerning the destruction of
God's people by their enemies; (c) Gog as the fulfilment of specific
extant OT prophecies, with candidates such as Joel 3:9–21; Zech 12:3–9
and 14:1–8. However, firm connections with the last-named texts are

---

120. For the history of research on Ezek 38–39, see Timothy John Mills, *The
"Gog Pericope and the Book of Ezekiel"* (Ph.D. diss., Drew University, 1989), 1–26.

121. Mitchell G. Reddish, "Gog and Magog," *ABD* 1:1056.

122. Daniel I. Block, "Gog in Prophetic Tradition: A New Look at Ezekiel
XXXVIII 17," *VT* 42 (1992): 159.

123. Ibid., 166.

lacking, whereas stronger commonalities with Isa 14:24–25 and Jer 4–6 have been noted. Block finds all these solutions unsatisfactory and challenges the assumption that the author of Ezekiel affirms Gog as being the one of whom former prophets spoke. He argues that Ezek 38:17 expresses a rhetorical question anticipating a *negative* response (e.g. see 2 Kgdms 7:5/1 Chr 17:4).[124] According to Block,

> Gog is in fact not the "foe from the north" of whom Jeremiah spoke. His role is entirely different. He is not commissioned by Yahweh to serve as his agent of judgement; he and his troops are brought down from the mountains for a single purpose; [*sic*] that the holiness of Yahweh might be manifested in the sight of all the nations (xxxviii 16, 23, xxxix 6–7; cf. *vv.* 22, 28).[125]

Regardless of whether Block is right about the meaning of Ezek 38:17, the LXX is our earliest witness to how the verse was actually perceived, and it was read affirmatively, viewing Gog as the fulfilment of previous prophecies:

> τάδε λέγει κύριος κύριος τῷ Γωγ σὺ εἶ περὶ οὗ ἐλάλησα πρὸ ἡμερῶν τῶν ἔμπροσθεν διὰ χειρὸς τῶν δούλων μου προφητῶν τοῦ Ισραηλ ἐν ταῖς ἡμέραις ἐκείναις καὶ ἔτεσιν τοῦ ἀγαγεῖν σε ἐπ' αὐτούς

> This is what the Lord says to Gog: You are the one of whom I spoke before the former days by a hand of my slaves, the prophets of Israel, in those days and years to bring you up against them. [NETS]

Such a reading of the verse would have understandably raised questions about previous prophecies and could perhaps have given licence to ancient interpreters to see prophecies older than Ezekiel's as pointing to Gog, the final foe. In a sense, the Greek version of Ezek 38:17 invites one to look for the "hidden" prophecies of Gog in the prophetic tradition preceding Ezekiel. Indeed, the "Gog" reading in LXX Num 24:7, the plethora of references to Gog in pseudepigraphical works, in Qumran, in the book of Revelation and in the Targums betrays a fascination with this eschatological figure (see the Appendix).[126] Although difficult to date, one example concerns the figures of Eldad and Medad (Num 11:26–29) who, according to Targum Pseudo-Jonathan and other rabbinic sources, prophesied about the assault upon Jerusalem, the end of days which would be brought about by a war involving Gog and Magog, and the

---

124.   Ibid., 170–71.
125.   Ibid., 171.
126.   See Nicholas Railton for the history of interpretation of Gog and Magog up to recent times. "Gog and Magog: The History of a Symbol," *EvQ* 75 (2003): 23–43.

defeat of evil at the hands of a royal Messiah.[127] Some traditions have found the earliest prophecy on Gog already in Balaam's oracle in Num 24:7 (LXX, Samaritan Pentateuch, Symmachus, Theodotion), presenting Gog as the strongest kingdom over which the Davidic Messiah would prevail.[128] Perhaps all the above were attempts at answering the question raised by Ezek 38:17.

Since it is widely accepted that LXX Pentateuch preceded the Greek translations of other books, we must take into account the possibility that the Greek translator of Amos was familiar with the Gog prediction in LXX Num 24:7.[129] To understand LXX Amos 7:1, one should not examine it in isolation, but as part of this existing tradition preserved in the LXX Pentateuch, of which the translator of Amos is heir and which had probably coloured the eschatological expectations of the time.[130] Horbury notes that, while Amos 7:1 could have been understood as an oracle about Sennacherib's invasion (so Jerome), in the light of LXX Num 24:7 it was more likely to be interpreted about a future adversary.[131]

However, it could also be argued that the Greek translator of Amos, in the light of Ezek 38:17, is attempting to uncover the secret meaning of the locust oracle in Amos 7:1, and so introduced Gog.[132]

The overall sense of the Greek version of Amos 7:1 is clearly greater than the sum of its parts. The locust plague envisaged by the prophet takes on the significance of an invading army whose king is Gog. The question we must now examine is why king Gog would be connected with a locust vision when there is no reference to locusts in Ezek 38–39.

---

127. *OTP* 2:463–64. Similarly, a marginal reading in Codex Reuchlinianus in Zech 12:10 describes the death of the Messiah, son of Ephraim, at the hand of the eschatological enemy Gog. Gordon supports the antiquity of the tradition reflected in this variant. "The Ephraimite Messiah and the Targum(s) to Zechariah 12.10," in *Hebrew Bible and Ancient Versions: Selected Essays by Robert P. Gordon* (SOTS; Aldershot: Ashgate, 2006), 347–56.

128. On the messianic connotations of this verse, see the Appendix.

129. John J. Collins is sceptical about discerning the eschatological views of the Greek translators of the Pentateuch. However, he grants that the translation of Agag as Gog in LXX Num 24:7 has turned the oracle into a prophecy about the end times and that it was received as such by Philo. "Messianism and Exegetical Tradition: The Evidence of the LXX Pentateuch," in Knibb, ed., *The Septuagint and Messianism*, 129–49.

130. So Rudolph, *Joel–Amos–Obadja–Jona*, 229.

131. William Horbury, *Jewish Messianism and the Cult of Christ* (London: SCM, 1998), 61.

132. Having Amos, a prophet preceding Ezekiel, mentioning Gog by name would have resolved the Ezek 38:17 problem.

Locust Symbolism
The image of locusts has a prominent role in Jewish tradition, primarily because of their association with the Exodus plague in Egypt (Exod 10; Ps 104[MT105]:34) and their identification with covenant curses (Deut 28:38; 3 Kgdms 8:37; 2 Chr 6:28; 7:13). However, the "locust" image has been used in various ways throughout the Old Testament. In Num 13:33, when Moses sent the leaders of the Israelite tribes to spy out the land, they perceived themselves as "locusts" before the giant inhabitants of Canaan. In this instance, locusts function as a symbol of weakness, smallness and frailty.[133]

On other occasions, it is their large number which makes them an apt element of comparison (e.g. Judg 6:5; 7:12; Ps 104[MT105]:34; Jer 26[MT46]:23; 28[MT51]:27). Because of the threat they posed to crops, locusts became a successful rhetorical element by which to characterize invading enemies (the Midianite armies—Judg 6:5; 7:12; Holofernes' army—Jdt 2:20; the army of the king of the Medes—Jer 28:14[MT51:11]; 28[MT51]:27).[134] Of the TP, Joel, and to a lesser degree Nahum, have also utilized the "locust" imagery.

Joel's Locusts. The book of Joel begins with the description of four types of locusts which devoured the produce of the land one after another, and this destruction seems to be identified in 1:6–7 with an invading nation too numerous to count (ὅτι ἔθνος ἀνέβη ἐπὶ τὴν γῆν μου ἰσχυρὸν καὶ ἀναρίθμητον).[135] In ch. 2 we have a more detailed description of the צפוני, this fierce enemy from the north (2:20; cf. Ezek 38:15–16).[136] This army is described in a fearsome way, and mounts an unprecedented attack in the history of Israel (2:2). Its like has never been seen, nor will be: ἐπὶ τὰ

133. Similarly, in Egyptian texts, it is usually the defeated enemies, not the attackers, who are compared to locusts. Egyptian similes emphasize the weakness of the locust, whereas Assyrian texts stress its destructiveness. John A. Thompson, "Joel's Locusts in the Light of Ancient Near Eastern Parallels," *JNES* 14 (1955): 52–53.

134. Comparison of invading armies to locusts is also present in the Ugaritic legend of King Keret and in many Assyrian royal annals. Ibid., 52. Also see Pablo R. Andiñach, "The Locusts in the Message of Joel," *VT* 42 (1992): 433–41.

135. Van Leeuwen's opinion is that this language is descriptive of the locusts. Cornelis van Leeuwen, "The 'Northern One' in the Composition of Joel 2,19–27," in *The Scriptures and the Scrolls: Studies in Honour of A. S. van der Woude on the Occasion of His 65th Birthday* (ed. F. García Martínez, A. Hilhorst, and C. J. Labuschagne; VTSup 49; Leiden: Brill, 1992), 85–99.

136. For an examination of the meaning of the "northern one" as relating to human enemies of Israel, eschatological powers or a literal host of locusts, see ibid. Van Leeuwen supports the literal interpretation (ibid., 98).

ὄρη λαὸς πολὺς καὶ ἰσχυρός ὅμοιος αὐτῷ οὐ γέγονεν ἀπὸ τοῦ αἰῶνος καὶ μετ᾽ αὐτὸν οὐ προστεθήσεται ἕως ἐτῶν εἰς γενεὰς γενεῶν. No greater enemy was expected to follow after this one; all previous attacks find their climax in this last and most threatening assault on God's people. In ch. 4[MT3], the battle has a worldwide dimension, as many nations gather together for war in the one valley (4[MT3]:9, 12), in language reminiscent of that used of Gog and his allies in Ezek 38.

The term צפוני is unique to Joel 2:20 and is translated as τὸν ἀπὸ βορρᾶ ("the northerner") by the Greek translator. This may have become a common way of referring to the northern enemy, since it is repeated in LXX Isa 41:25, with the definite article:

הַעִירוֹתִי מִצָּפוֹן   ἐγὼ δὲ ἤγειρα τὸν ἀπὸ βορρᾶ

וַיֵּאת מִמִּזְרַח־שֶׁמֶשׁ   καὶ τὸν ἀφ᾽ ἡλίου ἀνατολῶν

Commenting on Amos 7:1, Sellin hints at the connection that "locusts" might have had with Gog in Jewish thinking: "𝔊 hat für אַחַר גִּזֵּי gelesen אֶחָד גּוֹג; die sich darin verratende enge Verbindung zwischen Gog und Heuschrecken gibt uns einen bemerkenswerten Fingerzeig für die jüdischen Vorstellungen von dem eschatologischen Heere Gogs vgl. zu Joel 2."[137]

The symbolic significance of the locusts as foreign armies, especially as encouraged by Joel's locusts, must have been recognized by the Greek translator of Amos, as Bruce points out:

> [I]t would not have occurred to him to find Gog in this text [i.e. Amos 7:1] unless he already had in mind the association between these locusts of Amos and Joel's locusts, and the identity of Joel's locusts with Gog's army in Ezekiel. An interpretive tradition along these lines may already have been established, in the light of which it was easy for the translator to mistranslate as he did.[138]

Elsewhere Bruce states:

> True, a faded *Vorlage* may have been thought to read *gōg hammelek* at Amos vii 1 instead of *gizzē hammelek*, but the prior association with Joel's locusts and Ezekiel's invaders was father to the thought.[139]

137. Sellin, *Das Zwölfprophetenbuch*, 206. Marti also thinks that the LXX rendering reflects the thinking of the time. Marti, *Das Dodekapropheton*, 206.

138. F. F. Bruce, "Prophetic Interpretation in the Septuagint," *BIOSCS* 12 (1979): 19.

139. F. F. Bruce, "The Earliest Old Testament Interpretation," in *The Witness of Tradition: Papers Read at the Joint British–Dutch Old Testament Conference Held at Woudschoten, 1970* (ed. M. A. Beek et al.; Oudstestamentische Studiën 17; Leiden: Brill, 1972), 41. Cripps recognizes that the translators interpreted the references to locusts as an allusion to mythological armies. He says that "as Joel adorns the

Indeed, the Targum of Joel 2:25 may be preserving such an allegorical interpretation of the locusts, identifying them with foreign nations:[140] "And I shall repay you *good* years *in place of the years in which you were pillaged by peoples, tongues, governments, and kingdoms, the great retribution of my army*, which I sent against you."[141]

Perhaps the fourfold enumeration of Joel's locusts had triggered some interest in the allegorical interpretation of these locusts. Wolff points out that "[n]owhere else do we find four locust types with different names. Thus it is not surprising that the fourfold enumeration was already regarded in early times as an apocalyptic *topos*, marking the completeness of the report... Cf. already Jer 13:2–3; Ezek 14:21."[142]

In the Hebrew Bible we have numerous comparisons of people to locusts, but that is very different to locusts functioning as *symbols* concealing another reality.[143] As Wolff mentions above, this is an apocalyptic feature, analogous to Daniel's four metals in Dan 2, and four beasts in Dan 7.[144] Symbolism is found in Rev 9:1–11 where locusts function as symbols of an army with a king (ἔχουσιν ἐπ' αὐτῶν βασιλέα τὸν ἄγγελον τῆς ἀβύσσου, ὄνομα αὐτῷ Ἑβραϊστὶ Ἀβαδδών, καὶ ἐν τῇ Ἑλληνικῇ ὄνομα ἔχει Ἀπολλύων), a passage viewed as having some affinities to Rev 20:7–10 where Gog and Magog are mentioned.[145] An "allegorical" or "apocalyptic" reading is what Andersen and Freedman attribute to the Greek translator of Amos 7:1 as well. The LXX translation "points to a *Vorlage* already corrupt or else to great freedom in interpreting an obscure text allegorically and apocalyptically."[146]

'Northern Army' of locusts with mythical characteristics of the class of Gog-Magog prophecy, so Amos (according to the LXX) says that the locust plague *is* king Gog." Cripps, *A Critical and Exegetical Commentary on the Book of Amos*, 220 (also n. 2).

140. The allegorical interpretation of the locusts as nations is also present in various Church Fathers. See Josef Lössl, "When is a Locust Just a Locust? Patristic Exegesis of Joel 1:4 in the Light of Ancient Literary Theory," *JTS* NS 55 (2004): 575–99.

141. As Cathcart points out, the reference to "peoples, tongues," etc., recalls similar words in Dan 3:4, 7, 29, 31; 5:19; 6:26; 7:14; Rev 5:9; 7:9; 13:7; 14:6; 17:15. Cathcart and Gordon, *The Targum*, 70 n. 44.

142. Wolff, *Joel and Amos*, 28 (also n. 65).

143. Thompson observes that in extra-biblical literature "armies are compared with locusts or locusts with armies, but locusts are never *symbols* of armies." Thompson, "Joel's Locusts," 52.

144. Wolff, *Joel and Amos*, 28. The interest in finding the referents behind the four symbols was carried over into Christian interpretation. See Dines, "The Septuagint of Amos," 218–21.

145. Bøe, *Gog and Magog*, 65.

146. Andersen and Freedman, *Amos*, 742.

There are good reasons to suppose that Joel's message in its Hebrew form is intended to be "apocalyptic." Linville "unmasks" the presuppositions of various commentators on the book of Joel who try to pin it down to a certain historical referent. He recognizes that the literary world of the book operates on "cosmic, mythic themes" and he agrees with Deist that "the book was never intended to describe any real event that befell Judah. Thus, the locusts, droughts, fires and armies are all literary, not literal in character."[147] He concludes, with Deist, that, in general, the book is eschatological in character.[148] Garrett sees the "northerner" (Joel 2:20) applied to the Assyrians, the Babylonians, and more importantly to the apocalyptic army of Gog—but never a non-human army.[149] Joel's "northerner" surely carries a special, apocalyptic meaning.[150] Garrett notes that "Joel sees in the terror of a locust plague an image of an even more terrible enemy," in accordance with the apocalyptic day of Yahweh.[151] Likewise, Wolff notes that the "northerner" is a historical enemy in Jeremiah (1:14–15; 4:6; 6:1; 22) and Isaiah (5:26–30), but has mythical features in Ezek 38–39 (and Isa 13). What Joel is doing by using the unique designation, "the northerner" (הצפוני), following the dramatic description of 2:1–11, may be a "remythologizing." Wolff comments:

> The rising apocalypticism, which is clearly recognizable in Joel, begins to make use of mythological terminology as code words. This is connected with the fact that it wishes, on the one hand, to take up the prophetic proclamation, but is not able, on the other, to carry a historical identification. Rather, Joel sees in the natural event of the locust catastrophe a pledge that the prophetic eschatology of disaster will not become void. He can describe its fulfillment only in the form of locust-like apocalyptic creatures, however, and he similarly uses the cryptic term "the northerner," with its mythological ring, for the "last enemy."[152]

---

147. James R. Linville, "Bugs Through the Looking Glass: The Infestation of Meaning in Joel," in Rezetko, Lim, and Aucker, eds., *Reflection and Refraction*, 286, 291.

148. Ibid., 296–97. Ardiñach rejects the view that the locusts are a symbol of the eschatological army of God. He thinks that they are a metaphor characterizing a human army. Andiñach, "The Locusts in the Message of Joel," 441.

149. Moskala notes that in the OT the north is where the powers of chaos hostile to God reside, but in tradition beyond the OT the north was also regarded as a place of menace and mystery. Jiří Moskala, "Toward the Fulfillment of the Gog and Magog Prophecy of Ezekiel 38–39," *JATS* 18 (2007): 249.

150. Duane A. Garrett, "The Structure of Joel," *JETS* 28 (1985): 291–92.

151. Ibid., 293.

152. Wolff, *Joel and Amos*, 62. Already van Hoonacker notes the connections of Joel's הצפוני with Gog's army. *Les Douze Petits Prophètes*, 174–76.

If the above commentators are right and Joel is about the eschatological enemy of Israel, with apocalyptic or mythological dimensions, Gog would be the only enemy to fit these specifications.[153] The Greek translator could identify no one other than Gog and his army behind the locust imagery.

In LXX Amos 7:1, the Greek translator does not identify βροῦχος with a specific nation or king. Instead, Joel's primary identification of the four locusts with the worst and *last* enemy in history (1:6; 2:2) has led the translator to a parallel interpretation of Amos' locusts as the eschatological enemy Gog and his armies. This does not mean that the translator did not have a specific, historical nation in mind. The "universalized" use of Gog and Magog is an NT development. According to Bøe, John, the writer of Revelation, "is the first writer known to us who leaves the ethnic and national understanding of Gog and Magog as the enemy of Israel in particular."[154]

Nahum's Locusts. Nahum mentions the locusts in 3:15–17:

שָׁם תֹּאכְלֵךְ אֵשׁ תַּכְרִיתֵךְ	ἐκεῖ καταφάγεταί σε πῦρ ἐξολεθρεύσει σε
חֶרֶב תֹּאכְלֵךְ כַּיָּלֶק	ῥομφαία καταφάγεταί σε ὡς ἀκρίς καὶ
הִתְכַּבֵּד כַּיֶּלֶק הִתְכַּבְּדִי כָּאַרְבֶּה	βαρυνθήσῃ ὡς βροῦχος
הִרְבֵּית רֹכְלַיִךְ מִכּוֹכְבֵי	ἐπλήθυνας τὰς ἐμπορίας σου ὑπὲρ τὰ ἄστρα
הַשָּׁמָיִם יֶלֶק פָּשַׁט	τοῦ οὐρανοῦ βροῦχος ὥρμησεν
וַיָּעֹף מִנְּזָרַיִךְ כָּאַרְבֶּה	καὶ ἐξεπετάσθη ἐξήλατο ὡς ἀττέλεβος
וְטַפְסְרַיִךְ כְּגוֹב גֹּבָי הַחוֹנִים	ὁ σύμμικτός σου ὡς ἀκρίς ἐπιβεβηκυῖα
בַּגְּדֵרוֹת בְּיוֹם קָרָה שֶׁמֶשׁ	ἐπὶ φραγμὸν ἐν ἡμέραις πάγους ὁ ἥλιος
זָרְחָה וְנוֹדַד וְלֹא־נוֹדַע	ἀνέτειλεν καὶ ἀφήλατο καὶ οὐκ ἔγνω
מְקוֹמוֹ אַיָּם	τὸν τόπον αὐτῆς οὐαὶ αὐτοῖς

Although v. 15 is unclear in the MT, the locust seems to be compared to Nineveh's enemy (ἀκρίς [ילק]) and then to Nineveh itself (βροῦχος [ילק]/ארבה). In v. 17 the MT compares Nineveh's guards (מנזריך) and officials (טפסריך) with locusts settling on the wall on a cold day, until the sun rises and drives them away. The Greek translator probably did not recognize the two rare Hebrew nouns. The Targum, however, renders the first noun as "plates" ("*Behold, your plates gleam* like a locust swarm"), which probably refers to "plate-armour," thus comparing the scaled

153. Strazicich notes that the association of the locusts with Gog may be there already in the Hebrew text of Joel, as some commentators observe. The Exodus locust plague tradition and the burial of Gog seem to be merged together in Joel 2:20: Exod 10:19—the locusts thrown in סוף ים; Ezek 39:11—Gog will be thrown קדמת הים; Joel 2:20—the northerner will be thrown אל־הים הקדמני. Strazicich, *Joel's Use of Scripture*, 172–73.

154. Bøe, *Gog and Magog*, 388.

armour of the Assyrians to the scaled thoraces of the locusts (cf. Rev 9:9).[155] As a result, the neutral sense of the MT receives a military dimension in the Targum.

A military sense is probably what the LXX gives to the verse as well. LXX Nah 3:17a reads: ἐξήλατο ὡς ἀττέλεβος ὁ σύμμικτός σου ("Your commingled one hopped off like a locust" [NETS]). ἐξάλλομαι ("to leap up") is a plus in the LXX and it is often found in contexts of warfare (1 Macc 13:44; Joel 2:5; Hab 1:8) or joyous celebration (Mic 2:12; Isa 55:12). In the case of σύμμικτος, it is possible that the translator used it as a general term for the two rare Hebrew nouns, but it is obvious from various passages in the LXX that σύμμικτος typically renders עֶרֶב ("mixture, mixed company") or מַעֲרָב ("articles of exchange, merchandise").[156] The verb συμμίγνυμι may simply mean "to meet," and the general sense of the noun σύμμικτος is that of a "commingled, mixed crowd."[157] It is found as an adjective in Herodotus (*Histories* 7.55.6), describing an irregular army from all nations: Ἡγέοντο δὲ πρῶτα μὲν οἱ μύριοι Πέρσαι, ἐστεφανωμένοι πάντες· μετὰ δὲ τούτους ὁ σύμμικτος στρατὸς παντοίων ἐθνέων. In the LXX it is found as a substantive often designating an army made up of several nationalities (Jdt 1:16; Jer 32[MT25]:20).[158] The combination of ἐξάλλομαι (a term possibly implying an attack) and σύμμικτος shows that the translator had probably understood this verse to refer to an attacking multinational army which was compared to a locust—a sense not obvious in the MT. This image of the locust created by the LXX translator is not very different from the image portrayed in LXX Amos 7:1.[159]

Conclusion

Our analysis of LXX Amos 7:1 has shown that the meaning of the Greek verse was significantly changed by the Greek translator under the influence of Ezekiel's prophecy about Gog. Amos' locust vision was interpreted symbolically: the locusts are an army and one of them is Gog the king. In the light of what locusts represent in Joel and in the context of a fascination with Ezekiel's Gog around the time of the translation of the Greek TP, the phenomena observed in LXX Amos 7:1 seem naturally at home.

---

155.   Robert P. Gordon, "Loricate Locusts in the Targum to Nahum III 17 and Revelation IX 9," *VT* 33 (1983): 338–39.

156.   BDB 786.

157.   *Muraoka 2009*, 647.

158.   LEH 581.

159.   Another instance where locusts are mentioned is LXX Hos 13:3. מארבה ("from a window") is rendered ἀπὸ ἀκρίδων. See Joosten, "Exegesis in the Septuagint Version of Hosea," 72–73.

Summary and Conclusions

As the LXX is becoming increasingly important in studies of Second Temple Judaism, the interest of scholars is shifting away from the mere use of the version as an adjunct to the textual criticism of the Hebrew Bible. The process of sieving secondary readings in order to arrive at the "pure" form of the Hebrew text has been the main preoccupation of textual critics for centuries. LXX readings were commonly retroverted into Hebrew in order to offer more pristine readings than have survived in the MT. Other ways of explaining deviations (e.g. translational factors, influence of late Hebrew/Aramaic) were generally neglected and a different Hebrew *Vorlage* behind the LXX was commonly assumed.

The study of intertextuality is offering another angle of approach to the LXX version, attempting to explain deviations and peculiar renderings where other methods have been inadequate. The interests of an intertextual study are not directed towards restoring the Hebrew text. Instead, the translator, his literary competence and hermeneutical processes, conscious or unconscious, become the central foci. Consequently, through a better understanding of the translator and his intertextual matrix, some conclusions may be drawn regarding the interpretation of the biblical text in the circles inhabited by the LXX translator. This study has examined a broad spectrum of intertextuality (i.e. various types of intertextuality) in the LXX TP, with a special emphasis on the books of Hosea, Amos and Micah. While most of the chapters have been limited to these three books, my findings may have some validity for the rest of the LXX TP, given that a single translator was probably responsible for all twelve books. At the same time, not every book of the TP necessarily triggered intertextual connections for the translator in the same way as the others. Only an examination of the rest of the LXX TP would reveal the extent of the intertextual element in each case.

The aim of Chapter 2 was to ascertain whether LXX TP used the LXX Pentateuch as a kind of lexicon, since this has been argued by various scholars. It was shown that similarities between LXX Pentateuch and LXX TP could be explained otherwise, since the translators of both corpora had access to the same readily available Greek equivalents within their common Hellenistic milieu. Greek vocabulary peculiar to both corpora (e.g. neologisms, words with "forced" meaning) had quite conceivably arisen in the Jewish community prior to the writing down of the LXX Pentateuch, and the translator of the TP probably adopted it not from written translations but from oral tradition. The intertextual matrix of the translator of the TP is thus very broad, and no clear and direct connections between texts could be demonstrated. However, this chapter does show the translator's familiarity with the language and literary conventions of the Hellenistic period.

Chapter 3 dealt with the use of standard translations, that is, pre-existing, familiar, formulaic expressions which have become part of the religious jargon of the Greek translator and have their origin in a text other than the one being translated. This chapter, as well as subsequent ones, was limited to the books of Hosea, Amos and Micah in a search for cases where the translator deviates from his Hebrew *Vorlage* and translates by a Greek expression known from other biblical passages. The discussion shows that the translator's familiarity with certain expressions does not necessitate a direct "borrowing" from the original text containing the expression. The translator may have "quoted" from a secondary source or from common oral usage, since use of a familiar expression does not presuppose knowledge of the source from which it originated. Although exclusive dependence on particular texts was impossible to demonstrate, this type of intertextuality shows how the translator brings texts thematically related into closer, verbal correspondence. The fact that the translator feels free to incorporate these stock expressions in the text, instead of following the Hebrew literally, suggests that he understands there to be some sort of thematic unity between texts sharing similar language.

Chapter 4 examines how the Greek translator, in the process of reading and translating his Hebrew *Vorlage*, identifies certain catchwords which activate a connection with other biblical texts where the same catchword occurs. This type of connection left its mark on the way the translator rendered some passages. Such a type of reading approximates to the rabbinic exegetical category of *gezerah shavah* for, as some scholars have observed, the recognition of catchwords and their significance in biblical exegesis predates the exegetical work of the rabbis. The recognition of catchwords by the translator and their importance in the process of translation presuppose that he views the text as unified, "synchronic," and involving internal commentary on one text by another.

In Chapter 4 I have also included cases involving peculiar Greek renderings that, although they display connections apparently generated by catchwords and have been attributed by commentators to the initiative of the Greek translator, may be explained differently, as further examination has shown. These renderings can be explained as arising from the employment of other tools such as contextual exegesis, appeal to Post-Biblical Hebrew/Aramaic nuances for Classical Hebrew words, a different Hebrew *Vorlage*, or the use of imagery in accordance with Greek literary conventions.

The present chapter presents intertextuality in the form of allusions to specific biblical stories, events and characters. Unlike the cases discussed in the previous chapter, these allusions were not triggered by shared catchwords. The influence of the intertext is strong enough for the translator to "manipulate" his Hebrew *Vorlage* in order to "import" traces of the intertext into his translation. The cases included in this chapter give us a glimpse of stories and traditions which were of particular interest to the translator. Moreover, a couple of cases open up a window into the translator's attitude to prophecy and to eschatological expectations current in his time.

The above summary of the chapters allows us to make further observations on the translator of LXX TP, his LXX *Vorlage* and his approach to the biblical text:

(a) *Attitude to the Text*: First of all, the LXX *Vorlage* used by the TP translator appears to have been written in the Aramaic square script, given the frequent interchanges between ד and ר, as well as י and ו. Moreover, apart from a few instances where the LXX translation reveals a Hebrew *Vorlage* different from the MT (e.g. Amos 1:3, 15), this study justifies the assumption that the TP translator worked from a text belonging to the same family as the MT. As far as the translator's attitude to the biblical text is concerned, it is impossible to evaluate it simply from the methods that he employs in his translation. A *verbum de verbo* translation which represents every single element of the text betrays the need felt by the translator to present everything from the source text to the target audience. Thus the importance of the text is expressed in faithful word order and inclusion of every Hebrew symbol in the target language, even at the expense of Greek style. However, in a similar way, pluses, paraphrases and textual "manipulation" may also betray a high respect for the text, in that the intention of the translator is to communicate the full sense of the text accurately to the target audience, even at the expense of translational exactitude. However, the translator of LXX TP does not belong to either of these extremes. His normal practice lies somewhere in the middle, which is not to ignore the consonantal text or its word order, but nevertheless to maintain some freedom of manoeuvre. Often the translator's deviations are significant and display certain proto-midrashic or targumic tendencies on his part. The ingenuity observed at the points of deviation does not mean that the text is taken lightly by the translator. His licence to remove obscurities in the text is not proof that he thinks of his Hebrew text as inferior or problematic. Rather, deviations underline the translator's concern that the full sense of the text be understood by his audience, the implicit be made explicit and the rendering be in line with the literary conventions of his time.

(b) *Translator's Intellectual Status*: Intertextuality in LXX Hosea, Amos and Micah, especially where catchwords have been recognized, reveals the translator's broad knowledge of the Hebrew text, even of words which rarely occur in biblical books. He demonstrates familiarity, not only with the Pentateuch, but also with the historical books and the prophets. Moreover, the translator betrays a wide knowledge of Jewish tradition. By "tradition" I do not refer to his familiarity with a certain *reading* tradition. He most likely did not have the full pronounced form for each word available to him prior to the act of translation, but, instead, a semantic/syntactic scanning of the text he was reading preceded the full pronunciation of the words. However, the very act of reading was not done in a void. The translator read the text, not with a complete phonic tradition in his memory, but with interpretive traditions which, at times, affected decisions on vocalization. He was not a disinterested translator but one who moved in Jewish circles, was familiar with the Hebrew text and probably had prior exposure to various interpretations of it. This does not exclude the possibility that traditions also had their starting point in the process of translation.

One can also observe that some of the translator's methods display similarities with techniques attested in Alexandria (see "Judeo-Hellenistic Milieu" in the Introduction) and, at the same time, his translation approach presents affinities with hermeneutical approaches witnessed in Qumran writings. For example, the attitude of the LXX translator towards prophecy is that of understanding the text to be speaking primarily about his times, something which is also obvious in Qumran. Comparison can also be made in respect of "catchwords." As observed in various Qumran documents, associations between texts are made on the basis of common words, that is, catchwords. This technique is later accepted by the rabbis (*gezerah shavah*), but its roots are already observed in the LXX translation. These associations made on the basis of "catchwords" reveal that the translator's exegesis was sometimes "contextual." However, what the translator considers as "context" is much broader than the verses in close proximity. Indeed, his entire "bible" was the "context" within which he interpreted. A verse from an entirely different book might have more influence on the verse being translated than might its immediate context. The LXX translator views all scripture as synchronic, as having a single voice, thus allowing for even the most distant of texts to be mutually interpretive.

As far as knowledge of other LXX books is concerned, it is obvious that on many occasions agreements between the translator's Greek renderings and other LXX books are more likely to have come from oral memory, and not from a copy of the Greek Torah functioning as a reference source consulted by the translator. The majority of new forms of intertextuality introduced by the translator can be explained solely on the basis of his familiarity with other Hebrew texts. This, however, does not mean that the translator was unaware of existing Greek versions of other books, only that clear influence from Greek versions is rarely detectable.

For such studies which aim at a better understanding of the translational stage of the LXX, as opposed to the reception stage, it is necessary to keep the Hebrew and the Greek side by side. While many LXX scholars emphasize the LXX as a free-standing translation, Pietersma points out that even they are "forced by the evidence to have recourse to the parent text for essential linguistic information, in order to account for the Greek."[160] Moreover, as Pietersma observes, it is by recourse to the parent text that one can see the linguistic difficulties faced by the translator that forced him to change "gear" in the act of translating. He notes that it is "typically at such points of difficulty that the translator lapses into contextual interpretation, albeit seldom sustained over more than one or two verses. In other words, a specific translation problem arises and is solved locally."[161] This is the position that has evolved in the course of this study, which has not found sustained theological or other interventions by the translator, but which has mostly been engaged in uncovering the "disjointed" intertextual "solutions" provided by the translator at various points in his rendering of the Greek.

---

160. Albert Pietersma, "A New Paradigm for Addressing Old Questions: The Relevance of the Interlinear Model for the Study of the Septuagint," in *Bible and Computer: The Stellenbosch AIBI–6 Conference Proceedings of the Association Internationale Bible et Informatique "From Alpha to Byte." University of Stellenbosch 17–21 July, 2000* (ed. Johann Cook; Leiden: Brill, 2002), 355.

161. Ibid.

Appendix

NUMBERS 24:7 AND THE
EXTRA-BIBLICAL GOG TRADITION

MT   יִזַּל־מַיִם מִדָּלְיָו וְזַרְעוֹ בְּמַיִם רַבִּים וְיָרֹם מֵאֲגַג מַלְכּוֹ וְתִנַּשֵּׂא מַלְכֻתוֹ

LXX ἐξελεύσεται ἄνθρωπος ἐκ τοῦ σπέρματος αὐτοῦ καὶ κυριεύσει ἐθνῶν πολλῶν καὶ ὑψωθήσεται ἢ Γωγ βασιλεία αὐτοῦ καὶ αὐξηθήσεται ἡ βασιλεία αὐτοῦ

LXX Numbers 24:7 is considered one of the main Pentateuchal texts displaying the messianic beliefs of the LXX translator. The LXX reference to Γωγ (MT Agag), the only one in the Pentateuch,[1] gives the verse an eschatological dimension connecting it with Israel's end-time foe of Ezek 38 and 39. Moreover, the mention of ἄνθρωπος presents a royal messianic individual who will prevail over Gog.

Lust's View

In a series of essays, Lust sought to reexamine the way certain texts have been read messianically.[2] He advises that "One should not overlook the many passages in the Greek version where a 'messianising' translation might have been expected but where it is not given,"[3] "Neither should one overlook those texts in which the messianic connotation has been weakened or given a different nuance by the LXX."[4]

Lust concludes, contra Vermes who supports the messianizing interpretation of the LXX in Num 24:7,[5] that "one cannot say that the LXX

1. It is also found in some variant readings in Deut 3:1, 13; 4:47 (and Sir 48:17).
2. Johan Lust, *Messianism and the Septuagint: Collected Essays* (ed. K. Hauspie; BETL 178; Leuven: Leuven University, 2004).
3. Johan Lust, "Messianism and Septuagint," in *Messianism and the Septuagint*, 10.
4. Ibid., 11.
5. G. Vermes, *Scripture and Tradition in Judaism* (Leiden: Brill, 1961), 160–61. See also W. H. Brownlee, "The Servant of the Lord in the Qumran Scrolls II,"

as a whole displays a messianic exegesis. Most often the translation is literal, without any messianic bias. In other cases it shows a shift in accentuation, thereby weakening the royal messianic character of the text."[6]

However, arguing against a conscious messianic agenda on the part of the translator does not prove that it is impossible for us to discern occasionally his messianic beliefs in the way he translates certain verses. Lust attempts to explain the various elements in the third oracle of Balaam, Num 24:7, as follows:

(a) The Hebrew verb יזל was read as a form of the Aramaic verb אזל, meaning "go," and ἐξέρχομαι was chosen, perhaps under the influence of Mic 5:2 and Isa 11:1 where similar verbs are used.

(b) Instead of מדליו, the translator read מילדיו, "out of his children," or מדליותיו, "out of his branches" or "out of his seed." מים was overlooked, jumping to the preposition *mem* (מ) preceding דליו.

(c) The translator read זרע ("seed") as זרוע ("arm," "power," symbol of the ruler), and מים רבים ("many waters") as עמים רבים ("many nations").

(d) נשא was given the sense "grow up."

(e) 1 Chronicles 14:2, in both the Hebrew and the Greek, alludes to the third oracle of Balaam. The author of 1 Chr 14:2 chose למעלה, "highly," which probably suggests that he understood or read מאגג in Num 24:7 as מהגג ("[higher] than the roof"). According to Lust, the allusion in 1 Chr 14:2 as well as Philo's text in *De vita Mosis* 1.290 (πρὸς ὕψος, "on high") support an earlier version of LXX Num 24:7 which understood מאגג as מהגג ("[higher] than the roof").[7]

(f) Lust finds the presence of ἄνθρωπος very difficult to explain, but he doubts that it is a pre-Christian reading. He thinks that "The connection between Isa 11:1 with its 'branch' or ἄνθος and Num 24:17 may have facilitated the use of ἄνθρωπος in the Balaam oracle. In Num 24:7 it may have been introduced as an explicit subject to the verb אזל, in which case it may have simply meant 'somebody'."[8]

BASOR 135 (1954): 36–37 n. 30, and Frankel, *Über den Einfluss*, 182–85. Note his discussion of the LXX plus καὶ ἰδὼν τὸν Ὤγ in Num 24:23 (pp. 172 and 184).

6. Lust, "Messianism and Septuagint," 12.

7. Johan Lust, "The Greek Version of Balaam's Third and Fourth Oracles: The ἄνθρωπος in Num 24,7 and 17: Messianism and Lexicography," in *Messianism and the Septuagint*, 73–74.

8. Ibid., 86.

Lust also seems to suggest that the similar forms of ἄνθος and ἄνθρωπος, especially the abbreviated form of ἄνθρωπος ($\overline{ANO\Sigma}$), enhanced the connection between the two during the manuscript transmission stage.[9] Lust also questions Philo's version of Num 24:7, saying that "his quotation is rather free, and perhaps influenced by his vision of the final times as a fulfillment of primeval times in which the ἄνθρωπος had a prominent role. Thus the term ἄνθρωπος may belong to his own rewording of the verse. Christians may have adopted his use of it. They certainly would have appreciated it."[10]

We agree with Lust that one should not expect to find a consistent "messianizing" interpretive translation in the LXX. However, Lust may be trying too hard to explain away the instances where we do get a glimpse of an underlying messianic idea. His various attempts at explaining how each element in LXX Num 24:7 came about require a series of misreadings on the part of the translator in a verse of wide circulation and significance for Judaism. This would suggest that the translator was encountering this verse for the first time and struggled with every one of its elements. Apart from multiple misreadings, Lust is also open to the idea that Philo's interpretive use of ἄνθρωπος was adopted by Christians in their manuscript tradition, since it could be applied to Jesus, or that they were led by other Old Testament texts to adjust their manuscripts. Similar objections to those offered by Lust could be brought against his own views. Why did Christians refrain from "messianizing" other texts? Why is it more likely that the changes are of Christian origin, when already the ancient versions display a fair degree of interpretive translation, especially the Targums?[11] On the same note, Lust does mention the Samaritan Pentateuch's reading of Gog, as well as Aquila, Symmachus and Theodotion (according to some mss), but he does not attempt to explain it.[12]

Horbury's View

Horbury observes the eschatological interest shared by the Pentateuch and the Prophets, and he notes how the collection of the books and their editing "produces a series of what can be properly called messianic

9. Ibid., 83–84.

10. Ibid., 86.

11. For the Targums, see Gordon, "The Targumists as Eschatologists," in *Hebrew Bible and Ancient Versions*, 303–16; Bøe, *Gog and Magog*, 189–99.

12. Lust, "The Greek Version of Balaam's Third and Fourth Oracles," 71, 72 n. 9; Johan Lust, "Septuagint and Messianism, with Special Emphasis on the Pentateuch," in *Messianism and the Septuagint*, 149 n. 53.

prophecies, envisaging the future—sometimes evidently the immediate future."[13] This corpus makes it "natural to read the specifically messianic prophecies, like those in Ezekiel, Amos and Zechariah, in the context of the more general prophecies of the future among which they are interspersed."[14] Horbury notes further that "the prominence of a coherent series of prophecies will have been among the factors which led to the interpretation of still further oracles as messianic, and to still greater specificity in conceptions of the work of the expected ruler or rulers."[15]

Horbury sees the messianism of the second century B.C.E. and later as having organically developed from the collection of the books in the sixth and fifth centuries, with the LXX as one of the witnesses to this development. For LXX Num 24:7 Horbury says:

> "There shall come forth a man," probably from the third century BC, illustrates not only the addition of messianic value but also, with the word "Gog," the effect of combining Pentateuch and prophets; the "man" is implicitly identified as the victor over Ezekiel's Gog, the great opponent of the last days.[16]

> This "man" who shall rule an empire is then naturally identified, when Balaam returns to his prophecy and speaks of "the latter days" (Num. 24. 14), with the star of Jacob. "A star shall rise out of Jacob, and a man (Hebrew 'sceptre') shall rise up out of Israel" (Num. 24. 17 LXX). The messianic value of the title "man" appears among other places at Isa. 19. 20 LXX, "a man who shall save us,"…where the "saviour" of Egyptian Jews is evidently identified with the star-man of Balaam's prophecy. The pattern of the oracles in their LXX form, from Num. 23. 21 to 24. 17, is that already given in the Blessing of Jacob: a succession of rulers from Israel culminates in the advent of the great king who will crush the final adversary.[17]

The LXX versions of the oracles of the Pentateuch (e.g. Gen 49:10; Num 24:7; Deut 33:4–5), which belong to the third century, "presuppose, already at that time, a developed messianic interpretation which has given rise to a chain of exegetical interconnections, between these great prophecies within the Pentateuch and also between the Pentateuch and the books of the Prophets."[18] The language of 1 Chr 14:2, in both the Hebrew and the Greek, is close to the language of the oracle in

13. Horbury, *Jewish Messianism*, 29.
14. Ibid.
15. Ibid.
16. Ibid.
17. Ibid., 50.
18. Ibid., 51.

Num 24:7, linking it with the Davidic kingdom.[19] Moreover, without any reference to Gog, Philo is aware of the LXX version of this verse and displays a messianic understanding of it; in fact, this is "the single clear messianic reference in Philo."[20]

Bruce notes the various Qumran associations of the victory of the Davidic Messiah over the northern invaders, Gog and Magog.[21] Similarly, he has already noted that "The Septuagint contains two well-known passages in which the thinking of the translators has been influenced to such a degree by the figure of Gog that they have introduced his name in spite of his absence from the Hebrew text."[22]

The first passage is LXX Num 24:7, where ἄνθρωπος is further identified with the "star out of Jacob," a Messianic reference in both Jewish and Christian circles.[23] The second passage is LXX Amos 7:1, where the locusts are interpreted as invading armies on the basis of Joel's locusts, whose leader is Gog (Hebrew גוֹי).[24] LXX Numbers 24:7 would have formed part of the tradition inherited by the Greek translator of Amos, given that the Pentateuchal books were the first of the biblical corpus to be translated.

Bøe's View

Bøe notes the early shift from Agag to Gog in the LXX, and possibly in other Greek versions such as Theodotion, in the Vetus Latina and in the Samaritan Pentateuch. As Bøe says of the last-named, "This is surprising since Gog elsewhere is not witnessed in the Pentateuch, but rather in the latter prophets. These writings did not come to hold any canonical position for the Samaritan society."[25]

Nevertheless, in agreement with Gerleman, Bøe recognizes the weight of this tradition in pre-Christian times, meaning that Gog, not Agag, was the common reading. Normally it is a strong indication of a different *Vorlage* when the LXX and the Samaritan Pentateuch agree against the MT.[26] Bøe's thorough work on Gog and Magog covers a very broad range of extra-biblical tradition, some of which we shall summarize and use to

19. Ibid., 45, 130.
20. Ibid., 30. Also Bøe, *Gog and Magog*, 53.
21. Bruce, "The Earliest Old Testament Interpretation," 39.
22. Ibid., 40.
23. Ibid., 40–41, 41 n. 1.
24. Ibid., 41. See also Bruce, "Prophetic Interpretation," 17–21.
25. Bøe, *Gog and Magog*, 52.
26. Ibid., 52, 55, 58. For various explanations of the Gog reading, see pp. 54–57.

further our investigation.[27] Owing to space limitations we shall omit Gog and Magog in the book of Revelation, the rabbinic writings, the Church Fathers, and later literature.[28]

Gog and Magog in the Sibylline Oracles

All the passages relating to Gog and Magog are found in the third book (3.319–22, 512–13, 635–51, 657–731), which is generally believed to be the oldest section, probably dating from the middle of the second century B.C.E. in Alexandria. Only two of the above passages contain direct references to the names Gog and Magog and, apart from Ezek 38–39, these are the oldest passages known which combine the two names. There is little doubt of the direct use of Ezek 38–39 in *Sib. Or.* 3.[29] Charlesworth's comment on *Sib. Or.* 3.319–22 is that Gog and Magog may be understood as a general name for eschatological adversaries.[30]

Gog and Magog in the Book of Jubilees

There are two references to Magog (7.19; 9.7–8) and one to Gog (8.25) in the book of *Jubilees*. The dating of this book varies among scholars but the parameters have generally been set to approximately 170–100 B.C.E. It is possible that "Gog" has been understood as interchangeable with "Magog" and that the author was familiar with Ezek 38–39. Moreover, he combined his knowledge of the Magog tradition of Gen 10 with the Gog from Magog tradition of Ezek 38–39.[31]

Gog and Magog in Qumran

There are four references to Magog (4QpIsa a 8–10, III,21 [=4Q 161]; 1QapGen XII,12 and XVII,10.16), one to Gog (1QM XI,16), and one to Gog and Magog in combination (4Q523) in the writings published from Qumran. Three of the references to Magog (1QapGen XII,12 and XVII,10, 16) obviously relate to Gen 10:2 and hardly have any connection with Ezek 38–39. The reference to Magog in 4Q161 (the pesher on Isa 11:1–5) is connected with Ezek 38–39 and is eschatological as well as messianic. 1QM XI,16 is a section which has several allusions to Ezek 38–39, indicating an eschatological setting and including the duality of celestial warfare together with a terrestrial war waged by

---

27. For the history of interpretation of Gog and Magog, see also Railton, "Gog and Magog," 23–43.
28. For these consult the thorough study of Bøe, *Gog and Magog*.
29. Ibid., 140–50.
30. *OTP* 1:391.
31. Bøe, *Gog and Magog*, 150–59.

Israel. Bøe concludes: "The number of Gog and Magog references in writings found in Qumran...is high enough to assure us that the sectaries did occupy themselves with the eschatological prophecies in Ezekiel, and that the war with Gog and Magog was part of their future expectations."[32]

Collins, in his examination of apocalypticism in the Dead Sea Scrolls, identified the final war between Israel and the Gentiles as a recurring feature of the "end of days."[33] It was after the Babylonian invasion that the antagonism of the Gentiles was imagined on an even grander scale, and Gog from the land of Magog (Ezek 38–39) became the enemy of whom the Israelite prophets had spoken. The enemy's destruction on the mountains of Jerusalem (Ezek 39:2) is a scenario evoked in Dan 11:45 as well ("between the sea and the holy mountain"), predicting Antiochus Epiphanes' end.[34] Magog is mentioned in a *pesher* on Isaiah (4Q161) in company with the "war of the Kittim" and the Branch of David.[35] In the War Rule, we have a human leader, the Davidic messiah, and his place in the final conflict.[36] Collins notes that the Davidic messiah in the Dead Sea scrolls belongs to the complex of traditions associated with the nationalistic conflict between Israel and the nations, rather than to the cosmic war between the forces of light and darkness.[37]

Allusions to Ezekiel 38–39 in 1 Enoch *56:5–8*
Although the names Gog and Magog are not used in *1 En.* 56:5–8, the enemy in Ezekiel's Gog-oracles is identified as "the Parthians and the Medes." The indebtedness of this section to Ezek 38–39 is universally recognized. The section is possibly eschatological, looking forward to a future attack.[38]

Josephus on Magog
Josephus identifies Magog of Gen 10 with the nation of the Scythians (*Ant.* 1.122–23). He treats Magog as an ordinary name of an ancestor of a contemporary nation located to the east and to the north of the Roman world, and makes no associations between Magog and the Gog-oracles in Ezek 38–39.[39]

32. Ibid., 178.
33. John J. Collins, *Apocalypticism in the Dead Sea Scrolls* (London: Routledge, 1997), 91.
34. Ibid., 92.
35. Ibid., 93.
36. Ibid., 105.
37. Ibid., 106.
38. Bøe, *Gog and Magog,* 178–84.
39. Ibid., 184–86.

Magog in Liber Antiquitatum Biblicarum
There are four occurrences of the name "Magog" in *LAB*, also known as
Pseudo-Philo (*LAB* 4.1, 2, 4; 5.4). Magog is identified as Japheth's son,
Noah's grandson. As with Josephus, there are no associations with
Ezekiel's Gog oracles.[40]

Gog and Magog in the Targums
Gog and Magog are found in several places in the Targums. For
Tg. Ezek 38–39 Gog is Rome. Various Targums to Num 11:26 speak of
Eldad's and Medad's prophecies about Gog and Magog and their defeat
by the Messiah. Pseudo-Jonathan attributes the defeat to God's own
direct intervention. The Targums vary in their expectations of one or
more Messiahs and on the relationship between him/them and Gog. Gog
and Magog references are introduced in many different contexts (relating
to Zech 12:10; Isa 10:32; 33:22; Esth 5:1; Song 8:4), suggesting a wide
interest and familiarity with Gog and Magog expectations in the
formative years of the Targums.[41] Gordon notes that all the Targums tell
us about the Messiah son of Ephraim is that

> he would be killed while doing battle with that eschatological character
> Gog, the leader of Gentile resistance to the Messianic rule… Evidently it
> was expected in some quarters that the golden age of the Davidic Messiah
> would be preceded by the appearance, and the death, of a secondary
> Messianic figure. It is all the more surprising, then, and an illustration of
> the doctrinal pluralism of the Targums, that Targum Pseudo-Jonathan to
> Exod. xl 11 attributes the defeat of Gog to the hand of the Messiah son of
> Ephraim.[42]

Conclusion

The above survey of collected data and analysis by various scholars has
shown that LXX Num 24:7 was widely associated with the reading "Gog"
instead of "Agag" and was read messianically. The references to Gog
found in a wide variety of sources reveal familiarity with Ezek 38–39 in
early Judaism, and a certain fascination with this eschatological figure.

---

40. Ibid., 186–89.
41. Ibid., 189–99.
42. Gordon, "The Targumists as Eschatologists," 310.

BIBLIOGRAPHY

Ackroyd, P. R. "Hosea and Jacob." *VT* 13 (1963): 245–59.

Aejmelaeus, A. *Parataxis in the Septuagint: A Study of the Renderings of the Hebrew Coordinate Clauses in the Greek Pentateuch.* Annales Academiae Scientiarum Fennicae Dissertationes Humanarum Litterarum 31. Helsinki: Suomalainen Tiedeakatemia, 1982.

———. "'Rejoice in the Lord!' A Lexical and Syntactical Study of the Semantic Field of Joy in the Greek Psalter." Pages 501–22 in Baasten and Van Peursen, eds., *Hamlet on a Hill.*

———. "What We Talk About When We Talk About Translation Technique." Pages 531–52 in Taylor, ed., *X Congress of the IOSCS.*

Aichele, George, and Gary A. Phillips. "Introduction: Exegesis, Eisegesis, Intergesis." *Semeia* 69 (1995): 7–18.

Albright, W. F. "The Gezer Calendar." *BASOR* 92 (1943): 16–26.

Allen, Leslie C. *Ezekiel 20–48.* WBC 29. Dallas: Word, 1990.

———. *The Greek Chronicles: The Relation of the Septuagint of I and II Chronicles to the Masoretic Text.* Part 1, *The Translator's Craft.* VTSup 25. Leiden: Brill, 1974.

Alter, Robert. *The Art of Biblical Narrative.* London: George Allen & Unwin, 1981.

———. *The World of Biblical Literature.* London: SPCK, 1992.

Andersen, Francis I., and David Noel Freedman. *Amos.* AB 24A. New York: Doubleday, 1989.

———. *Hosea.* AB 24. New York: Doubleday, 1980.

Andiñach, Pablo R. "The Locusts in the Message of Joel." *VT* 42 (1992): 433–41.

Arieti, James A. "A Study in the Septuagint of Amos." Ph.D. diss., Stanford University, 1972.

———. "The Vocabulary of Septuagint Amos." *JBL* 93 (1974): 338–47.

Aristotle. Translated by H. Rackham. 23 vols. LCL. Cambridge, Mass.: Harvard University Press, 1990.

Ausloos, H., B. Lemmelijn, and M. Vervenne. *Florilegium Lovaniense: Studies in Septuagint and Textual Criticism in Honour of Florentino García Martínez.* BETL 224. Leuven: Peeters, 2008.

Avemarie, Friedrich. "Interpreting Scripture Through Scripture: Exegesis Based on Lexematic Association in the Dead Sea Scrolls and the Pauline Epistles." Pages 83–102 in *Echoes from the Caves: Qumran and the New Testament.* Edited by F. García Martínez. Leiden: Brill, 2009.

Baasten, M. F. J., and W. Th. Van Peursen, eds. *Hamlet on a Hill: Semitic and Greek Studies Presented to Professor T. Muraoka.* OLA 118. Leuven: Peeters, 2003.

Baer, David A. *When We All Go Home: Translation and Theology in LXX Isaiah 56–66.* JSOTSup 318. HBV 1. Sheffield: Sheffield Academic, 2001.

Bahrdt, C. F. Friederico. *Apparatus Criticus ad Formandum Interpretem Veteris Testamenti*, vol. 1. Leipzig: Schwickerti, 1775.

Baillet, M., J. T. Milik, and R. de Vaux. *Les "petites grottes" de Qumrân*. DJD III. Oxford: Clarendon, 1962.

Barclay, John M. G. *Jews in the Mediterranean Diaspora: From Alexander to Trajan (323 BCE–117 CE)*. Edinburgh: T. & T. Clark, 1996.

Barker, William D. "Isaiah 24–27: Studies in a Cosmic Polemic." Ph.D. diss., University of Cambridge, 2006.

Barr, James. "Did the Greek Pentateuch Really Serve as a Dictionary for the Translation of the Later Books?" Pages 523–43 in Baasten and Van Peursen, eds., *Hamlet on a Hill*.

———. "'Guessing' in the Septuagint." Pages 19–34 in *Studien zur Septuaginta—Robert Hanhart zu Ehren*. Edited by D. Fraenkel et al. MSU 20. Göttingen: Vandenhoeck & Ruprecht, 1990.

———. *The Semantics of Biblical Language*. Oxford: Oxford University Press, 1961.

———. *The Typology of Literalism in Ancient Biblical Translations*. MSU 15. Göttingen: Vandenhoeck & Ruprecht, 1979.

Barthélemy, D. *Critique Textuelle de l'Ancien Testament*. Tome 3, *Ézéchiel, Daniel et les 12 Prophètes*. OBO 50/3. Göttingen: Vandenhoeck & Ruprecht, 1992.

Barton, John. *Amos's Oracles Against the Nations: A Study of Amos 1.3–2.5*. SOTS Monograph Series 6. Cambridge: Cambridge University Press, 1980.

Beal, Timothy K. "Glossary." Pages 21–24 in Fewell, ed., *Reading Between Texts*.

———. "Ideology and Intertextuality: Surplus of Meaning and Controlling the Means of Productions." Pages 27–39 in Fewell, ed., *Reading Between Texts*.

Beentjes, Pancratius C. *The Book of Ben Sira in Hebrew*. VTSup 68. Leiden: Brill, 1997.

Bible d'Alexandrie. *Les Douze Prophètes: Osée*. 23.1. Paris: Cerf, 2002.

Bickerman, Elias J. "The Septuagint as a Translation." *PAAJR* 28 (1959): 1–39.

Blenkinsopp, J. *Ezekiel*. Interpretation. Louisville: John Knox, 1990.

———. *Isaiah 1–39*. AB 19. New York: Doubleday, 2000.

Block, Daniel I. "Gog in Prophetic Tradition: A New Look at Ezekiel XXXVIII 17." *VT* 42 (1992): 154–72.

———. *The Book of Ezekiel: Chapters 25–48*. NICOT. Grand Rapids: Eerdmans, 1997.

Bodi, Daniel. "Les *gillûlîm* chez Ézéchiel et dans l'Ancien Testament, et les différentes pratiques cultuelles associées à ce terme." *RB* 100 (1993): 481–510.

Bøe, Sverre. *Gog and Magog*. WUNT 2/135. Tübingen: Mohr Siebeck, 2001.

Bons, Eberhard. "Le vin filtré: Quelques remarques concernant les textes hébreu et grec d'Amos 6,6a et les sens de la tournure οἱ πίνοντες τὸν διυλισμένον οἶνον." Pages 71–83 in Ausloos, Lemmelijn, and Vervenne, eds., *Florilegium Lovaniense*.

Bovati, Pietro, and Roland Meynet. *Le livre du prophète Amos*. Paris: Cerf, 1994.

Boyarin, Daniel. *Intertextuality and the Reading of Midrash*. Indiana Studies in Biblical Literature. Bloomington: Indiana University Press, 1990.

Boyd-Taylor, Cameron. "Robbers, Pirates and Licentious Women." Pages 559–71 in *Die Septuaginta—Texte, Kontexte, Lebenswelten: Internationale Fachtagung veranstaltet von Septuaginta Deutsch (LXX.D), Wuppertal 20.–23. Juli 2006*. Edited by Martin Karrer and Wolfgang Kraus. WUNT 219. Tübingen: Mohr Siebeck, 2008.

Brock, Sebastian. "The Phenomenon of the Septuagint." *OtSt* 17 (1972): 11–36.

Brockington, L. H. *The Hebrew Text of the Old Testament*. Cambridge: Cambridge University Press. Oxford: Oxford University Press, 1973.

Brooke, George J. *Exegesis at Qumran: 4QFlorilegium in Its Jewish Context.* JSOTSup 29. Sheffield: JSOT, 1985.

———. "Shared Intertextual Interpretations in the Dead Sea Scrolls and the New Testament." No pages. Cited 16 January 2011. Online: http://orion.huji.ac.il/symposiums/1st/papers/Brooke96.html.

Brooke, George J., and Barnabas Lindars, eds. *Septuagint, Scrolls and Cognate Writings: Papers Presented to the International Symposium on the Septuagint and Its Relations to the Dead Sea Scrolls and Other Writings (Manchester, 1990).* SBLSCS 33. Atlanta: Scholars Press, 1992.

Brownlee, W. H. "The Servant of the Lord in the Qumran Scrolls II." *BASOR* 135 (1954): 33–38.

Bruce, F. F. "The Earliest Old Testament Interpretation." Pages 37–52 in *The Witness of Tradition: Papers Read at the Joint British–Dutch Old Testament Conference Held at Woudschoten, 1970.* Edited by M. A. Beek et al. Oudtestamentische Studiën 17. Leiden: Brill, 1972.

———. "Prophetic Interpretation in the Septuagint." *BIOSCS* 12 (1979): 17–26.

Büchner, Dirk. "The Thysia Soteriou of the Septuagint and the Greek Cult: Representation and Accommodation." Pages 85–100 in Ausloos, Lemmelijn, and Vervenne, eds., *Florilegium Lovaniense.*

Caird, G. B. "Homeophony in the Septuagint." Pages 74–88 in *Jews, Greeks and Christians: Religious Cultures in Late Antiquity: Essays in Honor of William David Davies.* Edited by Robert Hamerton-Kelly and Robin Scroggs. Leiden: Brill, 1976.

Camp, Claudia V., and Carole R. Fontaine, eds. *Women, War, and Metaphor: Language and Society in the Study of the Hebrew Bible.* Semeia 61. Atlanta: Scholars Press, 1993.

Carbone, Sandro P., and Giovanni Rizzi. *Il Libro di Amos: Lettura Ebraica, Greca e Aramaica.* Bologna: Dehoniane, 1993.

Cathcart, Kevin J., and Robert P. Gordon. *The Targum of the Minor Prophets: Translated, with a Critical Introduction, Apparatus, and Notes.* ArBib 14. Edinburgh: T. & T. Clark, 1989.

Charles, R. H., ed. *The Apocrypha and Pseudepigrapha of the Old Testament.* Vol. 2, *Pseudepigrapha.* Oxford: Clarendon, 1913. Repr., Berkeley: The Apocryphile, 2004.

Chilton, Bruce D. *A Galilean Rabbi and His Bible: Jesus' Own Interpretation of Isaiah.* London: SPCK, 1984.

———. *The Isaiah Targum: Introduction, Translation, Apparatus and Notes.* ArBib 11. Edinburgh: T. & T. Clark, 1987.

Churgin, Pinkhos. "The Targum and the Septuagint." *AJSL* 50 (1933): 41–65.

Coggins, Richard James. *Joel and Amos.* The New Century Bible Commentary. Sheffield: Sheffield Academic, 2000.

Collins, John J. *Apocalypticism in the Dead Sea Scrolls.* London: Routledge, 1997.

———. "Messianism and Exegetical Tradition: The Evidence of the LXX Pentateuch." Pages 129–49 in Knibb, ed., *The Septuagint and Messianism.*

Cook, Johann. "Intertextual Readings in the Septuagint." Pages 119–34 in *The New Testament Interpreted: Essays in Honour of Bernard C. Lategan.* Edited by Cilliers Breytenbach, Johan C. Thom, and Jeremy Punt. NovTSup 124. Leiden: Brill, 2006.

———. "Intertextual Relationships Between the Septuagint of Psalms and Proverbs." Pages 218–28 in Hiebert, Cox, and Gentry, eds., *The Old Greek Psalter.*

———. "The Relationship Between the Septuagint Versions of Isaiah and Proverbs." Pages 199–214 in van der Meer et al., eds., *Isaiah in Context.*

Coote, R. B. "Amos 1:11: RḤMYW." *JBL* 90 (1971): 206–8.

———. "Hosea XII." *VT* 21 (1971): 389–402.

Cordes, Ariane. *Die Asafpsalmen in der Septuaginta: der griechische Psalter als Übersetzung und theologisches Zeugnis.* Herders Biblische Studien 41. Freiburg: Herder, 2004.

Craven, Toni. *Artistry and Faith in the Book of Judith.* SBLDS 70. Chico: Scholars Press, 1983.

Cripps, Richard S. *A Critical and Exegetical Commentary on the Book of Amos.* London: SPCK, 1929.

Croughs, Mirjam. "Intertextuality in the Septuagint: The Case of Isaiah 19." *BIOSCS* 34 (2001): 81–94.

Cuffey, Kenneth H. "Gog," *ABD* 2:1056.

Dahmen, Ulrich. "Zur Text- und Literarkritik von Am 6,6a." *BN* 32 (1986): 7–10.

Dalman, Gustaf Hermann. *Arbeit und Sitte in Palästina, Schriften des Deutschen Palästina-Instituts.* 1928. 7 vols. Repr., Hildesheim: Georg Olms, 1964.

Danby, Herbert. *The Mishnah.* London: Oxford University, 1933.

Daniel, Suzanne. *Recherches sur le Vocabulaire du Culte dans la Septante.* Études et Commentaires LXI. Paris: Klincksieck, 1966.

Darvill, Timothy. *The Concise Oxford Dictionary of Archaeology.* Oxford: Oxford University Press, 2008. Cited 31 July 2009. Online: http://www.oxfordreference.com/views/ENTRY.html?subview=Main&entry=t102.e645.

De Moor, Johannes C., ed. *Intertextuality in Ugarit and Israel: Papers Read at the Tenth Joint Meeting of The Society for Old Testament Study and Het Oudtestamentisch Werkgezelschap in Nederland en België; Held at Oxford, 1997.* Leiden: Brill, 1998.

De Waard, Jan. "Do You Use 'Clean Language'? Old Testament Euphemisms and Their Translation." *Bible Translator* 22 (1971): 107–15.

———. "A Greek Translation-Technical Treatment of Amos 1:15." Pages 111–18 in *On Language, Culture and Religion: In Honor of Eugene A. Nida.* Edited by Matthew Black and William A. Smalley. Approaches to Semiotics 56. The Hague: Mouton, 1974.

———. "Translation Techniques Used by the Greek Translators of the Book of Amos." *Bib* 59 (1978): 339–50.

De Waard, Jan, and William A. Smalley. *A Handbook on the Book of Amos.* UBS Handbook Series. New York: United Bible Societies, 1994.

Déaut, R. Le, and J. Robert. *Targum des Chroniques:* Tome I—*Introduction et Traduction.* Analecta Biblica 51. Rome: Biblical Institute, 1971.

———. *Targum des Chroniques:* Tome II—*Texte et Glossaire.* Analecta Biblica 51. Rome: Biblical Institute, 1971.

Delitzsch, Franz. *Die Psalmen.* 5th ed. Giessen: Brunnen, 1984.

Demetrius. Edited and Translated by Doreen C. Innes. LCL. Cambridge, Mass.: Harvard University Press, 1995.

Demsky, Aaron. "Dark Wine from Judah." *IEJ* 22 (1972): 233–34.

Dines, J. M. "The Septuagint of Amos: A Study in Interpretation." Ph.D. diss., Heythrop College, University of London, 1992.

———. "The Twelve Among the Prophets." Unpublished draft of a paper presented as a Grinfield Lecture on the Septuagint, Oxford, March 1, 2007.

Diodorus of Sicily. Translated by C. H. Oldfather. 12 vols. LCL. Cambridge, Mass.: Harvard University Press, 1979.

Dogniez, Cécile. "L'indépendence du traducteur grec d'Isaïe par rapport au Dodekapropheton." Pages 229–46 in van der Meer et al., eds., *Isaiah in Context*.

———. "L'intertextualité dans la LXX de Zacharie 9–14." Pages 81–96 in García Martínez and Vervenne, eds., *Interpreting Translation*.

Dorival, Gilles. "Les phénomènes d'intertextualité dans le livre grec des Nombres." Pages 253–85 in *Κατὰ τοὺς ο´ "selon les Septante": Trente études sur la Bible grecque des Septante. En hommage à Marguerite Harl*. Edited by Gilles Dorival and Olivier Munnich. Paris: Cerf, 1995.

Driver, G. R. "Babylonian and Hebrew Notes." *WO* 2 (1954): 20–21.

Driver, S. R. *Joel and Amos*. Cambridge Bible. Cambridge: Cambridge University Press, 1897.

———. *Notes on the Hebrew Text and the Topography of the Books of Samuel*. 2d ed. Oxford: Clarendon, 1913.

Edgill, Ernest Arthur. *The Book of Amos*. 2d ed. London: Methuen, 1926.

Edwards, Tim. "Aquila and the Rabbis on Hapax Legomena in the Psalms." Paper presented at ESAJS "Greek Scripture and the Rabbis" Conference. OCHJS, Yarnton Manor, Oxford, June 21, 2010.

Eichrodt, Walther. *Ezekiel: A Commentary*. Translated by Cosslett Quin. OTL. London: SCM, 1970. German ed., *Der Prophet Hesekiel*. Das Alte Testament Deutsch 22/1–2. Göttingen: Vandenhoeck & Ruprecht, 1965–66.

Ellingworth, Paul, and Aloo Mojola. "Translating Euphemisms in the Bible." *Bible Translator* 37 (1986): 139–43.

Emerton, John A. "Some Difficult Words in Isaiah 28.10 and 13." Pages 39–56 in *Biblical Hebrew, Biblical Texts: Essays in Memory of Michael P. Weitzman*. Edited by Ada Rapoport-Albert and Gillian Greenberg. JSOTSup 333. HBV 2. Sheffield: Sheffield Academic, 2001.

Epstein, Isidore. *The Babylonian Talmud*, vols. 1–18. London: Soncino, 1948–1952.

Eslinger, L. M. "Hosea 12:5a and Genesis 32:39: A Study in Inner Biblical Exegesis." *JSOT* 18 (1980): 94.

Evans, Craig A. "Listening for Echoes of Interpreted Scripture." Pages 47–51 in *Paul and the Scriptures of Israel*. Edited by Craig A. Evans and James A. Sanders. JSNTSup 83. SSEJC 1. Sheffield: JSOT, 1993.

Ferguson, Everett. "Wine as a Table-drink in the Ancient World." *ResQ* 13 (1970): 141–53.

Fernández Marcos, Natalio. *The Septuagint in Context: Introduction to the Greek Versions of the Bible*. Translated by Wilfred G. E. Watson. Leiden: Brill, 2000.

Fewell, Danna Nolan, ed. *Reading Between Texts: Intertextuality and the Hebrew Bible*. Louisville: John Knox, 1992.

Field, F. *Origenis Hexaplorum Quae Supersunt: Sive Veterum Interpretum Graecorum in Totum Vetus Testamentum Fragmenta*. 2 vols. Oxford: Clarendon, 1875.

Fishbane, Michael. *Biblical Interpretation in Ancient Israel*. Oxford: Clarendon, 1985.

———. "The Treaty Background of Amos 1[11] and Related Matters." *JBL* 89 (1970): 313–18.

Flashar, M. "Exegetische Studien zum Septuagintapsalter (IV)." *ZAW* 32 (1912): 161–89.

Frankel, Rafael. *Wine and Oil Production in Antiquity in Israel and Other Mediterranean Countries*. JSOT/ASOR Monograph Series 10. Sheffield: Sheffield Academic, 1999.

Frankel, Z. *Über den Einfluss der Palästinischen Exegese auf die Alexandrinische Hermeneutik.* Leipzig: Barth, 1831. Repr., Farnborough: Gregg International, 1972.

Freedman, David Noel, and Jeffrey G. Geochegan. "Another Stab at the Wicked Priest." Pages 17–24 in *The Bible and the Dead Sea Scrolls: The Princeton Symposium of the Dead Sea Scrolls.* Edited by James H. Charlesworth. Waco: Baylor University Press, 2006.

Freedman, H., and Simon Maurice, eds. *Midrash Rabbah.* 10 vols. London: Soncino, 1939.

Fuller, R. E. "The Minor Prophets Manuscripts from Qumran, Cave IV." Ph.D. diss., Harvard University, 1988.

———. "Textual Traditions in the Book of Hosea and the Minor Prophets." Pages 247–56 in *The Madrid Qumran Congress*, vol. 1. Edited by J. Trebolle Barrera and L. V. Montaner. Leiden: Brill, 1992.

García Martínez, F., and M. Vervenne, eds. *Interpreting Translation: Studies on the LXX and Ezekiel in Honour of Johan Lust.* BETL 192. Leuven: Peeters, 2005.

Garrett, Duane A. *Hosea, Joel.* NAC 19A. Nashville: Broadman & Holman, 1998.

———. "The Structure of Joel." *JETS* 28 (1985): 289–97.

Gehman, H. S. "Hebraisms of the Old Greek Version of Genesis." *VT* 3 (1953): 141–48.

Gelston, A. *The Peshiṭta of the Twelve Prophets.* Oxford: Clarendon, 1987.

———. "Some Hebrew Misreadings in the Septuagint of Amos." *VT* 52 (2002): 493–500.

Gentry, Peter J. "Old Greek and Later Revisors: Can We Always Distinguish Them?" Pages 301–27 in *Scripture in Transition: Essays on Septuagint, Hebrew Bible, and Dead Sea Scrolls in Honour of Raija Sollamo.* Edited by Anssi Voitila and Jutta Jokiranta. JSJSup 126. Leiden: Brill, 2008.

Gerleman, G. *Studies in the Septuagint.* Vol. 2, *Chronicles.* LUÅ, I/43, 3. Lund, 1946.

Gertner, M. "The Masora and the Levites: Appendix on Hosea XII." *VT* 10 (1960): 241–84.

Gibson, John C. L. *Textbook of Syrian Semitic Inscriptions.* Oxford: Clarendon, 1971.

Ginsberg, H. L. "Hosea's Ephraim, More Fool than Knave: A New Interpretation of Hosea XII: 1–14." *JBL* 80 (1961): 339–47.

Glenny, W. E. *Finding Meaning in the Text: Translation Technique and Theology in the Septuagint of Amos.* VTSup 126. Leiden: Brill, 2009.

———. "Hebrew Misreadings or Free Translation in the Septuagint of Amos?" *VT* 57 (2007): 524–47.

Good, E. M. "Hosea and the Jacob Tradition." *VT* 16 (1966): 137–51.

Gooding, D. W. "On the Use of the LXX for Dating Midrashic Elements in the Targum." *JTS* 25 (1974): 1–11.

———. "Two Possible Examples of Midrashic Interpretation in the Septuagint Exodus." Pages 39–48 in *Wort, Lied und Gottesspruch: Beiträge zur Septuaginta. Festschrift für Joseph Ziegler herausgegeben von Josef Schreiner.* Forschung zur Bibel 1. Edited by Josef Schreiner. Würzburg: Echter Verlag Katholisches Bibelwerk, 1972.

Gordon, R. P. *1 & 2 Samuel: A Commentary.* Exeter: Paternoster, 1986.

———. "The Ephraimite Messiah and the Targum(s) to Zechariah 12.10." Pages 347–56 in *Hebrew Bible and Ancient Versions.*

———. *Hebrew Bible and Ancient Versions: Selected Essays by Robert P. Gordon.* SOTS. Aldershot: Ashgate, 2006.

———. "Loricate Locusts in the Targum to Nahum III 17 and Revelation IX 9." *VT* 33 (1983): 338–39.

___ "The Targumists as Eschatologists." Pages 303–16 in *Hebrew Bible and Ancient Versions*.

Graetz, Heinrich. *Emendationes in Plerosque Sacrae Scripturae Veteris Testamenti Libros.* Edited by G. Bacher. 3 vols in 1. Breslau, 1892–94.

Gray, George Buchanan. *A Critical and Exegetical Commentary on the Book of Isaiah: I–XXXIX*, vol. 1. Edinburgh: T. & T. Clark, 1928.

Grossouw, Willem. *The Coptic Versions of the Minor Prophets.* MBE 3. Rome: Pontifical Biblical Institute, 1938.

Gunkel, Hermann. *Genesis.* Translated by Mark E. Biddle, 1901. Macon: Mercer University Press, 1997.

Hadot, Jean. *Penchant Mauvais et Volonté Libre dans la Sagesse de Ben Sira.* Brussels: University of Brussels Press, 1970.

Hammershaimb, Erling. *The Book of Amos: A Commentary.* Translated by John Sturdy. Oxford: Blackwell, 1970.

Hamori, Esther J. "The Spirit of Falsehood." *CBQ* 72 (2010): 15–30.

Hanhart, Robert. "The Translation of the Septuagint in Light of Earlier Tradition and Subsequent Influences." Pages 339–79 in Brooke and Lindars, eds., *Septuagint, Scrolls and Cognate Writings*.

Harl, Marguerite. "La Bible d'Alexandrie." Pages 181–97 in Taylor, ed., *X Congress of the IOSCS*.

———. *La Langue de Japhet: Quinze Études sur la Septante et le Grec des Chrétiens.* Paris: Cerf, 1994.

Harper, William Rainey. *A Critical and Exegetical Commentary on Amos and Hosea.* 1905. Repr., ICC. Edinburgh: T. & T. Clark, 1936.

Harrill, J. Albert. "Cannibalistic Language in the Fourth Gospel and Greco-Roman Polemics of Factionalism (John 6:52–66)." *JBL* 127 (2008): 133–58.

Harrington, Daniel J., and Anthony J. Saldarini. *Targum Jonathan of the Former Prophets.* ArBib 10. Edinburgh: T. & T. Clark, 1987.

Harrison, C. Robert, Jr., "The Unity of the Minor Prophets in the LXX: A Reexamination of the Question." *BIOSCS* 21 (1988): 55–72.

Hatch, Edwin, and Henry A. Redpath, eds. *A Concordance to the Septuagint: And the Other Greek Versions of the Old Testament (Including the Apocryphal Books).* Oxford: Clarendon, 1897–1906. 2d ed. Grand Rapids: Baker, 1998.

Hayes, John H. *Amos the Eighth Century Prophet: His Times and His Preaching.* Nashville: Abingdon, 1988.

Hays, Richard B. *Echoes of Scripture in the Letters of Paul.* New Haven: Yale University Press, 1989.

———. "Who Has Believed our Message?" Pages 34–45 in *The Conversion of the Imagination: Paul as Interpreter of Israel's Scripture.* Grand Rapids: Eerdmans, 2005.

Hayward, Robert. *Interpretations of the Name Israel in Ancient Judaism and Some Early Christian Writings: From Victorious Athlete to Heavenly Champion.* Oxford: Oxford University Press, 2005.

———. "Observations on Idols in Septuagint Pentateuch." Pages 40–57 in *Idolatry: False Worship in the Bible, Early Judaism and Christianity.* Edited by Stephen C. Barton. London: T. & T. Clark, 2007.

Hedley, P. L. "ΔΙΑΒΟΥΛΙΑ." *JTS* 34 (1933): 270.

Hiebert, Robert J. V., Claude E. Cox, and Peter J. Gentry, eds. *The Old Greek Psalter: Studies in Honour of Albert Pietersma.* JSOTSup 332. Sheffield: Sheffield Academic, 2001.

Hock, Hans Henrich. *Principles of Historical Linguistics.* Trends in Linguistics—Studies and Monographs 34. Berlin: de Gruyter, 1986.

Holladay, W. L. "Chiasmus, the Key to Hosea XII 3–6." *VT* 16 (1966): 53–64.

Hoonacker, Albin van. *Les Douze Petits Prophètes Traduits et Commentés.* Études Bibliques. Paris: Gabalda, 1908.

Horbury, William. *Jewish Messianism and the Cult of Christ.* London: SCM, 1998.

Horgan, Maurya P. *Pesharim: Qumran Interpretations of Biblical Books.* CBQMS 8. Washington: Catholic Biblical Association of America, 1979.

Hornblower, Simon, and Antony J. S. Spawforth. *The Oxford Classical Dictionary.* Oxford: Oxford University, 2009. No pages. Cited 31 July 2009. Online: http://www.oxfordreference.com/views/ENTRY.html?subview=Main&entry=t111.e1341.

Horsley, G. H. R. *New Documents Illustrating Early Christianity.* Vol. 1, *A Review of the Greek Inscriptions and Papyri Published in 1976.* Sydney: Macquarie University, 1981.

———. *New Documents Illustrating Early Christianity.* Vol. 4, *A Review of the Greek Inscriptions and Papyri Published in 1979.* North Ryde: The Ancient History Documentary Research Centre Macquarie University, 1987.

Howard, G. E. "Some Notes on the Septuagint of Amos." *VT* 20 (1970): 108–12.

———. "To the Reader of the Twelve Prophets." Pages 777–81 in NETS.

Huizenga, Leroy A. *The New Isaac: Tradition and Intertextuality in the Gospel of Matthew.* NTSup 131. Leiden: Brill, 2009.

Hyatt, J. Philip. "The Translation and Meaning of Amos 5,23.24." *ZAW* 68 (1956): 17–24.

Hyvärinen, Kyösti. *Die Übersetzung von Aquila.* ConBOT 10. Uppsala: Almqvist & Wiksell, 1977.

Ibn Ezra, Abraham ben Meïr, 1092–1167. *The Commentary of Abraham Ibn Ezra on the Pentateuch.* Vol. 3, *Leviticus.* Translated by Jay F. Schachter. Hoboken: Ktav, 1986.

Jellicoe, Sidney. *The Septuagint and Modern Study.* Oxford: Clarendon, 1968.

Jobes, Karen H. "Distinguishing the Meaning of Greek Verbs in the Semantic Domain of Worship." *Filología Neotestamentaria* 4 (1991): 183–91.

Jobes, Karen H., and Moisés Silva. *Invitation to the Septuagint.* Grand Rapids: Baker, 2000.

Johnson, Sherman E. "The Septuagint Translators of Amos." Ph.D. diss., University of Chicago, 1936.

Jones, Barry Alan. *The Formation of the Book of the Twelve: A Study in Text and Canon.* SBLDS 149. Atlanta: Scholars Press, 1995.

Joosten, Jan. "Exegesis in the Septuagint Version of Hosea." Pages 62–85 in de Moor, ed., *Intertextuality in Ugarit and Israel.*

———. "A Septuagintal Translation Technique in the Minor Prophets: The Elimination of Verbal Repetitions." Pages 217–23 in García Martínez and Vervenne, eds., *Interpreting Translation.*

Josephus. Translated by H. St J. Thackeray et al. 10 vols. LCL. Cambridge, Mass.: Harvard University Press, 1926–1965.

Kalmin, Richard. "Levirate Law." *ABD* 4:296–97.

Kaminka, Armand. *Studien zur Septuaginta an der Hand der Zwölf Kleinen Prophetenbücher.* SGFWJ 33. Frankfurt: J. Kauffman, 1928.

Keil, Friedrich. *The Twelve Minor Prophets*. Clark's Foreign Theological Library 17–18. 4th series. Edinburgh: T. & T. Clark, 1871.

Kelley, Page H. *The Book of Amos: A Study Manual*. Shield Bible Study Outlines. Grand Rapids: Baker, 1966.

Kennicott, Benjamin, ed. *Vetus Testamentum Hebraicum: Cum Variis Lectionibus*. 2 vols. Oxford: Clarendon, 1776.

Klauck, Hans-Josef. "θυσιαστηριον. Eine Berichtigung." *ZNW* 71 (1980): 274–77.

Knibb, M. A. *The Septuagint and Messianism*. BETL 195. Leuven: Peeters, 2006.

Koenig, Jean. *L'Herméneutique Analogique du Judaïsme Antique*. VTSup 33. Leiden: Brill, 1982.

Kristeva, Julia. *Desire in Language: A Semiotic Approach to Literature and Art*. Translated by Thomas Gora, Alice Jardine, and Leon Roudiez. New York: Columbia University Press, 1980.

Kruger, Paul A. "The Evildoer in Hosea 6:8–9." *JNSL* 17 (1991): 17–22.

Kutscher, E. Y. *The Language and Linguistic Background of the Isaiah Scroll (1QIsaᵃ)*. Leiden: Brill, 1974. Hebrew edition: Jerusalem: Magnes, 1959.

Lee, J. A. L. *A Lexical Study of the Septuagint Version of the Pentateuch*. SBLSCS 14. Chico: Scholars Press, 1983.

Leeuwen, Cornelis van. "The 'Northern One' in the Composition of Joel 2,19–27." Pages 85–99 in *The Scriptures and the Scrolls: Studies in Honour of A. S. van der Woude on the Occasion of His 65th Birthday*. Edited by F. García Martínez, A. Hilhorst, and C. J. Labuschagne. VTSup 49. Leiden: Brill, 1992.

Lentin, Rachel. "Seeing Double: Strategies for Understanding Imagery with Reference to the Wine-Related Images of the Hebrew Bible." Ph.D. diss., University of Cambridge, 2008.

Leonhardt-Balzer, Jutta. "A Case of Psychological Dualism: Philo of Alexandria and the Instruction on the Two Spirits." Pages 27–45 in *Early Christian Literature and Intertextuality*. Vol. 2, *Exegetical Studies*. Edited by Craig A. Evans and H. Daniel Zacharias. Library of New Testament Studies 392. London: T&T Clark, 2009.

Lévi, Israel. *The Hebrew Text of the Book of Ecclesiasticus*. SSS 3. Leiden: Brill, 1904.

Lieberman, Saul. *Hellenism in Jewish Palestine: Studies in the Literary Transmission, Beliefs and Manners of Palestine in the 1 Century B.C.E.–IV Century C.E.* Texts and Studies of the Jewish Theological Seminary of America 18. New York: The Jewish Theological Seminary of America, 1950.

Lindars, Barnabas. "Introduction." Pages 1–7 in Brooke and Lindars, eds., *Septuagint, Scrolls and Cognate Writings*.

Linville, James R. "Bugs Through the Looking Glass: The Infestation of Meaning in Joel." Pages 299–314 in Rezetko, Lim, and Aucker, eds., *Reflection and Refraction*.

Lössl, Josef. "When Is a Locust Just a Locust? Patristic Exegesis of Joel 1:4 in the Light of Ancient Literary Theory." *JTS* NS 55 (2004): 575–99.

Lundbom, Jack R. "Contentious Priests and Contentious People in Hosea IV·1–10." *VT* 36 (1986): 52–70.

Lust, J. "The Cult of Molek/Milchom: Some Remarks on G. H. Heider's Monograph." *ETL* 63 (1987): 361–66.

———. "The Greek Version of Balaam's Third and Fourth Oracles: The ἄνθρωπος in Num 24,7 and 17: Messianism and Lexicography." Pages 69–86 in *Messianism and the Septuagint*.

————. "Idols? גלולים and εἴδωλα in Ezekiel." Pages 317–33 in Ausloos, Lemmelijn, and Vervenne, eds., *Florilegium Lovaniense*.

————. "Messianism and Septuagint." Pages 9–26 in *Messianism and the Septuagint*.

————. *Messianism and the Septuagint: Collected Essays*. BETL 178. Edited by K. Hauspie. Leuven: Leuven University Press, 2004.

————. "Septuagint and Messianism, with Special Emphasis on the Pentateuch." Pages 129–51 in *Messianism and the Septuagint*.

————. "The Use of Textual Witnesses for the Establishment of the Text." Pages 7–20 in *Ezekiel and His Book: Textual and Literary Criticism and Their Interrelation*. BETL 74. Leuven: Leuven University Press, 1986.

————. "The Vocabulary of the LXX Ezekiel and Its Dependence Upon the Pentateuch." Pages 529–46 in *Deuteronomy and the Deuteronomic Literature*. Edited by M. Vervenne and J. Lust. BETL 133. Leuven: Peeters, 1997.

Lust, J. et al., eds. *A Greek–English Lexicon of the Septuagint*. Stuttgart: Deutsche Bibelgesellschaft, 1992, 1996.

Macintosh, A. A. *A Critical and Exegetical Commentary on Hosea*. ICC. Edinburgh: T. & T. Clark, 1997.

Margolis, M. L. "Notes on Some Passages in Amos." *AJSL* 17 (1901): 170–71.

Marti, Karl. *Das Buch Jesaja*. KHC. Tübingen: J. C. B. Mohr, 1900.

————. *Das Dodekapropheton*. KHC. Tübingen: J. C. B. Mohr, 1904.

Martin-Achard, Robert, and Paul S. Re'emi. *God's People in Crisis*. International Theological Commentary. Edinburgh: Handsel. Grand Rapids: Eerdmans, 1984.

Mays, James Luther. *Hosea: A Commentary*. OTL. London: SCM, 1969.

McCarter, P. Kyle. *II Samuel*. AB 9. New York: Doubleday, 1984.

McCarthy, Carmel. *The Tiqqune Sopherim and Other Theological Corrections in the Masoretic Text of the Old Testament*. OBO. Göttingen: Vandenhoeck & Ruprecht, 1981.

McComiskey, Thomas Edward, ed. *The Minor Prophets: An Exegetical and Expository Commentary: Hosea, Joel, and Amos*, vol. 1. Grand Rapids: Baker, 1992.

McKenzie, Steven L. "The Jacob Tradition in Hosea XII 4–5." *VT* 36 (1986): 311–22.

Michaelis, Wilhelm. "Der Beitrag der Septuaginta zur Bedeutungsgeschichte von πρωτότοκος." Pages 313–20 in *Sprachgeschichte und Wortbedeutung: Festschrift Albert Debrunner*. Edited by G. Redard. Berne: Francke, 1954.

Milgrom, Jacob. *Leviticus 23–27*. AB 3B. New York: Doubleday, 2000.

Millard, Alan. "'Scriptio Continua' in Early Hebrew: Ancient Practice or Modern Surmise?" *JSS* 15 (1970): 2–15.

Mills, Timothy John. "The Gog Pericope and the Book of Ezekiel." Ph.D. diss., Drew University, Madison, N.J., 1989.

Miscall, Peter D. "Isaiah: New Heavens, New Earth, New Book." Pages 41–56 in Fewell, ed., *Reading Between Texts*.

Moore, Carey A. *Judith*. AB 40B. New York: Doubleday, 1985.

Moskala, Jiří. "Toward the Fulfillment of the Gog and Magog Prophecy of Ezekiel 38–39." *JATS* 18 (2007): 243–73.

Motyer, J. Alec. *The Prophecy of Isaiah: An Introduction and Commentary*. Downers Grove: IVP, 1993.

Moulton, J. H., and G. Milligan. *The Vocabulary of the Greek New Testament*. London: Hodder & Stoughton, 1930. Repr., 1952.

Mowvley, Harry. *The Books of Amos and Hosea.* Epworth Commentaries. London: Epworth, 1991.

Mozley, F. W. *The Psalter of the Church: The Septuagint Psalms Compared with the Hebrew, with Various Notes.* Cambridge: Cambridge University Press, 1905.

Muraoka, T. "Hebrew Hapax Legomena and Septuagint Lexicography." Pages 205–22 in *VII* Congress of the IOSCS. Edited by C. Cox. SBLSCS 31. Atlanta: Scholars Press, 1989.

———. "Hosea IV in the Septuagint Version." *AJBI* 9 (1983): 24–64.

———. "Hosea V in the Septuagint Version." *Abr-Nahrain* 24 (1986): 120–38.

———. "Hosea 6 in the Septuagint." Pages 335–49 in Ausloos, Lemmelijn, and Vervenne, eds., *Florilegium Lovaniense.*

———. "In Defence of the Unity of the Septuagint Minor Prophets." *AJBI* 15 (1989): 25–36.

———. Is the Septuagint Amos viii 12–ix 10 a Separate Unit?" *VT* 20 (1970): 496–500.

———. "Literary Device in the Septuagint." *Textus* 8 (1973): 20–30.

———. "Towards a Septuagint Lexicon." Pages 255–76 in *VI Congress of the IOSCS: Jerusalem 1986.* Edited by Claude E. Cox. SBLSCS 23. Atlanta: Scholars Press, 1986.

———. "Translation Techniques and Beyond." Pages 13–22 in Sollamo and Sipilä, eds., *Helsinki Perspectives.*

Neal, Tamara. "Blood and Hunger in the *Iliad.*" *CP* 101 (2006): 15–33.

Ngunga, Abi T. "Messianism in the Old Greek of Isaiah: An Intertextual Analysis." Ph.D. diss., University of Aberdeen, 2010.

Nogalski, James D. "The Redactional Shaping of Nahum 1 for the Book of the Twelve." Pages 193–202 in *Among the Prophets: Language, Image and Structure in the Prophetic Writings.* Edited by Philip R. Davies and David J. A. Clines. JSOTSup 144. Sheffield: Sheffield Academic, 1993.

———. "Intertextuality and the Twelve." Pages 102–24 in *Forming Prophetic Literature: Essays on Isaiah and the Twelve in Honor of John D. W. Watts.* Edited by James W. Watts and Paul R. House. JSOTSup 235. Sheffield: Sheffield Academic, 1996.

North, Christopher R. *The Second Isaiah.* Oxford: Clarendon, 1964.

Nowack, W. *Die kleinen Propheten.* 2d ed. HKAT 3/4. Göttingen: Vandenhoeck & Ruprecht, 1903.

Olofsson, Staffan. *The LXX Version: A Guide to the Translation Technique of the Septuagint.* ConBOT 30. Stockholm: Almqvist & Wiksell, 1990.

Palmer, James K. "'Not Made with Tracing Paper': Studies in the Septuagint of Zechariah." Ph.D. diss., University of Cambridge, 2004.

Park, Aaron W. *The Book of Amos as Composed and Read in Antiquity.* StBL 37. New York: Lang, 2001.

Parry, Donald W., and Elisha Qimron. *The Great Isaiah Scroll (1QIsaᵃ): A New Edition.* STDJ 32. Leiden: Brill, 1999.

Paul, Shalom M. "Classifications of Wine in Mesopotamian and Rabbinic Sources." *IEJ* 25 (1975): 42–44.

———. *A Commentary on the Book of Amos.* Hermeneia. Minneapolis: Fortress, 1991.

———. "Euphemistically 'Speaking' and a Covetous Eye." *HAR* 14 (1994): 193–204.

———. "Fishing Imagery in Amos 4:2." *JBL* 97 (1978): 183–90.

Payne Smith, J. *A Compendious Syriac Dictionary.* Oxford: Clarendon, 1903.

Perkins, Larry. "Greek Exodus and Greek Isaiah: Detection and Implications of Interdependence in Translation." *BIOSCS* 42 (2009): 18–33.

Philo. Translated by F. H. Colson. 10 vols. LCL. Cambridge, Mass.: Harvard University Press, 1929–1953.

Pietersma, Albert. "A New Paradigm for Addressing Old Questions: The Relevance of the Interlinear Model for the Study of the Septuagint." Pages 337–64 in *Bible and Computer: The Stellenbosch AIBI–6 Conference Proceedings of the Association Internationale Bible et Informatique "From Alpha to Byte." University of Stellenbosch 17–21 July, 2000.* Edited by Johann Cook. Leiden: Brill, 2002.

Plato. Translated by W. R. M. Lamb. 12 vols. Cambridge, Mass.: Harvard University Press, 1925.

Plutarch. *Moralia.* Translated by Paul A. Clement and Herbert B. Hoffleit. 16 vols. LCL. Cambridge, Mass.: Harvard University Press, 1969.

Polaski, Donald C. *Authorizing an End: The Isaiah Apocalypse and Intertextuality.* BIS 50. Leiden: Brill, 2001.

Porton, Gary G. "Hermeneutics: A Critical Approach." *EOM* 1:250–68.

Power, Edmond. "Note to Amos 7,1." *Biblica* 8 (1927): 87–92.

Prijs, Leo. *Jüdische Tradition in der Septuaginta: Die grammatikalische Terminologie des Abraham ibn Esra.* Leiden: Brill, 1948. Repr., Hildesheim: Georg Olms, 1987.

Probert, Philomen. *Ancient Greek Accentuation: Synchronic Patterns, Frequency Effects, and Prehistory.* Oxford: Oxford University Press, 2006.

Puech, Émile. "Milkom, le Dieu Ammonite, en Amos I 15." *VT* 27 (1977): 117–25.

Rabin, Chaim. "The Translation Process and the Character of the Septuagint." *Textus* 6 (1968): 1–26.

Railton, Nicholas M. "Gog and Magog: The History of a Symbol." *EvQ* 75 (2003): 23–43.

Rajak, Tessa. "Dying for the Law: The Martyr's Portrait in Jewish-Greek Literature." Pages 99–133 in *The Jewish Dialogue with Greece and Rome: Studies in Cultural and Social Interaction.* Leiden: Brill, 2001.

———. *Translation and Survival: The Greek Bible of the Ancient Jewish Diaspora.* Oxford: Oxford University Press, 2009.

Reddish, Mitchell G. "Gog and Magog." *ABD* 1:1056.

Reese, James M. *Hellenistic Influence on the Book of Wisdom and Its Consequences.* Analecta Biblica 41. Rome: Biblical Institute, 1970.

Reider, Joseph. *An Index to Aquila: Greek–Hebrew, Hebrew–Greek, Latin–Hebrew with the Syriac and Armenian Evidence.* VTSup 12. Leiden: Brill, 1966.

Renaud, B. *La Formation du Livre de Michée: Tradition et Actualisation.* Etudes bibliques. Paris: Gabalda, 1977.

Rezetko, Robert, Timothy H. Lim, and W. Brian Aucker, eds. *Reflection and Refraction: Studies in Biblical Historiography in Honour of A. Graeme Auld.* VTSup 113. Leiden: Brill, 2007.

Riffaterre, Michael. *Semiotics of Poetry.* 1978. London: Methuen, 1980.

Rudolph, Wilhelm. *Joel–Amos–Abadja–Jona.* KAT 13/2. Gütersloh: Gerd Mohn, 1971.

———. *Micha–Nahum–Habakuk–Zephanja.* KAT 13/3. Gütersloh: Gerd Mohn, 1975.

Saint Cyril, Patriarch of Alexandria. *Commentary on the Twelve Prophets*, vol. 1. Translated by Robert C. Hill. The Fathers of the Church 115. Washington: Catholic University Press of America, 2007.

Sanders, James A. "Isaiah in Luke." Pages 14–25 in *Luke and Scripture: The Function of Sacred Tradition in Luke–Acts.* Edited by Craig A. Evans and James A. Sanders. Minneapolis: Fortress, 1993.

Sarason, Richard S. "Liturgy, Midrash in." *EOM* 1:463–92.

Sarna, Nahum M. *The JPS Torah Commentary, Genesis: The Traditional Hebrew Text with the New JPS Translation.* Philadelphia: Jewish Publication Society, 1989.

Sawyer, John F. A. "'Those Priests in Damascus': A Possible Example of Anti-Sectarian Polemic in the Septuagint Version of Amos 3:12." *ASTI* 8 (1970–1971): 123–30.

Schaper, Joachim. "Messianism in the Septuagint of Isaiah and Messianic Intertextuality in the Greek Bible." Pages 371–80 in Knibb., ed., *The Septuagint and Messianism.*

Schart, Aaron. "The Jewish and the Christian Greek Versions of Amos." Pages 157–77 in *Septuagint Research: Issues and Challenges in the Study of the Greek Jewish Scriptures.* Edited by Wolfgang Kraus and Glenn Wooden. SBLSCS 53. Atlanta: SBL, 2006.

Schiffman, L. H. "The Septuagint and the Temple Scroll: Shared 'Halakhic' Variants." Pages 277–97 in Brooke and Lindars, eds., *Septuagint, Scrolls and Cognate Writings.*

Schmidt, Heinrich J. *Synonymik der Griechischen Sprache.* 4 vols. Leipzig: Teubner, 1876–86.

Schorch, Stefan. "The Septuagint and the Vocalization of the Hebrew Text of the Torah." Pages 41–54 in *XII Congress of the IOSCS: Leiden, 2004.* Edited by Melvin K. H. Peeters. SBLSCS 54. Leiden: Brill, 2006.

Schultz, Richard L. *The Search for Quotation: Verbal Parallels in the Prophets.* JSOTSup 180. Sheffield: Sheffield Academic Press, 1999.

Schwantes, Siegfried J. "Note on Amos 4:2b." *ZAW* 79 (1967): 82–83.

Schwertheim, E. ed. *Die Inschriften von Hadrianoi und Hadrianeia.* Bonn: Habelt, 1987.

Seeligmann, I. L. *The Septuagint Version of Isaiah: A Discussion of Its Problems.* Ex oriente lux 9. Leiden: Brill, 1948. Repr. edited by R. Hanhart and H. Spieckermann. FAT 40. Tübingen: Mohr Siebeck, 2004.

Sellers, Ovid R. "Stages of Locust in Joel." *AJSL* 52 (1935–36): 81–85.

Sellin, Ernst. *Das Zwölfprophetenbuch.* KAT 12. Leipzig: Deichert, 1922.

Shipp, G. P. *Modern Greek Evidence for the Ancient Greek Vocabulary.* Sydney: Sydney University Press, 1979.

Sinclair, L. A. "Hebrew Text of the Qumran Micah Pesher and Textual Tradition of the Minor Prophets." *RevQ* 11 (1983): 253–63.

Smith, Billy K., and Frank S. Page. *Amos, Obadiah, Jonah.* NAC 19B. Nashville: Broadman & Holman, 1995.

Smith, Gary V. *Amos.* Rev. ed. Fearn: Christian Focus, 1998.

———. *Isaiah 1–39.* NAC 15A. Nashville: Broadman & Holman, 2007.

Snaith, Norman, H. *The Book of Amos.* Part Two, *Translation and Notes.* Study Notes on Bible Books. London: Epworth, 1946.

Soggin, Alberto J. *The Prophet Amos: A Translation and Commentary.* London: SCM, 1987.

Sollamo, Raija. "Introduction." Pages 7–12 in Sollamo and Sipilä, eds., *Helsinki Perspectives.*

Sollamo, Raija, and Seppo Sipilä, eds. *Helsinki Perspectives on the Translation Technique of the Septuagint.* PFES 82. Göttingen: Vandenhoeck & Ruprecht, 2001.

Soulen, Richard N. *Handbook of Biblical Criticism.* 3d ed. Louisville: Westminster John Knox, 2001.

Sperber, Daniel. "Varia Midrashica IV. 1: Esau and His Mother's Womb—A Note on Amos 1:11." *REJ* 137 (1978): 149–53.

Sperling, S. David. "Biblical *rḥm* I and *rḥm* II." *JANES* 19 (1989): 149–59.

Staalduine-Sulman, Eveline van. *The Targum of Samuel.* SAIS 1. Leiden: Brill, 2002.

Strazicich, John. *Joel's Use of Scripture and Scripture's Use of Joel: Appropriation and Resignification in Second Temple Judaism and Early Christianity.* Leiden: Brill, 2007.

Stuart, Douglas. *Hosea–Jonah.* WBC 31. Waco: Word, 1987.

Stuart, G. H. Cohen. *The Struggle in Man Between Good and Evil: An Inquiry into the Origin of the Rabbinic Concept of Yeṣer Haraʾ.* Kampen: Kok, 1984.

Sweeney, Marvin A. *The Twelve Prophets,* vol. 1. Berit Olam. Collegeville: Liturgical, 2000.

Talmon, Shemaryahu. "Aspects of the Textual Transmission of the Bible in the Light of Qumran Manuscripts." *Textus* 4 (1964): 95–132.

Talshir, Zipora. *I Esdras: From Origin to Translation.* SBLSCS 47. Atlanta: SBL, 1999.

Tate, Marvin E. *Psalms 51–100.* WBC 20. Dallas: Word, 1990.

Taylor, Bernard A., ed. *X Congress of the IOSCS, Oslo, 1998.* SBLSCS 51. Atlanta: SBL, 2001.

Thackeray, H. St J. "The Greek Translators of Ezekiel." *JTS* 4 (1903): 398–411.

———. "The Greek Translators of Jeremiah." *JTS* 4 (1903): 245–66.

———. "The Greek Translators of the Prophetical Books." *JTS* 4 (1903): 578–85.

———. *The Septuagint and Jewish Worship: A Study in Origins.* The Schweich Lectures 1920. London: Oxford University Press, 1921.

Theodore, Bishop of Mopsuestia, *Commentary on the Twelve Prophets.* Translated by Robert C. Hill. The Fathers of the Church 108. Washington: The Catholic University Press of America, 2004.

Thompson, John A. "Joel's Locusts in the Light of Ancient Near Eastern Parallels." *JNES* 14 (1955): 52–55.

Tov, E. "Biliteral Exegesis of Hebrew Roots in the Septuagint?" Pages 459–82 in Rezetko, Lim, and Aucker, eds., *Reflection and Refraction.*

———. "Compound Words in the LXX Representing Two or More Hebrew Words." *Biblica* 58 (1977): 199–201.

———. "Greek Words and Hebrew Meanings." Pages 83–125 in *Melbourne Symposium on Septuagint Lexicography.* Edited by Takamitsu Muraoka. SCS 28. Atlanta: Scholars Press, 1990.

———. "The Impact of the LXX Translation of the Pentateuch on the Translation of the Other Books." Pages 577–93 in *Mélanges Dominique Barthélemy: Études Bibliques Offertes à l'Occasion de son 60e Anniversaire.* Edited by Pierre Casetti, Othmar Keel, and Adrian Schenker. OBO 38. Göttingen: Vandenhoeck & Ruprecht, 1981.

———. "Midrash-Type Exegesis in the Septuagint of Joshua." Pages 153–64 in *The Greek and Hebrew Bible: Collected Essays on the Septuagint.* VTSup 72. Leiden: Brill, 1999.

———. *The Septuagint Translation of Jeremiah and Baruch: A Discussion of an Early Revision of the LXX of Jeremiah 29–52 and Baruch 1:1–3:8.* HSM 8. Missoula: Scholars Press, 1976.

———. "Some Reflections on the Hebrew Texts from which the Septuagint was Translated." *JNSL* 19 (1993): 107–22.

———. *The Text-critical Use of the Septuagint in Biblical Research.* 2d ed. JBS 8. Jerusalem: Simor, 1997.

————. *Textual Criticism of the Hebrew Bible*. Minneapolis: Fortress, 1992.

————. "Three Dimensions of LXX Words." *RB* 83 (1976): 529–44.

Tov, E., and Frank Polak, eds. *The Revised CATSS Hebrew/Greek Parallel Text.* Jerusalem, 2005. Accessed on *Bible Works 8*, 2009–2010.

Trench, R. C. *Synonyms of the New Testament*. New ed. London: Kegan Paul, Trench, Trübner, 1915.

Tychsen, O. G. *Testamen de Variis Codicum Hebraicorum Vet. Test. MSS*. Rostock, 1772.

Ulrich, Eugene. "The Septuagint Manuscripts from Qumran: A Reappraisal of Their Value." Pages 49–80 in Brooke and Lindars, eds., *Septuagint, Scrolls and Cognate Writings.*

Ulrich, E., F. M. Cross, R. E. Fuller, J. E. Sanderson, P. W. Skehan, and E. Tov. *Qumran Cave 4.X: The Prophets*. DJD XV. Oxford: Clarendon, 1997.

Van der Kooij, Arie. "Isaiah and Daniel in the Septuagint: How Are These Two Books Related?" Pages 465–73 in Ausloos, Lemmelijn, and Vervenne, eds., *Florilegium Lovaniense.*

————. "On the Use of βωμός in the Septuagint." Pages 601–7 in Baasten and Van Peursen, eds., *Hamlet on a Hill.*

————. *The Oracle of Tyre: The Septuagint of Isaiah XXIII as Version and Vision.* VTSup 71. Leiden: Brill, 1998.

————. "The Septuagint of Psalms and the First Book of Maccabees." Pages 229–47 in Hiebert, Cox, and Gentry, eds., *The Old Greek Psalter.*

————. "The Septuagint of Zechariah as Witness to an Early Interpretation of the Book." Pages 53–64 in *The Book of Zechariah and Its Influence*. Edited by Christopher Tuckett. Aldershot: Ashgate, 2003.

Van der Louw, Theo A. W. *Transformations in the Septuagint: Towards an Interaction of Septuagint Studies and Translation Studies*. CBET 47. Leuven: Peeters, 2007.

Van der Meer, Michaël N. "Papyrological Perspectives on the Septuagint of Isaiah." Paper presented at Colloquium on "The Old Greek of Isaiah: Issues and Perspectives." University of Leiden, Leiden, April 10–11, 2008.

————. "The Question of the Literary Dependence of the Greek Isaiah Upon the Greek Psalter Revisited." Pages 162–200 in *Die Septuaginta—Texte, Theologien, Einflüsse. 2. Internationale Fachtagung veranstaltet von Septaginta Deutsch (LXX.D), Wuppertal 23.–27.7.2008*. Edited by Wolfgang Kraus and Martin Karrer. WUNT 252. Tübingen: Mohr Siebeck, 2010.

Van der Meer, Michaël N., Percy van Keulen, Wido van Peursen, and Bas ter Haar Romeny, eds. *Isaiah in Context: Studies in Honour of Arie van der Kooij on the Occasion of His Sixty-Fifth Birthday*. VTSup 138. Leiden: Brill, 2010.

Vellas, V. *Ἀμώς*. Athens: Astir, 1947.

Vermes, Geza. "Bible and Midrash: Early Old Testament Exegesis." Pages 199–231 in *Cambridge History of the Bible*, vol. 1. Edited by P. R. Ackroyd and C. F. Evans. Cambridge: Cambridge University Press, 1970.

————. *Scripture and Tradition in Judaism*. Leiden: Brill, 1961.

Verwijs, Petra. "The Septuagint in the Peshitta and Syro-Hexapla Translations of Amos 1:3–2:16." *BIOSCS* 38 (2005): 25–40.

Wallace, Daniel B. *Greek Grammar Beyond the Basics*. Grand Rapids: Zondervan, 1995.

Walters, Peter. *The Text of the Septuagint: Its Corruptions and Their Emendation*. Edited by D. W. Gooding. Cambridge: Cambridge University Press, 1973.

Waltke, Bruce. *A Commentary on Micah*. Grand Rapids: Eerdmans, 2007.

Walton, John H., Victor H. Matthews, and Mark W. Chavalas. *The IVP Bible Background Commentary: Old Testament*. Downers Grove: IVP, 2000.

Weissert, David. "Alexandrinian Analogical Word-Analysis and Septuagint Translation Techniques." *Textus* 8 (1973): 31–44.

Weitzman, M. P. *The Syriac Version of the Old Testament: An Introduction*. University of Cambridge Oriental Publications 56. Cambridge: Cambridge University Press, 1999.

Wellhausen, J. *Die Kleinen Propheten: Übersetzt und Erklärt*. Berlin: de Gruyter, 1963. Originally published by Georg Reimer, 1892.

Wevers, John William. *Notes on the Greek Text of Exodus*. SBLSCS 30. Atlanta: Scholars Press, 1990.

———. *Notes on the Greek Text of Genesis*. SBLSCS 35. Atlanta: Scholars Press, 1993.

———. *Notes on the Greek Text of Leviticus*. SBLSCS 44. Atlanta: Scholars Press, 1997.

———. *Notes on the Greek Text of Numbers*. SBLSCS 46. Atlanta: Scholars Press, 1998.

———. *Text History of the Greek Deuteronomy*. Abhandlungen der Akademie der Wissenschaften in Göttingen. MSU 13. Göttingen: Vandenhoeck & Ruprecht, 1978.Williams, Tyler F. "Towards a Date for the Old Greek Psalter." Pages 248–76 in Hiebert, Cox, and Gentry, eds., *The Old Greek Psalter*.

Williamson, H. G. M. *Ezra, Nehemiah*. WBC 16. Waco: Word, 1985.

Wolff, Hans Walter. *Hosea*. Translated by Gary Stansell. Hermeneia. Philadelphia: Fortress, 1974.

———. *Joel and Amos*. Translated by Waldemar Janzen, S. Dean McBride, Jr., and Charles A. Muenchow. Hermeneia. Philadelphia: Fortress, 1977.

———. *Micah: A Commentary*. Translated by Gary Stansell. Minneapolis: Augsburg Fortress, 1990.

Wong, Ka Leung. "The Masoretic and Septuagint Texts of Ezekiel 39,21–29." *ETL* 78 (2002): 130–47.

Wright, Benjamin J. "The Jewish Scriptures in Greek: The Septuagint in the Context of Ancient Translation Activity." Pages 197–212 in *Praise Israel for Wisdom and Instruction: Essays on Ben Sira and Wisdom, the Letter of Aristeas and the Septuagint*. JSJSup 131. Leiden: Brill, 2008.

Wutz, F. X. *Die Transkriptionen von der LXX bis zu Hieronymus*. BWAT 2/9. Stuttgart: Kohlhammer, 1933.

Xenophon. *Symposium and Apology*, vol. 4. Translated by O. J. Todd. LCL. Cambridge, Mass.: Harvard University Press, 1979.

Ziegler, J. *Beiträge zum griechischen Dodekapropheton*. Nachrichten von der Akademie der Wissenschaften. Göttingen: Vandenhoeck & Ruprecht, 1943.

———. *Duodecim Prophetae*, vol. XIII. Septuaginta Vetus Testamentum Graecum. Göttingen: Vandenhoeck & Ruprecht, 1943.

———. "Die Einheit der Septuaginta zum Zwölfprophetenbuch." Pages 29–42 in *Sylloge: Gesammelte Aufsätze zur Septuaginta*. MSU 10. Göttingen: Vandenhoeck & Ruprecht, 1971. Originally published: *Die Einheit der LXX zum Zwölfprophetenbuch*. Beilage zum Vorlesungsverzeichnis der Staatlichen Akademie zu Braunsberg im WS 1934/35. Braunsberg, 1934.

———. "Einleitung." Pages 1–145 in *Duodecim Prophetae,* vol. XIII.

————. *Sylloge: Gesammelte Aufsätze zur Septuaginta.* MSU 10. Göttingen: Vandenhoeck & Ruprecht, 1971.

————. *Untersuchungen zur Septuaginta des Buches Isaias.* Alttestamentliche Abhandlungen 12/3. Münster i. W.: Aschendorffschen, 1934.

Zimmerli, Walther. *Ezekiel, II: A Commentary on the Book of the Prophet Ezekiel, Chapters 25–48.* Translated by James D. Martin. Neukirchen–Vluyn: Neukirchener Verlag, 1969. Hermeneia. Philadelphia: Fortress, 1983.

INDEXES

INDEX OF REFERENCES

INDEX OF AUTHORS